PENGUIN BOOKS

ESSAYS

Michel Eyquem, Seigneur de Montaigne, was born in 1533, the son and heir of Pierre, Seigneur de Montaigne (two previous children dying soon after birth). He was brought up to speak Latin as his mother tongue and always retained a Latin turn of mind; though he knew Greek, he preferred to use translations. After studying law he eventually became counsellor to the *Parlement* of Bordeaux. He married in 1565. After following the royal court in Paris and Rouen, he retired in 1571 to his lands at Montaigne, devoting himself to reading and reflection and to composing his *Essais* (1580). He loathed the fanaticism and cruelties of the religious wars of the period, but sided with Catholic orthodoxy and legitimate monarchy. He was twice elected Mayor of Bordeaux (1581 and 1583) a post he held for four years. He died at Montaigne (1592) while preparing another edition of his *Essais*.

J. M. Cohen, born in London in 1903 and a Cambridge graduate, was the translator of many volumes for the Penguin Classics, including versions of Cervantes, Rabelais and Montaigne. For some years he assisted E. V. Rieu in editing the Penguin Classics. He collected the three books of *Comic and Curious Verse* and anthologies of Latin American and Cuban writing. With his son Mark Cohen he also edited the *Penguin Dictionary of Quotations* and the two editions of its companion *Dictionary of Modern Quotations*. He frequently visited Spain and made several visits to Mexico, Cuba and other Spanish American countries. J. M. Cohen died in 1989.

Michel de Montaigne

ESSAYS

Translated with an Introduction by
J. M. COHEN

PENGUIN BOOKS

PENGUIN BOOKS

Published by the Penguin Group
Penguin Books Ltd, 27 Wrights Lane, London W8 5TZ, England
Penguin Books USA Inc., 375 Hudson Street, New York, New York 10014, USA
Penguin Books Australia Ltd, Ringwood, Victoria, Australia
Penguin Books Canada Ltd, 10 Alcorn Avenue, Toronto, Ontario, Canada M4V 3B2
Penguin Books (NZ) Ltd, 182–190 Wairau Road, Auckland 10, New Zealand

Penguin Books Ltd, Registered Offices: Harmondsworth, Middlesex, England

This translation first published in Penguin Classics 1958
Reprinted in Penguin Books 1993
3 5 7 9 10 8 6 4 2

Copyright © J. M. Cohen, 1958
All rights reserved

Printed in England by Clays Ltd, St Ives plc
Set in Monotype Garamond

TO
Mark

CONTENTS

INTRODUCTION

I

Montaigne's Essays are, in effect, an extended autobio-graphy, the only one ever to be written in this way. Other autobiographers begin with the writer's birth, and carry on, with more or less digressions, to that moment when he picks up the pen to sketch out his first chapter. Montaigne, however, does not proceed along the line of time; he does not tell us what event succeeded what other. His aim is to present a portrait of himself in a frame of timelessness; to build up from a number of partial sketches the essential man; not as an unchanging being, but as one who retained a core of identity more important as a subject than the events that befell him.

Montaigne, as he says several times, is following a new method. In order to leave this portrait of himself as a memorial for his friends and relations, he makes a number of *trials* – for such is the meaning of the word *essai*, which he invented as a literary term – in order to test his response to different subjects and situations. He writes on education and friendship, on the uncertainty of our judgement and the strength of the imagina-tion, or develops what appears to be an entirely wayward reflec-tion on the subject of cannibals or coaches. But all the time he is making a trial of himself and his opinions, in an endeavour to see which of them are permanent and which temporary; which of them arise from the passing circumstances of his life and the particular climate of his times, with its pedantic scholarship, its religious dissensions, and its cruel civil wars, and which belong to the man himself, Michel de Montaigne.

This constant reference back to the man himself might sug-gest that it is a monstrous egoist we shall be meeting. If he can consider nothing for its own sake, then Montaigne must surely take an inflated view of his own personality. This is certainly not so. One of the greatest charms that has drawn readers to the *Essays* throughout the four centuries since they were first published, is that of Montaigne himself, as he is revealed in them. He is modest, truthful, humorous, and objective; he is clear-sighted, unprejudiced, and a great conversationalist. He has, in fact, all the qualities that the most exacting man could desire in a friend.

Montaigne is, moreover, tireless in his search for the truth; neither humbug nor easy theories could convince him. The first forty years of his life were devoted to a search for it in objective form. Yet in 1576, at the age of 42 he ordered his famous medal to be struck with the inscription, *Que sçais-je?* – What do I know? He had come to recognize by experience and reading that the intellect was powerless to discover those truths about which he was most curious. This is the period of his so-called scepticism, which was far less complete than his pious detractors have supposed. He was never a sceptic in the modern sense. The astronomical theories of Copernicus, and travellers' tales from the New World, showed him that Western Man, with his classical culture and his revealed religion, was not the centre of the Universe. What passed as truth was often a matter of climate and upbringing, of passion and prejudice, depending entirely on the inquirer's viewpoint. 'When I play with my cat, who knows whether she is amusing herself with me, or I with her?' he asks.

Montaigne could not shrug his shoulders, however, and become, like some men of our own century, a mere conforming relativist. He could not say to his neighbour, in Pirandello's phrase: 'That's the truth if you think it is.' Most things were, as he now saw, unknowable. But there remained one subject about which a man might discover something: himself.

Those great men of the past whose books were Montaigne's most constant reading and to whom he most frequently refers in his writings – Plato and Seneca, Cicero and Plutarch – had found an approach to truth by way of self-knowledge and self-discipline: twin virtues upon which, in Montaigne's opinion, all the classical philosophies depended. So he resolved to follow their example, and in no egoistic spirit set out to study the one subject available to him. In his reflections on death (Book Two, Chapter 19) he observes that in this last act there can be no more pretence. 'We must use plain words', he goes on, 'and display such goodness or purity as we have at the bottom of the pot.' Montaigne's purpose in his writings is to discover just what there is at the bottom of his pot.

Most autobiographers are anxious to build up a personality, to present themselves as more consistent, more resolute, more far-sighted, and built on an altogether grander scale than they would have appeared to their wives or their intimates. Their ambition, in the words of M. Ramon Fernandez,* is to foist a *false personality* upon the world. Fernandez divides the makers of false personalities into two classes. 'The first', he says, 'claim to possess an individual self, endowed with a positive existence, but one that cannot be projected beyond the boundaries of their own mind without being either distorted or destroyed.' The real truth about themselves, they say, can never be told. 'Men of the second class wish us to judge them', he goes on, 'by certain external signs which they believe will be sufficient to make us accept their pretensions.' Goethe presents himself in *Dichtung und Wahrheit* solely as a poet; the rest is not our concern. But the more commonplace inventor of an external false personality involves himself in continuous posturings and pretences. To defend his vanity and sustain the role he has adopted, he must perpetually do violence to whatever he truly is. But the internal kind of false portraiture, though rarer, is even more insidious; and its classic exemplar is Jean-Jacques Rousseau.

'Rousseau', says Fernandez, 'gives an account of his morality in terms of his desires. He makes the person he was coincide with the person he would like to be by explaining his intentions after the event.' The *Confessions* are full of incidents that show Rousseau pretending to emotions that he never had, and that clearly belonged to an imaginary self, whose secret, by Fernandez' definition, could never be revealed. Rousseau takes it for granted that this romantic ego was really in control of events and aware of situations at the moment when they happened, that it was, in fact, capable of consciously, and sometimes mysteriously, planning his life.

* *De la personnalité*. Paris, au Sans Pareil, 1928.

Rousseau must therefore explain, though he cannot explain away, any incident in which he fell short of the ideal picture of himself which he cherished in his imagination. Montaigne never explained his actions in this way; he merely noted them down. The word that he uses to describe this recording process is *constater*: a verb which implies no suggestion of moral or wishful criticism. Had he been guilty of a meanness like some of Rousseau's, he would no doubt have noted it down. Indeed he notes down many things that would be to the discredit of an ideal Michel de Montaigne, if he had carried one about with him. He confesses in his essay on Presumption (Book Two, Chapter 17) to writing a rough style – which we would consider a gross self-libel – to speaking with a provincial accent, to being rather dull in company, and to having largely forgotten his Latin. When Rousseau made such admissions, it was chiefly in the interests of his own glory. If he confessed to an inferior intellect, it was in order to throw into greater relief the alleged purity of his emotions.

Montaigne, on the other hand, by *testing* himself in a number of situations, discovers that, in Fernandez' words, 'his ego is no more than a tendency to act in this or that fashion; it is his knowledge of what he can and cannot do'. His essential personality is, in fact, a kind of observer which, although incapable of controlling the complete mechanism of his life, is able to prevent its springing too many surprises on him. It was to nourish and strengthen this observer that the *Essays* were written.

In Montaigne's view, says Fernandez, 'a man must not identify himself with his impressions and his passions; he is not truly himself except in so far as he refrains from following the promptings of his senses to the end'. Montaigne's watchword, like Goethe's, is *Restraint* (*Je m'abstiens*), which he took from the Greek sceptics, and inscribed, in Greek, on the reverse side of his famous medal.

The reward for restraint was, as Montaigne saw it, consistency:

What I do, I do habitually; and I go forward all of a piece. Hardly anything stirs in me that is secret or hidden from my reason; hardly anything takes place that has not the consent of every part of me, without divisions and without inner rebellion. My judgement takes the complete credit or the complete blame for my actions; and once it takes the blame, it keeps it for ever. For almost since my birth it has been undivided, with the same inclinations, the same methods, and the same strength; and in the matter of general opinions, I adopted even as a child the position in which I was to remain.*

Such is Montaigne as he appears in one of his final essays, when he has passed from a mood of scepticism to a final and lively acceptance of all experience, even the most painful. In the first forty-seven years of his life, much of his knowledge had been drawn from books. As a young man, he had been at Court, and he had practised as a lawyer at Bordeaux, but the centre to which he constantly returned was his library, which he had built in one of the towers of his country-house. Into it he had retreated in 1571, at the age of 38, to begin his writings in the next year, which was that of the Massacre of Saint Bartholomew. But in 1580, with the first two books of the *Essays* composed and published, though not in their final form, he re-emerged to make a journey from spa to spa of Italy and Germany, in search of a cure for the gall-stones from which he had begun to suffer. Henceforth, his life was more active; and it is this new activity that enabled him to carry his self-analysis further. He had seen himself in comfort, and in the company of his books; now he found himself among men, in strange society, travelling through unfamiliar scenery, and often in severe pain. All this gave him fresh means for self-examination.

He was recalled home from Italy by the news that he had been elected Mayor of Bordeaux, a post once filled by his father. His immediate task was to hold the city for the Catholics, and pacify the countryside. He had friends, however, in both parties; which prevented his gaining political advancement – supposing he had desired it – from his partial success in this task. He left Bordeaux when his second term of office was over, and did not return, since the plague was raging there. After making some detours to avoid infection, he returned to his estate. Some accused him of deserting his responsibilities. But in his own

* Book Three, Chapter 10, 'On the control of the will'.

district, scarcely less deadly than the plague, were bands of robbers disguised as religious partisans, who were laying waste the countryside, murdering the peasants, and holding the land-owners to ransom. Once he was captured by a company of free-booters, once they invaded his home, and often he was forced to ride out in pursuit of them; and all the while he was subject to attacks of his cruel complaint, that did not, however, prevent him either from hunting, which he had always enjoyed, or from performing his military duties.

Montaigne's reflections now were always practical. If he quoted a book it was because it provided an interesting parallel to his own experience. Many autobiographers have retired into some private place from which they could look back on their past life, and make their actions conform in retrospect to the idea they had formed of themselves. Montaigne, on the other hand, emerged from his retirement to finish his portrait. Now the active side of his nature was called in to supplement the passive; and at intervals during the last three years of his life he wrote the new essays of his third book, or added a relevant experience or example to the more theoretical arguments of the first two.

The picture that he leaves of himself is an entirely pleasing one. Not only was he, as has already been noted, modest, truthful, and unprejudiced, not only had he a sound knowledge of his own limitations, but he had also great and endearing powers of admiration for all that he found excellent in books and in his fellow-men. By cast of mind he was a country gentle-man, but one who had undergone the influence of the New Learning, which was strongly established in France in his boy-hood. Brought up to speak Latin as a child, by a system of education comparable to that instituted by Gargantua for the young Pantagruel, Montaigne came to know and love some Latin writers – Ovid, Virgil, Horace, and Seneca in particular – at an age when children under looser discipline were enjoying the romances of chivalry. Latin he always read fluently and easily, but he knew little Greek, and was familiar with Plato, Plutarch, and Xenophon only in contemporary French translations.

As he again and again insists, Montaigne was no scholar. He seldom read books through, but preferred to dip into them in search of arguments, anecdotes, and observations that threw light on his current interests. He did not care for the apparatus of learning, with its lengthy preliminaries, its strictly marshalled pleadings and proofs. He was always impatient to come quickly to the heart of the matter.

An intelligent man with little taste for scholarship, an active man without the guile, patience, or partisanship to achieve political advancement, Montaigne was rich on the emotional side by reason of a single relationship; his loving admiration for his older friend Étienne de la Boétie. With him only did he establish community of spirit. 'If I were pressed to say why I love him,' he writes in his essay 'On friendship' (Book One, Chapter 28), 'my only reply could be: "Because it was he, because it was I". ... At our first meeting ... we found ourselves so captivated, so familiar, so bound to one another, that from that time nothing was closer to either than each was to the other.' The friendship lasted for five years, beginning when Montaigne was 25 and ending with la Boétie's premature death in 1563. La Boétie, a judge at Bordeaux and a Hellenist, undoubtedly fostered Montaigne's taste for speculative writing; his influence lasted with his younger friend to the end of his life.

Montaigne tells us something of his father, but hardly anything of his mother, his brothers, his children, or his wife. With them it would seem, his relations were, to quote his own definition, 'natural and social'. One can feel some warmth in his references to his father, but he can have experienced very little emotion in his family life. The highest of all relationships was in his eyes a spiritual communion that could not coincide with the tie of kinship or sex. He found it again at the end of his life in his attachment to his adopted daughter, Mlle de Gournay, who was attracted to him, as he tells us, by his writings long before she met him face to face.

Though Montaigne hardly mentions his wife, he says a good deal about his amours, sometimes in rather frank detail, since they provided interesting material for his observations. We know his sexual preferences as we know his domestic habits, his hours of sleeping and waking, and the processes of his digestion. Until he met Mlle de Gournay, emotion seems to have been absent from his relations with women, whom he thought incapable of the highest kind of friendship. It was in large part absent too from his religion, which was a mere conforming Catholicism. Many of his relatives belonged to the Huguenot party. And he himself would willingly have pared away much of the old religion's dogma, if churchmen had not insisted that the Church's whole teaching hung together.* In fact, he kept his religion apart from his life, seeing God as just, but so far above man that He communicates with him only from a distance. The idea of any direct and mystical relationship is quite foreign to Montaigne.

We may speak of power, truth, and justice, which are words that mean something very great; but we cannot see this thing at all, or even conceive of it. We say that God fears, that God is angry, that God loves,

Immortalia mortali sermone notantes†

but these are agitations and emotions that can have no place in God in the form they take in us; nor can we imagine them as they are in Him. It belongs to God alone to know Himself and interpret His works.‡

Montaigne accepted a double truth; the sphere of faith and the sphere of reason were to him entirely separate. He paid formal tribute to the first, and concentrated his attention on the second, in which, despite his awareness of its practical limitations, he found his own method of spiritual attainment.

Such an attitude was still possible in Montaigne's day, when Humanism had not yet spent its force. Once the Counter-Reformation gained strength, however, and Protestantism was contained, it was attacked and condemned under the name of Fideism;§ and, finally in 1676, when the *Essays* had been

* See Book One, Chapter 27, 'That it is folly to measure truth and error by our own capacity'.

† 'Expressing immortal things in mortal words.' Lucretius, v, 121.

‡ Book Two, Chapter 12, 'The Apology for Raimond Sebond'.

§ For Fideism and its subsequent history, see Alan M. Boase, *The Fortunes of Montaigne*. Methuen, 1935.

freely circulating for close on a century, they were placed on the Index.

The views that Montaigne advanced in the very long twelfth essay of his second book, 'The Apology for Raimond Sebond', depended on the proposition that the existence of God and the immortality of the soul are incapable of proof. They must be accepted by faith. The scholastic philosophy maintained that such faith could be supplemented by reason. Montaigne, and with him many thinkers of his time, held that reason was here incompetent. Theology and philosophy were thus separated; and such scientific discoveries of the age as the new astronomy, which was steadfastly combated by the Church, could thus be accepted as a matter of reason, without any theological conclusions being drawn from them. Montaigne could find virtue in the pagan Greeks and Romans, or in the idolatrous Brazilians, without reminding himself or his reader, except in passing, that this must be of an inferior kind, since they had not received the Christian revelation.

Montaigne's own practical philosophy derived from the Classical forms of self-discipline, which he found in Socrates and the Stoics. The religions of worship and mystical revelation, whether Greek or Christian, were incomprehensible to him. He found no virtue in asceticism, but saw every reason to grant the mind and the body their ordinary comforts. He took great pains to discover what conditions suited them best. But his watchword was always sobriety, and none of his essays is more sober, more reasonable, or more level-headed than that upon prayer.* Prayer was clearly not his way. On the subject of controlling the will and bowing to reason, he comes near, however, to a religious attitude.

One sees, as one reads him, how broad his mind was, and how many of the ideas of the next two centuries he grasped by anticipation. Even Rousseau's *noble savage* is implicit in his account of Brazil, compiled from the information of captains who had made the Atlantic voyage. But far more affecting than his breadth of mind is the spectacle which we receive from his last

* Book One, Chapter 56.

essays of the steadfastness with which he bore his increasing loneliness, his frequent bouts of pain, and the dangers of his disorderly times: conditions which provided him with a limitless testing-ground, on which he learnt to accept the ineluctable facts of life and death, and to feel his way towards what lies beyond them.

2

Michel de Montaigne was born on 28 February 1533, the son of Pierre Eyquem, a soldier, lawyer, and landowner of Bordeaux and Montaigne in the Dordogne valley, and his wife Antoinette de Louppes, the wealthy descendant of a Spanish or Portuguese Jewish family, whose name had originally been López. Of his childhood and early education he tells us a great deal in the essay devoted to that topic;* and he gives some account of his affection for his father in that on the relations between parents and children.† By the time he was sent to the Collège de Guienne, at the age of 6, his mother had borne two more boys and one girl. She bore five sons and three daughters in all. At 13 Montaigne probably began to read philosophy, and at 16 he transferred from the University of Bordeaux to that of Toulouse, which enjoyed a higher reputation. At 21 he obtained a legal post at Périgueux, and in the same year his father was elected mayor of Bordeaux, to which town Montaigne was himself transferred in 1557. In the next year began his friendship with his senior colleague Étienne de la Boétie. Bordeaux soon fell into great disorder, with Huguenot plots and riots, which culminated in the execution by burning of a rich Huguenot merchant. Such events no doubt strengthened Montaigne's prejudices in favour of tolerance, which was granted to the Protestants by the edict of 1562, much against the will of the high Tribunal or Parlement of Bordeaux.

In 1561 Montaigne was sent to Court on a mission which lasted for a year and a half. In 1562 he followed the King to Rouen, which had just been captured from the Huguenots, and

* Book One, Chapter 26.   † Book Two, Chapter 8.

18

there saw those Brazilian natives whom he described in his essay on Cannibals.* During this time he may have had political ambitions, but these were short-lived.

In 1563, just before his thirtieth birthday, he returned to Bordeaux, and six months afterwards received the news of la Boétie's premature death. This was followed, two years later, by Montaigne's marriage to Françoise de la Chassagne, who brought him a considerable dowry; and in 1568 came his father's death, by which he inherited the estates of Montaigne.

Next year he published his first literary work, the *Natural Theology* of the Catalan Raimond Sebond, whose defence he was later to write. This was a translation made at his father's request of a work which set out to expound the Christian faith in the light of 'human and natural reason'. The study of Sebond, together with his earlier reading, of which we learn something from the essays, and the influence of la Boétie, prepared him for the life of reflection to which he gave himself up in 1571, when he abandoned the law and retired to his estates.

The greater part of the essays in Book One were composed in their first form in 1572 and 1573. Almost all of them were short, and took the form of notes on his reading. They were, indeed, as originally written, little more than a tissue of quotations, held together by a few reflections, on a number of conventional subjects. Nevertheless, when he wrote of friendship and education, Montaigne had already much of his own to say.

His writing was now interrupted by the events of the civil war, in which he took part; and he was not free to retire again to his library until 1576, the year of the *Que sçais-je?* medal, in which he began to write the 'Apology for Raimond Sebond'. This work occupies almost two-fifths of his second book, which was finished, and one or two essays, in particular that on Cannibals, added to its predecessor, in time for the publication of both volumes together in 1580, when Montaigne was 47.

Immediately after giving his essays to the printer, Montaigne set off in search of a cure for the stone, from which he had been suffering for the past two or three years. He visited Germany

* Book One, Chapter 31.

and Italy, stopping at Baden, Augsburg, Munich, Venice, Florence, and Rome, in which last city he was received in audience by the Pope, and had all his books confiscated.

He was taking the waters at Lucca when news came that he had been elected Mayor of Bordeaux. During his first term of office, he was able to make a business journey to Paris, and to escape often enough to Montaigne to add considerable passages to his essays, touching principally on his Italian journey. A second and enlarged edition was published in 1583, in which year his sixth and last daughter was born. Only one of his children, his daughter Leonor, survived more than a few months.

Next year he was re-elected mayor and received a visit from Henry of Navarre, now heir to the throne, who had thought well of him for many years. But though Montaigne was able to be of service to Henry, he was no longer ambitious on his own behalf. No sooner was his second term of office over than he was compelled to take his family wandering, as he puts it, to avoid the plague. Once he was able to return to Montaigne, he began to resume his reading; and in 1586 he was composing the autobiographical essays of the third book. A fourth edition, including these and many fresh additions to the first two books, was published in 1588. But, though political unrest and war continually disturbed him, Montaigne continued to expand his book, always making it more personal and revealing. In 1590 he refused a post offered him by Henry of Navarre, and on 13 September 1592 died, at the age of 59. An edition of the *Essays* containing all his additional material was published by his adopted daughter, Mlle de Gournay, in 1595. His popularity, which had begun in his lifetime, continued for more than half a century, and was revived after a brief decline by Voltaire and his generation, never to decrease again.

3

The present translation follows the text established by Albert Thibaudet (Édition de la Pléiade, 1950) which is based on Montaigne's own annotated copy with the last additions in his own hand, which has been compared with Mlle de Gournay's edition of 1595. I have, however, omitted, in the interests of straightforward reading, the marginal letters, which have been introduced by recent French editors to indicate what passages were added in each edition. It seems satisfactory enough to me that these essays are in the form in which Montaigne left them. The identification of the successive strata helps no one to follow his argument. In general, one can say that the later the writing the more intimate it is.

I have chosen as fairly as I could, from all three books, essays that will show their author in all his principal aspects. I would willingly defend every one of my inclusions, but should find it more difficult to justify my exclusions except on grounds of space. For a complete Montaigne would fill more than three volumes of this size. There is hardly one of the essays, however, which does not contain something of Montaigne's best; and once a man has established an acquaintance with him, he will gladly listen to him on any topic. In each of these twenty-six choices this very great Frenchman speaks both from heart and from head.

The *Essays* have been translated at least five times into English. The first to attempt them was the Italian Protestant refugee John Florio, the friend of Philip Sidney and possibly of Shakespeare. Though his version is considered one of the greatest Elizabethan translations, its virtues lie in the vigour of its English rather than in the truth of its rendering. Though repeatedly reprinted, Florio is far from Montaigne in the spirit, and not too accurate in the word. Charles Cotton's translation of 1685 is stylistically much closer to the original, and much more certain in its interpretation of Montaigne's actual meaning. Two American versions of this century, while far more scholarly than that of Izaak Walton's friend, appear to base themselves largely on him. I too have, on occasions, found him a reliable guide. The most recent rendering made on this side of the Atlantic is by E. J. Trechmann (Oxford University Press, 1927).

In translating Montaigne's foreign quotations, I have put

all those that are in prose into English, and shown by a note the sources from which he took them. The verse I have left in the original, since there is no adequate substitute for Virgil, Horace, or Lucretius. I have, however, rendered them into plain English, to appear as footnotes for the aid of the reader without Latin. Montaigne's quotations are frequently inaccurate. Sometimes they have been deliberately distorted to suit the point they have to illustrate, but often they appear to have been set down from memory – and Montaigne admitted that his memory was bad! My own versions are rough and ready, perhaps sometimes impressionistic, their only purpose being to give the general purport of the passage.

For reading and criticizing the whole of my text, and particularly the classical quotations, I am very grateful to Miss Rachel Levy, to whom I also owe my reintroduction, after almost forty years' neglect, to Latin poetry as a whole.

March, 1957 J. M. C.

The Essays of Montaigne

TO THE READER

This, reader, is an honest book. It warns you at the outset that my sole purpose in writing it has been a private and domestic one. I have had no thought of serving you or of my own fame; such a plan would be beyond my powers. I have intended it solely for the pleasure of my relatives and friends so that, when they have lost me — which they soon must — they may recover some features of my character and disposition, and thus keep the memory they have of me more completely and vividly alive.

Had it been my purpose to seek the world's favour, I should have put on finer clothes, and have presented myself in a studied attitude. But I want to appear in my simple, natural, and everyday dress, without strain or artifice; for it is myself that I portray. My imperfections may be read to the life, and my natural form will be here in so far as respect for the public allows. Had my lot been cast among those peoples who are said still to live under the kindly liberty of nature's primal laws, I should, I assure you, most gladly have painted myself complete and in all my nakedness.

So, reader, I am myself the substance of my book, and there is no reason why you should waste your leisure on so frivolous and unrewarding a subject.

Farewell then, from Montaigne,
this first day of March, 1580.

BOOK ONE

BOOK ONE: Chapter 7

That our actions should be judged by our intentions

DEATH, it is said, releases us from all our obligations. But I know some who have taken this saying in a special sense. King Henry the Seventh of England made an agreement with Don Philip, son of the Emperor Maximilian – or, to give him a higher title, father of the Emperor Charles V – that the said Philip should deliver into his hands his enemy the Duke of Suffolk of the White Rose, who had fled for refuge to the Netherlands, but this on condition that Henry should make no attempt on the life of the said Duke. But when the English king came to die, he commanded his son in his last will to put Suffolk to death immediately after his decease.

More recently in the tragedy of Count Horn and Count Egmont, which the Duke of Alva staged for us at Brussels, a certain incident occurred, among many others worthy of note. Count Egmont, upon whose pledge and assurance Count Horn had surrendered to the Duke, earnestly entreated that he might be the first to die, so that by his death he might be released from his obligation to Count Horn.

Death did not, in my opinion, excuse the English king from his promise, and I think that Egmont would have been excused from his even if he had not died. We cannot be held responsible beyond our strength and means, since the resulting events are quite outside our control and, in fact, we have power over nothing except our will; which is the basis upon which all rules concerning man's duty must of necessity be founded. Count Egmont, therefore, since he considered his whole mind and will to be pledged to his promise, though the power to keep it was not in his hands, would indubitably have been absolved from it even if he had outlived Count Horn. But the English king, having deliberately gone back on his word, cannot be excused merely because he postponed the performance of his treachery till after his death, any more than can the King of Egypt's mason in Herodotus, who kept the secret of his master's treasure faithfully so long as he lived, but revealed it to his children at his death.

I have known several men in my own time whose consciences have pricked them for retaining other men's property, and who have attempted in their wills to set things right after their decease. But it will not help them to fix a term in so urgent a matter; no attempt to redeem an injury at so small a cost and sacrifice to themselves will be of any avail. They owe something of what is really their own. And the more distressing and inconvenient the payment, the more just and meritorious is the restitution. Penitence must be felt as a weight.

It is even worse when a man who has concealed some spiteful feelings against a neighbour for the whole of his life gives vent to them in his last will. He is showing little regard for his own reputation in thus rousing the injured man's anger against his memory, and still less for his conscience in this failure to stifle his malice even in the presence of death, and in extending its life beyond his own. It is an unjust judge who postpones his judgements until the case is outside his jurisdiction.

I shall see to it, if I can, that my death makes no statement that my life has not made already.

BOOK ONE: Chapter 8

On idleness

As we see ground that lies fallow, teeming, if rich and fertile, with countless kinds of wild and useless plants, and observe that, to keep it serviceable, we must master it and sow it with various crops of use to ourselves; and as we see that women, of themselves, sometimes bring forth inanimate and shapeless lumps of flesh, but to produce a sound and natural birth must be fertilized with different seed, so it is with our minds. If we do not occupy them with some definite subject which curbs and restrains them, they rush wildly to and fro in the ill-defined field of the imagination,

> *Sicut aquae tremulum labris ubi lumen ahenis*
> *sole repercussum, aut radiantis imagine Lunae*
> *omnia pervolitat late loca, iamque sub auras*
> *erigitur, summique ferit laquearia tecti.**

And there is no folly or fantasy that they will not produce in this restless state.

> *velut aegri somnia, vanae*
> *finguntur species.*†

The mind that has no fixed aim loses itself, for, as they say, to be everywhere is to be nowhere.

> *Quisquis ubique habitat, Maxime, nusquam habitat.*‡

When lately I retired to my house resolved that, in so far as I could, I would cease to concern myself with anything except the passing in rest and retirement of the little time I still have to live, I could do my mind no better service than to leave it in complete idleness to commune with itself, to come to rest, and to grow settled; which I hoped it would thenceforth be able to do more easily, since it had become graver and more mature with time. But I find,

> *variam semper dant otia mentem,*§

that, on the contrary, like a runaway horse, it is a hundred times more active on its own behalf than ever it was for others. It presents me with so many chimeras and imaginary monsters, one after another, without order or plan, that, in order to contemplate their oddness and absurdity at leisure, I have begun

---

* 'As water, trembling in a brass bowl, reflects the sun's light or the form of the shining moon, and so the bright beams flit in all directions, darting up at times to strike the lofty fretted ceilings.' Virgil, *Aeneid*, VIII, 22.

† 'Unreal monsters are imagined, like a sick man's dreams.' Horace, *Ars Poetica*, 7.

‡ 'A man who lives everywhere, Maximus, lives nowhere.' Martial, VII, 73.

§ 'Leisure always breeds an inconstant mind.' Lucan, IV, 704.

to record them in writing, hoping in time to make my mind ashamed of them.

BOOK ONE: Chapter 9

On liars

THERE is no man so unsuited for the task of speaking about memory as I am, for I find scarcely a trace of it in myself, and I do not believe there is another man in the world so hideously lacking in it. All my other faculties are poor and ordinary, but in this I think I am most rare and singular, and deserve to gain name and fame thereby.

Besides the natural inconvenience that I suffer on this account – for assuredly, considering how necessary it is, Plato was right in calling memory a great and powerful goddess – in my country, when they want to say that a man has no sense, they say that he has no memory; and when I complain of the short-comings of my own, people correct me and refuse to believe me, as if I were accusing myself of being a fool. They can see no difference between memory and intellect.

This makes me look much worse off. But they wrong me, for experience shows that, on the contrary, excellent memories are often coupled with feeble judgements. They also wrong me in this, that the same words which indicate my infirmity, signify ingratitude as well – and I am nothing if I am not a good friend. They blame my affections instead of my memory, and turn an involuntary defect into a wilful one. 'He has forgotten this request or that promise,' they say. 'He doesn't remember his friends. He did not remember to do this, to say that, or to keep quiet about the other, for my sake.' Certainly I am prone enough to forgetfulness, but as for neglecting, out of indifference, a service which a friend has asked of me, that I do not do. Let them be content with my misfortune and not turn it into a kind of ill-will, a kind quite foreign to my character.

But I find some consolation, first because I have derived from this evil my principal argument against a worse evil, which might have taken root in me: the evil of ambition. For lack of memory is an intolerable defect in anyone who takes on the burden of the world's affairs.

Then, as several similar examples of nature's workings show, she has generously strengthened other faculties in me in proportion as this one has grown weaker. I might easily have let my intelligence and judgement follow languidly in other men's footsteps, as all the world does, without exerting their own power, if other people's ideas and opinions had ever been present with me by favour of my memory.

Again, my speech is consequently briefer, for the storehouse of the memory is generally better stocked with material than that of the invention. If my memory had been good, I should have deafened all my friends with my chatter, since any subject that calls out such powers as I have of argument and development warms and extends my eloquence. This would have been lamentable, as I have learned in the case of some of my intimate friends. In proportion as their memory gives them a complete and first-hand view of their subject, so they push their narrative back into the past and burden it with useless details. If the story is a good one, they smother its virtues; if it is not, you curse their fortunate powers of memory or their unfortunate lack of judgement. Once one is well on the road, it is difficult to close a discourse and break it off. There is no better way of proving a horse's strength than by pulling him up short and sharp. Even among men who keep to the point, I find some who would like to break off but cannot. While they are searching for a place at which to stop, they go maundering and trailing on like a man who is losing strength. Particularly dangerous are old men who retain the memory of past events, but do not remember how often they have repeated them. I have known some very amusing tales to become most tiresome when told by some gentlemen whose whole audience has been sated with them a hundred times.

I find some consolation, also, in the reflection that I have, in the words of a certain ancient author,* a short memory for

* Cicero, speaking of Caesar, *Pro Ligario*, xii.

the injuries I have received. Like Darius, I should need a
prompter. Wishing not to forget the insult he had suffered from
the Athenians, the Persian King made one of his pages come
and repeat three times in his ear, each time he sat down to table:
'Sire, remember the Athenians'; and it consoles me too that the
places I revisit and the books I re-read always smile upon me
with the freshness of novelty.

Not without reason is it said that no one who is not conscious of having a sound memory should set up to be a liar. I
know quite well that grammarians make a distinction between
telling an untruth and lying. They say that to tell an untruth is to
say something that is false, but that we suppose to be true, and
that the meaning of the Latin *mentiri*, from which our French
word for lying derives, is to go against one's conscience, and
that consequently it applies only to those who say the opposite
of what they know; and it is of them I am speaking.

Now liars either invent the whole thing, or they disguise and
alter an actual fact. If they disguise and alter, it is hard for them
not to get mixed up when they refer to the same story again and
again because, the real facts having been the first to lodge in the
memory and impress themselves upon it by way of consciousness and knowledge, they will hardly fail to spring into the
mind and dislodge the false version, which cannot have as firm
or assured a foothold. The circumstances, as they were first
learned, will always rush back into the thoughts, driving out
the memory of the false or modified details that have been
added.

If liars make a complete invention, they apparently have
much less reason to be afraid of tripping up, in as much as there
is no contrary impression to clash with their fiction. But even
this, being an empty thing that offers no hold, readily escapes
from the memory unless it is a very reliable one. I have often
had amusing proof of this, at the expense of those who profess
to suit their speech only to the advantage of the business in
hand, and to please the great men to whom they are speaking.
The circumstances to which it is their wish to subordinate their
faith and their conscience being subject to various changes,

their language has also to change from time to time; and so they call the same thing grey one moment and yellow the next, say one thing to one man, and another to another. Then, if these listeners happen to bring all this contrary information together as a common booty, what becomes of all their fine art? Besides they trip up so often when they are off their guard. For what memory could be strong enough to retain all the different shapes they have invented for the same subject? I have seen many in my time who have desired a reputation for this subtle kind of discretion, not seeing that the reputation and the end in view are incompatible.

Lying is indeed an accursed vice. We are men, and we have relations with one another only by speech. If we recognized the horror and gravity of an untruth, we should more justifiably punish it with fire than any other crime. I commonly find people taking the most ill-advised pains to correct their children for their harmless faults, and worrying them about heedless acts which leave no trace and have no consequences. Lying – and in a lesser degree obstinacy – are, in my opinion, the only faults whose birth and progress we should consistently oppose. They grow with a child's growth, and once the tongue has got the knack of lying, it is difficult to imagine how impossible it is to correct it. Whence it happens that we find some otherwise excellent men subject to this fault and enslaved by it. I have a decent lad as my tailor, whom I have never heard to utter a single truth, even when it would have been to his advantage.

If, like the truth, falsehood had only one face, we should know better where we are, for we should then take the opposite of what a liar said to be the truth. But the opposite of a truth has a hundred thousand shapes and a limitless field.

The Pythagoreans regard good as certain and finite, and evil as boundless and uncertain. There are a thousand ways of missing the bull's eye, only one of hitting it. I am by no means sure that I could induce myself to tell a brazen and deliberate lie even to protect myself from the most obvious and extreme danger. An ancient father* says that we are better off in the company of a dog we know than in that of a man whose language we do not understand. Therefore those of different nations do not regard

* St Augustine.

one another as men,* and how much less friendly is false speech than silence!

King Francis the First boasted of having by this means drawn circles round Francesco Taverna, ambassador of Francesco Sforza, Duke of Milan – a man of great reputation in the art of speechmaking. Taverna had been sent to make his master's excuses to His Majesty in a matter of great importance, which was this: the King wished to have constant channels of information in Italy, from which he had recently been expelled, and especially in the Duchy of Milan. He had decided, therefore, to keep a gentleman of his own at the Duke's court, an ambassador in effect, but in appearance a private individual ostensibly there on his own personal business. For the Duke very much depended on the Emperor – especially at that moment when he was negotiating a marriage with his niece, the King of Denmark's daughter, now the Dowager Duchess of Lorraine – and he could not establish open relations or intercourse with us without great prejudice to himself. A Milanese gentleman named Merveille, one of the King's equerries, was chosen for this office, and was despatched with secret credentials and instructions as ambassador, also with letters of recommendation to the Duke in the matter of his own private affairs as a mask and a show. However, he was at Court so long that the Emperor began to grow suspicious; and it was this, we believe, that gave rise to the subsequent events, which were that one fine night the Duke had Merveille's head cut off on a false charge of murder, his whole trial having been hurried through in a couple of days!

Francesco Taverna had come with a long falsified account of the affair – for the King had addressed himself to all the princes in Christendom, as well as to the Duke, demanding satisfaction – and he was received in audience one morning. In support of his case he advanced several plausible justifications of the deed, carefully prepared for the purpose. He pleaded that his master had never taken our man for anything but a private gentleman and a subject of his own, who had come to Milan on his own business and resided there in no other character. He denied all knowledge that Merveille was a member of the King's household or was even known to the King, much less that he was his

* Pliny, *Natural History*, VII, i.

32

ambassador. King Francis, in his turn, pressed objections and questions upon him, attacking him from all sides and cornering him at last on the point of the execution, carried out at night and apparently in secret. To which the poor embarrassed man replied, as if to put an honest face on the matter, that out of respect for His Majesty the Duke would have been sorry to let the execution take place in daylight. You can guess how quickly he was caught out in this clumsy self-contradiction, made in the presence of such a nose* as King Francis had.

Pope Julius the Second having sent an ambassador to the King of England, to incite him against King Francis,† and having stated his case, the English King, in his reply, dwelt on the difficulties he would find in making the necessary preparations for attacking so powerful a king, and put forward certain reasons for them. The ambassador then, ill-advisedly, answered that he had himself considered these difficulties, and had put them before the Pope. From this statement, so foreign to his purpose, which was to urge him to immediate war, the King of England at once inferred what he afterwards found to be the case, that this ambassador was privately inclined to the French side. When he informed the Pope of this, the ambassador's property was confiscated, and he barely escaped with his life.

BOOK ONE: Chapter 19

That no man should be called happy until after his death

Scilicet ultima semper
expectanda dies homini est, dicique beatus
ante obitum nemo supremaque funera debet.‡

EVERY child knows the story of King Croesus: how he was captured by Cyrus, how he was condemned to death, how, on the point of execution, he cried out: 'O Solon, Solon!', and

* See any portrait of Francis I.

† Probably Louis XII, since Pope Julius died before Francis I came to the throne.

‡ 'One should always wait till a man's last day, and never call him happy before his death and funeral.' Ovid, *Metamorphoses*, III, 135.

how, when these words were reported to Cyrus, he asked what they meant. His captive's answer was that now he was learning for himself the truth of a warning that Solon had once given him, to the effect that no man should be called happy, however kindly Fortune might smile on him, until the last day of his life was over. For human affairs are uncertain and variable, and the slightest shock may change them from one state to another wholly different. It was the same reason that prompted Agesilaus' well-known answer. Someone had called the Persian king happy for having reached his exalted station while still so young. 'Yes,' exclaimed Agesilaus, 'but Priam was not unhappy at his age either.'

We may see kings of Macedon, successors to the great Alexander, reduced to the level of carpenters or scribes at Rome, and Sicilian tyrants who have become schoolmasters at Corinth. The conqueror of half the world and commander of many armies is turned into a miserable suppliant to the rascally officers of an Egyptian king; such was the price paid by Pompey the Great for the prolongation of his life by some five or six months. And in our fathers' day, Lodovico Sforza, tenth duke of Milan, under whose foot all Italy had trembled for so long, died in prison at Loches, though not until he had lain there for ten years: which was the worst part of his bargain. And did not that most beautiful queen,* widow of the greatest king in Christendom, fall only yesterday beneath the executioner's axe?

There are countless other examples. For as storms and tempests are provoked by the pride and loftiness of our buildings, so there seem to be spirits above who are envious of our grandeurs here below.

> *Usque adeo res humanas vis abdita quaedam*
> *obterit, et pulchros fasces saevasque secures*
> *proculcare, ac ludibrio sibi habere videtur.*†

Fortune appears sometimes purposely to wait for the last year of our lives in order to show us that she can overthrow in one

---

* Mary, Queen of Scots.

† 'There is a dark power, hostile to human affairs, that tramples the fine (consular) fasces and cruel axes underfoot, and makes a silly toy of them.' Lucretius, v, 1233.

moment what she has taken long years to build. Then she makes us cry out with Laberius: 'Today I have lived too long by just one day.'*

So we have good reason to heed Solon's warning. He was a philosopher, however, and such men are not moved to happiness or unhappiness by Fortune's favours or her slights; for them greatness and power are accidents of an almost trivial nature. I think, therefore, that he was probably looking further into the future. In my opinion, what he meant was that since this mortal happiness of ours depends on the calm and contentment of a noble mind, on the resolution and assurance of a well-ordered soul, it should never be attributed to a man until we have seen him perform the last act of his drama, which will certainly be the most difficult. All the others allow of some disguise; our fine philosophical speeches may be only an outward show, or we may not be so hard pressed by our misfortunes as not to be able to keep our features composed. But in this last scene between ourselves and death, there is no more pretence. We must use plain words, and display such goodness or purity as we have at the bottom of the pot.

> *Nam verae voces tum demum pectore ab imo*
> *eliciuntur, et eripitur persona, manet res.*†

That is why the earlier acts of our lives must be proved on the touchstone of our last breath. There comes the supreme day, the day that is judge of all the rest. 'It is the day,' as one of the ancients says, 'that must judge all my past years.'‡ I leave the fruit of my studies for death to taste. We shall see then whether my speeches come from my mouth or my heart.

I have known many by their deaths confer a reputation for good or ill on their whole lives. By a worthy death Pompey's father-in-law Scipio redeemed the bad name that had dogged him up to his last day. When they asked Epaminondas which of the three he thought the best, Chabrias, Ephicrates, or himself,

---

* Macrobius, *Saturnalia*, II, vii.

† 'Not till then are true words drawn up from the depths of the heart; the mask is torn off and the reality is exposed.' Lucretius, III, 57.

‡ Seneca.

he answered: 'No one can decide that question till he has seen us all die.' Indeed, he himself would come off much less well if we were to weigh him up without regard to his great and honourable end.

God has ordered things as He has pleased; but three of the most execrable and infamous men of my time, whom I have seen in all the abomination of their lives, have died most proper deaths, in complete and perfect composure.

Some deaths are brave and fortunate. I have seen death cut the thread of a man's* days when he was on the point of magnificent achievement. In the flower of his age, he made so fine an end that I do not believe even his most ambitious and courageous designs attained a splendour equal to that of the moment that cut them short. Without moving towards it, he obtained his goal more grandly and more gloriously than he can have hoped or desired. And he gained by his fall a more ample power and fame than he had aspired to in his whole career. In judging another man's life, I always inquire how he behaved at the last; and one of the principal aims of my life is to conduct myself well when it ends – peacefully, I mean, and with a calm mind.

BOOK ONE: Chapter 21

On the power of the imagination

'A STRONG imagination brings on the event,' say the scholars. I am one of those who are very much affected by the imagination. Everyone feels its impact, but some are knocked over by it. On me it makes an intense impression, and my practice is rather to avoid it than to resist it. I wish I could consort only with the healthy and the cheerful, for the sight of another's anguish gives me real pain, and my body has often taken over the sensations of some person I am with. A perpetual cougher irritates my lungs and my throat; and I am more reluctant to visit a sick man to whom I am bound by duty and

* Probably a reference to Étienne de la Boétie.

interest than one who has a smaller claim on my attention and consideration. As I observe a disease, so I catch it and give it lodging in myself. It is no surprise to me that the imagination should bring fevers and death to those who allow it free play and encourage it. Simon Thomas was a great physician in his day, and I remember meeting him once at the house of a rich old man who suffered with his lungs. When the patient asked him how he could be cured, Master Thomas answered that one way would be for him to infect me with a liking for his company. Then if he were to fix his gaze on the freshness of my complexion, and his thoughts on the youthful gaiety and vigour with which I overflowed, and if he were to feast his senses on my flourishing state of health, his own condition might well improve. What he forgot to say was that mine might at the same time deteriorate.

Gallus Vibius so taxed his mind to understand the nature and periodicity of insanity that he completely lost his senses and was never able to recover them; he might have boasted that he had gone mad by learning. There are some who from fear anticipate the executioner's hand; and there was one who, when they unbound his eyes so that his pardon might be read to him, was found to be stark dead on the scaffold, slain by no other stroke than that of his imagination. We sweat, we tremble, we turn pale, we flush, beneath our imagination's impact; deep in our feather-beds, we feel our bodies shaken by its onslaughts, sometimes almost to the point of death; and fervent youth grows so heated in its sleep that it satisfies its amorous desires even in dreams,

> *Ut quasi transactis saepe omnibus rebus profundant*
> *fluminis ingentes fluctus, vestemque cruentent.**

Although there is nothing strange in seeing horns grow in the night on foreheads that had none at bedtime, there is something memorable about the case of Cippus, King of Italy. During the day he had been a passionate spectator at the bull-fight, and all night long he had worn horns in his dreams. His

* 'As if they were performing the entire act, the mighty wave gushes forth and stains their garments.' Lucretius, IV, 1305.

forehead had actually sprouted them by the power of the imagination. Anger gave Croesus' son* the voice that Nature had denied him, and Antiochus fell into a fever because Stratonice's beauty had become too deeply imprinted on his mind. Pliny says that he saw Lucius Cossitius change from a woman into a man on his wedding-day; and Pontanus and others record similar metamorphoses that have occurred in Italy in more recent times. By his own vehement desire and his mother's,

Vota puer solvit, qui femina voverat Iphis.†

Passing through Vitry-le-François, I was shown a man whom the Bishop of Soissons had confirmed under the name of Germain, but whom all the village's inhabitants had both known and seen to be a girl, and who had been called Marie up to the age of twenty-two. He was then old, had a heavy growth of beard, and was unmarried. He said that as he was straining to take a jump his male organs appeared; and the girls of that neighbourhood still sing a song in which they warn one another not to take long strides or they may turn into boys, like Marie Germain. It is not very surprising that this sort of accident happens frequently, for the imagination is so continually drawn to this subject that, supposing it has any power over such things, it would be better for it to incorporate the virile member in a girl once and for all, rather than subject her so often to the same thoughts and the same violence of desire.

Some people attribute the scars of King Dagobert and St Francis‡ to the power of the imagination. It is said sometimes to lift bodies from their places. Celsus tells of a priest whose soul was ravished by such an ecstasy that his body would remain for a long time without breath or feeling. St Augustine makes mention of another who no sooner heard some melancholy or doleful cry than he would fall into a sudden swoon, and be so

* According to Herodotus, he had been dumb from birth, but had found his voice when he saw his father in peril of death.

† 'Iphis as a man fulfilled the vows he had made as a woman.' Ovid, *Metamorphoses*, IX, 793.

‡ Dagobert's scars were caused by fear of the gangrene; St Francis's were the stigmata.

violently transported out of himself that it was no use shaking him or shouting at him, pinching him or scorching him, until he came to of his own accord. Then he would say that he had heard voices, but as if from far away, and would become aware of his bruises and burns. That this was no obstinate pretence, no concealment of his real sensations, was shown by the fact that all the time he had neither pulse nor breath.

It is probable that the belief in miracles, visions, enchantments, and such extraordinary occurrences springs in the main from the power of the imagination acting principally on the minds of the common people, who are the more easily impressed. Their beliefs have been so strongly captured that they think they see what they do not. I am also of the opinion that those comical impediments which so embarrass our society that they talk of nothing else are most likely caused by apprehensions and fears. I have personal knowledge of the case of a man for whom I can answer as for myself, and who could not fall under the least suspicion of impotence or of being under a spell. He had heard a comrade of his tell of an extraordinary loss of manhood that had fallen on him at a most inconvenient moment; and, when he was himself in a like situation, the full horror of this story had suddenly struck his imagination so vividly that he suffered a similar loss himself. Afterwards the wretched memory of his misadventure so devoured and tyrannized over him that he became subject to relapses. He found some remedy for this mental trick in another trick; by himself confessing this weakness of his and declaring it in advance, he relieved the strain on his mind and the mishap being expected, his responsibility for it diminished and weighed upon him less. When he had an opportunity of his own choosing – his thought being disengaged and free and his body in its normal state – he would have his virility tested, seized, and taken unawares, by previous arrangement with the other party. He was then completely and immediately cured of his infirmity. For once a man has been capable with a certain woman, he will never be incapable with her again unless out of real impotence.

This mishap is only to be feared in an enterprise where the

mind is immoderately torn between desire and respect, and particularly when the opportunity is unforeseen and urgent. There is no way of overcoming the trouble. I know someone who found it a help to come to it with his body already partially sated elsewhere. Thus the heat of his passion was allayed. Now, in old age, he finds himself less impotent because less potent. And I know another man who was greatly helped by a friend's assurance that he was furnished with a counter-battery of enchantments, certain to protect him. But it would be better if I were to explain how this came about.

A Count of very good family and an intimate friend of mine married a beautiful lady who had been courted by someone who was present at the marriage feast. This greatly perturbed his friends, and especially one old lady, a relation of his, who was presiding over the festivities and in whose house they were given. She was very much afraid of these sorceries and told me of her fears. I asked her to rely on me. Luckily, I had in my luggage a small flat piece of gold, with celestial figures engraved on it, as a charm against sunstroke and a remedy for headaches. It had to be worn just on the suture of the skull and, to keep it in place, a ribbon was sewn on to it, to be tied under the chin: a fantastic notion, but relevant to the subject we are discussing. Jacques Pelletier* had given me this odd present, and I decided to put it to good use. I warned the Count that he might encounter the same bad luck as other men had, certain persons being present who would like to play him a trick, but that he could boldly go to bed since I would act as his friend. I promised him that at need I would not withhold a miracle, which it was in my power to perform, provided that he would swear on his honour to keep it absolutely secret. He was merely to let me know by a certain sign when they brought in the midnight refreshment, if things had gone badly with him. This idea had been so dinned into his ears and into his brain that he found himself impeded by his disturbed imagination, and made me the sign. I told him then to get up under pretence of chasing us from the room and, as if in sport, to pull off the bed-robe I was

* Jacques Pelletier (1517–82), physician, mathematician, and humanist.

wearing – we were much of a height. This he was to put on him-self, and wear it until he had carried out my instructions. These were that, when we had gone, he should retire to make water, repeat certain prayers three times and go through certain motions. On each of these three occasions he must tie round his waist the ribbon that I put in his hands and very carefully place the medal which was attached to it over his kidneys with the figure in a certain position. After that, having made the ribbon quite tight so that it could not get untied or fall out of place, he should return to the business in hand, and not forget to throw my robe on the bed, so that it covered them both.

These monkey-tricks play the main part in the matter, for we cannot get it out of our minds that such strange practices must be based on some occult knowledge. Their absurdity lends them weight and gains them respect. In short, my talisman certainly proved itself more Venerian than Solar, more active than preventive. It was a sudden and odd impulse that led me to do a thing so alien to my nature. I am an enemy to all subtle deeds of deception, and I hate to take part in trickery, not only in sport but even to obtain an advantage; if the action is not wicked, the way to it is.

Amasis, King of Egypt, married a very beautiful Greek girl called Laodice; but though he had shown himself a regular gallant everywhere else, he found himself unable to enjoy her. Believing that there was some sorcery in this, he threatened to kill her. But she, considering his trouble to be of the imagina-tion, sent him to his devotions. He made his vows and promises to Venus, and on the first night after the performance of his oblations and sacrifices found his potency divinely restored.

It is wrong of women to receive us with pouting, querulous, and shrinking looks that quell us even as they kindle us. The daughter-in-law of Pythagoras said that a woman who goes to bed with a man ought to lay aside her modesty with her skirt, and put it on again with her petticoat. The mind of the assailant, disturbed by so many different alarms, is easily dismayed; and once the imagination has subjected a man to this disgrace – and it never does so except at the first encounter, because the desires are then more turbulent and strong, and because at the outset one has a much greater fear of failing – the fact that he has begun badly throws him into a fever, and vexation at his mischance carries over to succeeding occasions.

Married men, with time at their command, need not hurry, nor need they attempt the enterprise if they are not ready. It is better to accept the disgrace and refrain from inaugurating the marriage-bed when feverish and full of agitations, and to await another more private and less disturbed opportunity, than to be thrown into a perpetual misery by the surprise and disappointment of an initial failure. Before possession is taken, one who suffers from the imagination should by sallies at different times make gentle essays and overtures without any strain or persistence, in order definitely to convince himself of his powers. Those who know their members to be obedient by nature need only take care to out-manoeuvre the imagination.

We have reason to remark the untractable liberties taken by this member, which intrudes so tiresomely when we do not require it and fails us so annoyingly when we need it most, imperiously pitting its authority against that of the will, and most proudly and obstinately refusing our solicitations both mental and manual. Yet if on being rebuked for rebellion and condemned on that score he were to engage me to plead his cause, I might perhaps cast some suspicion on our other members, his fellows, of having framed this fictitious case against him out of pure envy of the importance and pleasure attached to his functions. I might arraign them for plotting to make the world his enemy by maliciously blaming him alone for their common fault. For I ask you to consider whether there is a single part of our bodies that does not often refuse to work at our will, and does not often operate in defiance of it. Each one of them has its own passions that rouse it and put it to sleep without our leave.

How often do the involuntary movements of our features reveal what we are secretly thinking and betray us to those about us! The same cause that governs this member, without our knowing it governs the heart, the lungs, and the pulse, the sight of a charming object imperceptibly spreading within us the flame of a feverish emotion. Are these the only muscles and veins that swell and subside without the consent, not only of our will, but even of our thoughts? We do not command our hair to stand on end, or our skin to quiver with desire or fear. The hand often goes where we do not send it. The tongue is paralysed and the voice choked, each at its own time. Even when, having nothing to cook, we could gladly prevent it, the appetite for food and drink does not fail to stir those parts that are subject to it, in just the same way as this other appetite; and it forsakes us just as unseasonably when it chooses to. The organs that serve to discharge the bowels have their own dilations and contractions outside the control of the wishes and contrary to them, as have those that serve to relieve our kidneys. And though, to vindicate the supreme power of our will, St Augustine claims to have seen a man who could command his bottom to break wind as often as he wished, and Vives, his commentator, caps him with another case from his own day of a man who could synchronize his blasts to the metre of verses that were read to him, this does not imply the complete obedience of this organ. For usually it is most unruly and mutinous. Indeed, I know one such that is so turbulent and so intractable that for the last forty years it has compelled its master to break wind with every breath. So unremittingly constant is it in its tyranny that it is even now bringing him to his death.

But let us take our will, on whose behalf we are preferring this charge. How much more justifiably can we brand it with rebellion and sedition, on account of its constant irregularities and disobedience! Does it always desire what we wish it to desire? Does it not often desire, to our obvious disadvantage, what we forbid it to? Does it let itself be guided, either, by the conclusions of our reason?

In short, I ask you on behalf of my noble client kindly to reflect that, although his case in this matter is inseparably and indistinguishably joined with that of an accomplice, nevertheless he alone is attacked, and with such arguments and accusations as, seeing the condition of the parties, cannot possibly appertain to or concern the said accomplice. Wherefore the malice and manifest injustice of his accusers is apparent.

Be that as it may, protesting that the wranglings and sentences of lawyers and judges are in vain, nature will go her own way. Yet she would have been quite justified in endowing that member with some special privileges, since it is the author of the sole immortal work of mortal man. For this reason Socrates held that procreation is a divine act, and love a desire for immortality as well as an immortal spirit.

One man, perhaps, by this working of the imagination, may leave the king's evil behind him, while his companion carries it back to Spain. That is why in such cases the mind must generally be prepared in advance. Why do doctors begin by practising on the credulity of their patients with so many false promises of a cure, if not to call the powers of the imagination to the aid of their fraudulent concoctions? They know, as one of the masters of their craft has given it to them in writing, that there are men on whom the mere sight of medicine is operative.

All this nonsense has come into my head through my recalling a tale told me by an apothecary who served in the household of my late father. He was a simple man and a Swiss – a people not much given to vanity and lying. He had known, some years before, a merchant of Toulouse who was sickly and subject to stone, and who often resorted to enemas, which he had made up for him by the physicians in different ways according to the phases of his disease. When they were brought to him none of the usual formalities was omitted; and he often tried them to see if they were too hot. Imagine him then, lying on his stomach, with all the motions gone through except that no application had been made! This ceremonial over, the apothecary would retire, and the patient would be treated just as if he had taken the enema; the effect was the same as if he actually had. And if the doctor found the action insufficient, he would administer two or three more in precisely the same way. My witness swears that when, to save the expense – for he paid for the enemas as if he had really taken them – the patient's wife tried sometimes to make do with warm water, the result

44

betrayed the fraud; this method was found useless and they had
to return to the first.

A certain woman, imagining that she had swallowed a pin
with her bread, shrieked and writhed as if she had an unbearable pain in her gullet, where she thought she could feel it
sticking. But, there being no swelling and no outward sign, a
clever fellow concluded that this was just fancy, and that the
idea had been suggested by a piece of crust that had scraped her
throat as it went down. So he made her vomit, and stealthily
threw a bent pin into what she threw up. Believing that she had
thrown up the pin, the woman was immediately relieved of her
pain. I know of a gentleman too who, three or four days after
having entertained a large party in his house, bragged, by way
of a joke – for there was nothing in it – that he had made them
eat cat in a pasty. One young lady in the company was thereupon so horrified that she was seized with a severe dysentery
and fever, and nothing could be done to save her. Even animals
can be seen, like us, to be subject to the power of the imagination, as witness those dogs who pine away with grief for the loss
of their masters. We also see them barking and trembling, and
horses whinnying and struggling, in their dreams.

But all this may be attributed to the close connexion between
the mind and the body, whose fortunes affect one another. It is
another matter when the imagination works, as it sometimes
does, not on one's own body but on someone else's. Just as one
body passes a disease to its neighbour, as we see in the case of
plague, smallpox, and pink-eye, which one person catches from
another –

> Dum spectant oculi laesos, laeduntur et ipsi,
> multaque corporibus transitione nocent,*

so, when the imagination is violently disturbed, it launches
shafts that may hit a distant object. The ancients believed that
certain women in Scythia, if aroused and angry with a man,
could kill him with a single glance. Tortoises and ostriches
hatch their eggs merely by looking at them – a proof that their

* 'When their eyes behold others in pain, they feel pain themselves, and
so many ills pass from body to body.' Ovid, De Remedio Amoris, 615.

eyes have some ejaculative power. And as for sorcerers, they are said to have an evil eye, which is capable of working mischief:

Nescio quis teneros oculus mihi fascinat agnos.*

I do not put much trust in magic. But we know by experience that women imprint the marks of their fancies on the children they are carrying in their womb, as witness the mother who gave birth to a blackamoor.† And there was that girl from a village near Pisa, who was all rough and hairy. When she was presented to the Emperor Charles, King of Bohemia, her mother said the child had been conceived like that because of a picture of St John the Baptist that hung above her bed.

It is the same with animals, as witness Jacob's sheep, and those partridges and hares that are turned white by the snow on the mountains. Someone in my house recently saw a cat watching a bird at the top of a tree. After they had gazed fixedly at one another for some time, the bird dropped, apparently dead, between the cat's paws, either stupefied by its own imagination or drawn by some power of attraction in the cat. Lovers of hawking have heard the story of the falconer who fixed his glance firmly on a kite in the air, and wagered that he would bring it down simply by the power of his eyes. They say that he did so.

For the anecdotes that I borrow I rely on the consciences of those from whom I have them. The inferences are my own, and depend on the evidence of common reasoning, not of experience. Anyone may add his own examples, and if he has none, the number and variety of occurrences being so great, he may still be sure that plenty exist. If my own comments are not sound, let someone else comment for me. In this study of our manners and behaviour that I am undertaking, fabulous incidents are as good as true ones, so long as they are feasible. Whether they happened or not, in Paris or in Rome, to John or to Peter, there is always some turn of the human mind about which they

* 'Some evil eye has bewitched my young lambs.' Virgil, *Eclogues*, III, 103.

† An anecdote related by St Jerome.

give me useful information. I note and draw profit from these anecdotes, whether they are shadowy or substantial. Of the various readings that the histories often provide, I make use of the most unusual and memorable. There are some authors whose purpose is to relate actual events. Mine, if I could fulfil it, would be to tell what might happen. The schools are rightly permitted to invent examples when they have none. I do not do this, however, and in that respect I surpass the most faithful historians in scrupulous reverence for truth. In the examples which I am drawing here from what I have heard, done, or said, I have refused to be so bold as to change even the most trivial and unimportant details. Consciously I do not falsify one iota; I cannot answer for my knowledge.

In this connexion I sometimes wonder whether it can be right for a prudent theologian, philosopher, or other such person of precise and delicate conscience to write history. How can they pledge their word on a popular belief? How can they answer for the thoughts of unknown persons, and advance their own conjectures as valid coin? They would refuse to give sworn testimony before a magistrate concerning actions involving several parties that had actually taken place before their eyes; and there is nobody whom they know so intimately that they would undertake to answer fully for his intentions. I consider it less dangerous, however, to write of the past than of present affairs, in as much as the writer has then only to produce some borrowed facts. Some people urge me to write a chronicle of my own times. They consider that I view things with eyes less disturbed by passion than other men, and at closer range, because fortune has given me access to the heads of various factions. But they do not realize that I would not undertake the task for all the fame of Sallust; that I am a sworn foe to constraint, assiduity, and perseverance; and that nothing is so foreign to my style as an extended narrative. So often I break off for lack of breath. I have no proper skill in composition or development, and am more ignorant than a child of the words and phrases used for the most ordinary things. Therefore I have undertaken to say only what I can say, suiting my matter to my powers. Were I to select some subject that I had to pursue, I might not be able to keep up with it. Besides, the liberties I take being so complete, I might publish opinions that reason, and even my own judgement, would find unwarrantable and blameworthy. Plutarch would readily tell us that if the examples he cites in his works are wholly and in every way true the credit is due to other writers; if they are of use to posterity, on the other hand, and are presented with a brilliance that lights us on the way to virtue, the credit for that is his own. An ancient tale is not like a medicinal drug; whether it is so or so, there is no danger in it.

BOOK ONE: Chapter 22

That one man's profit is another's loss

DEMADES the Athenian condemned a man of his city whose trade was to sell what is needed for funerals, on the ground that he asked too high a profit, and that he could only make this profit by the death of a great many people. This seems an ill-reasoned judgement, since no profit can be made except at another's expense, and so by this rule we should have to condemn every sort of gain.

The merchant only thrives on the extravagance of youth; the farmer on the high price of grain; the architect on the collapse of houses; the officers of the law on men's suits and contentions; even the honour and practice of ministers of religion depend on our deaths and our vices. No physician takes pleasure in the health even of his friends, says the ancient Greek comedy-writer,* no soldier in the peace of his city, and so on. And what is worse, let anyone search his heart and he will find that our inward wishes are for the most part born and nourished at the expense of others.

As I was reflecting on this, the fancy came upon me that here nature is merely following her habitual policy. For natural

* Philemon.

48

scientists hold that the birth, nourishment, and growth of each thing means the change and decay of something else:

> *Nam quodcumque suis mutatum finibus exit,*
> *continuo hoc mors est illius, quod fuit ante.**

BOOK ONE: Chapter 26

On the education of children

to Madame Diane de Foix, Comtesse de Gurson

I HAVE never known a father refuse to acknowledge his son however scabby or deformed the boy may be. Yet this is not to say that, unless he is absolutely besotted by paternal affection, he does not perceive these defects, but the fact remains that it is his own son. I too see, better than anyone else, that these are only the idle musings of a man who in his youth just nibbled the outer crust of learning, and who has retained only a general and amorphous impression of it – a little of everything and nothing thoroughly, after the French fashion. In short, I know that there is a science of medicine, one of jurisprudence, and four divisions of mathematics, and also roughly what their purposes are. I know too, perhaps, how much the sciences in general have contributed to our lives. But as for plunging any deeper, or for biting my nails over the study of Aristotle, the monarch of modern learning, or stoutly pursuing any particular branch of knowledge, that I have never done. Nor is there any art of which I could sketch even the elementary outlines. There is no child in the middle forms who cannot lay claim to more learning than I, who am incapable of examining him in his first lessons. At least I cannot do so in due form and, if I must, am compelled, ineptly enough, to pick out some matter of general interest, and to judge his natural understanding by that; to give him a lesson, in fact, that is as strange to him as his lessons are to me.

I have never settled down to any solid book except Plutarch

* 'Whenever a thing changes and alters its nature, at that moment comes the death of what it was before.' Lucretius, II, 753, and III, 519.

and Seneca, into which I dip like the Danaïds, filling and emptying my cup incessantly. Some part of my reading sticks to this paper, but to myself little or nothing sticks.

History is my favourite pursuit, or poetry, for which I have a special affection. For to quote Cleanthes, just as the voice, confined in the narrow channel of a trumpet, comes out sharper and stronger, so, in my opinion, a thought, compressed in the strict metres of verse, springs out more briskly and strikes me with a livelier impact. As for the natural faculties within me, of which my writing is the proof, I feel them bending under the burden. My ideas and my judgement merely grope their way forward, faltering, tripping, and stumbling; and when I have advanced as far as I can, I am still not at all satisfied. I can see more country ahead, but with so disturbed and clouded a vision that I can distinguish nothing. And when I venture to write indifferently of whatever comes into my head, relying only on my own natural resources, I very often light upon the matter I am trying to deal with in some good author, as I did just now in Plutarch, in his discourse on the strength of the imagination. Then I realize how weak and poor, how heavy and lifeless I am, in comparison with them,* and feel pity and contempt for myself.

Yet I take pleasure in the fact that my opinions have often the honour of coinciding with theirs and that I follow them, though far behind, proclaiming their virtues. I am glad too that I have the advantage, which many have not, of recognizing the great difference between them and myself. And yet I allow my own ideas to run their course, feeble and trivial as when I first conceived them, without plastering and patching the defects revealed to me by this comparison. A man must have strong legs if he intends to keep up with people like that. The injudicious writers of our century who scatter about their valueless works whole passages from old authors, in order to increase their own reputations, do just the reverse. For the infinitely greater brilliance of the ancients makes their own stuff look so pale, dull, and ugly that they lose much more than they gain.

Here are two contrary points of view. The philosopher

* Seneca and Plutarch.

Chrysippus dropped into his books not just passages but whole works by other authors, including in one instance the complete *Medea* of Euripides; and Apollodorus said that if all that was not his own were to be cut out of his works the paper would be quite blank. Epicurus, on the other hand, did not introduce a single quotation into any of the three hundred volumes that he left behind him.

I happened the other day to light on such a passage.* I had been languidly following a string of French words, so bloodless, fleshless, and devoid of substance and meaning that they were just words of French and no more. Then at the end of this long and tiresome road I came upon a rich and lofty sentence which towered into the clouds. If I had found the slope gentle and the ascent somewhat gradual, it would have been excusable. But the rise was so sheer and precipitous that after the first six words I felt myself flying into another world, from which I recognized the depth of the abyss out of which I had come. So deep was it that I have never had the heart to plunge into it again. If I were to load one of my discourses with such rich spoils, it would throw too much light on the stupidity of the rest.

To censure my own faults in some other person seems to me no more incongruous than to censure, as I often do, another's in myself. They must be denounced everywhere, and be allowed no place of sanctuary. I know very well how boldly I myself attempt at every turn to rise to the level of my purloinings and to remain there, even rashly hoping that I can prevent the judicial eye from discovering them. In this endeavour my industry plays as great a part as my inventive powers. And then, I do not contend with those ancient champions in the mass and hand to hand, but only in repeated brushes, in slight and trivial encounters. I do not press them hard; I merely try their strength and never go as far as I hesitatingly intend. If I could hold my own with them I should be doing well, for I only attack them at their strongest points.

To cover themselves, as I have seen some writers doing, so completely in other men's armour as not to leave even their

* One in which the thought of an ancient author coincided with his own.

finger-tips showing; to compose a work from pieces gathered here and there among the ancients – an easy task for a man of learning who is treating an ordinary subject – and then to attempt to conceal the theft and pass it all off as their own; this is in the first place criminal and cowardly, in that having no private resources with which to make a display, they try to boost themselves with other men's wealth; and secondly, it is very foolish to be satisfied by gaining the ignorant approbation of the vulgar through trickery, while discrediting oneself in the eyes of the intelligent. For their praise alone carries any weight, and they turn up their noses at all this borrowed decoration. For my part, I would do anything rather than that. I only quote others to make myself more explicit.

This criticism does not apply to those *centos** which are published as such; and I have seen some very clever ones in my time, among them – not counting the ancients – one published under the name of Capilupus. There are talents that can reveal themselves as well in this way as in any other; Lipsius, for instance, in his learned and laborious compilation, the *Politics*.

Whatever my borrowings, I mean, and whatever my clumsiness, I have not set out to conceal them, any more than I would conceal a portrait of myself, bald and grizzled, in which the painter had presented no ideal countenance; I give them out as my own beliefs, not as what I expect others to believe. My sole aim is to reveal myself; and I may be different tomorrow if some new lesson changes me. I have no authority to exact belief, nor do I desire it, for I do not feel myself to be well enough instructed to instruct others.

Someone who had read the preceding chapter said to me at my house the other day that I ought to have enlarged a little on the subject of children's education. Well, Madame, if I had any competence on the subject, I could make no better use of it than to present it to that little man who threatens shortly to make a happy departure from your womb – for you have too noble a nature not to begin with a boy. Having played so large a part in the arrangement of your marriage, I have some right to be

* A poem manufactured from fragments of other poems.

interested in the greatness and prosperity of all that shall spring from it. Besides, I am bound by the old claim that you have on my service to desire the honour, welfare, and profit of everything that concerns you. But really I know nothing about the subject, except that the most difficult and important problem confronting human knowledge seems to be that of the right rearing and education of children.

Just as in agriculture the operations that precede planting, and the planting itself, are certain and easy, but once the plant has taken life there are a variety of ways of cultivation and many difficulties; so with men, it requires little skill to plant them, but once they are born, training them and bringing them up demands care of a very different kind, involving much fear and tribulation.

The evidence of their inclinations is so slight and obscure at that tender age, and their promise so uncertain and deceptive, that it is hard to arrive at any solid judgement of them. Look at Cimon, look at Themistocles and a thousand others, how greatly they belied their expectations! The young of bears and dogs show their natural dispositions. But men, falling immediately under the sway of custom, opinion, and law, easily change or assume disguises. Yet it is difficult to overcome the natural bent; and so it happens that, having chosen the wrong course, we often labour to no purpose, and spend much of our lives training children up to callings in which they cannot establish themselves. But my advice is that, this being a great difficulty, they should always be directed towards what is best and most profitable, and that we should pay little heed to the slight conjectures and prognostications which we base on their childish actions. Even Plato in his *Republic* seems to me to attach too much importance to them.

Learning is a great ornament, Madame, and a tool of marvellous utility, particularly to persons raised to such a degree of fortune as yours. In fact, in low and menial hands it is not properly employed. It takes much more pride in lending its powers to the conduct of a war, to the ruling of a people, to cultivating the friendship of a prince or a foreign nation, than in devoting itself to the composition of a dialectical argument, or in arguing an appeal, or in prescribing a packet of pills. So, Madame, I believe that you will not neglect this part of your children's training, you who have savoured its pleasures and are yourself of a lettered race – for we still possess the books of those ancient Comtes de Foix from whom you and your husband are descended; and Bishop François de Candale, your uncle, every day produces more writings that will extend your family's fame for these qualities by many centuries. But I should like to give you just one idea of my own on the subject. It is at variance with common usage, and it is all the service that I can offer you in this matter.

The functions of the tutor whom you will choose for your son, upon your choice of whom the whole success of his education depends, will involve many other important duties upon which I will not touch, since I cannot say anything of value about them; and on this one point about which I venture to offer him my advice, he should only trust me in so far as he sees reason to do so. In the case of a child of good family who seeks learning not for profit – for so low an aim is unworthy of the Muses' grace and blessing, and anyhow depends on the cultivation of other men's favour – and not so much for external advantages as for his own good, and for his inward enrichment and adornment – one, in fact, who is more anxious to become an accomplished man than a scholar – I should wish great care to be taken in the selection of a guide with a well-formed rather than a well-filled intellect. One should look for a man who has both, but should put good morals and understanding before book-learning, and should require him to fulfil his functions in a new way.

The usual way is to bawl into a pupil's ears as if one were pouring water into a funnel, and the boy's business is simply to repeat what he is told. I would have the tutor amend this state of things, and begin straight away to exercise the mind that he is training, according to its capacities. He should make his pupil taste things, select them, and distinguish them by his own powers of perception. Sometimes he should prepare the way for him, sometimes let him do so for himself. I would not have him start everything and do all the talking, but give his pupil a turn and listen to him. Socrates, and after him Arcesilaus, made his pupils speak first and then spoke to them. 'The authority of those who teach is very often a hindrance to those who wish to learn.'*

It is well for a tutor to make his charge trot in front of him, so that he may judge his pace and decide to what extent he should himself hold back to keep in step with him. If this adjustment is not made we spoil everything. But to strike the right proportion and duly to conform with it is one of the hardest tasks that I know. It takes a lofty and very powerful mind to conform with a child's gait and to guide it. I walk with a steadier and firmer step uphill than down. When, according to our common practice, a teacher undertakes to school several minds of very different structure and capacity with the same lessons and the same measure of guidance, it is no wonder that, among a whole multitude of children, he scarcely finds two or three who derive any proper profit from their teaching.

A tutor must demand an account not just of the words of his lesson, but of their meaning and substance, and must judge of its benefit to his pupil by the evidence not of the lad's memory but of his life. He must make him consider what he has just learnt from a hundred points of view and apply it to as many different subjects, to see if he has yet understood it and really made it his own; and he must judge his pupil's progress by Plato's dialectical method. It is a sign of rawness and indigestion to disgorge our meat the moment we have swallowed it. The stomach has not performed its function if it has not changed the condition and character of what it was given to digest.

Our minds never work except on trust; they are bound and controlled by their appetite for another man's ideas, enslaved and captivated by the authority of his teaching. We have been so subjected to our leading-strings that we have lost all freedom of movement. Our vigour and independence are extinct. 'They

* Cicero, *De Natura Deorum*, I, v.

never cease to be under guidance.'* I had some private conversation at Pisa with an excellent man, but such an Aristotelean as to accept as his universal dogma, that the touchstone and measure for all sound opinion and all truth is its conformity with the teaching of Aristotle, and that outside this there is nothing but illusions and inanities. He believes that Aristotle saw and said everything. This standpoint, somewhat too broadly and unfairly interpreted, once brought him, and for a long time kept him, in great danger from the Inquisition at Rome.

The tutor should make his pupil sift everything, and take nothing into his head on simple authority or trust. Aristotle's principles must no more be principles with him than those of the Stoics or the Epicureans. Let their various opinions be put before him; he will choose between them if he can; if not, he will remain in doubt. Only fools are certain and immovable.

Che non men che sapper dubbiar m'aggrada.†

For if he embraces the opinions of Xenophon and Plato by his own reasoning, they will no longer be theirs but his. Who follows another follows nothing. He finds nothing, and indeed is seeking nothing. 'We are not under a king: each man should look after himself.'‡ Let him know what he knows at least; he must imbibe their ways of thought, not learn their precepts; and he may boldly forget, if he will, where he has learnt his opinions, so long as he can make them his own. Truth and reason are common to all men, and no more belong to the man who first uttered them than to him that repeated them after him. It is no more a matter of Plato's opinion than of mine, when he and I understand and see things alike. The bees steal from this flower and that, but afterwards turn their pilferings into honey, which is their own; it is thyme and marjoram no longer. So the pupil will transform and fuse together the passages that he borrows from others, to make of them something entirely his own; that is to say, his own judgement. His education, his labour, and his study have no other aim but to form this.

* Seneca, *Letters*, XXXIII.
† 'It pleases me as much to doubt as to know.' Dante, *Inferno*, XI, 93.
‡ Seneca, *Letters*, XXXIII.

Let him conceal all that has helped him, and show only what he has made of it. Plunderers and borrowers make a display of their buildings and their purchases, not of what they have taken from others. You do not see a high-court judge's *perquisites*; you see the alliances he has made and the honours he has won for his children. Nobody renders a public account of his receipts; everyone displays his profits. The profit from our studies is to become better and wiser men.

It is the understanding, said Epicharmus, that sees and hears: it is the understanding that turns everything to profit, that arranges everything, that acts, directs, and rules: everything else is blind, deaf, and soulless. Certainly we make it servile and cowardly by refusing it the liberty to do anything for itself. Has anyone ever asked his pupil what he thought of rhetoric or grammar, or of this or that sentence from Cicero? Our masters stuff these things into our memory, fully feathered, like oracles in which the letters and syllables are the substance of the matter. Knowing by heart is no knowledge; it is merely a retention of what has been given into the keeping of the memory. What we really know we can make use of without looking at the model, without turning our eyes to the book. How poor is the proficiency that is merely bookish! I would have it be an ornament, not a foundation; and this was Plato's opinion when he said that firmness, faith, and sincerity are the true philosophy, and that other sciences that are directed to other ends are just face-painting.

I should like to see Paluel or Pompey, those splendid dancers of our day, teaching us capers merely by demonstrating them to us while we sit in our seats, as these men set out to inform our understanding without setting it to work. I should like to see us taught to manage a horse, or a pike, or a lute, or to sing, without any practice, as these men try to teach us to form a sound judgement and to speak well without exercising us either in judgement or in speech. For the instruction that I propose anything that we witness will serve as sufficient book; a page's trick, a servant's stupidity, a conversation at table, are so many fresh subjects.

Human society is wonderfully adapted to this end, and so is travel in foreign countries, not merely for the sake of recording, as our French nobles do, the exact measurements of the Holy Rotunda, or the embroidery on Signora Livia's drawers, or of noting, like some others, how much longer or broader the face of Nero is on some old ruin than on a medal of equal antiquity, but for the principal purpose of discovering the characteristics and customs of the different nations, and of rubbing and polishing our wits on those of others. I should like a boy to be sent abroad very young; and first, in order to kill two birds with one stone, to those neighbouring countries whose languages differ most from our own, and to which the tongue cannot adapt itself if it is not trained early.

It is also a generally accepted opinion that it is wrong for a child to be reared in its parents' lap; their natural affection makes them too soft and tender, even the wisest of them. Parents are incapable of punishing a child's faults, or of letting him be brought up roughly and carelessly, as he should be. They cannot bear to see him come back sweating and dusty from his exercise, or drinking when he is hot or when he is cold, or see him on a restive horse, or facing a skilful fencer, foil in hand, or handling his first musket. But there is no help for it; if one wants to make him into a man of parts, one must certainly not spare him in youth and must often transgress the laws of medicine.

> *vitamque sub dio et trepidis agat*
> *in rebus.**

It is not enough to harden his mind; we must also toughen his muscles. The mind will suffer too much strain if it is not backed up; it is too much for it to perform a double function alone. I know how mine labours in the company of a most delicate and sensitive body that leans so heavily upon it. Often in my reading I have found my masters commending as models of great-heartedness and high courage men who were more remarkable, I believe, for a tough skin and hard bones. I have seen men, women, and children so constituted by nature that a

* 'To live under the open sky, and among dangers.' Horace, *Odes,* III, ii, 5.

beating to them is less than a flick of the finger to me, and who do not utter a sound or blink an eyelid under the blows they receive. When athletes ape the endurance of philosophers, it is rather out of strong nerves than a steadfast heart. To be used to hard labour is to be used to pain: for 'Labour hardens us against pain'.* A boy must be broken in to the discomfort and hardship of exercise, in preparation for the discomfort and hardship of a dislocation, the colic, cauteries, gaol, and torture. For he might fall a victim even to these last two which, as the times are, threaten the good as well as the bad. We are experiencing this at the present day, for when people fight against the law, even the best of men are threatened with a whipping and the halter.

Moreover, the tutor's authority, which ought to be supreme with the child, is checked and hindered by the presence of parents. I might add too that the respect paid to him by the household, and his consciousness of the power and greatness of his house are, in my opinion, considerable disadvantages at that age.

In this school of human intercourse there is one vice that I have often noted: instead of paying attention to others, we make it our whole business to call attention to ourselves, and are more concerned to sell our wares than to acquire a new stock. Silence and modesty are very proper qualities in human relations. The boy will be trained to be sparing and economical with his accomplishments, when he has acquired them, and not to contradict the idle sayings or silly stories that are spoken in his presence. For it is both rude and tiresome to quarrel with everything that is not to our liking. He should be content to correct himself, and not seem to condemn in others everything that he would not himself do, or to set himself up in opposition to general custom. 'A man can be wise without display and without arousing enmity.'† Let him avoid these overbearing and discourteous airs, also the puerile ambition of trying to appear cleverer because he is different, and of getting a name for censoriousness and originality. As it is unbecoming for any but

* Cicero, *Tusculans*, II, 15. † Seneca, *Letters*, CIII.

a great poet to indulge in the licences of his art, so it is intolerable for any but great and illustrious minds to claim any unusual privileges. 'Because a Socrates and an Aristippus acted contrary to general usage and custom, one must not suppose that one is similarly privileged; only their great and godly virtues authorized this liberty.'*

The pupil must be taught only to enter into conversation or discussion where he sees a champion worthy of his steel, and even then not to use all the resources that may help him, but only those that will serve him best. He should be trained to choose and sift his arguments with subtlety, also to be a lover of pertinence, and so of brevity. But above all, he should be taught to yield to the truth, and to lay down his arms as soon as he discovers it, whether it appear in his opponent's argument, or to himself in his own second thoughts. For he will not be sitting in a professorial chair to repeat a set lecture. He will be pledged to no cause except in so far as he approves it; nor will he be of that profession in which the freedom to repent and think again is sold for good ready money. 'No necessity compels him to defend all that is prescribed and enjoined.'†

If his tutor be of my way of thinking he will school him to be a very loyal, devoted, and courageous servant to his prince. But he will discourage any desire he may have to attach himself to that master except out of public duty. Not to speak of the many other ways in which our liberty is prejudiced by these personal obligations, either the judgement of a man who is bought and receives wages must be less free and honest, or he will be taxed with indiscretion and ingratitude. A courtier can have neither the right nor the will to think or speak other than favourably of a master who has chosen him from among his many thousand subjects to be fostered and advanced by his own hand. This favour and advantage will, not unreasonably, impair his freedom and bedazzle him. Therefore we generally find such people talking a language different from any other spoken in the state, and find them to be untrustworthy in state affairs.

* Cicero, *De Officiis*, I, 41.   † Cicero, *Academica*, II, 3.

The pupil's conscience and virtue should shine out in his speech, and should take reason alone for their guide. It must be explained to him that to admit any mistake he may find in what he has said, even though no one has noticed it but himself, is an act of good judgement and sincerity, the chief virtues that he is pursuing; that obstinacy and contentiousness are common qualities, generally to be found in the meanest minds; and that to change one's opinion and correct oneself, to give up a false position at the climax of a heated exposition, is a rare, strong, and philosophical virtue.

He must be warned that when in company he should have his eyes everywhere. For I find that the highest places are usually seized by the least capable men, and that great fortune and ability are seldom found together. I have been present when those at the head of the table were chatting about the tapestry or the taste of the malmsey, while many fine sayings were lost at the other end. He must sound every man's capacity. A herdsman, a mason, a passing stranger, he must draw upon them all and borrow from each according to his wares, for everything has some household use. Even other men's folly and weakness will be instructive to him. By noting each one's graces and manners, he will foster in himself a liking for good manners and a dislike for bad.

Let an honest curiosity be instilled in him, so that he may inquire into everything; if there is anything remarkable in his neighbourhood let him go to see it, whether it is a building, a fountain, a man, the site of an ancient battle, or a place visited by Caesar or Charlemagne:

> *Quae tellus sit lenta gelu, quae putris ab aestu,*
> *ventus in Italiam qui bene vela ferat.**

Let him inquire into the characters, resources, and alliances of this prince and that. Such things are very interesting to learn, and very useful to know.

In this study of man I would have him include, most particularly, those men who live only by the memories they have

* 'What land is benumbed with cold, what land crumbling with heat, and which is the fair wind that blows towards Italy.' Propertius, IV, iii, 39.

left in books. By means of histories, he will be in touch with the great minds of the best ages. It is a profitless study if one makes it so; but if one has the will, it can also be of inestimable value. It was the only study, as Plato tells us, that the Lacedaemonians thought worth while. What profit will he not reap in this respect by reading the *Lives* of our favourite Plutarch? But let his tutor remember the purpose of his duties, and impress upon his pupil the qualities of Hannibal and Scipio rather than the date of the fall of Carthage, and not so much where Marcellus died as why it was inconsistent with his duty that he should die there. Let him be taught not so much the facts of history as how to judge them. It is, I believe, of all subjects the one to which our minds apply themselves in the most various ways. I have read a hundred things in Livy that another has not. Plutarch read a hundred more in him than ever I have found, or than the historian ever put in, perhaps. To some it is a purely grammatical study, to some the anatomy of philosophy by which the deepest parts of our nature can be explored.

There are in Plutarch many extended reflections that richly deserve study. He is, in my opinion, the master craftsman in this field. But there are a thousand others on which he barely touches; he merely points with his finger to the way that we can go, if we please, and is sometimes content to make a single thrust at the heart of a question. We must draw out his points and bring them to full view. Take as an example, that remark of his that the peoples of Asia were subject to one man because they did not know how to pronounce the single syllable, No; which perhaps gave la Boétie the idea and the material for his *Voluntary Servitude*. Only to see Plutarch pick out some slight action in a man's life, or a remark that seems of no significance, is a treatise in itself. It is a pity that men of understanding are so fond of brevity; no doubt their reputations profit by it, but the loss is ours. Plutarch would rather have us applaud his judgement than his knowledge; he prefers to leave us not satiated but still hungry for more. He knew that even on the greatest subjects too much can be said, and that Alexandridas was right to reproach the man who made an excellent speech before the

Ephors, but was too long-winded. 'Stranger,' he said, 'what you say is right, but you are saying it in the wrong way.' Men that have thin bodies stuff them out with padding; those whose substance is slender puff it out with words.

Mixing with the world has a marvellously clarifying effect on a man's judgement. We are all confined and pent up within ourselves, and our sight has contracted to the length of our own noses. When someone asked Socrates of what country he was he did not reply, 'of Athens', but 'of the world'. His was a fuller and wider imagination; he embraced the whole world as his city, and extended his acquaintance, his society, and his affections to all mankind; unlike us, who look only under our own feet. When the vines in my village are nipped by the frost, my priest immediately argues that God is angry with the human race, and concludes that the Cannibals must already be stricken with the pip. Who does not cry out at the sight of our civil wars, that the fabric of the world is being overthrown, and that Judgement Day has us by the throat? He fails to reflect that many worse things have happened, and that people are thoroughly enjoying themselves in ten thousand other parts of the world just the same. For myself, when I consider the licence and impunity with which these wars are fought, I am surprised to find them so mild and restrained. When hailstorms are falling on a man's head, he thinks that the whole hemisphere has been struck by a raging tempest. And a Savoyard used to say that if that fool of a French king had known how to look after his interests, he might have become steward to the Duke of Savoy. The man's imagination could conceive no grandeur more exalted than his master's. Unconsciously, we all make this mistake; a most harmful mistake with serious consequences. But whoever calls to his mind, as in a picture, the great image of our mother nature in all her majesty; whoever reads in her face her universal and constant variety; whoever sees himself in it, and not only himself but a whole kingdom, like a dot made by a very fine pencil; he alone estimates things according to their true proportions.

This great world, which some still reckon to be but one

example of a whole genus, is the mirror into which we must look if we are to behold ourselves from the proper standpoint. In fact, I would have this be my pupil's book. So many dispositions, sects, judgements, opinions, laws, and customs teach us to judge sanely of our own, and teach our understanding how to recognize its imperfections and natural weaknesses; which is no trivial lesson. So many national revolutions and changes of public fortune teach us to consider our own no great miracle. So many names, so many victories, so many conquests buried in oblivion, render ridiculous our hope of eternalizing our own names by the capture of ten insignificant troopers or of a henroost, known only by the fact of its fall. The pride and arrogance of so much foreign display, the swollen majesty of so many courts and great houses, steadies us and enables our eyes to endure the brilliance of our own without blinking. All those millions of men buried before our time encourage us not to fear our departure to another world where we shall find so much good company. And so with all the rest.

Our life, said Pythagoras, is like the great and crowded assembly at the Olympic games. Some exercise the body in order to win glory in the contests; others bring merchandise there to sell for profit. There are some – and these are not the worst – whose only aim is to observe how and why everything is done, and to be spectators of other men's lives, in order to judge and regulate their own.

Fit examples can be chosen for all the most profitable teachings of philosophy to which human actions ought to be referred, as to a standard. Our pupil should be told:

> *quid fas optare, quid asper*
> *utile nummus habet, patriae carisque propinquis*
> *quantum elargiri deceat, quem te deus esse*
> *iussit et humana qua parte locatus es in re, ...*
> *quid sumus et quidnam victuri gignimur,* *

* 'What it is right to desire, what hard-earned money is useful for, how much should be bestowed on country and dear kindred, what sort of man God intended you to be, and for what place in the commonwealth he marked you out ... what we are and what life we are born to lead.' Persius, *Satires*, III, 69–72 and 67.

what it is to know and not to know, what the aim of his study should be; what courage, temperance, and justice are; what the difference is between ambition and greed, servitude and submission, licence and liberty; by what signs one may recognize genuine and solid contentment; to what extent we should fear death, suffering, and shame,

Et quo quemque modo fugiatque feratque laborem,*

by what springs we move; and the reason for all the different impulses within us. For it seems to me that the first ideas which his mind should be made to absorb must be those that regulate his behaviour and morals, that teach him to know himself, and to know how to die well and live well.

Among the liberal arts, let us start with the one that makes us free. They are all of some service in teaching us how to live and employ our lives, as is everything else to a certain extent. But let us choose the one that serves us directly and professedly. If we knew how to restrict our life-functions within their just and natural limits, we should find that most of the branches of knowledge in current usage are valueless to us; and that even in those which are valuable, there are quite profitless stretches and depths which we should do better to avoid. Following Socrates' instructions, we must limit the extent of our studies in those branches which are lacking in utility.

> *sapere aude:*
> *incipe. qui recte vivendi prorogat horam,*
> *rusticus expectat dum defluat amnis: at ille*
> *labitur et labetur in omne volubilis aevum.*†

It is very foolish to teach our children

> *Quid moveant Pisces animosaque signa Leonis,*
> *lotus et Hesperia quid Capricornus aqua,*‡

---

* 'And how to avoid or endure each kind of hardship.' Virgil, *Aeneid,* III, 459 (rightly *fugiasque ferasque*).

† 'Dare to be wise! Begin now. The man who puts off the day when he will live rightly is like the peasant who waits for the river to drain away. But it flows on, and will flow on for ever.' Horace, *Epistles,* I, ii, 40.

‡ 'What is the influence of Pisces, and of the fierce constellation of the Lion, and of Capricorn bathed in the Hesperian Sea.' Propertius, IV, i, 85.

the science of the stars and the movement of the eighth sphere before we teach them their own.

> Τί πλειάδεσσι κἀμοί
> Τί δ᾽ ἀστράσι βοώτεω.*

Anaximenes wrote to Pythagoras: 'How can I meditate on the secrets of the stars when I have death or slavery always before my eyes?' For at that time the kings of Persia were preparing a war against his country. Everyone should ask himself this question: 'Beset as I am by ambition, avarice, temerity, and superstition, and having so many other enemies of life within me, shall I start speculating about the motions of the world?'

After the pupil has been told what serves to make him wiser and better, he must be taught the purpose of logic, physics, geometry, and rhetoric: his judgement once formed, he will very soon master whichever branch he may choose. His instruction should be given him sometimes verbally, sometimes by book; sometimes his tutor will put into his hands the author most suitable for that part of his instruction; sometimes he will give him the marrow and substance of the volume ready prepared. And if he is not himself familiar enough with books to find all the fine passages in them that suit his purpose, some man of letters can be associated with him who can supply him with the necessary provisions to be dealt and dispensed to his pupil. Who can doubt that this way of teaching is easier and more natural than that of Gaza?† His precepts are thorny and disagreeable, his words empty and fleshless, giving you nothing to catch hold of, nothing to rouse the spirits. But in the new method, the mind has something to bite and feed on. Its fruit is incomparably greater, and yet will be much sooner ripe.

It is a great pity that things have reached such a pass in our age, and that philosophy is now, even to men of intelligence, a vain and chimerical name, a thing of no use or value either in the popular opinion or in reality. The cause, I think, lies in these

* 'What do I care about the Pleiades or the constellation of the Ploughman?' Anacreon, *Odes*, XVII, 10.

† Theodorus Gaza (1398–1478), a Greek scholar, the author of a grammar and translator of Aristotle.

quibblings which have blocked the approach to it. It is very wrong to describe it to children as the unapproachable study, and as frowning, grim, and terrible of aspect. Who has disguised it in this wan and hideous mask? Nothing can be gayer, more agile, more cheerful, and I might almost say more sportive. It preaches nothing but jollity and merry-making. A sad and dejected air shows that here philosophy is not at home. When Demetrius the grammarian found a bunch of philosophers seated together in the temple at Delphi, he said to them: 'To judge by your serene and cheerful faces, I should say that you are engaged in no deep discourse.' To which one of them, Heracleon of Megara, replied: 'It is for those who inquire whether the future of the verb βάλλω should have a double λ, or who seek the derivation of the comparatives χεῖρον and βέλτιον, and of the superlatives χείριστον and βέλτιστον to wrinkle their brows as they discuss their subject. But philosophical conversation quickly enlivens and delights those who take part in it; it does not depress them or make them sad.'

> *Deprendas animi tormenta latentis in aegro*
> *corpore, deprendas et gaudia; sumit utrumque*
> *inde habitum facies.** *

The mind that harbours philosophy should, by its soundness, make the body sound also. It should make its tranquillity and joy shine forth; it should mould the outward bearing to its shape, and arm it therefore with a gracious pride, with an active and sprightly bearing, with a happy and gracious countenance. The <u>most manifest sign of wisdom is a constant happiness</u>; its state is like that of things above the moon: always serene. It is *Baroco* and *Baralipton*† that make their servants so dirty and smoke-begrimed; not philosophy, which they know only by hearsay. Why, philosophy's object is to calm the tempests of the soul, to teach hunger and fever how to laugh, not by a few imaginary epicycles‡ but by natural and palpable arguments!

* 'You can detect the mental torments concealed within a sick body, and you can also detect joy: the face reflects both states.' Juvenal, *Satires*, IX, 18.

† Terms of the old scholastic logic.

‡ Scientific term of the sixteenth century.

Its aim is virtue, which does not, as the schoolmen allege, stand on the top of a sheer mountain, rugged and inaccessible. Those who have approached it have found it, on the contrary, dwelling on a fair, fertile plateau, from which it can clearly see all things below it. But anyone who knows the way can get there by shady, grassy, and sweetly flowering paths, pleasantly and up an easy and smooth incline, like that of the vault of heaven. Through unfamiliarity with this sovereign, beautiful, triumph-ant virtue, which is both delicate and courageous, which is the professed and irreconcilable enemy of bitterness, trouble, fear, and constraint; and which has nature for guide, and good-fortune and delight for companions, they have created in their feeble imaginations this absurd, gloomy, querulous, grim, threatening, and scowling image, and placed it on a rock apart, among brambles, as a bogey to terrify people.

My tutor, who knows that he should fill his pupil's mind as much – or rather more – with affection for virtue than with respect for it, will tell him that poets have the feelings of com-mon men. He will give him palpable proof that the gods have made it a sweatier toil to approach to the chambers of Venus than those of Minerva. Then when the lad comes to be self-critical, and is offered the choice between Bradamante and Angelica* as a mistress to be enjoyed – a natural, vigorous, spirited beauty, not mannish but manly, in contrast to a soft, affected, delicate, and artificial one, the former dressed as a boy, with a glittering helmet on her head, the latter in girlish clothes and adorned with a pearl head-dress – his tutor will judge even his love to be a manly one if he differs entirely in his choice from the effeminate shepherd of Phrygia.†

He will then teach his pupil this new lesson: that the value and height of true virtue lies in the ease, the profit, and the pleasure of its practice, which is so far from being difficult that it is within the reach of children as well as men, of the simple as well as the subtle. Moderation as its instrument, not force. Socrates, virtue's first favourite, deliberately renounced all

* See Ariosto, *Orlando furioso.*
† Paris, who chose Venus rather than Juno or Minerva.

effort, to glide towards her by natural and easy stages. She is the foster-mother of human joys. By making them righteous, she makes them certain and pure; by moderating them, she keeps them in breath and appetite; by cutting off those that she rejects, she whets our desire for those that she leaves us and, like a mother, she leaves us an abundance of all those that nature requires, even to satiety, if not to exhaustion; unless, perhaps, we choose to say that the authority which stops the drinker short of drunkenness, the eater short of indigestion, and the lecher before he loses his hair, is an enemy to our pleasures. If common happiness plays her false, virtue rises above it or does without it, or makes another happiness of her own, that is neither fickle nor unsteady. She knows how to be rich, powerful, and learned, and to lie on perfumed beds. She loves life; she loves beauty, glory, and health. But her proper and peculiar function is to know how to use these good things in a disciplined way, and how to be steadfast when she loses them: a duty that is noble rather than laborious, and without which the whole course of life is unnatural, turbulent, and distorted. Lack of virtue is the most plausible reason for the rocks, brambles, and phantoms with which life is strewn.

If the pupil proves to be of so perverse a disposition that he would rather listen to some idle tale than to the account of a glorious voyage or to a wise conversation, when he hears one; if he turns away from the drum-beat that awakens young ardour in his comrades, to listen to another tattoo that summons him to a display of juggling; if he does not fervently feel it to be pleasanter and sweeter to return from a wrestling-match, dusty but victorious, with the prize in his hand, than from a game of tennis or a ball, I can see no other remedy than for his tutor to strangle him before it is too late, if there are no witnesses. Alternatively, he should be apprenticed to a pastry-cook in some substantial town, even if he is the son of a duke, in compliance with Plato's precept, that children should be placed not according to their father's qualities but to the qualities of their own minds.

Since it is philosophy that teaches us how to live, and childhood, like other ages, has lessons to learn from it, why are children never instructed in it?

Udum et molle lutum est, nunc nunc properandus et acri fingendus sine fine rota.

When life is over, we are taught to live. A hundred scholars have caught the pox before coming to read Aristotle *On Temperance*. Cicero used to say that though he should live two men's lives he would never have the leisure to read the lyric poets; and I consider those sophists even more deplorably useless. Our pupil has much less time to spare: he owes the pedagogues only the first fifteen or sixteen years of his life; the rest he owes to action. Let us devote this very short time to the necessary instruction. Away with all these thorny subtleties of dialectic, by which our life cannot be improved; they are wasteful. Take the simple arguments of philosophy, learn how to pick them and make fit use of them; they are easier to understand than a tale by Boccaccio. A newly weaned child is more capable of doing this than of learning to read or write. Philosophy has teachings for man at his birth as well as in his decrepitude.

I agree with Plutarch, that Aristotle did not waste his great pupil's time on lessons in the construction of syllogisms, or on the principles of geometry, but taught him wise precepts on the subject of valour, prowess, magnanimity, temperance, and that assurance which knows no fear; and he sent him out thus provided, while still a boy, to conquer the Empire of the world with only 30,000 foot-soldiers, 4000 horsemen, and 42,000 crowns. As for the other arts and sciences, says Aristotle, Alexander honoured them no doubt, and praised their virtues and attractions; but as for taking pleasure in them himself, he was not easily surprised by any desire to practise them.

petite hinc puerique senesque
finem animo certum miserisque viatica canis.†

This is what Epicurus said, at the beginning of his letter to

* 'The clay is moist and soft, let us hasten and shape it on the sharp, revolving wheel.' Persius, *Satires*, III, 23.

† 'Young men and old, take from here, a fixed aim for your minds, and provide for the wretchedness of old age.' Persius, *Satires*, V, 64.

Meniceus: 'Let not the youngest shun philosophy or the oldest grow weary of it. To do so is equivalent to saying either that the time for a happy life has not yet come or that it is already past.'

For all these reasons I would not have our pupil kept a prisoner. I would not have him given over to the melancholy humours of a hot-tempered schoolmaster. I do not want to spoil his mind by keeping it, as others do, always on the rack, toiling for fourteen or fifteen hours a day like a porter. Nor should I approve if, out of a solitary and brooding disposition, he were to apply himself immoderately to the study of his books. Were I to see this propensity in him, I should not encourage it. It unfits boys for social intercourse, and deflects them from better occupations. How many men have I seen in my time brutalized by this uncontrolled avidity for learning! Carneades was so besotted with it that he had no time to look after his hair or his nails. Neither should I wish the pupil's noble manners to be spoilt by contact with the incivility and barbarism of others. French wisdom was once proverbial for taking root early but having little hold. We still find, in fact, that there is nothing so charming in France as the young children. But they generally disappoint the hopes that are conceived of them, and when they are grown men we find them to excel in nothing. I have heard men of understanding maintain that it is the colleges to which they are sent – of which there is such an abundance – that make them into such brutes.

For our pupil, a little room, a garden, table and bed, solitude, company, morning and evening; all hours shall be alike to him, and all places will be his study. For philosophy, since it is the moulder of judgement and manners, shall be his principal lesson; and it has the privilege of entering everywhere. When Isocrates the orator was asked at a banquet to speak about his art, everyone thought him right to reply: 'Now is not the time for what I can do, and what it is now time to do I cannot do.' For to offer harangues or rhetorical disputations to a company assembled for laughter and merry-making, would be to create a most unseemly discord; and the same might be said of all other

71

forms of learning. As for philosophy, however, in so far as it treats of man, his duties and functions, all sages have agreed that its conversation is too charming for it ever to be denied admission to feasts or to sports. When Plato invited Philosophy to his Banquet, we see how pleasantly she discoursed to the company, in a fashion suitable to the time and place, although this is one of his loftiest and most salutary Dialogues.

> *Aeque pauperibus prodest, locupletibus aeque,*
> *et, neglecta, aeque pueris senibusque nocebit.**

Thus, doubtless, he will have fewer holidays than the rest. But as the steps that we take walking in a gallery may be three times as many, but tire us less than if they were taken on a fixed journey, so our lessons, occurring as it were accidentally, without being bound to time or place, and mingling with all our other actions, will glide past unnoticed. Even games and exercises will form a good part of his study: running, wrestling, music, dancing, hunting, the management of horses and of weapons. I would have the pupil's outward graces, his social behaviour, and his personal demeanour, formed at the same time as his mind. It is not a soul or a body that one is training, but a man; the two must not be separated. And, as Plato says also, we must not train one without the other, but must drive them side by side, like a pair of horses harnessed to the same shaft. When we listen to him, does he not seem to devote more time and more care to the exercise of the body, and to reckon that the mind will get its exercise at the same time, rather than vice versa?

 soul & body are trained together

For the rest, this education ought to be conducted with a gentle severity, and not as it is at present. Instead of being invited to study, children are now confronted with terror and cruelty. Away with violence and compulsion! There is nothing, in my opinion, that is so debasing and stupefying to a noble nature. If you want him to fear shame and punishment, do not inure him to them. Inure him to sweat and to cold, to wind, to sun, and to dangers, which he should despise. Rid him of all

* 'It is equally profitable to poor and rich and, to neglect it, will harm boys and old men alike.' Horace, *Epistles*, 1, i, 25.

fastidiousness and delicacy in regard to his clothes and his bed, his food and his drink. Accustom him to everything. He must be no pretty boy, no fancy fellow, but a sturdy, vigorous young man. I have always been of this opinion, in childhood, in manhood, and in old age.

The discipline of most of our schools has always been a thing of which I have disapproved. If they had erred on the side of indulgence, they might have erred less lamentably. But they are veritable gaols in which imprisoned youth loses all discipline by being punished before it has done anything wrong. Visit one of these colleges when the lessons are in progress; you hear nothing but the cries of children being beaten and of masters drunk with anger. What a way of arousing an appetite for learning in these young and timid minds, to lead them to it with a terrifying visage and an armful of rods! This is a wicked and pernicious system. Besides, as Quintilian very well observed, such imperious authority has some very dangerous consequences, particularly in the matter of punishment. How much more fitting it would be if the classrooms were strewn with flowers and leaves than with bits of bloodstained switches! I would have my school hung with pictures of Joy and Gladness, and of Flora and the Graces, as the philosopher Speusippus had his. Where their profit is, let their pleasure be also. One should sweeten the food that is healthy for a child, and dip what is harmful in gall. It is remarkable how solicitous Plato shows himself in his *Laws* for the pleasure and amusement of the youth of his city, and how much attention he pays to their races, games, songs, leapings, and dancings, the ordering and patronage of which he says the ancients gave to the gods themselves: to Apollo, the Muses, and Minerva. He dwells on a thousand precepts for his *gymnasia*, but pays very little attention to literary studies. Poetry in particular he recommends chiefly for the music's sake.

Anything singular or idiosyncratic in our habits and bearing should be avoided as an impediment to social intercourse, and as unnatural as well. No one could fail to be astonished by the constitution of Alexander's steward Demophon, who sweated in the shade and shivered in the sun. I have seen men run from the smell of an apple more rapidly than from a volley of musketry, others frightened by a mouse, others vomit at the sight of cream, and others at the making of a feather-bed; and Germanicus could not endure the sight or the crowing of cocks. There may perhaps be some occult influence in all this, but I think it could be dispelled if taken in good time. Training has done so much for me – though not without some trouble, it is true – that, except for beer, my stomach accommodates itself indifferently to anything it is offered. While the body is still pliable, therefore, one ought to condition it to all fashions and customs. Provided that we can keep a young man's will and appetites under control, let us boldly make him used to all nations and all countries, to irregularity and excess, if need be. In his practice he should follow custom. He should be able to do everything, but only like doing what is good. Even philosophers do not find it praiseworthy in Callisthenes that he forfeited the favour of his master, Alexander the Great, by refusing to keep up with him in drinking. He should laugh and sport and debauch himself with his prince. Even in his debauches I would have him surpass his companions in vigour and persistency, and refrain from evil-doing not from lack of strength or skill, but only from lack of inclination. 'There is a great difference between a man who does not want to sin and one who does not know how to.'*

I thought I was honouring a certain nobleman who is as far removed from such excesses as any man in France, when I asked him, in good company, how many times in his life he had got drunk in Germany in the interest of the King's business. Taking this in the right spirit, he answered 'Three times', and told us the circumstances. I know some who through lack of that faculty have got into great difficulties when they had to deal with Germans. I have often reflected most admiringly on the wonderful constitution of Alcibiades, who adapted himself so

* Seneca, *Letters*, xc. This paragraph was condemned by the Sacred College in Rome, when Montaigne was there in 1580. He promised to correct it, but did not do so.

easily to very diverse customs without injury to his health, sometimes outdoing the Persians in pomp and luxury, sometimes the Lacedaemonians in austerity and frugality. He was as much the ascetic in Sparta as in Ionia he was the voluptuary;

*Omnis Aristippum decuit color, et status, et res.**

I would train my pupil as one,

quem duplici panno patientia velat
mirabor, vitae via si conversa decebit,
personamque feret non inconcinnus utramque.†

These are my precepts; they will be more profitable to the man who puts them into practice than to the man who merely learns them. If you see him, you listen to him; if you listen to him, you see him. 'God forbid,' says someone in Plato, 'that to philosophize should mean simply to learn a number of things and discuss the arts!' 'Instruction in right living, the most fruitful of all the arts, is to be gained by life itself rather than by study.'‡

When asked by Leo, prince of the Phalasians, what science or art he professed, Heraclides of Pontus answered: 'I know neither science nor art, but am a philosopher.' Someone reproached Diogenes for being ignorant yet dabbling in philosophy. 'That makes me all the fitter to dabble in it,' he replied. Hegesias begged him to read him some book. 'You are joking,' said he, 'you prefer real, natural figs to painted ones. Why do you not also prefer real and natural exercises to written ones?'

Our pupil should not so much say his lesson as perform it. He should repeat it in his actions. We shall then see whether there is any wisdom in his plans, any goodness and justice in his conduct, any judgement and grace in his speech, any fortitude in his bearing of sickness, any moderation in his amusements, any temperance in his pleasures, any indifference in his

* 'Every condition, situation, and circumstance fitted Aristippus.' Horace, *Epistles*, I, xvii, 23.

† 'Who after carefully dressing himself in a lined garment, can change his way of life, and can play both roles with equal ease. Such a man I admire,' Horace, *Epistles*, xvii, 25–6 and 29.

‡ Cicero, *Tusculans*, IV, iii.

taste for flesh, fish, wine, or water, any order in his expenditure, and whether he 'regards what he is taught not in the light of knowledge, but as a rule of life, whether he is his own master and obeys his own principles'.* The conduct of our lives is the true reflection of our thoughts.

When asked why the Lacedaemonians did not commit the rules of bravery to writing and give them to their young people to read, Zeuxidamus answered that it was because they wanted to accustom them to deeds not words. Compare such a pupil, after fifteen or sixteen years, to one of these college Latinists, who will have spent as much time in simply learning to speak. The world is all babble, and I have never met a man who did not talk more, rather than less, than he should; yet half our lives are wasted in this way. They keep us four or five years learning words and stringing them together in clauses; as many more building them up into a long speech, duly divided into four or five parts; and another five, at least, learning to mingle them succinctly and weave them together in some subtle fashion. Let us leave this to those who make a special profession of it.

One day, on my way to Orléans, I met in the open country this side of Cléry, two Masters of Arts, travelling fifty paces apart towards Bordeaux. A little way behind them I saw a troop of horsemen with their captain at their head – it was the late Comte de la Rochefoucaut. One of my men inquired of the leading scholar who the gentleman was that was coming after him. Not having observed the company in the rear, he thought that I was referring to his colleague, and replied facetiously, 'He is not a gentleman, but a grammarian; and I am a logician.'

But our object is, on the contrary, not to make a grammarian, or a logician, but a gentleman. So we should leave them to their time-wasting. We have business elsewhere. Our pupil should be well supplied with things, and the words will follow only too freely; if they do not come of their own accord, he will force them to do so. I hear some people apologize for their inability to express themselves, and pretend to have their heads full of good things which they cannot bring out through lack of

* Cicero, *Tusculans*, II, iv.

eloquence. This is a delusion. Do you know what I think? These
are shadows cast upon their minds by some half-shaped ideas
which they cannot disentangle and clear up inwardly, and therefore are unable to express outwardly; they do not yet understand themselves. Only watch them stammering on the point of
parturition, and you will see that their labour is not at the stage
of delivery but of conception. They are only licking a formless
embryo. I personally believe – and with Socrates it is axiomatic
– that anyone who has a clear and vivid idea in his mind will express it, either in rough language, or by gestures if he is dumb:

> *Verbaque provisam rem non invita sequentur.**

And as another author said just as poetically in prose, 'When
things have seized the mind, the words come of themselves.'†
And yet another, 'The subject itself seizes on the words.'‡ He
knows no ablative, subjunctive, substantive, or grammar;
neither does his servant, or a fishwife on the Petit Pont. Yet they
will give you your fill of talk if you will listen, and will very
likely make no more mistakes in the linguistic rules than the
best Master of Arts in France. He knows no rhetoric, nor how,
by way of preface, to *capture the benevolence of the candid reader*; nor
has he any wish to do so. In fact, all such fine tricks are easily
eclipsed by the light of a simple, artless truth. These refinements
serve only to divert the vulgar, who are incapable of swallow-
ing solider and stronger food, as Afer§ very clearly shows in
Tacitus. The Samian ambassadors had come to Cleomenes, King
of Sparta, prepared with a fine long speech urging him to declare
war against the tyrant Polycrates. After hearing them to the end,
the Spartan King gave them their answer: 'As for your introduction and exordium, I no longer remember them, or the middle of
your speech either; and as for your conclusion, I will do nothing
of the sort.' There is a fine answer, I think, with the speechifiers
well rebuffed.

* 'When the matter is ready the words will follow freely.' Horace, *Ars
Poetica*, 311.
† Seneca, *Dialogues*, III, Introduction.
‡ Cicero, *De Finibus*, III, v.
§ Properly Aper. Montaigne is misconstruing a passage in the *Dialogue
on Orators*.

And what of this other example? The Athenians had to choose one of two architects to put up a great building. The first and more plausible came forward with a finely prepared speech on the subject of the projected work and swung the popular opinion in his favour. But the second used no more than three words: 'Noble Athenians, what this man has said I will do. ...'

When Cicero was at the height of an eloquent harangue, many were moved to admiration. But Cato only said with a laugh: 'We have an amusing consul.' A useful thought or a good stroke of wit is always seasonable, whether it comes early or late. If it does not fit either what goes before it or what follows, still it is good in itself. I am not one of those who think that good rhythm makes a good poem. Let the poet make a short syllable long, if he will; it is no great matter. If the idea is pleasing, if thought and judgement have played their part well, then I will say, 'Here's a good poet, but a bad versifier,'

*Emunctae naris, durus componere versus.**

Let a poet's work, says Horace, lose all its measures and joints,

tempora certa modosque, et quod prius ordine verbum est
posterius facias, praeponens ultima primis,
invenias etiam disiecti membra poetae.†

its character will not be changed by this; even the fragments will be beautiful.

When Menander was reproved because the day on which he had promised to deliver a comedy was drawing near and he had not yet started to write it, he replied to similar effect: 'It is composed and ready; all that remains is to fit it with verses.' Having the subject and material prepared in his mind, he thought very little of the rest. Since Ronsard and du Bellay have established

* 'His nose is good, but he composes harsh verses.' Horace, *Satires*, 1, v, 8.

† 'Take away the rhythm and the metre, and put the first word last and the last first; still the scattered limbs are those of a poet.' Horace, *Satires*, 1, v, 58–9 and 62.

— the eloquence, meter + form are of little importance the content is what's really important

the reputation of our French poetry, every little novice, it seems to me, puffs up his words and manages his cadences almost as well as they. 'It is more sound than sense.'* In the popular opinion there were never so many poets before. But while it has been quite easy for lesser men to reproduce their rhythms, they fall very far short of imitating Ronsard's rich descriptions and the delicate thought of du Bellay.

Yes, but what if our pupil is confronted with the sophistical subtlety of some syllogism? 'Ham makes one drink, drink quenches thirst, therefore ham quenches thirst.' Why, he should laugh at it. There is more subtlety in that laugh than in any answer. Let him borrow this amusing counter-finesse from Aristippus: 'Why should I untie it since it is tiresome enough tied up?' When someone advanced some dialectical subtleties against Cleanthes, Chrysippus said: 'Keep those tricks for playing on children. Do not divert the serious thoughts of a mature man with such stuff.' If these absurd quibbles, these 'involved and subtle fallacies'† are likely to persuade him of a falsehood, that is dangerous; but if their only effect on him is to move him to laughter, I do not see why he need be on his guard against them. There are some men who are so foolish as to go a good mile out of their way in pursuit of a witty remark, or who, 'instead of suiting their words to their subject drag in extraneous matters, to which their words will fit'.‡ And as another author says, 'There are some who are tempted by the charm of an attractive phrase to write about something they had not intended.'§ I prefer to twist a good saying in order to weave it into my argument, rather than twist my argument to receive it. Far from that, it is the business of words to serve and follow, and if French will not do it, Gascon may. I would have the subject be paramount, and so fill the hearer's mind that he has no memory of the words. The speech that I love is a simple and natural speech, the same on paper as on a man's lips: a pithy, sinewy, short, and concise speech, sharp and forcible rather than mincing and delicate:

* Seneca, *Letters*, XL.　　　　† Cicero, *Academica*, II, 24.
‡ Quintilian, VIII, iii.　　　　§ Seneca, *Letters*, LIX.

*Haec demum sapiet dictio, quae feriet,**

rather rough than tedious, void of all affectation, free, irregular
and bold; not pedantic, not friar-like, not lawyer-like, but
soldierly rather, as Suetonius says Julius Caesar's was, though
I do not see very well why he calls it so.

I have been in the habit of copying the careless manner of
dress adopted by our young men: the cloak worn negligently
with the hood over one shoulder, and the stockings ungartered;
which shows a proud contempt for all foreign adornments and
a careless neglect of artifice. But I find this carelessness still
better applied to the method of speech. All affectation is unbecoming in the courtier, especially in France where we are so
gay and so free; and in a monarchy every nobleman ought to
model himself on the fashion of the Court. We do well, therefore, to incline a little towards the artless and negligent.

I do not like a texture in which the joints and seams are
visible, just as in a lovely body one should not be able to count
the bones and the veins. 'Speech aids truth in so far as it is un-
studied and natural.'† 'Who makes a study of speech except
the man who wishes to talk affectedly?'‡ Eloquence is harmful
to the subject when it calls our attention to itself.

Just as in dress, any attempt to make oneself conspicuous by
adopting some peculiar and unusual fashion is the sign of a
small mind, so in language, the quest for new-fangled phrases
and little-known words springs from a puerile and pedantic
pretension. I wish that I could limit myself to the language of
the Paris markets. Aristophanes the grammarian was off the
mark when he criticized Epicurus for the simplicity of his
language and the purpose of his rhetoric, which was simply to
make his speech plain. The imitation of speech is so easy that
a whole people follows a new mode immediately; but the imitation of opinions and ideas does not proceed so fast. When the
ordinary reader discovers a similarity of dress, he most mis-
takenly thinks that he is dealing with a similar body. Strength
and sinews cannot be borrowed; the attire and the cloak may be.

* 'Striking speech is good speech.' *Epitaph* of Lucan.
† Seneca, *Letters*, XL.   ‡ op. cit., LXXV.

ON THE EDUCATION OF CHILDREN

The majority of those who consort with me talk like these essays of mine, but I do not know whether they have the same thoughts.

The Athenians, says Plato, pay particular attention to copiousness and elegance of speech; the Lacedaemonians aim at brevity; and the Cretans at fertility of thought rather than of language: the last are the best. Zeno used to say that he had two kinds of disciples: one that he called φιλολόγους, curious to learn things, who were his favourites; and the other λογοφίλους, who were concerned only with the words. This is not to say that good expression is not a fine and excellent thing; but it is not as excellent as it is made out to be, and it vexes me that our whole life should be devoted to it. I would wish first to know my own language well, and that of my neighbours with whom I have most dealings. Greek and Latin are undoubtedly an admirable ornament, but we buy them too dearly. I will describe here a method of getting them at less than the usual price, which was tried in my case. Let anyone make use of it who will.

My late father, in his search for a perfect method of education, made every inquiry that a man can among scholars and men of judgement, and was apprised of the disadvantages of the method then in use. He was told that the length of time we spend in learning tongues which cost the ancients none is the sole reason for our failure to reach the spiritual and intellectual grandeur of the Greeks and Romans. I do not believe that this is the sole reason. However, the expedient that my father found was this: while I was at nurse and before the first loosing of my tongue, he put me in charge of a German, totally ignorant of our language and very well versed in Latin. He later became a famous physician here in France, where he died. This man, whom he had engaged for the purpose at a very high salary, carried me around constantly; and with him he had two others less learned, to look after me and relieve him. None of them spoke to me in any language but Latin. As for the rest of the house, it was an inviolable rule that neither my father nor my mother, nor any manservant or maid, should utter in my presence anything but such Latin words as each of them had learned in order to chat with me. It was wonderful how much they all profited by this. My father and mother picked up enough Latin to understand it, and acquired sufficient skill to speak it at need; and so did those members of the household who had most to do with my upbringing. In fact, we were so Latinized that it spread to the villages round about us, where one still hears some craftsmen and their tools called by Latin names that have taken root by usage. As for me, I was over 6 before I understood any more French or Périgordin than I did Arabic. Without system, without books, without grammar or rules, without whipping, and without tears, I learnt a Latin as pure as my master's own, for I had no way of adulterating or confusing it. If, by way of test, they wanted to give me a theme, as is done in colleges, whereas other boys are given theirs in French, mine had to be given to me in bad Latin, to be turned into good. And Nicholas Groucchi, who wrote *De comitiis Romanorum*, Guillaume Guerente, the commentator on Aristotle, George Buchanan, the great Scottish poet, and Marc-Antoine Muret, whom France and Italy recognize as the best orator of our day, who were my private tutors, have often told me that in my childhood I had the language so readily at my disposal that they were shy of starting a conversation with me. Buchanan, whom I afterwards met in the suite of the late Marshal de Brissac, told me that he was then writing a book on the education of children, and that he was taking mine as a pattern. He was tutor at the time to that Comte de Brissac who has since shown himself so brave and so valiant.

As for Greek, of which I have hardly any knowledge at all, my father planned to have me taught it artificially, but by a new method, as an amusement and an exercise. We tossed our declensions to and fro in the manner of those who learn arithmetic and geometry by certain table games. For amongst other things, he had been advised to make me relish learning and duty not by forcing my inclinations but by leaving me to my own desires, and to train my mind in all gentleness and freedom, without rigour or constraint. He did this, let me say, to such an over-scrupulous degree that, because some hold that it troubles the tender brains of children to wake them in the morning with a start, and rouse them suddenly and violently out of their sleep – which is much deeper with them than with us – he used to have me woken by the playing of some instrument; and he was never without a man who could do this for me.

This detail which serves as an example of all the rest, speaks eloquently too for the wisdom and affection of my very good father, who must by no means be blamed if the fruits he gathered did not correspond to such meticulous cultivation. There were two reasons for this. In the first place, a sterile and unsuitable soil; for although I had strong and sound health, and with it a mild and tractable disposition, yet I was at the same time so heavy, sluggish, and drowsy that they could not rouse me from my idleness even to play. What I saw, I saw clearly, and beneath my heavy disposition harboured bold ideas and opinions in advance of my age. But I had a slow mind that would go no further than it was led, a tardy understanding, a weak imagination, and, worst of all, an incredibly defective memory. It is no wonder that my father could extract little that was of value from all this.

In the second place, like those who are urged by a frantic desire for a cure and so follow all sorts of advice, the good man was so afraid of failing in a project so close to his heart that he finally allowed himself to be carried away by the common opinion which, like the cranes, always follows anyone that takes the lead. He conformed to custom. Having no longer around him the persons who had given him his first ideas, which he had back from Italy, he sent me at the age of about 6 to the College of Guienne, which was then very flourishing and the best in France. Here he took every possible care in the choice of competent private tutors, and over all the other details of my education, reserving for me a number of special privileges contrary to the usage of schools. But for all that, it was still a school. My Latin immediately grew corrupt, and through lack of practice I have since lost all use of it. The only service that this new method of education did me was to let me skip the lower classes at the beginning. For when I left the school, at 13, I had finished the course – as they call it – and really without any benefit that I can now note in its favour.

The first taste that I had for books came to me from my pleasure in the fables of Ovid's *Metamorphoses*. For, at the age of 7 or 8, I would steal away from every other amusement to read them, because the book was written in my mother tongue, and was the easiest that I knew, and because, owing to its subject-matter, it was the best suited to my tender years. As for the Lancelots of the Lake, the Amadises, the Huons of Bordeaux, and other such trashy books as children waste their time on, I did not so much as know their names; and even now I do not know their contents, so strict was my discipline. I became more negligent, therefore, in the study of my other prescribed lessons. But here I was extremely lucky in having a man of intelligence as my tutor, for he was clever enough to connive at this irregularity of mine and at others of the same nature. Thus it was that I ran straight through Virgil's *Aeneid*, then Terence, then Plautus, and some Italian comedies, always lured on by the charm of the subject. Had he been foolish enough to interrupt this pursuit of mine, I think I should have come away from school, like almost all young noblemen, with nothing but a detestation of books. He behaved with great ingenuity, and pretended to see nothing. Thus by allowing me to feast on these books only by stealth and keeping me gently to my task in my other, regular studies, he sharpened my appetite. The principal qualities that my father sought in those into whose charge he put me, were friendliness and an easy disposition. For my only faults of character being sloth and idleness, the danger was, not that I should do wrong, but that I should do nothing. Nobody prophesied that I should become wicked, but merely useless. They foresaw a distaste for work, but no mischief.

I am conscious that it has turned out as they predicted. The complaints that resound in my ears are to this effect: 'Lazy, indifferent to the bonds of friendship and kinship, and to public duties; too withdrawn.' The most critical do not say: 'Why did he take that? Why did he not pay for it?', but, 'Why does he not fulfil expectations? Why does he give nothing?' I ought to be thankful that I am found wanting only in such acts of supererogation. But it is unjust of them to demand of me what I do not owe, much more rigorously than they ask of themselves what they do owe. By that demand, they deny the gratuitous character of my action, and so refuse me the thanks that should be my due. For active well-doing ought to count for more, coming from me, seeing that I am under no obligation whatever. I am the freer to dispose of my fortune for its being all my own. However, if I were a great blazoner of my own deeds, I could perhaps rebut these reproaches, and point out to some of my critics that what offends them is not so much my failure to do enough, but the fact that I could do much more than I do.

Yet all this time my mind was vigorously and ceaselessly active on its own account; it made clear and confident judgements on subjects within its knowledge and digested them alone, communicating them to nobody. And, among other things, I believe that it would have been truly incapable of yielding to force and violence.

Shall I add to the reckoning a certain faculty of my childhood: the power of commanding my expression, and suiting my voice and gestures to any part that I undertook? For, in advance of my years,

*Alter ab undecimo tum me iam acceperat annus.**

I had played the chief parts in the Latin tragedies of Buchanan, Guerente, and Muret, of which dignified performances were given in our College of Guienne. In this, as in all other branches of his duties, our principal, Andreas Goveanus, was incomparably the best principal in France, and I was considered a first-class performer. Acting does not seem to me an unsuitable pastime for children of good family; and I have seen our princes lend themselves to it in person, after the example of some of the ancients, in a most honourable and commendable way. In Greece it was even permissible for men of quality to make acting their profession: 'He confided in Ariston, the tragic actor, a man of good family and fortune, whose calling did not

* 'I had hardly reached the age of twelve.' Virgil, *Eclogues*, VIII, 40.

prejudice his position, for it is not considered disgraceful among the Greeks.'*

I have always thought it unreasonable to condemn this amusement, and unjust to refuse entrance into our large cities to actors who are worth seeing, thus begrudging the populace a public entertainment. Wise administrators take care to assemble and unite their citizens, not only for the serious duties of religion, but for sports and spectacles as well, to the enhancement of good-fellowship and friendship among them. And no more orderly amusements could be found for them than those that take place with everyone present and beneath the eye of the magistrate himself. For my part, I should think it reasonable if the magistrate and the prince were sometimes to give the people a show at their own expense, out of paternal kindness and affection, and if in populous cities there should be places appointed and set apart for these spectacles – as a diversion from worse actions performed in secret.

To return to my subject, there is nothing like tempting the appetite and the interest; otherwise we shall produce only book-laden asses. With strokes of the birch we put a pocketful of learning into our pupils' keeping. But if it is to be of any use, it should not merely be kept within. It should be indissolubly wedded to the mind.

BOOK ONE: Chapter 27

That it is folly to measure truth and error by our own capacity

IT is perhaps not without reason that we consider credulity and the readiness to be persuaded to be signs of simplicity and ignorance. For I was once taught, I think, that belief is like an impression made upon the mind, and that the softer and less resistant the mind, the easier it is to impress something upon it. 'As the scale of the balance must necessarily sink when weights

* Livy, xxiv, xxiv.

are placed upon it, so the mind must yield to clear proof.'* The
emptier a mind is, and the less counterpoise it has, the more
easily it sinks under the weight of the first argument. That is why
children, the common people, women, and the sick are particularly apt to be led by the ears. But then, on the other hand, it
is a stupid presumption to go about despising and condemning
as false anything that seems to us improbable; this is a common
fault in those who think they have more intelligence than the
crowd. I used to be like that once, and if I heard talk of ghosts
walking, or prognostications of future events, of enchantments
or sorceries, or some other tale that I could not swallow,

> *Somnia, terrores magicos, miracula, sagas,*
> *nocturnos lemures portentaque Thessala,†*

I would pity the poor people who were taken in by such nonsense. And now I find that I was at least as much to be pitied
myself: not that experience has since shown me anything that
transcends my former beliefs, though this has not been for lack
of curiosity; but reason has taught me that to condemn anything so positively as false and impossible is to claim that our
own brains have the privilege of knowing the bounds and
limits of God's will, and of our mother nature's power. I have
learnt too that there is no more patent folly in the world than to
reduce these things to the measure of our own power and
capacity. If we call everything beyond the reach of our reason a
prodigy or miracle, how many such are continually appearing
before our eyes? When we consider through what mists and
how gropingly we are led to our knowledge of most of the things
within our grasp, we shall assuredly conclude that it is familiarity rather than knowledge that takes away their strangeness,

> *Iam nemo, fessus satiate videndi,*
> *suspicere in coeli dignatur lucida templa,‡*

and if these same things were presented to us newly, we should
think them as incredible as any others, or even more so,

* Cicero, *Academica*, II, 12.

† 'Dreams, superstitious horrors, wonders, witches, nocturnal spectres,
and Thessalian prodigies.' Horace, *Epistles*, II, ii, 208.

‡ 'Weary and sated with seeing, no man today deigns to lift his eyes to
the luminous spaces of the sky.' Lucretius, II, 1038.

si nunc primum mortalibus adsint
ex improviso, ceu sint objecta repente,
nil magis his rebus poterat mirabile dici,
*aut minus ante quod auderent fore credere gentes?**

The man who had never seen a river thought that the first he met with was the Ocean; and things that are the biggest within our knowledge seem to us the utmost that nature can create of that kind:

Scilicet et fluvius, qui non est maximus, ei est
qui non ante aliquem maiorem vidit, et ingens
arbor homoque videtur; et omnia de genere omni
maxima quae vidit quisque, haec ingentia fingit.†

'The habitual sight of things makes the mind accustomed to them; it feels no wonder and asks no questions about what is constantly before the eyes.'‡ It is the novelty rather than the greatness of things that prompts us to inquire into their causes.

We must bring more reverence and a greater recognition of our ignorance and weakness to our judgement of nature's infinite power. How many improbable things there are, vouched for by trustworthy people, about which we should at least preserve an open mind, even if they do not convince us! For to condemn them as impossible is rashly and presumptuously to pretend to a knowledge of the bounds of possibility. If we really knew the difference between the impossible and the unusual, and between what contradicts the order and course of nature and what goes counter to the common beliefs of man, neither believing hastily nor easily disbelieving, we should observe the rule of *Nothing too much*, prescribed by Chilo.

When we find in Froissart that the Comte de Foix knew, in Béarn, of King John of Castile's defeat at Juberoth the day

* 'If these things were, for the first time, unexpectedly presented to mortals, or were suddenly exposed before them, could anything be thought of as more marvellous, or less like what people had previously dared to think possible?' Lucretius, II, 1033.

† 'So it is that a river which is not very great seems so to one who has never seen one greater. A tree or a man appears huge in the same way. Everything of any kind seems to a man colossal if he has not seen anything bigger.' Lucretius, VI, 674.

‡ Cicero, *De Natura Deorum*, II, xxxviii.

after it happened, and read his account of the circumstances, we may well smile; and so we may too when our annals tell that on the very day when King Philip Augustus died at Mantes, Pope Honorius publicly solemnized his funeral rites, and ordered that the same should be done throughout Italy. For the authority of these witnesses is perhaps not weighty enough to restrain us. But what when Plutarch, after citing several examples from antiquity, tells us that, in Domitian's time, to his certain knowledge, the news of a battle lost by Antonius in Germany was made public in Rome, many days' journey away, and spread all around on the actual day of the defeat? And if Caesar maintains that the report has very frequently preceded the event, shall we say that these simple men have let themselves be taken in like the vulgar, being not so clear-sighted as we? Can any mind be clearer, livelier, or more discriminating than Pliny's, when he chooses to bring it into play, or any less prone to be lightly swayed? Setting aside the excellence of his learning, by which I set less store, in which of these two qualities do we in any way surpass him? And yet the very smallest schoolboy can convict him of falsehood, and give him a lesson on the progress of nature's works.

When we read in Bouchet* of the miracles performed by St Hilary's relics – well! – his reputation is not great enough to rob us of our liberty to contradict. But to condemn all such stories altogether seems to me strangely overbold. The great St Augustine testifies to having seen a blind child recover its sight upon the relics of St Gervais and St Protasius at Milan, and a woman at Carthage cured of cancer by the sign of the cross made upon her by another woman, newly baptized. He also states that Hesperius, an intimate friend of his, drove out the spirits that infested his house with a little earth from Our Lord's sepulchre, and that when this earth was afterwards taken to the church, a paralytic was suddenly cured by it; and that when a woman in a procession rubbed her eyes with a nosegay which she had just brushed against St Stephen's shrine, she recovered her sight, which she had lost some time before. He speaks of

* *Annals of Aquitaine.*

several other miracles too, of which he says he was himself a witness. What accusation shall we bring against him and the two holy bishops Aurelius and Maximinus, whom he calls on to confirm him? Shall it be of ignorance, of simplicity, of credulity, or of malice and imposture? Is there any man of our day bold enough to think himself their equal, either in virtue or piety, or in learning, judgement, and ability? 'Even if they brought forward no proof, their very authority would convince me.'*

It is a dangerous and serious presumption, and argues an absurd temerity, to condemn what we do not understand. For, having by virtue of your excellent intellect established the boundaries of truth and error, and found yourself compelled to believe stranger things than those you deny, you are then obliged to abandon those boundaries. Now what seems to me to bring so much confusion into our minds in our present religious troubles is the partial abandonment of their belief on the part of the Catholics. They imagine themselves to be displaying moderation and understanding when they concede some of the points in dispute to their opponents. Not only do they fail to see what an advantage it is to the attacker when you begin to give him ground and to retire, and how much it encourages him to pursue his advantage, but the very points that they choose as the most trivial are sometimes very important indeed. Either we must submit entirely to the authority of our ecclesiastical government, or we must dispense with it altogether. It is not for us to settle what degree of obedience we owe it.

And I can say this, moreover, from my own experience, since I formerly exercised this liberty of discrimination and personal choice, dismissing as negligible certain points in our Church ceremonial which had the appearance of being either too meaningless or too strange. But when I came to discuss them with learned men, I found that these things have a substantial and very solid foundation, and that it is only stupidity and ignorance that make us accept them with less reverence than the rest. Why do we not remember how many contradictions we find

* Cicero, *Tusculans*, I, xxi.

even in our own opinions, how many things we regarded yesterday as articles of faith that seem to us only fables today? Pride and curiosity are the two scourges of our souls. The latter prompts us to poke our noses into everything, and the former forbids us to leave anything unresolved and undecided.

BOOK ONE: Chapter 28

On friendship

As I was observing the way in which a painter in my employment goes about his work, I felt tempted to imitate him. He chooses the best spot, in the middle of each wall, as the place for a picture, which he elaborates with all his skill; and the empty space all round he fills with grotesques; which are fantastic paintings with no other charm than their variety and strangeness. And what are these things of mine, indeed, but grotesques and monstrous bodies, pieced together from sundry limbs, with no definite shape, and with no order, sequence, or proportion except by chance?

*Desinit in piscem mulier formosa superne.**

I am at one with my painter in this second point, but I fall short of him in the other and better part. For my skill is not such that I dare undertake a fine, finished picture that follows the rules of art. It has occurred to me, therefore, to borrow one from Étienne de la Boétie, which will grace all the rest of this work. It is a treatise to which he gave the name of *The Voluntary Servitude*; but others who did not know this have since very fitly renamed it *The Protest.*† He wrote this as an essay in his early youth, in praise of liberty and against tyrants. It has for a long time been circulating among men of understanding, not without singular and well-deserved commendation, for it is as fine and perfect as it could be. Yet it is far short of the best that he

* 'A beautiful woman that tails off into a fish.' Horace, *Ars Poetica*, 4.

† Montaigne would have included it in his *Essays* if the Protestants had not printed it under this title in a collection of pamphlets published in 1576.

could do; and if in his maturer years, when I knew him, he had conceived a plan, like this of mine, of committing his thoughts to writing, we should now see many rare things which would make our age almost as famous as antiquity. For, in natural gifts particularly, I know of no one who could compare with him. But he left nothing behind him except this treatise – and this only by chance, as I believe he never saw it after it left his hands – and some observations on that January Edict,* famous in our civil wars, which will perhaps yet find a place elsewhere. That is all that I have been able to recover from his possessions except the little book of his works which I have already published. To me he bequeathed in a will made when he was in the very grip of death his library and his papers, with a most loving message; and I owe a particular debt to this treatise because it was the means of our first acquaintance. For it was shown to me a long time before I met him, and gave me my first knowledge of his name, thus preparing the way for that friendship which we preserved as long as God willed, a friendship so complete and perfect that its like has seldom been read of, and nothing comparable is to be seen among the men of our day. So many circumstances are needed to build it up that it is something if fate achieves it once in three centuries.

There is nothing for which nature seems to have given us such a bent as for society. And Aristotle says that good lawgivers have paid more attention to friendship than to justice. Of a perfect society friendship is the peak. For, generally speaking, all those relationships that are created and fostered by pleasure and profit, by public or private interest, are so much the less fine and noble, and so much the less *friendships*, in so far as they mix some cause, or aim, or advantage with friendship, other than friendship itself. Nor do the four kinds recognized by the ancients – natural, social, hospitable, and sexual – separately or in combination, come up to it.

The feeling of children for their parents is rather respect. Friendship is fed on familiar intercourse, which cannot exist

* The Edict of January 1571, which granted the Huguenots the freedom of public worship.

parents & children cannot be friends

between them because of their over-great disparity; and it might well conflict with their natural obligations. For a father's secret thoughts cannot all be communicated to his children for fear they may give rise to an unbecoming intimacy, nor can admonitions and reproofs, which are one of the first duties of friendship, be administered by children to their parents. There have been nations in which it was the custom for children to kill their fathers, and others in which the fathers killed their children, to avoid embarrassment which they might one day cause one another, for by nature the prosperity of one depends on the ruin of the other. There have been philosophers – witness Aristippus – who have disdained this natural tie. When someone insisted on the affection that he owed his children, since they came out of him, he began to spit, saying that this came out of him too, and that we also breed lice and worms. And there was that other whom Plutarch tried to reconcile with his brother. 'I do not value him any more highly,' he said, 'for having come out of the same hole.'

The name of brother is indeed a beautiful and affectionate one and it was with it that we pledged our alliance. But this joining of property, these sharings, and the riches of one being the poverty of the other, wondrously weaken and relax the fraternal bond. Since brothers have to pursue the advancement of their fortunes along the same path and at the same pace, it is no wonder that they jostle and clash with one another. Besides, why should that resemblance and harmony which gives rise to true and perfect friendships be found between them? Fathers and sons may be of entirely different natures, and so may brothers. He is my son, he is my kinsman, but he is a barbarian, a rascal, or a fool. Moreover, in proportion as these friendships are imposed upon us by natural law and obligation, there is less of our own choice and free-will in them; and our free-will produces nothing that is more properly its own than affection and friendship. It is not that I lack experience of all that is possible on the side of kinship; I had the best father that ever was, and the most indulgent, even into his extreme old age, and I come of a family famous for generations as models of brotherly concord,

brothers aren't friends

et ipse
*notus in fratres animi paterni.**

As for comparing with it the affection that we feel for women, though this is born of our own choice, it cannot be placed in the same class. Its flame, I admit,

neque enim est dea nescia nostri
quae dulcem curis miscet amaritiem,†

is more active, hotter, and fiercer. But it is a reckless and fickle flame, wavering and changeable, a feverish fire prone to flare up and die down, which only catches us in one corner. In friendship there is a general and universal warmth, temperate, moreover, and uniform, a constant and settled warmth, all gentleness and smoothness, with no roughness or sting about it. What is more, in sexual love there is only a frantic desire for what eludes us:

Come segue la lepre il cacciatore
Al freddo, al caldo, alla montagna, al lito;
Ne più l'estima poi che presa vede,
Et sol dietro a chi fugge affretta il piede.‡

As soon as it enters into the bounds of friendship – that is to say, into a consonance of wills – it weakens and languishes; fruition destroys it, since its aim is carnal and subject to satiety. Friendship, on the other hand, is enjoyed even as it is desired; it is bred, nourished, and increased only by enjoyment, since it is a spiritual thing and the soul is purified by its practice. During our perfect friendship these fleeting affections used once to seize hold of me, and also of him, as he reveals only too clearly in his poetry. Thus these two passions have entered into me, each aware of the other but never in competition, the first keeping its course on proud and lofty wing, and looking disdainfully down on the other, as it pursues its way far below.

* 'Noted for my fatherly love for my brothers.' Horace, *Odes*, II, ii, 6. The first two words are supplied by Montaigne.

† 'For I am not unknown to the goddess who mingles a sweet bitterness with her tortures.' Catullus, *Epigrams*, LXVIII, 17.

‡ 'So the hunter follows the hare, in cold and heat, on the mountain and along the shore; but once he has caught it, he cares no more for it, he only chases what flies from him.' Ariosto, *Orlando furioso*, x, vii.

As for marriage, not only is it a bargain to which only the entrance is free, continuance in it being constrained and compulsory, and depending upon other things than our will, but it is a bargain commonly made for other ends. There occur in it innumerable extraneous complications which have to be unravelled, and are enough to break the thread and disturb the course of a lively affection, whereas in friendship there is no business or traffic with anything but itself. Moreover, the normal capacity of women is, in fact, unequal to the demands of that communion and intercourse on which the sacred bond is fed; their souls do not seem firm enough to bear the strain of so hard and lasting a tie. And truly, if that were not so, if such a free and voluntary relationship could be established in which not only the soul had its perfect enjoyment, but the body took its share in the alliance also, and the whole man was engaged, then certainly it would be a fuller and more complete friendship. But there has never yet been an example of a woman's attaining to this, and the ancient schools are at one in their belief that it is denied to the female sex.

As for that alternative, permitted by the Greeks, our morality rightly abhors it. But since, according to their custom, there was necessarily a great disparity of age and difference of station between the lovers, it corresponded no better to the perfect union and harmony that we here demand. 'For what after all is this love of friends? Why should we never love an ugly youth or a handsome old man?'* Even the picture that the Academy† draws of it will not, I think, refute me when I say that since this first frenzy inspired by Venus' son in a lover's heart is for an object in the flower of tender youth, and since every wild and passionate action that immoderate ardour can produce is then permitted, the whole thing is simply founded upon external beauty, a deception designed by the forces of natural reproduction. It cannot be born of the mind, which has not yet revealed itself, since it is only newly born and not yet budding.

* Cicero, *Tusculans*, IV, 33.
† See Plato's *Symposium*, particularly Pausanias' speech.

Now if this frenzy seized on a base heart, the means by which it pressed its suit were riches, gifts, favour in advancement to high places, and other such low merchandise as the Academy condemns. If it seized on a nobler heart, the means were then nobler also: instruction in philosophy; lessons in religious reverence and in obedience to the laws; encouragement to die for the good of the country; examples of valour, wisdom, and justice, the lover studying how to make himself acceptable by the charm and beauty of his mind, that of his body having long ago faded, and hoping by this mental comradeship to make a stronger and more lasting union.

When this courtship had its effect in due season – for while they did not require of the lover that he should take time and exercise discretion in his wooing, they did strictly demand this of the loved one, since he had to assess the lover's inward beauty, which was difficult to recognize and hard to discover – then there was born in the loved one the desire for a spiritual conception implemented by a spiritual beauty. This was for him the principal thing: the physical was fortuitous and secondary, whereas with the lover it was just the opposite. That is why the Greeks rate the loved one more highly, and maintain that the gods do so too; and they take the poet Aeschylus severely to task for his description of the love of Achilles and Patroclus, in which he gives the lover's part to Achilles, who was in the first and beardless bloom of his youth and the handsomest of the Greeks. They say that from the complete relationship in which the chief and worthier partner plays the predominating part there spring results useful both to the individuals and to the community; that it constituted the strength of those countries in which it prevailed, and was the chief bulwark of equity and freedom; as witness the salutary loves of Harmodius and Aristogeiton. Therefore they call it sacred and divine and, to their thinking, only the violence of tyrants and the baseness of the people are opposed to it. In brief, all that can be said in favour of the Academy's conception is that it is a love which terminates in friendship, a definition which does not disagree with that of the Stoics, 'that love is an attempt to gain the friendship of someone whose beauty has attracted us'.*

I return to my description of a more right and proper kind of friendship: 'In general you cannot judge a relationship until the partners have attained strength and stability in mind and in years.'† For the rest, what we commonly call friends and friendships are no more than acquaintanceships and familiarities, contracted either by chance or for advantage, which have brought our minds together. In the friendship I speak of they mix and blend one into the other in so perfect a union that the seam which has joined them is effaced and disappears. If I were pressed to say why I love him, I feel that my only reply could be: 'Because it was he, because it was I.'

There is, beyond all my reasoning, and beyond all that I can specifically say, some inexplicable power of destiny that brought about our union. We were looking for each other before we met, by reason of the reports we had heard of each other, which made a greater impression on our emotions than mere reports reasonably should. I believe that this was brought about by some decree of Heaven. We embraced one another by name. And at our first meeting, which happened by chance at a great feast and gathering in the city, we found ourselves so captivated, so familiar, so bound to one another, that from that time nothing was closer to either than each was to the other. He wrote an excellent Latin satire, which has been published, in which he excuses and explains the suddenness of our understanding, which so quickly grew to perfection. Having so short a time to live, and having begun so late, for we were both grown men and he some years the elder, it had no time to lose, and none in which to conform to the regular pattern of those mild friendships that require so many precautions in the form of long preliminary intercourse. Such a friendship has no model but itself, and can only be compared to itself. It was not one special consideration, nor two, nor three, nor four, nor a thousand; it was some mysterious quintessence of all this mixture which possessed itself of my will, and led it to plunge and lose itself in his; which possessed itself of his whole will, and led it, with a

* Cicero, *Tusculans*, IV, xxxiv.   † Cicero, *De Amicitia*, xx.

similar hunger and a like impulse, to plunge and lose itself in mine. I may truly say *lose*, for it left us with nothing that was our own, nothing that was either his or mine.

When the Roman consuls had condemned Caius Gracchus, and were proceeding against all those who had been in his confidence, Laelius, in their presence, inquired of Caius Blossius, who was his chief friend, how much he would have been willing to do for him. His reply was, 'Everything.' 'How, everything?' demanded Laelius. 'And what if he had ordered you to set fire to our temples?' 'He would never have told me to do that,' answered Blossius. 'But if he had,' Laelius insisted. 'Then I should have obeyed him,' said he. If he was so wholly the friend of Gracchus as the histories say, he had no business to offend the consuls by this last foolhardy admission. He should not have deviated from his confidence in Gracchus' intentions. However, those who condemn his answer as seditious have no proper understanding of the problem, and fail to take into account the fact that he held Gracchus' will in the palm of his hand, since he both influenced it and knew it. They were friends before they were citizens, friends to one another before they were either friends or enemies to their country, or friends to ambition and revolt. Having absolutely given themselves up to one another, each had absolute control over the reins of the other's inclinations. Therefore, supposing this team to have been guided by virtue and governed by reason – and it could not have been driven otherwise – Blossius' answer was as it should have been. If their actions did not fit together, they were, according to my measure, neither friends to one another nor to themselves.

What is more, his reply rings no more true than mine would if I were asked: 'If your will told you to kill your daughter, would you kill her?', and should answer, Yes. For that would be no evidence of my readiness to do the deed, because I have no doubts about my will, and just as little about the will of such a friend. It is beyond the power of all the arguments in the world to upset my certainty of my friend's intentions and judgements. No action of his could be put before me in any aspect that I should not immediately discern its motive. Our souls travelled so unitedly together, they felt so strong an affection for one another, and with this same affection saw into the very depths of each other's hearts, that not only did I know his as well as my own, but I should certainly have trusted myself more freely to him than to myself.

Let no one put other, everyday friendships in the same rank as this. I knew them as well as anyone, and very perfect examples of their kind. But I should advise no one to measure them by the same rules; he would be making a grave mistake. In these other friendships one must go forward, bridle in hand, prudently and with precautions; the knot is never so secure that one has not reason to distrust it. 'Love him,' said Chilo, 'as if one day you may come to hate him; hate him as if you may one day come to love him.' This precept, abhorrent though it is in this supreme and perfect relationship, is sound when applied to commonplace and everyday friendships, to which we must apply Aristotle's habitual phrase: 'O my friends, there is no friend!'

In this noble relationship services and kindnesses, which keep other friendships alive, do not deserve even to be taken into account, by reason of the complete fusion of the wills. For just as my own love for myself is not increased by the help I give myself at need, whatever the Stoics may say, and as I feel no gratitude to myself for any service that I do myself; so the union of such friends, being truly perfect, causes them to lose consciousness of these duties, and to hate and banish from their thoughts these words that imply separation and difference: benefit, obligation, gratitude, request, thanks, and the like. Everything being in effect common between them – will, thoughts, opinions, goods, wives, children, honour, and life – and their agreement being that of one soul in two bodies, according to Aristotle's very proper definition, they can neither lend nor give one another anything. This is why the lawmakers, to honour marriage by some imaginary comparison with this union, forbid gifts between husband and wife, intending thereby to infer that everything should belong to each, and that they have nothing to divide or share out between them. If, in the sort of friendship of which I am speaking, one could give to the other, it would be the one who received the benefit that would be laying his friend under an obligation. For since the principal study of each is to confer benefits on the other, it is the one who provides the matter and occasion that plays the truly liberal part, by giving his friend the pleasure of acting towards him as he most desires. When the philosopher Diogenes had need of money, he used to say that he asked it *back* from his friends, not that he asked them for it. And to show how this works out in practice, I will relate a singular example of it.

Eudamidas of Corinth had two friends, Charixenus of Sicyon and Aretheus of Corinth. Being a poor man, and his two friends being rich, when he came to die he made his will in this form: 'To Aretheus I leave the task of supporting my mother and providing for her old age, and to Charixenus the duty of finding a husband for my daughter and giving her the biggest dowry he can afford; and in case either of them should die I appoint the survivor to take his place.' The first to see this will laughed at it, but when the heirs were notified they accepted it with extreme satisfaction. And when one of them, Charixenus, died five days later and the succession fell on Aretheus, he took scrupulous care of the mother and, out of his estate of five talents, gave two and a half as a dowry to his only daughter and two and a half to the daughter of Eudamidas, celebrating both their weddings on the same day.

This example is quite complete but for one detail: the number of friends. For this perfect friendship of which I speak is indivisible. Each gives himself so absolutely to his friend that he has nothing to dispose of elsewhere. On the contrary, he is sorry that he is not double, triple, or quadruple, and that he has not several souls and several wills, so that he can bestow them all on this one object.

Common friendships are divisible; one may love one person for his beauty, another for his ease of manner, another for his liberality, this one for his paternal affection, and that one for his brotherly love, and so on. But that friendship which

[handwritten margin note: -You can only be true friends w/ one person at a time]

possesses the soul and rules over it with complete sovereignty cannot possibly be divided in two. If two called on you for help at the same time, to which of them would you run? If they asked contradictory services of you, how would you reconcile them? If one of them told you a secret which it would be useful for the other to know, how would you get out of the quandary? A unique and dominant friendship dissolves all other obligations. The secret that I have sworn to reveal to no other, I may without perjury communicate to him who is not another – but is myself. It is a sufficient miracle for a man to divide himself in two, and those who speak of dividing themselves in three do not know the greatness of it. Nothing is superlative that has its like. And anyone who supposes that I can love two equally and that they can love one another and me as much as I love them, is multiplying into a brotherhood something absolutely single and indivisible, one sole example of which is the hardest thing in the world to find.

The ending of the tale entirely confirms what I was saying. Eudamidas bestows on his friends the grace and favour of employing them in his need. He makes them heirs of his own liberality by thus putting into their hands the means of benefiting him. Beyond all doubt, the power of friendship is much more richly displayed in the terms of his will than in Aretheus' actions.

To conclude, the experience is beyond the imagination of anyone who has not tasted it; and therefore I greatly admire the young soldier's reply to Cyrus, when he was asked how much he would take for a horse on which he had just won first prize in a race, and whether he would exchange him for a kingdom. 'Certainly not, Sire,' he answered, 'but I would gladly part with him to gain a friend, if I could find anyone worthy of such a fellowship.' He was right to say 'if I could find'. For it is easy enough to find men fit for a superficial acquaintance, but here, where a man commits himself from the depths of his heart, keeping nothing back, it is essential that all the springs of action be perfectly clean and reliable.

In those connexions which only hold by one end, we have

only to provide against the imperfections that particularly affect that end. It cannot matter of what religion are my doctor and my lawyer. This consideration has nothing to do with the friendly services they do me; and, in the domestic relations between my servants and myself, I take the same attitude. I do not look closely into a footman's chastity, but I do inquire if he does his duty. I am not so much afraid of a muleteer's gambling as of his being a fool, and I would rather have a cook swear than be incompetent. I do not go about telling people what they ought to be doing in the world. There are enough others to do that – but I say what I do myself.

*Mihi sic usus est; tibi, ut opus est facto, face.**

As familiar company at table, I choose the amusing rather than the wise; in bed I prefer beauty to goodness; and for serious conversation, I like ability even combined with dishonesty; and similarly in other things.

As the man who was found astride a broomstick, playing with his children, asked the friend who surprised him to make no comment until he was himself a father, reckoning that the affection which would then arise in his heart would make him a fair judge of such an act, so I wish I could speak with people who have experienced what I am describing. But, knowing how far from common, indeed how rare, such a friendship is, I have no expectation of finding a competent judge. Even the treatises which antiquity has left us on this subject seem flat to me in comparison with my own feeling. For, in this particular, the reality surpasses even the precepts of philosophy.

Nil ego contulerim iucundo sanus amico.†

Menander, of old, called a man happy if he had met only with the shadow of a friend. He was assuredly right, and especially if he spoke from experience, for indeed if I compare all the rest of my life which, by God's mercy, has been pleasant, easy, and, except for the loss of this rare friend, free of any grievous

* 'This is my habit; as for you, do as you think best.' Terence, *Heautontimoroumenos*, 1, i, 28.

† 'So long as I am in my senses, I shall find nothing to compare with a pleasant friend.' Horace, *Satires*, 1, v, 44.

affliction, a life passed in spiritual tranquillity since I have been content with my natural and original advantages, and have not sought others – if, I say, I compare it all with the four years that I was permitted to enjoy of that man's sweet and companionable society, it is but smoke, nothing but a dark and tedious night. Since the day when I lost him,

> *quem semper acerbum,*
> *semper honoratum (sic, di, voluistis) habebo,* *

I have dragged out but a languishing existence, and even such pleasures as come to me, far from consoling me, redouble my grief for his loss. We were equal partners in everything, and I seem to be robbing him of his share,

> *Nec fas esse ulla me voluptate hic frui*
> *decrevi, tantisper dum ille abest meus particeps.*†

I had grown so accustomed to be his second self in everything that now I seem to be no more than half a man.

> *Illam meae si partem animae tulit*
> *maturior vis, quid moror altera,*
> *nec carus aeque, nec superstes*
> *integer? Ille dies utramque*
> *duxit ruinam.*‡

There is no action or thought of mine in which I do not miss him, as he would have missed me. For just as he infinitely surpassed me in every other talent and virtue, so did he also in the duties of friendship.

> *Quis desiderio sit pudor aut modus*
> *tam cari capitis?*§

* 'Which will ever be bitter to me and ever sacred – such, O Gods, has been your will!' Virgil, *Aeneid*, v, 49.

† 'I have resolved to enjoy no pleasures, while he is not here to share them with me.' Terence, *Heautontimoroumenos*, I, i, 97 (adapted).

‡ 'If a premature death has taken away the half of my life, why should I, the other half, linger on, since I love myself less and have not survived whole? The same day destroyed us both.' Horace, *Odes*, II, xvii, 5 (adapted).

§ 'What shame or restraint should there be, in mourning so dear a head?' Horace, *Odes*, I, xxiv, 1.

O misero frater adempte mihi!
Omnia tecum una perierunt gaudia nostra,
  quae tuus in vita dulcis alebat amor.
Tu mea, tu moriens fregisti commoda, frater;
  tecum una tota est nostra sepulta anima,
cujus ego interitu tota de mente fugavi
  haec studia atque omnes delicias animi.
alloquar? audiero nunquam tua verba loquentem?
  Nunquam ego te, vita frater amabilior,
aspiciam posthac? at certe semper amabo.*

But let us listen a little to this boy of sixteen.

I have learnt, however, that this work† has in the meantime been published, and for a disreputable purpose, by men whose aim is to upset and change the form of our government, without the least care whether they improve it or not. They have, moreover, included it amongst writings of their own concoction. I have therefore decided not to place it here; and in order that its publication may not prejudice the author's memory in the eye of those who could have no first-hand acquaintance with his opinions and actions, I would inform them that the treatise was written by him in his boyhood, and by way of exercise only, as a common theme which has been a thousand times worn threadbare in different books. I have no doubt that he believed what he wrote, for he was too conscientious to deceive even in jest. I know too that if he had had his choice, he would rather have been born at Venice‡ than at Sarlac; and with good reason. But he had another maxim deeply imprinted on his soul: that he must most religiously obey and submit to the laws under which he was born. There was never a better citizen, nor one who cared more for his country's peace; no one more hostile to the

* 'How sad I am to have lost you, brother! With you have perished all the joys which your sweet friendship gave to my life. In your death, brother, you have destroyed all my comforts, and both our souls are buried with you. Since you died I have completely abandoned reading and all the delights of the mind. Shall I speak with you again? Shall I never hear you talk again? Shall I never look on you again, oh brother dearer to me than life? But certainly I shall always love you.' Catullus, lxviii, 20, and lxv, 9 (much adapted).

† *The Voluntary Servitude*, mentioned at the beginning of the essay.

‡ In a republic rather than in a monarchy.

commotions and revolutions of his times. He would much rather have devoted his talents to suppressing them than to providing matter that would rouse them to greater violence. His mind was fashioned on the model of another age than this.

Now, instead of this serious work, I shall insert another, produced in the same period of his life, but more gallant and entertaining.*

BOOK ONE: Chapter 31

On cannibals

HAVING surveyed, during his invasion of Italy, the marshalling of the army that the Romans had set out against him, King Pyrrhus remarked: 'I do not know what barbarians these are' – for so the Greeks called all foreign nations – 'but the ordering of the army before me has nothing barbarous about it.' The Greeks said the same of the forces with which Flaminius invaded their country; and Philip also, when from a little hill he saw the orderly arrangement of the Roman camp, set up in his kingdom under Publius Sulpicius Galba. We see from this how chary we must be of subscribing to vulgar opinions; we should judge them by the test of reason and not by common report.

I had with me for a long time a man who had lived ten or twelve years in that other world which has been discovered in our time, in the place where Villegaignon landed,† and which he called Antarctic France. This discovery of so vast a country seems to me worth reflecting on. I should not care to pledge myself that another may not be discovered in the future, since so many greater men than we have been wrong about this one. I

* Montaigne originally intended, as already noted, to print la Boétie's treatise on Voluntary Servitude. But this, as he says, had already appeared in a collection of Huguenot pamphlets. He therefore substituted, in the editions of the *Essays* published in his lifetime, 29 Sonnets by la Boétie. But when these were printed in 1588 in a collection of la Boétie's works, Montaigne crossed them out in his own copy. They once formed the greater part of Chapter 27.

† Brazil.

am afraid that our eyes are bigger than our stomachs, and that
we have more curiosity than understanding. We grasp at everything, but catch nothing except wind.

Plato interpolates a story told by Solon, and learnt by him
from the priests of Sais in Egypt, to the effect that there was,
long ago before the Deluge, a great island called Atlantis, right
at the mouth of the Straits of Gibraltar, which contained more
land than Asia and Africa put together. The kings of that
country not only possessed the island, but had extended so far
on to the mainland that they held the whole breadth of Africa
as far as Egypt, and the length of Europe as far as Tuscany.
They proposed to push on into Asia, and conquer all the
nations on the Mediterranean shores as far as the Black Sea, and
therefore crossed Spain, Gaul, and Italy, on their way to Greece,
where they were halted by the Athenians. But some time later
both the Athenians, and they and their island, were swallowed
up by the Deluge.

It is very probable that this immense inundation made strange
alterations in the inhabited earth, by which it is thought that the
sea cut Sicily off from Italy,

> *Haec loca, vi quondam et vasta convulsa ruina,*
> *dissiluisse ferunt, cum protinus utraque tellus*
> *una foret;*[*]

Cyprus from Syria, and the isle of Euboea from the mainland of
Boeotia; and that elsewhere it united lands that were once
separate, filling the straits between them with sand and mud,

> *sterilisque diu palus aptaque remis*
> *vicinas urbes alit, et grave sentit aratrum.*[†]

But it is not very probable that the new world we have lately
discovered is, in fact, that island. For it almost touched Spain,
and it would have been an incredible effect of an inundation to
have pushed it back where it is, more than twelve hundred

---

[*] 'They say that these lands were once violently rent by a great con-
vulsion. Until then the two lands were one.' Virgil, *Aeneid*, III, 414.

[†] 'Long a sterile marsh, on which men rowed, it now feeds the neighbouring towns and feels the weight of the plough.' Horace, *Ars Poetica*,
65.

leagues away. Besides, recent voyages have made it almost certain that it is not an island, but a mainland, which connects with the East Indies on one side, and with the lands that lie beneath the two poles on the others; or, if it is divided from them, it is by so narrow a strait or distance that it is not entitled to be called an island.

It would seem that there are movements, some natural and some feverish, in these great bodies, as in our own. When I consider the encroachment that my own river, the Dordogne, is making at present on its right bank, and that in twenty years it has gained so much, undermining the foundations of several buildings, I clearly see that this disturbance is no ordinary one. For if it had always done so at this rate or were always to do so, the face of the world would be totally transformed. But rivers are subject to changes; sometimes they overflow one bank, and sometimes the other; and sometimes they keep to their channels. I am not speaking of sudden floods, of which the causes are clear to us. In Médoc, beside the sea, my brother, the Sieur d'Arsac, sees one of his estates being swallowed up by the sand that the sea is throwing up on it. The roofs of some buildings are still visible, but his rents and property have been transformed into very poor pasture. The inhabitants say that for some time the sea has been advancing on them so hard that they have lost four leagues of land. These sands are her outriders; we see great piles of moving dunes marching half a league before her, and occupying the land.

The other testimony from antiquity with which some would connect this discovery is in Aristotle – at least if the little book *On Unheard-of Wonders* is his. He there relates that certain Carthaginians, after sailing for a very long time through the Straits of Gibraltar out into the Atlantic Sea, finally discovered a large fertile island, well covered with woods and watered by broad, deep rivers. It was very far from any mainland, but they, and others after them, attracted by the goodness and fertility of the soil, went there with their wives and children, and there settled. When the rulers of Carthage saw their country being gradually depopulated, they expressly forbade any more of their people to go there, under pain of death; and they drove the new inhabitants out, fearing, it is said, that in course of time they might so multiply as to supplant themselves and ruin the state of Carthage. This tale of Aristotle's relates no more closely to our new lands than Plato's.

This man who stayed with me was a plain, simple fellow, and men of this sort are likely to give true testimony. Men of intelligence notice more things and view them more carefully, but they comment on them; and to establish and substantiate their interpretation, they cannot refrain from altering the facts a little. They never present things just as they are but twist and disguise them to conform to the point of view from which they have seen them; and to gain credence for their opinion and make it attractive, they do not mind adding something of their own, or extending and amplifying. We need either a very truthful man, or one so ignorant that he has no material with which to construct false theories and make them credible: a man wedded to no idea. My man was like that; and besides he has on various occasions brought me seamen and merchants whom he met on his voyage. Therefore I am satisfied with his information, and do not inquire what the cosmographers say about it.

We need topographers to give us exact descriptions of the places where they have been. But because they have this advantage over us, that they have seen the Holy Land, they claim the additional privilege of telling us news about all the rest of the world. I would have everyone write about what he knows and no more than he knows, not only on this, but on all other subjects. One man may have some special knowledge at firsthand about the character of a river or a spring, who otherwise knows only what everyone else knows. Yet to give currency to this shred of information, he will undertake to write on the whole science of physics. From this fault many great troubles spring.

Now, to return to my argument, I do not believe, from what I have been told about this people, that there is anything barbarous or savage about them, except that we all call barbarous anything that is contrary to our own habits. Indeed we seem to have no other criterion of truth and reason than the type and kind of opinions and customs current in the land where we live. There we always see the perfect religion, the perfect political system, the perfect and most accomplished way of doing everything. These people are wild in the same way as we say that fruits are wild, when nature has produced them by herself and in her ordinary way; whereas, in fact, it is those that we have artificially modified, and removed from the common order, that we ought to call wild. In the former, the true, most useful, and natural virtues and properties are alive and vigorous; in the latter we have bastardized them, and adapted them only to the gratification of our corrupt taste. Nevertheless, there is a special savour and delicacy in some of the uncultivated fruits of those regions that is excellent even to our taste, and rivals our own. It is not reasonable that art should win the honours from our great and mighty mother nature. We have so loaded the riches and beauty of her works with our inventions that we have altogether stifled her. Yet, wherever she shines forth in her purity, she makes our vain and trivial enterprises marvellously shameful.

Et veniunt ederae sponte sua melius,
surgit et in solis formosior arbutus antris,
*et volucres nulla dulcius arte canunt.**

With all our efforts we cannot imitate the nest of the very smallest bird, its structure, its beauty, or the suitability of its form, nor even the web of the lowly spider. All things, said Plato, are produced either by nature, or by chance, or by art; the greatest and most beautiful by one or other of the first two, the least and most imperfect by the last.

These nations, then, seem to me barbarous in the sense that they have received very little moulding from the human intelligence, and are still very close to their original simplicity. They are still governed by natural laws and very little corrupted by our own. They are in such a state of purity that it sometimes saddens

* 'The ivy grows best when it grows wild, and the arbutus is most lovely when it grows in some solitary cleft; birds sing most sweetly untaught.' Propertius, I, ii, 10.

me to think we did not learn of them earlier, at a time when there were men who were better able to appreciate them than we. I am sorry that Lycurgus and Plato did not know them, for I think that what we have seen of these people with our own eyes surpasses not only the pictures with which poets have illustrated the golden age, and all their attempts to draw mankind in the state of happiness, but the ideas and the very aspirations of philosophers as well. They could not imagine an innocence as pure and simple as we have actually seen; nor could they believe that our society might be maintained with so little artificiality and human organization.

This is a nation, I should say to Plato, in which there is no kind of commerce, no knowledge of letters, no science of numbers, no title of magistrate or of political superior, no habit of service, riches or poverty, no contracts, no inheritance, no divisions of property, only leisurely occupations, no respect for any kinship but the common ties, no clothes, no agriculture, no metals, no use of corn or wine. The very words denoting lying, treason, deceit, greed, envy, slander, and forgiveness have never been heard. How far from such perfection would he find the republic that he imagined: 'men fresh from the hands of the gods'.*

Hos natura modos primum dedit.†

For the rest, they live in a land with a very pleasant and temperate climate, and consequently, as my witnesses inform me, a sick person is a rare sight; and they assure me that they never saw anyone palsied or blear-eyed, toothless or bent with age. These people inhabit the seashore, and are shut in on the landward side by a range of high mountains, which leave a strip about a hundred leagues in depth between them and the sea. They have a great abundance of fish and meat which bear no resemblance to ours, and they eat them plainly cooked, without any other preparation. The first man who brought a horse there, although he had made friends with them on some earlier voyages, so terrified them when in the saddle that they shot him

* Seneca, *Letters*, xc.

† 'These are the first laws that nature gave.' Virgil, *Georgics*, II, 20.

to death with arrows before recognizing him.

Their buildings are very long and capable of holding two or three hundred people. They are covered with strips of bark from tall trees, tethered at one end to the ground and attached at the other for mutual support to the roof beam, after the manner of some of our barns whose roofing comes down to the ground and serves for side walls. They have a wood so hard that they can cut with it, and make it into swords and grills to roast their meat. Their beds are of woven cotton, hung from the roof like those on our ships; and each has his own, for the women sleep apart from their husbands. They get up with the sun, and immediately after rising they eat for the whole day, for they have no other meal. They do not drink at the same time, but like some Eastern peoples described by Suidas, always apart from their meals. They drink several times a day, and a great deal. Their beverage is made of some root, and is of the colour of our red wine. They drink it only warm, and it will not keep for more than two or three days. It is rather sharp in taste, not at all heady, good for the stomach, and laxative to those who are not used to it; it is a very pleasant drink to those who are. Instead of bread they use a white stuff like preserved coriander, which I have tasted; the flavour is sweetish and rather insipid.

They spend the whole day dancing. Their young men go hunting after wild beasts with bows and arrows. Some of their women employ themselves in the meantime with the warming of their drink, which is their principal duty. In the morning, before they begin to eat, one of their old men preaches to the whole barnful, walking from one end to the other, and repeating the same phrase many times, until he has completed the round – for the buildings are quite a hundred yards long. He enjoins only two things upon them: valour against the enemy and love for their wives. And he never fails to stress this obligation with the refrain that it is they who keep their drink warm and well-seasoned for them.

There may be seen in a number of places, including my own house, examples of their beds, of their ropes, of their wooden swords, of the wooden bracelets with which they protect their wrists in battle, and of the great canes, open at one end, which they sound to beat time for their dancing. They are close-shaven all over, and perform the operation much more cleanly than we, with only a razor of wood or stone. They believe in the immortality of the soul, and that those who have deserved well of the gods have their abode in that part of the sky where the sun rises; and those who are damned in the West.

They have some sort of priests and prophets, who very seldom appear among the people, but have their dwelling in the mountains. When they come, a great festival and solemn assembly of several villages is held. Each of these barns which I have described forms a village, and they are about one French league apart. The prophet speaks to them in public, exhorting them to virtue and to do their duty. But their whole ethical teaching contains only two articles; resolution in battle and affection for their wives. He prophesies things to come, and tells them what outcome to expect from their enterprises; he encourages them to war, or dissuades them from it; but all this with the proviso that should he make a false prophecy, or should things not turn out for them according to his predictions, they will cut him into a thousand pieces if he is caught, and condemn him as a false prophet. For this reason, one of them who has made a miscalculation is never seen again.

Divination is a gift of God. Therefore its abuse should be treated as a punishable imposture. Among the Scythians, when diviners failed in their predictions, they were laid, bound hand and foot, in a little ox-drawn cart filled with brushwood, and there burned. Those who undertake matters that depend only on the human capacities for guidance, are to be excused if they merely do their best. But these others who come deluding us with pretensions to some extraordinary faculty beyond our understanding should surely be punished for their bold impostures, when they fail to carry out their promises.

They have their wars against the people who live further inland, on the other side of the mountains; and they go to them quite naked, with no other arms but their bows or their wooden swords, pointed at one end like the heads of our boar-spears. It is remarkable with what obstinacy they fight their battles, which never end without great slaughter and bloodshed. As for flight and terror, they do not know what they are. Every man brings home for a trophy the head of an enemy he has killed, and hangs it over the entrance of his dwelling. After treating a prisoner well for a long time, and giving him every attention he can think of, his captor assembles a great company of his acquaintances. He then ties a rope to one of the prisoner's arms, holding him by the other end, at some yards' distance for fear of being hit, and gives his best friend the man's other arm, to be held in the same way; and these two, in front of the whole assembly, despatch him with their swords. This done, they roast him, eat him all together, and send portions to their absent friends. They do not do this, as might be supposed, for nourishment as the ancient Scythians did, but as a measure of extreme vengeance. The proof of this is that when they saw the Portuguese, who had allied themselves with their enemies, inflicting a different sort of death on their prisoners – which was to bury them to the waist, to shoot the rest of their bodies full of arrows, and then to hang them – they concluded that these people from another world who had spread the knowledge of so many wickednesses among their neighbours, and were much more skilled than they in all sorts of evil, did not choose this form of revenge without a reason. So, thinking that it must be more painful than their own, they began to give up their old practice and follow this new one.

I am not so anxious that we should note the horrible savagery of these acts as concerned that, whilst judging their faults so correctly, we should be so blind to our own. I consider it more barbarous to eat a man alive than to eat him dead; to tear by rack and torture a body still full of feeling, to roast it by degrees, and then give it to be trampled and eaten by dogs and swine – a practice which we have not only read about but seen within recent memory, not between ancient enemies, but between neighbours and fellow-citizens and, what is worse, under the cloak of piety and religion – than to roast and eat a man after he is dead.

Chrysippus and Zeno, the heads of the Stoic sect, did indeed consider that there was no harm in using a dead body for any need of our own, or in consuming it either, as our own ancestors did during Caesar's blockade of the city of Alexia, when they resolved to relieve the hunger of the siege with the bodies of the old men, women, and other persons who were incapable of fighting.

> *Vascones, fama est, alimentis talibus usi*
> *produxere animas.**

Physicians, too, are not afraid to use a corpse in any way that serves our health, and will apply it either internally or externally. But no man's brain has yet been found so disordered as to excuse treachery, disloyalty, tyranny, and cruelty, which are our common faults.

We are justified therefore in calling these people barbarians by reference to the laws of reason, but not in comparison with ourselves, who surpass them in every kind of barbarity. Their fighting is entirely noble and disinterested. It is as excusable, and beautiful too, as is compatible with this disease of humanity, their only motive for war being the desire to display their valour. They do not strive for conquest of new territories since their own still possess such natural fertility as to yield them all their necessities without labour or trouble, in such abundance that they have no need to extend their borders. They are still at the happy stage of desiring no more than their simple appetites demand; everything beyond that is to them a superfluity.

If of the same age they generally call one another brothers; those who are younger are called children, and the old men are fathers to all the rest. They leave to their heirs the undivided possession of their property, to be held in common, with no other title than the plain one which nature bestows on her creatures when she brings them into the world. If their neighbours cross the mountains to attack them and win a victory over them, the victors gain nothing but glory, and the advantage of a proved superiority in valour and virtue. For the rest, they have

* 'They say that the Gascons prolonged their lives with such food.' Juvenal, xv, 93.

no use for the possessions of the conquered, and so return to their country, where they are not short of any necessity, nor yet of that great gift of knowing how to enjoy their happy condition in perfect content. The seaboard peoples do the same. They ask no ransom of their prisoners but only the confession and acknowledgement that they have been beaten: but there has never been one, in a whole century, who has not chosen death rather than yield, either by word or behaviour, one single jot of their magnificent and invincible courage; not one of them has ever been known who has not preferred to be killed and eaten rather than beg to be spared. Prisoners are treated with all liberality so that their lives may be the more dear to them, and are usually plied with threats of their imminent death. They are reminded of the tortures that they are to suffer, of the preparations then being made to that end, of the lopping off of their limbs, and of the feast that will be held at their expense. All this is done solely in order to extort from their lips some weak or despondent word, or to rouse in them a desire to escape; its only purpose is to gain the advantage of having frightened them and shaken their constancy. For, properly understood, a true victory rests on that point alone,

*victoria nulla est
quam quae confessos animo quoque subjugat hostes.**

The Hungarians of old, who were very bellicose fighters, never pursued their advantage further once they had brought their enemy to ask for mercy. Having once extorted this admission from them, they let them go unhurt and without any ransom, compelling them, at the most, to give their word never to bear arms against them again.

Many of the advantages that we gain over our enemies are only borrowed advantages, not truly ours. To have stouter legs and arms is the quality of a porter, not a sign of valour; skill is a dead and physical possession; it is a stroke of luck that causes our enemy to stumble or his eyes to be dazzled by the sunlight; it is a trick of art and science that makes one who may easily be

* 'There is no victory, except when the enemy in his own mind acknowledges himself beaten.' Claudian, *On the Sixth Consulate of Honorius*, 248 (adapted).

cowardly and worthless into a nimble fencer. A man's value and reputation depend on his heart and his resolution; there his true honour lies. Valour is strength, not of leg or arm, but of the heart and soul; it lies not in the goodness of our horse or our weapons, but in our own. He who falls with a firm courage, 'will, though fallen, fight on his knees'.* The man who yields no jot to his steadfastness for any threat of imminent death, who, as he yields up his soul, still gazes on his enemy with a firm and disdainful eye, is beaten not by us but by fortune; he is killed but he is not vanquished. The most valiant are sometimes the most unfortunate.

There are defeats, therefore, that are as splendid as victories. Never did those four sister triumphs of Salamis, Plataea, Mycale, and Sicily – the fairest on which the sun ever gazed – dare to oppose all their combined glories to the glorious defeat of King Leonidas and his men at the pass of Thermopylae.

What captain ever rushed with a more glorious and ambitious desire to win a battle than did Ischolas to lose one?† Who in all the world took more ingenious pains to ensure his safety than he for his own destruction? He was instructed to defend a certain Peloponnesian pass against the Arcadians. Finding that the nature of the place and the inferior numbers of his forces made it quite impossible for him to do so, he concluded that all who confronted the enemy must inevitably fall where they stood. On the other hand, he thought it unworthy of his own courage and noble spirit, and of the Lacedaemonian name, to fail in his charge. So between these two extremes he took a middle course, which was this: the youngest and most active of his troops he reserved for the defence and service of their country, and sent them back. Then, with those whose loss would be least felt, he decided to defend the pass, and by their death to make the enemy purchase his passage at the highest possible price. Thus it fell out. For soon they were hedged in on every side by the Arcadians; and after making a great slaughter he and his men were all put to the sword. Is there any trophy which is a victor's due that was not more truly earned by these

* Seneca, *On Providence*, II.   † See Diodorus Siculus, xv, 64.

men in their defeat? The true victory lies in battle rather than in survival; the prize of valour in fighting, not in winning.

To return to our narrative, these prisoners are so far from giving in, whatever their treatment, that all through these two or three months of their captivity they show a cheerful face, and urge their masters to be quick in putting them to the test. They defy them, insult them, and reproach them with cowardice, counting over the number of battles in which their own people have defeated them. I have a ballad made by one prisoner in which he tauntingly invites his captors to come boldly forward, every one of them, and dine off him, for they will then be eating their own fathers and grandfathers, who have served as food and nourishment to his body. 'These muscles,' he says, 'this flesh, and these veins are yours, poor fools that you are! Can you not see that the substance of your ancestors' limbs is still in them? Taste them carefully, and you will find the flavour is that of your own flesh.' A shaft of wit that by no means savours of barbarism. Those who tell us how they die, and describe their executions, depict the prisoner spitting in the faces of his killers and grimacing defiantly. In fact, up to their last gasp they never cease to brave and defy them with word and gesture. Here are men who compared with us are savages indeed. They must be so, indubitably, if we are not, for there is an amazing difference between their characters and ours.

Their men have many wives; the higher their reputation for valour the larger the number; and one very beautiful thing about their marriages is that whereas our wives anxiously keep us from enjoying the friendship and kindliness of other women, their wives are equally anxious to procure just those favours for their husbands. Being more concerned for the honour of their men than for anything else, they take pains to find and keep as many companions as they can, in as much as this is a testimony to their husband's worth.

Our wives will exclaim that this is a miracle. It is not. It is a proper marital virtue, but of the highest order. And in the Bible Leah, Rachel, Sarah, and Jacob's wives* gave their beautiful

* Jacob's wives were Leah and Rachel; Montaigne seems to be confused.

handmaidens to their husbands; Livia too aided Augustus in his passions, to her own disadvantage; and Stratonice, the wife of King Deiotarus, not only lent her husband a very beautiful young servant-maid of hers as a concubine, but carefully brought up the children he had by her, and supported them in their claim to their father's estates.

It should not be supposed that all this is done out of simple and servile bondage to common usage, or under weight of the authority of their ancient customs, without reflection or judgement. The minds of this people are not so dull that they cannot take another course; and to prove this I will give some examples of their capabilities. In addition to the verse I have just quoted from one of their war-songs, I have another, a love-song, which begins like this: 'Adder, stay. Stay, adder, so that my sister may follow the pattern of your markings, to make and embroider a fine girdle for me to give to my beloved. So shall your beauty and markings be preferred for ever above all other serpents.' This first verse forms the refrain of the song. Now I have enough acquaintance with poetry to form this judgement: that far from there being anything barbaric in its conception, it is quite Anacreontic. Their language, moreover, is a soft one, and has a pleasant sound; it is much like Greek in its terminations.

Not knowing how costly a knowledge of this country's corruptions will one day be to their happiness and repose, and that from intercourse with us will come their ruin – which, I suppose, is far advanced already – three men of their nation – poor fellows to allow themselves to be deluded by the desire for things unknown, and to leave the softness of their own skies to come and gaze at ours – were at Rouen at the time when the late King Charles the Ninth visited the place. The King talked with them for some time; they were shown our way of living, our magnificence, and the sights of a fine city. Then someone* asked them what they thought about all this, and what they had found most remarkable. They mentioned three things, of which I am sorry to say I have forgotten the third. But I still remember the other

* Montaigne himself.

two. They said that in the first place they found it very strange that so many tall, bearded men, all strong and well armed, who were around the King – they probably meant the Swiss of his guard – should be willing to obey a child, rather than choose one of their own number to command them. Secondly – they have a way in their language of speaking of men as halves of one another – that they had noticed among us some men gorged to the full with things of every sort while their other halves were beggars at their doors, emaciated with hunger and poverty. They found it strange that these poverty-stricken halves should suffer such injustice, and that they did not take the others by the throat or set fire to their houses.

I talked to one of them for some time; but I had an interpreter who followed my meaning so badly, and was so hindered by stupidity from grasping my ideas, that I could hardly get any satisfaction from him. When I asked the visitor what advantage he gained by his superior position among his own people – for he was a captain and our sailors called him the king – he said, the privilege of marching first into battle. And by how many men was he followed? He pointed to a piece of ground, to indicate that they were as many as would fill a space of that size. It might have been four or five thousand. And when there was no war, did all his authority cease? He answered that it remained, and that when he visited the villages that depended upon him, paths were cleared for him through their thickets, so that he could travel at his ease. All this does not seem too bad. But then, they do not wear breeches.

BOOK ONE: Chapter 36

On the custom of wearing clothes

WHEREVER I wish to turn, I have to break through some barrier of custom, so carefully has custom blocked all our approaches. In this chilly season, I was questioning whether the fashion in these lately discovered countries of going entirely naked is forced on them by the heat of the air, as we assume with the Indians and the Moors, or whether it is the original custom of mankind. Since everything under the heavens, as Holy Writ declares, is subject to the same laws,* in questions like these, where we must distinguish between natural laws and those which are man-made, scholars generally turn for evidence to the general order of the world, in which there can be no disguises. Now all other creatures being suitably provided with the needle and thread to keep themselves alive, it is truly incredible that we alone should be brought into the world in a defective and indigent condition, a condition indeed that cannot be maintained without foreign assistance. I believe, therefore, that as plants, trees, animals, and all living things are furnished by nature with sufficient covering to protect them from the assaults of the weather,

> *Proptereaque fere res omnes aut corio sunt,*
> *aut seta, aut conchis, aut callo, aut cortice tectae,†*

so too were we. But like those who by artificial light put out the light of day, by borrowed means we have destroyed our own. And we can easily see that it is custom which makes some things impossible for us that are not really so. For some of those peoples who have no knowledge of clothing live in climates roughly similar to ours, and, moreover, our own most delicate parts are those which are always exposed: the eyes, the mouth, the nose and the ears, and in the case of peasants, as with our ancestors, the breast and the belly. If we were born with the need for petticoats and breeches, nature would no doubt have armed with a thicker skin those parts that she exposes to the rigours of the seasons, just as she has done the finger-tips and the soles of the feet.

Why does this seem difficult to believe? I see a far greater difference between my way of dressing and a peasant's of my own district than between his and that of a man who wears nothing but his skin.

* Ecclesiastes, 9, 3.

† 'And for this reason almost all things are covered with hide, or bristles, or shells, or hard skin, or bark.' Lucretius, IV, 935. The Oxford text differs.

How many men, especially in Turkey, go naked out of religious devotion! Someone asked one of our beggars, whom he saw in his shirt in the depth of winter, as cheerful as anyone muffled up to the ears in sables, how he could have such endurance. 'But you, sir,' he replied, 'have your face exposed. Well, I am all face.' The Italians tell a story which is about the Duke of Florence's fool, I think. His master asked him how, in his poor clothing, he could endure the cold, when it was almost beyond his own bearing. 'Follow my rule,' answered the fool, 'and pile on all your clothes, as I do mine. Then you will feel it no more than I do.' King Massinissa could not be induced to cover his head even in his extreme old age, however cold, stormy, or showery it might be; and the same is held of the Emperor Severus.

In describing the battles between the Egyptians and the Persians, Herodotus records a remarkable fact noticed both by himself and by others. Of those left dead on the field, the Egyptians had incomparably harder skulls than the Persians because the latter invariably covered their heads, first with bonnets and then with turbans, while the former were close-shaven from infancy and went bare-headed.

And King Agesilaus, until his extreme old age, had the habit of wearing the same clothes in winter as in summer. Caesar, says Suetonius, always advanced at the head of his army, and generally on foot, with his head bare whether in sunshine or rain; and the same is said of Hannibal,

tam vertice nudo
*excipere insanos imbres coelique ruinam.**

A Venetian who lived for a long while in the kingdom of Pegu, from which he has lately returned, writes that both men and women there, though they clothe the rest of their bodies, always go barefoot, even on horseback. And Plato gives us this remarkable advice, that for the health of our whole bodies, we should give the feet and the head no other covering than nature has provided. The King whom the Poles chose to succeed our

* 'With bare head he received the furious rain, and torrents falling from heaven.' Silius Italicus, I, 250.

own Duke and who is, indeed, one of the greatest princes of our time,* never wears gloves, nor changes in the hardest winter weather the bonnet that he wears indoors.

While I cannot bear to be unbuttoned and unlaced, the labouring men of my district would feel shackled were they otherwise. Varro holds that when it was ordained that we should stand bare-headed in the presence of gods or rulers, this was for our health's sake and to harden us against the weather rather than as a sign of respect.

Now that we are on the subject of cold and, being Frenchmen, are accustomed to wearing motley colours – not I myself for, like my father before me, I seldom wear anything but black or white – let me add a story of another sort, told by Captain Martin du Bellay. He says that, when marching through Luxemburg, he met with frosts so sharp that the wine provided for the army had to be cut with axes and hatchets and distributed to the troops by weight, and that they carried it away in baskets. And Ovid says much the same thing:

> *Nudaque consistunt formam servantia testae*
> *vina, nec hausta meri, sed data frusta bibunt.†*

At the mouth of Lake Maeotis, the frosts are so hard that in the very same place where Mithridates' lieutenant had fought the enemy dry-shod and defeated them, he defeated them once more in a naval battle when summer came round. The Romans suffered a grave handicap in the engagement they fought with the Carthaginians near Placentia. They went into the fight with their blood congealed and their limbs stiff with cold, whereas Hannibal had had fires lit throughout his camp, to warm his soldiers. He had distributed oil among the ranks too, so that they should anoint themselves, thus making their muscles more limber and supple, and protecting their pores against the atmosphere and the freezing wind that was then blowing.

The Greeks' retreat from Babylon to their own country is famous for the hardships and discomforts that they had to over-

* Stephen Bathory, who succeeded Henri, Duke of Anjou.

† 'And the wine ready for serving keeps the shape of the jar. They do not drink it neat, but hand it out in lumps.' Ovid, *Tristia*, III, x, 25.

come. One of these was that in the mountains of Armenia they were overtaken by a terrible snowstorm, and lost all knowledge of the country and the roads. It suddenly hemmed them in, and for a day and a night they were without food or drink. The greater part of their cattle died, and so did many of them. Many too were blinded by the hail and the dazzle of the snow, many had their extremities frozen, and many were stiff, numb, and paralysed with the cold, though still in full possession of their senses. Alexander saw a people who buried their fruit-trees in winter, to protect them from the frost.

On the subject of clothes, the King of Mexico used to change his garments four times a day, and never wore them a second time, but used them for his continual charities and as rewards. In the same way, no pot or dish, or kitchen or table utensil was ever put before him twice.

BOOK ONE: Chapter 47

On the uncertainty of our judgement

THERE is truth in the line:

'Επέων δὲ πολὺς νόμος ἔνθα καὶ ἔνθα*

there is much to be said everywhere on both sides. For example:

*Vinse Hannibal, et non seppe usar' poi
Ben la vittoriosa sua ventura.†*

Anyone who agrees with this point of view, and will impress on our people what a mistake it was that we did not follow up our stroke at Montcontour, or who will attack the King of Spain for not having known how to make the most of the advantage that he gained over us at Saint Quentin, may say that the error proceeded from a soul intoxicated with its success, or from a spirit brimming over with the beginnings of good

* Homer.

† 'Hannibal conquered, but then did not know how to make profitable use of his victory.' Petrarch, *Sonnet*, LXXXVII.

fortune, which loses its appetite for more, being already too glutted to digest what it has. The victor whose arms are full and who cannot grasp more is unworthy of the gift that fortune has placed in his hands. For what advantage does he reap by it if, notwithstanding, he gives his enemy the chance to recover? What hope can there be that he will dare to attack their forces again, when they have rallied and reformed, and when anger and revenge have given them fresh arms, if he neither dared nor knew how to pursue them when they were broken and dismayed?

*Dum fortuna calet, dum conficit omnia terror.**

What better, in fact, can he expect than what he has just lost? It is not as in fencing, where the number of hits decides the victory. So long as the enemy is on his feet, it is a matter of beginning over again; it is no victory unless it has put an end to the war. In the skirmish in which Caesar was worsted near the town of Oricum, he taunted Pompey's men by telling them that he would have been lost if their general had known how to win a fight; and he clapped on his spurs in a very different way when it came to his turn.

But why should we not argue, on the other hand, that it is the sign of a headstrong and insatiable spirit to be unable to limit its greed; that an attempt to make God's favours exceed the measure that He has prescribed for them is an abuse of those favours; that to expose oneself to fresh dangers after gaining a battle is to throw victory back into fortune's lap, and that one of the wisest maxims in the art of war is never to drive the enemy to despair.

After defeating the Marsi in the Civil War, Sulla and Marius, seeing a remnant of the enemy's troops returning to hurl themselves upon them with the desperation of wild beasts, thought it better not to await the fury of their attack. Had Monsieur de Foix' ardour not led him into too fierce a pursuit of the stragglers from his victory at Ravenna, he would not have marred the day by his death. However, the memory of his recent ex-

* 'When fortune is aglow, and terror is all-conquering.' Lucan, VII, 734.

ample was instrumental in saving Monsieur d'Enghien from a similar disaster at Cérisoles. It is dangerous to attack a man whom you have deprived of every means of escape except by fighting, for necessity is a violent schoolmistress. 'Most terrible is the bite of enraged necessity.'*

Vincitur haud gratis iugulo qui provocat hostem.†

That is why Pharax prevented the King of Lacedaemon, who had just won the day against the Mantineans, from provoking the thousand Argives who had escaped unhurt from the defeat, but left them free to slip away rather than put their valour to the test when it was goaded and exasperated by misfortune. After his victory over Gondemar, King of Burgundy, Clodomir, King of Aquitaine, pursued his conquered and fugitive enemy and forced him to turn about. But this persistence lost him all the fruit of his victory, for he died on the field.

Likewise, if a general had to choose whether to have his soldiers richly and luxuriously equipped, or simply armed as need required, he might argue in favour of the first course, which was that of Sertorius, Philopoemen, Brutus, Caesar, and others, that it is always a spur to honour and glory for a soldier to see himself in fine array, and that he is then the more stubborn in battle since he has his arms to save, which are his possessions and his inheritance. This, said Xenophon, is the reason why the Asiatics carried their wives and concubines, together with their jewels and richest possessions, along with them to the wars.

But then it might be argued, on the other hand, that a soldier ought to be made less rather than more careful about saving his skin, and that to be generously equipped will double his fear of taking risks; and, what is more, that the enemy's desire for victory will be heightened by the prospect of rich spoils. It has been observed, too, that this prospect wonderfully encouraged the Romans of old in their fight against the Samnites. When Antiochus showed Hannibal the army that he was preparing

* Portius Latro, as quoted by Justus Lipsius. *Politics*, v, xviii.

† 'A man who offers his throat to an enemy sells his life dear.' Lucan, VII, 734.

against Rome, which was splendidly provided with fine equipment of every sort, he asked him, 'Will this army be enough for the Romans?' 'Enough for them?' exclaimed Hannibal. 'Yes, it will be quite enough, however greedy they are for booty.' Lycurgus forbade his soldiers not only all sumptuous equipment, but also the despoiling of their conquered enemies. He wished poverty and frugality, as he said, to be as conspicuous as their other qualities in battle.

In sieges and elsewhere, when occasion brings us close to the enemy, we readily allow our soldiers to defy him, to taunt him, and to abuse him with all manner of insults. There is some colour of reason for this, since there is some advantage in making it clear to one's men that they can hope for no mercy and expect no terms from an enemy whom they have so violently provoked, and that their only salvation lies in victory. Yet it is true that this was the undoing of Vitellius. He was fighting against Otho, whose men, being long unaccustomed to deeds of war and enervated by city pleasures, had much less courage than his own. But in the end he so infuriated them by his stinging speeches, in which he taunted them with cowardice, and with their regrets for the ladies and the banquets they had lately left behind them at Rome, that he gave them fresh heart, which no exhortations had been able to do, and drew down on himself an attack into which no one had so far been able to push them. And indeed when insults strike to the quick, they can easily make a man who is only sluggishly pursuing his king's quarrel, enter with a different spirit into what has become his own.

When we think how important is the safety of an army's commander, and that the enemy's aim is chiefly directed against that head upon which all the rest depend, it would seem impossible to question the plan which we see to have been followed by many great captains, of changing their dress and disguising themselves on going into an engagement. Yet the disadvantage incurred by this means is no less than that which it is designed to avoid. For if the captain is not recognized by his men, the courage they derive from his example and his presence gradually deserts them; and when they fail to see his usual insignia and banners they think that he is either dead, or has lost hope of success and fled. So far as experience goes, we sometimes see it favouring one viewpoint, sometimes the other. Pyrrhus's adventures in the battle that he fought against the consul Laevinus in Italy will serve to illustrate both. For by choosing to disguise himself in Demogacles' armour and to give that captain his own, he no doubt preserved his own life, but he came near to incurring the other disaster of losing the battle. Alexander, Caesar, and Lucullus liked to make themselves conspicuous in battle by their rich accoutrements and armour, of an unusual and brilliant colour; Agis, Agesilaus, and the great Gylippus, on the other hand, went to war meanly accoutred and without the insignia of a commander.

Among the criticisms of Pompey's conduct at the battle of Pharsalia is that he halted his army to await the enemy with a firm stance. 'For this' – I will here borrow Plutarch's words, which are worth more than mine – 'lessens the vigour which a charge lends to the first blows, and at the same time prevents that clash of the combatants, rank against rank, which is more prone than anything else to fill them with fire and fury. When they rush violently against one another, their courage is increased by their running and their cries. But immobility chills, so to speak, and freezes the soldier's ardour.' That is his opinion of such tactics. But if Caesar had lost, might it not just as well have been said on the other side that the strongest and firmest position is one in which a man stands firmly and does not budge, and that if he comes to a halt and keeps his strength husbanded, ready for the time of need, he will have a great advantage over an opponent who is shaken up and has already expended half his breath in running? Besides, an army being a body with so many different limbs, it is impossible for it to move, in this state of excitement, with such accuracy as not to break or change its array. The nimblest man, in fact, will be at grips with the enemy before his comrade can support him.

In that disastrous battle between the two Persian brothers,*

* Cyrus and Artaxerxes Mnemon, who fought at Cunaxa.

Clearchus the Lacedaemonian, who commanded the Greeks on Cyrus's side, led them quite deliberately to the attack, without any haste. But at fifty paces he put them into a run, hoping for that short distance both to preserve their order and husband their breath, but to give them by this impetus an advantage both of impact and aim. Others have settled the question for their armies in this way: 'If your enemy rushes upon you, await him with a firm stance; if he awaits you with a firm stance, then rush upon him.'

When the Emperor Charles V invaded Provence, King Francis was left to choose whether to advance and meet him in Italy, or wait for him on his own territory. He well knew what a great advantage it is to keep one's own dominions clear and untouched by the troubles of war, so that, with strength unimpaired, they may continue to supply men and money at need; that war necessarily implies devastation at every turn, which cannot readily be inflicted on one's own lands; that the peasant does not bear the depredations of his own party as mildly as those of the enemy, and that, as a result, seditions and commotions may easily be kindled among one's own people; that the licence to pillage and plunder, which cannot be granted on one's own territory, greatly relieves the fatigues of war, and that a man with no other prospect of gain than his bare pay is hard to keep to his duty when he is only two steps from his wife and home; that it is he who lays the cloth that pays the cost of the meal; that it is more cheering to attack than to defend; that the shock of losing a battle in the heart of one's own country is so violent that it is hard to prevent the whole body from crumbling, seeing that no emotion is so contagious as that of fear, none so easily taken on trust and so quick to spread; and that cities which have heard the rattle of the tempest at their gates, which have opened them to receive their captains and soldiers still trembling and breathless are in danger of rushing, in the heat of the moment, into some evil course of action. Yet, in spite of all these reasons, King Francis chose to recall the army that he had on the other side of the mountains, and to wait for the enemy to come to him.

But he may have thought, on the other hand, that being at home among his own friends, he could not fail to have an abundance of all commodities; that the rivers and passes, being under his own control, would bring him both provisions and money in complete safety and without the need of convoys; that the nearer the danger the more affection he would have from his subjects; that having so many cities and defences to protect him, it would be in his power to choose the hour of battle to suit his own opportunities and advantages; that if it pleased him to temporize, he might, in sheltered ease, watch the enemy catching cold and defeating himself in his battle against the difficulties that would confront him, since he was fighting on hostile territory, where everything before him, behind him, and on every side, would make war on him; where he would have no means of renewing or reinforcing his army if disease attacked it, or of lodging his wounded under cover; no money and no victuals except at the lance's point; no chance of resting or of taking breath; no knowledge of the places or the country to secure him from ambushes and surprises, and no way of saving the remains of his army, if he should lose a battle. In fact, there was no lack of examples on both sides.

Scipio thought it much better to go and attack his enemies' territory in Africa than to defend his own and fight them in Italy, where he was; and it was well for him that he did so. But Hannibal, on the other hand, in that same war, ruined himself by abandoning the conquest of a foreign land to return and defend his own. The Athenians left the enemy in their land in order to cross over to Sicily, and had fortune against them, but Agathocles, King of Syracuse, found it with him when he crossed over into Africa and left the war on his own soil.

So we are accustomed to say, and with good reason, that events and results, especially in war, depend for the most part on fortune, which will not conform or subject itself to our reason and foresight, as these lines say:

> *Et male consultis pretium est: prudentia fallax,*
> *nec fortuna probat causas sequiturque merentes;*
> *sed vaga per cunctos nullo discrimine fertur;*

scilicet est aliud quod nos cogatque regatque
*maius, et in proprias ducat mortalia leges.**

But to understand things aright, it seems that our opinions and deliberations depend upon fortune just as much, and that she involves our reason too in her uncertainties and confusion. 'We reason rashly and at random,' says Timaeus in Plato, 'because our judgements, like ourselves, have in them a large element of chance.'

BOOK ONE: Chapter 50

On Democritus and Heraclitus

THE judgement is applicable to all subjects, and has a hand in everything. For these trials,† therefore, which I am making of it, I take advantage of every kind of occasion. If there is a subject that I do not understand, I try it out for that very reason, sounding the ford from a distance; and if I find the water too deep for my stature, I keep to the bank. And this power of knowing when it cannot cross is a part of its efficacy – indeed that part of which it is proudest. Sometimes, with a vain and insubstantial subject, I try to see whether my judgement can find some way of giving it body, something on which to prop and support it. At other times I address it to some noble and outworn theme, in which it can make no discoveries of its own, the road being so well-worn that it can only walk in others' footsteps. In that case it plays its part by choosing the track that seems to it best; out of a thousand paths it says that this one or that is the best choice.

I take the first subject that chance offers me. All are for me equally good. And I never set out to cover them completely. For I never see the whole of anything; nor do those who pro-

* 'Often bad advice is of value, while good is deceptive. Fortune does not examine reasons or reward the deserving, but wanders where it will, guided by no discrimination. There is indeed a stronger power which controls us and rules us, and holds mortal laws subject to its own laws.' Manilius, IV, 95.

† *Essais*: the literary term *essay* derives from Montaigne's use of this word.

mise to show it to us. Of the hundred parts and aspects that each thing has, I take one, sometimes merely licking it, sometimes scraping its surface, and sometimes pinching it to the bone. I stab it as deeply, but not as widely as I can; and I generally like to seize it from some unaccustomed viewpoint. If I knew myself less well, I should take the risk of treating some subject thoroughly. But, since I scatter a word here and a word there, samples torn from their piece and separated without plan or promise, I am not bound to answer for them, or to keep to them, but can change them when it suits me. I am free to give myself up to doubt and uncertainty, and to my predominant quality which is ignorance.

Every action reveals us. That same mind of Caesar's that is apparent in the ordering and direction of the battle of Pharsalia can also be seen in the ordering of his idle and amorous intrigues. One judges a horse not only by seeing it ridden at a gallop, but also by its walk, and even by the sight of it resting in its stable.

Among the mind's functions are some of a lowly order; and anyone who does not see it engaged in these has no perfect knowledge of it. And perhaps it is best observed going at its simple pace. It is more apt to be seized by the winds of passion in its lofty moments. Moreover, the mind applies itself completely to each matter, giving it its whole attention, and never treating more than one thing at a time. And this it treats not according to the nature of the thing, but in accordance with itself.

Things in themselves perhaps have their own weights, measures, and states; but inwardly, when they enter into us, the mind cuts them to its own conceptions. Death is terrible to Cicero, but of no consequence to Socrates. Health, conscience, authority, knowledge, riches, beauty, and their opposites are all stripped on entry and reclothed by the mind, in whatever colour it pleases: brown, green, light, dark, bitter, sweet, deep or superficial, according to the pleasure of each. For they have not agreed together upon their styles, rules, and shapes; each mind is ruler in its own dominions. Let us not therefore use the external qualities of things as an excuse; we must hold ourselves responsible for them. Our good and our evil depend only on ourselves. Let us make our offerings and our vows to ourselves and not to fortune, which has no power over our moral nature. On the contrary character drags fortune in its train, and moulds it to its own form.

Why should I not judge of Alexander at table, talking and drinking rather too much, or when he is handling the chessmen? What chord of his mind was not plucked and played upon by that stupid and puerile game? I hate and avoid it, because it is not enough of a game. It is too serious for an amusement, and I am ashamed to give it an attention that might be employed on some good action. It absorbed Alexander quite as much as the direction of his glorious expedition into India, and engrosses another no less than the unravelling of some passage on which the whole salvation of mankind depends. See how our minds magnify and exaggerate this absurd pastime, how every nerve is strained over it! What a full opportunity it affords everyone to know and judge rightly of himself! There is no situation in which I have a fuller sight and feeling of myself than in this. What passion does it not arouse? Anger, spite, hatred, impatience, and a violent ambition to win, in a situation where a wish to be beaten would be more excusable. For rare and outstanding excellence in some trivial matter is unfitting to a man of honour. What I say of this example may be applied to all others. Any particle and any occupation of a man betrays and displays him as well as any other.

Democritus and Heraclitus were two philosophers, of whom the first, finding the human state vain and ridiculous, never appeared in public except with a mocking and ribald expression. Heraclitus, on the other hand, felt pity and compassion for this state of ours, so his expression was always melancholy and his eyes full of tears.

> alter
> *ridebat, quoties a limine moverat unum*
> *protuleratque pedem; flebat contrarius alter.**

I prefer the first humour, not because it is pleasanter to laugh

* 'The one laughed from the moment he put one foot over his doorstep, the other, on the contrary, wept.' Juvenal, x, 28.

than to weep, but because it expresses more contempt and is more condemnatory of us than the other. I do not think we can ever be despised as much as we deserve. Wailing and commiseration imply some valuation of the object bewailed; what we mock at we consider worthless. There is, in my opinion, not so much misery in us as emptiness, not so much malice as folly. We are not so full of evil as of inanity, nor so wretched as we are base. Therefore Diogenes, who played the fool to himself, rolling his tub, and turning up his nose at the great Alexander, esteeming us as flies or bladders puffed up with wind, was a sharper and more biting – and consequently, in my opinion, juster – judge than Timon who was nicknamed the man-hater. For what a man hates, he takes seriously. Timon wished us ill, was passionately desirous of our ruin, and avoided our company, since he considered us wicked and depraved by nature. But Diogenes valued us so little that contact with us could neither disturb nor affect him; he gave up our company, not out of fear but of contempt for our society. He thought us incapable of doing either good or harm.

Statilius replied in just that strain when Brutus invited him to join the conspiracy against Caesar. He considered the enterprise a just one, but did not think that men were worth taking any trouble about. This agrees with the teaching of Hegesias, who said that a wise man should do nothing except for himself, since he alone was worth doing anything for; also with Theodorus' saying that it is wrong for a wise man to risk himself for the good of his country, and endanger wisdom for fools. Our own peculiar condition is as capable of exciting laughter as of giving us any cause to laugh.

BOOK ONE: Chapter 55

On smells

IT is recorded of some men, among them Alexander the Great, that their sweat exhaled a sweet odour, owing to some rare and extraordinary property, of which Plutarch and others sought to find out the cause. But the common run of bodies are quite otherwise, and the best state they can be in is to be free from odour. Even the purest breath can be no sweeter or more excellent than to lack all offensive odours, as healthy children do. That is why, says Plautus,

Mulier tum bene olet, ubi nihil olet,*

a woman smells most perfectly when she does not smell at all, just as her deeds are said to smell sweetest when they are un-noticed and unheard. And those fine foreign perfumes are rightly regarded as suspicious in those who use them; it may be thought that their purpose is to cover some natural defect in that quarter. Thence proceed those paradoxes of the ancient poets, that to smell sweet is to stink,

Rides nos, Coracine, nil olentes,
malo quam bene olere, nil olere.†

And again:

Posthume, non bene olet, qui bene semper olet.‡

Yet I very much like to be regaled with good smells, and particularly loathe bad ones, which I can detect at a greater distance than anyone else:

Namque sagacius unus odoror,
Polypus, an gravis hirsutis cubet hircus in alis,
quam canis acer ubi lateat sus.§

The simplest and most natural smells seem to me the most pleasant; and this applies chiefly to the ladies. In the heart of barbarism, the women of Scythia are accustomed, after bathing, to powder and plaster their whole body and face with a certain sweet-smelling herb that grows in their country; and when they

* 'A woman has a good smell when she has no smell.' *Mostellaria*, I, iii, 117.

† 'You laugh at me, Coracinus, because I use no scent. I had rather smell of nothing than smell sweet.' Martial, VI, lv, 4.

‡ 'Posthumus, the man who always smells sweet does not smell sweet.' Martial, II, xii, 4.

§ 'For my nose is sharper, Polypus, at smelling the rank goat-smell of hairy armpits, than a dog at scenting out hidden game.' Horace, *Epodes*, XII, 4.

remove this paint to come to their husbands, they remain both sleek and perfumed.

Whatever the odour, it is remarkable how it clings to me, and how prone my skin is to absorb it. He who reproaches nature for failing to furnish man with the means of bringing smells to his nose is wrong, for they bring themselves. But in my case it is my moustache, which is thick, that performs that duty. If I touch it with my gloves or my handkerchief, it holds the scent for the whole day. It betrays the place where I have been. The close, luscious, greedy, long-drawn kisses of youth would adhere to it in the old days, and would remain for several hours afterwards. And yet I do not find myself much prone to epidemic diseases, which are either caught by contact, or arise from the contagion of the air; I have escaped those of my time, of which there have been several varieties in our cities and our armies. We read of Socrates that, though he never left Athens during the many visitations of plague that affected the city, he alone was never the worse for them.

Physicians might, I believe, make greater use of scents than they do, for I have often noticed that they cause changes in me, and act on my spirits according to their qualities; which make me agree with the theory that the introduction of incense and perfume into churches, so ancient and widespread a practice among all nations and religions, was for the purpose of raising our spirits, and of exciting and purifying our senses, the better to fit us for contemplation.

To form a better opinion of this, I should like to have tried the art of those cooks who are able to blend foreign odours with the flavour of their meats, as was particularly noticed of those in the service of that King of Tunis who landed at Naples in our own day to confer with the Emperor Charles. His meats were stuffed with sweet-smelling herbs at such expense that to dress a peacock and two pheasants in this way cost a hundred ducats; and then they were carved, not only the banqueting hall but every room in the palace, and even the near-by houses, were filled with a very sweet vapour, which did not disappear for some time afterwards.

My chief precaution in choosing my lodgings is to avoid a heavy and unwholesome atmosphere. The affection that I have for those beautiful cities Venice and Paris is lessened by their offensive smells, which arise from the marshes of the former and the mud of the latter.

BOOK TWO

BOOK TWO: Chapter 8

On the affection of fathers for their children

To Madame d'Estissac

MADAME, if strangeness and novelty do not save me – and these qualities generally give things a value – I shall never come off with honour from this foolish enterprise. But my purpose is so fantastic, and so very different from the common custom, that this will perhaps enable it to pass. It was a melancholy – and so one greatly opposed to my natural disposition – engendered by the sad solitude into which I was plunged some years ago, that first put this idle fancy of writing into my head. And then, finding myself entirely unprovided and empty of other material, I proposed myself to myself for argument and subject. This is the only book in the world of its kind, and its plan is both wild and extravagant. In fact, there is nothing remarkable about this whole project except its singularity. For the best craftsman in the world could never have given so vain and worthless a subject a form that would entitle it to anyone's consideration.

Now, Madame, since I have undertaken to draw a lifelike portrait of myself, I should have omitted an important feature had I not recorded the honour in which I have always held your merits. And I have decided to declare it explicitly at the head of this chapter for the special reason that the love you have shown to your children ranks among the first of your many good qualities. Whoever knows the age at which Monsieur d'Estissac, your husband, left you a widow; the great and honourable proposals* that have been made to you – as many as to any lady

* She remarried in 1580, the year of the *Essays'* first publication.

of your condition in France; the constancy and firmness with which, for so many years and midst such thorny difficulties, you have borne the burden of managing their affairs, which have bustled you from one corner of France to another and still press you hard; the successful way in which you have guided them by your own unaided wisdom or good fortune – whoever knows all this, I say, will readily conclude with me that we have no example of maternal affection more outstanding than yours in our time.

I praise God, Madame, that it has been so well employed. For the good hopes that your son, Monsieur d'Estissac, gives of himself are a sufficient assurance that, when he comes of age, you will be rewarded with the obedience and gratitude of a very good son. But since, because of his youth, he has been unable to recognize the very great services he has so abundantly received from you, I should like him to hear from me – if these pages one day fall into his hands, when I shall have neither mouth nor voice with which to tell him – this very true testimony, which will be even more vividly affirmed to him by the good results of your work on his behalf. These, please God, will make him conscious that no gentleman in France owes more to his mother than he, and that he cannot, in future, give more certain proof of his goodness and virtue than by recognizing your devotion to him.

If there is any true law of nature, that is to say any instinct seen to be universally and unchangeably implanted in animals and in men – which is not beyond dispute – I can say that, in my opinion, after the care that all beasts have for their own preservation, and to avoid what does them harm, the affection which the parent feels for its progeny holds the second place. And because nature seems to have recommended this affection to us, with a view to the spread and advancement of the successive parts of this machine of hers, it is no wonder if the love of children for their parents, since it goes in reverse, is rather less great.

To this may be added that other, Aristotelean reflection*

* See the *Nicomachean Ethics*, ix, vii.

that a man who has conferred a benefit on his fellow, loves him more than he is loved in return; and that one to whom something is owing loves more than his debtor; and every workman loves his work better than his work would love him in return, if it had feeling. For it is Being that is dear to us, and Being lies in movement and action. Consequently everyone exists, in some sort, in his work. He who confers a benefit performs a fine and honourable action, but the act of receiving one is merely useful. Now the useful is much less lovable than the beautiful. A beautiful action is stable and permanent; it furnishes a constant gratification to its performer. A useful action, on the other hand, easily disappears and is lost; and the memory of it is neither so fresh nor so pleasing. Those things are dearest to us that have cost us most; and it is harder to give than to receive.

Since it has pleased God to endow us with some capacity for reason, so that we may not be, like the beasts, slavishly subject to the general laws, but may adapt ourselves to them by judgement and free-will, we ought indeed to yield a little to the simple authority of nature, but not to let ourselves be tyrannically carried away by her. Reason alone should guide us in our inclinations.

I, for my part, have a strange disgust for those propensities which arise within us without the control and intervention of our judgement. Touching my present subject, for instance, I cannot entertain that passion for caressing new-born infants, that have neither mental activities nor recognizable bodily shape by which to make themselves lovable; and I have never willingly suffered them to be fed in my presence.

A true and regular affection should spring up and increase with our growing knowledge of them. Then if they are deserving of it, our natural inclination keeping step with our reason, we shall cherish them with a truly paternal regard; and we shall pass judgement on them also if they are unworthy, deferring always to reason, notwithstanding the force of nature. Very often it is quite the reverse; and we are generally more moved by our children's frolickings, games, and infantile nonsense than afterwards by their mature acts. It is as if we had loved them for our amusement, as monkeys, not as human beings. Many a parent is very liberal in supplying his children with toys, but becomes close-fisted over the slightest sum that they need once they are of age. It really looks as if our jealousy at seeing them come out and enjoy the world when we are on the point of leaving it, makes us more sparing and niggardly towards them. We are vexed that they should tread on our heels, as if to urge our departure. But if this were something to be feared, the order of things decreeing that they cannot, in fact, be nor live except at the expense of our being and our life, we should never have allowed ourselves to be fathers.

For my part, I think that it is both cruel and unjust not to admit them to a share and partnership in our property, and give them a full and friendly knowledge of our domestic affairs when they are capable of it. We ought to retrench and restrict our comforts to provide for theirs, since it is to this end that we have begotten them. It is unjust that an old, broken-down, half-dead father should, alone in his chimney-corner, enjoy wealth that would suffice for the advancement and support of several children, and that he should let them, meanwhile, waste their best years, for lack of the means to advance themselves in reputation and in the public service. They are driven in desperation to seek any way, however wicked, of providing for their needs. In my own day I have seen many young men of good family become such confirmed thieves that no reproof could deter them. I know one very well-connected person whom I once reproved at the request of his brother, a most honourable and gallant gentleman. The lad answered me with a blunt confession that he had been led into these beastly habits by the severity and avarice of his father, but that he was now so used to them that he could not control himself. He had just been caught stealing the rings of a lady at whose levée he had been present with many others.

He put me in mind of a story that I had heard about another gentleman, who had become so used to this noble art from the time of his youth, and so skilled in it, that when he afterwards succeeded to his estate and decided to abandon the practice, he still could not prevent himself, if he passed a shop in which he saw something that he needed, from snatching it up, even though he had to send and pay for it afterwards. I have seen many so habituated and inured to this vice that they stole even from their friends, though with the intention of restoring what they had taken.

I am a Gascon, and yet there is no vice for which I feel less sympathy. I loathe it instinctively even more than I condemn it by reason. I never so much as desire anything that belongs to another. This province has, in plain truth, a rather worse reputation for theft than other parts of the French kingdom. Yet we have on various occasions recently seen men of good family in other provinces in the hands of justice, convicted of many abominable robberies. I am afraid that we must to some extent attribute their vices to the avarice of their fathers.

If someone should answer me, as a gentleman of very good understanding did one day, that he was husbanding his wealth for no other benefit or advantage but to win the respect and attentions of his kin; and that, old age having deprived him of all other power, it was his sole remaining means of keeping his authority over his family, and preventing himself from falling into general contempt and disrepute – and truly not old age alone, but every weakness is, according to Aristotle, a promoter of avarice – there is something in what he says; but this is the remedy for a disease which we should prevent from ever arising. It is a very poor father that has no other hold on his children's affection than the need they have of his assistance – always supposing that this can be called affection at all. He should win their respect by his virtue and abilities, and their love by his goodness and sweetness of character. Even the ashes of a rich substance have their value; and we have grown accustomed to respecting and venerating the bones and relics of men of honour.

No old age can ever be so foul and decrepit in a man who has lived an honourable life that it should not be revered, especially by his children, whose minds he should have trained in their duties by reason, not by necessity and dependence, or by force and harshness,

et errat longe, mea quidem sententia,
qui imperium credat esse gravius aut stabilius
*vi quod fit, quam illud quod amicitia adiungitur.**

I condemn all violence in the education of a tender soul that is being trained for honour and freedom. There is something servile in harshness and constraint; and I believe that what cannot be accomplished by reason, and by wisdom and tact, can never be accomplished by force. That is how I was brought up. They tell me that in all my childhood I was only whipped twice, and then very mildly. I owed the same upbringing to my own children. They all died at nurse, except Leonor, my one daughter who escaped this unhappy fate. She has reached the age of more than 6 without anything but words, and very gentle words, being used to guide her and correct her childish faults. Her mother's indulgence readily concurred in this. And even if my hopes in her should be disappointed, there will be enough other causes for this without blaming my educational system, which I know to be both just and natural. I should have followed it still more scrupulously with sons, who are born less subservient and are freer by nature. I should have loved to build up their courage by honest and frank treatment. I have never seen any other effects of a whipping than to make the soul more cowardly and more perversely obstinate.

If we wish to be loved by our children, if we wish to take from them all reason to desire our death – though no reason for so dreadful a desire can be either just or pardonable; 'no crime is based on reason'† – let us reasonably supply their lives with everything that is within our power. With this in view, we should not marry so young that their maturity almost coincides with ours. For this inconvenience throws us into many great difficulties. I am speaking especially of the nobility, whose state is one of idleness, and who live, as they say, only on their rents. For with people of other classes, who work for their livelihood, the addition of a number of children is an advantage to the

* 'A man is very wrong, at least in my opinion, who believes that power is stronger and more durable when imposed by force than when procured by friendship.' Terence, *Adelphi*, I, i, 40.

† Livy, xxviii, xxviii.

household; they are so many additional tools and instruments by which it can grow rich.

I married at 33, and agree with Aristotle's reported opinion, that 35 is the best age. Plato would have no one marry before 30, but he rightly laughs at those who perform their connubial duties after 55, and considers their offspring undeserving of life and sustenance. Thales set the truest limits; when he was young and his mother urged him to marry, he answered that it was not yet time; and when advanced in years, that it was too late. We should allow no opportunities for inopportune actions. The ancient Gauls thought it most reprehensible to have relations with a woman before the age of 20, and particularly urged those who wanted to be trained for war to preserve their virginities till they were well advanced in years, since courage is weakened and diverted by intercourse with women.

> *Ma hor congiunto a giovinetta sposa,*
> *Lieto homai de' figli, era invilito*
> *Negli affetti di padre e di marito.**

Greek history observes of Iccus of Tarentum, of Chryso, of Astylus, of Diopompus, and others that to keep their bodies strong for racing in the Olympic games, for wrestling and for other exercises, they abstained from all sexual intercourse for so long as their training lasted. Muley-Hassan, that King of Tunis whom the Emperor Charles the Fifth restored to his throne, upbraided his father's memory for his frequent visits to women, calling him weak, effeminate, and a begetter of children. In a certain country of the Spanish Indies, the men were forbidden to marry until they were over 40, and yet the girls were allowed to do so at 10.

When a gentleman is 35, it is too early for him to give place to a son of 20; he is still able to make a good showing both in military expeditions and at his prince's court. He has need of his possessions; and though he should certainly share them he should not part with so much as to neglect himself in another's

---

* 'But now, wedded to a young wife and blessed with children, his affections as husband and father had weakened him.' Tasso, *Gerusalemme liberata*, x, 39.

favour. Such a man may indeed justifiably repeat that saying which is commonly on the tip of a father's tongue: 'I will not take off my clothes before I go to bed.'

But a father weighed down by old age and infirmities, barred by his weakness and ill-health from the common society of man, is doing a wrong both to himself and his children if he squats uselessly on a great pile of riches. He has come to the state in which, if he is wise, he will wish to strip, not to his shirt but to a nice warm nightgown, and go to bed. His remaining luxuries, for which he has no further use, he should voluntarily present to those who ought, by the natural order of things, to possess them. It is only right that he should leave the enjoyment to them, since nature has deprived him of it; any other course would surely be spiteful and envious. The Emperor Charles V never performed a finer action than in recognizing, after the example of certain ancients of his own quality, that reason quite clearly commands us to undress when our robes grow too heavy and encumber us, and to go to bed when our legs fail us. He resigned his possessions, his greatness, and his power to his son, when he found himself failing in strength and vigour to conduct his affairs with the glory that their management had hitherto won him.

> *Solve senescentem mature sanus equum, ne*
> *peccet ad extremum ridendus, et ilia ducat.**

The mistake of not realizing in time the impotence and complete alteration that old age naturally brings both to body and mind – to both equally, in my opinion, unless indeed the mind be the worse afflicted – has destroyed the reputations of most of the world's great men. I have in my own time met and been intimately acquainted with persons of great authority who, as could very easily be seen, had suffered a marvellous diminution of their former power, of which I knew from the fame that it had gained them in their best years. For their honour's sake, I could heartily have wished that they had retired comfortably to their homes, freed from their public and military commands,

* 'Be wise in time, and unharness the ageing horse, lest in the end he fail ridiculously, and become broken winded.' Horace, *Epistles*, i, i, 8.

which were now too heavy for their shoulders.

I was once an habitual visitor at the house of a gentleman*
who was a widower and very old, yet still in a fairly green old
age. He had several marriageable daughters and a son old
enough to appear in the world. This burdened his household
with many expenses, and with visits from strangers which gave
him little pleasure, not only on the score of economy, but also
because, by reason of his age, he had adopted a mode of life very
different from ours. I said to him one day, somewhat boldly as is
my custom, that he would do better to give place to us and let
his son have his principal house – for he had no other that was
well situated and furnished – and himself retire to a near-by
estate of his, where no one would disturb his repose. Otherwise,
considering his children's condition, he would not be able to
avoid our tiresome company. He afterwards took my advice,
and found the advantage of it.

This does not mean that a man should transfer his property
to his children by a bond that he can never revoke. I, who am
myself old enough to play this part, would give them the enjoyment of my house and property, but with the right to change
my mind if they should give me cause. I should leave the use to
them because it no longer suited me; and I should reserve for
myself as much authority over general matters as I chose. For I
have always considered that it must be very satisfactory to an
aged father himself to teach his children the management of his
affairs, and to have the power, during his lifetime, of controlling
their conduct, whilst giving them instruction and advice based
on his own experience of business matters. He must be glad to
watch the ancient honour and order of his house when it is in
the hands of his successors, and thus to safeguard such hopes
as he may have formed of their future conduct.

With this in view, I should not avoid their society, but should
observe them closely and take part in their feasts and merri-
ments, in so far as my age permitted. If I did not live among
them – which I could not do without troubling their gatherings
with my old man's gloom and with the tyranny of my ailments,

* Probably Jean de Lusignan of Agen.

and without also straining and doing violence to the regular way of life that I should then have adopted – I should at least live beside them in a wing of my house, not in the most elegant, but in the most comfortable quarters. I would not live like a certain Dean of St Hilaire of Poitiers,* whom I saw a few years ago reduced to such isolation by the pressure of his melancholy that when I entered his room it was twenty-two years since he had been out of the door. And yet he had free and easy use of all his faculties, but for a chill which he had caught in his stomach. Hardly once a week would he allow anyone in to see him; he constantly kept himself shut up in his room, alone except for a servant who brought him food once a day, but merely came in and went out. His occupation was to walk to and fro and read a few books – for he was something of a scholar – and he persisted in remaining like this till he died, as he did soon afterwards.

I would try, by kindly dealings, to foster in my children a warm friendship and unfeigned good feeling towards myself; which from noble natures are not hard to win. But if they are savage brutes, such as our age produces in profusion, they must be loathed and shunned as such. I dislike the custom of forbidding children to call us *Father*, and insisting that they use some more distant appellation, to show greater respect; as if nature had not sufficiently provided us with authority. We call God *Almighty Father*, yet disdain to let our children use the name. I have corrected this fault in my family.†

It is also wrong and foolish to deprive the young of familiarity with their fathers when they grow up and to maintain a remote and austere attitude towards them, in the hope of thus keeping them in awe and obedience. For this is a most futile farce, which makes fathers distasteful and, what is worse, ridiculous to their children. They are in possession of youth and strength, and therefore enjoy the world's goodwill and favour; and they have nothing but mockery for the fierce and tyrannical airs of a man

* Jean d'Estissac, d. 1576.
† This last sentence appears in the edition of 1595, but not in the *Édition Municipale*, which I am following.

146

who has no blood left either in his heart or in his veins – a veritable scarecrow in a hemp field! Even if I had the power to inspire fear, I should still prefer to make myself loved.

There are so many kinds of failings in old age, and such feebleness, and it is so open to contempt, that the best thing a man can win is the love and affection of his family; authority and fear are no longer his weapons. A certain gentleman whom I knew* was in his youth kept under very strict control; and now that he is advanced in years, although he behaves as reasonably as he can, he strikes, bites, and swears, and is the most tempestuous master in France. He is wearing himself out with cares and precautions. All this is nothing but a farce to which his very family conspires; of his storeroom, his cellar, and even his purse, others have the main use, while he keeps the keys in his wallet, as if they were dearer to him than his eyes. While he congratulates himself on the economy and parsimony of his table, everything is being squandered in various parts of the house; it is all gambling and extravagance, and amusing tales about his futile furies and niggardliness. Everyone watches him like a sentinel. If by chance some wretched serving-man becomes attached to him, he immediately becomes an object of suspicion: a sentiment at which old age bites readily enough of itself. How many times he has boasted to me of the check he has imposed on his household, of the punctilious obedience and respect that he receives, and of the insight he has into his own affairs!

Ille solus nescit omnia.†

I do not know anyone who can claim more qualities, natural and acquired, that fit him to maintain authority. Yet he has, childishly, lost it. That is why I have chosen him, among many similar cases that I know, as the best example.

It would be a subject for scholastic disputation, whether he is better thus, or otherwise. In his presence, all defer to him in every way. This idle tribute is paid to his authority, that he is

* This is probably Gaston de Foix, Marquis de Trans, a powerful neighbour of Montaigne's.

† 'He alone is in complete ignorance.' Terence, *Adelphi*, IV, ii, 9.

never opposed; he is believed, feared, and respected to his
heart's content. If he dismisses a servant, the man packs his
bundle and is gone – but only out of his sight. The steps of old
age are so slow, and its senses so dull that the man will live and
do his work in the very house for a whole year unnoticed. And
when a seasonable opportunity occurs, piteous and imploring
letters will arrive from some distant place, full of promises to
amend; and on the strength of these the man will be received
back into favour. Does Monsieur make a bargain or send a
letter of which they disapprove? It is suppressed, and reasons
enough are invented afterwards to excuse the lack of performance, or of an answer. Since letters from outside are never
delivered straight to him, he only sees those that it is thought
convenient for him to see. If he happens to get hold of them
first, it being his custom to rely on a certain person to read them
to him, that person promptly invents what he thinks fit, and
often contrives to have somebody or other asking the old
gentleman's pardon when he is actually insulting him in that
very letter. In short, he sees his affairs only in a planned and
contrived shape, as satisfactory to himself as they can make it,
in order not to arouse his displeasure and wrath. I have seen,
under various forms, many households managed like this, consistently and for long periods, with very similar results.

Women are always prone to disagree with their husbands.
They seize with both hands every pretext for opposing them;
the first excuse serves for plenary justification. I have known
one who robbed her man wholesale, in order, as she told her
confessor, to give more liberal alms to the poor. Believe in that
pious excuse if you will! No household authority seems to them
grand enough if it comes as a concession from the husband.
They must usurp it either by cunning or by effrontery, and
always offensively, if it is to have charm and dignity in their
eyes. When, as in the case I have been speaking of, they are
opposing a poor old man on behalf of their children, then they
seize on this pretext and triumphantly turn it to their purpose;
and, as if in common servitude, readily intrigue against the
husband's domination and control.

If there are grown sons, in the flower of their youth, they promptly suborn, either by force or favour, both the steward and the bursar, and all the rest. Those who have neither wife nor sons fall into this misfortune less easily, but suffer even more cruelly and ignobly. The elder Cato said in his day, 'So many servants, so many enemies.' Consider whether, our age being so much less pure than his, he did not mean to warn us that wife, son, and servant are for us so many enemies. It is as well for old age that it provides us with the welcome blessings of imperceptiveness, ignorance, and an easy credulity. If we struck back, what would be our fate, especially in these days, when the judges who have to decide our disputes are commonly interested parties, and on the side of youth?

If the trick escapes my sight, at least I do not fail to see that I am very easy to cheat. And can anyone ever say enough about the value of a friend, and of how different friendship is from these civil ties? Even the reflection of it that I see in beasts is so pure that I regard it with reverence. If I am deceived by others, at least I do not deceive myself into thinking that I am capable of protecting myself, or rack my brains for a means of becoming so. I turn to my own bosom as a refuge from these treacheries; I do not give myself up to restless and disturbing cares, but deliberately apply my mind to other things. When I hear an account of some man's predicament, I do not waste my thoughts on him; I immediately look inwards upon myself, to see how it is with me. Whatever touches him concerns me. His case is a warning to me, and makes me watch out in that direction. Every day and every hour, we say things of others that we might more properly say of ourselves, if we could but turn our observation inwards as well as direct it outwards. Thus many authors prejudice their own cause by rushing headlong against the cause they are attacking, and hurling shafts at their enemies that can be hurled back at them.

The late Maréchal de Monluc, whose son – a truly brave and most promising gentleman – died on the island of Madeira, when talking to me of his sorrow, greatly stressed, among his many regrets, the heartbroken grief that he felt at never having opened his heart to the boy. He had always put on the stern face of paternal gravity, and had thus lost the opportunity of really knowing and appreciating his son, also of revealing to him the deep love he bore him, and the deservedly high opinion he had of his virtues. 'And that poor lad', he said, 'never saw anything of me but a grim and scornful frown, and has died in the belief that I could neither love him nor value him at his proper worth. For whom was I saving the revelation of the singular affection that I felt for him in my soul? Was it not he who should have had all the pleasure and all the obligation? I constrained and tortured myself to keep on this foolish mask, thus losing the delight of his companionship, and of his affection too. For his feelings towards me cannot have been anything but cool, since all he had ever received from me was gruffness, and my bearing towards him was always tyrannical.' I think his lament was well-founded and justifiable. As experience has only too conclusively taught me, there is no consolation so sweet, on the loss of a friend, as that which comes from our consciousness that we have held nothing back from him, but enjoyed a perfect and complete communion.

I am open with my family, to the extent of my powers. I quite freely reveal to them the state of my feelings for them, also my opinion of them, and of everyone else. I make haste to disclose and make myself clear to them; for I wish for no misunderstandings, either in my favour or my disfavour.

Caesar tells us that among the peculiar customs of our ancient Gauls was this: that male children did not appear before their fathers or venture to be seen with them in public till they began to bear arms; as if to signify that this was also the time for their fathers to admit them into their society and companionship.

I have observed yet one more error of judgement in some fathers of my day. Not content with having deprived their children during their own long lives of the share they should naturally have had in their wealth, they leave to their wives after them the same control over all their property, with authority to dispose of it at their pleasure. I knew a certain lord, one of the chief officers of the crown,* who, despite his expectations of an annual revenue of more than fifty thousand crowns, by right of succession, died in want and loaded with debts, when over 50, while his mother, in her extreme old age, still enjoyed all his property by the will of his father, who had himself lived to be nearly eighty. This seems to me most unreasonable.

Therefore, I do not think that it is of much advantage to a man whose affairs are prosperous to look for a wife who will encumber him with a great dowry; there is no foreign debt that brings more disaster to a family. My ancestors have generally been of this opinion and have acted on it, as I did myself. But those who advise us against marrying rich wives, for fear they may be less tractable and kind, are mistaken; indeed, we may lose a real benefit on this frivolous assumption. It costs an un-reasonable woman no more to override one consideration than another. She is best pleased with herself when she is most in the wrong. But as injustice attracts her, so a good woman is at-tracted by the honour of virtuous actions; and the more riches she brings, the better her nature; just as the greater her beauty, the more gladly and proudly a woman remains chaste.

It is right to leave the administration of affairs to mothers, so long as the children are not of a legal age to take charge. But the father has brought them up very badly if he cannot expect that, once they are of age, they will have more wisdom and ability than his wife, considering the common weakness of her sex. Yet it would, truly, be more unnatural to make the mother de-pendent on the discretion of her children. She should be liberally provided with sufficient means to maintain herself ac-cording to the standing of her house and her years, since want and shortage are much more unsuitable, and much harder to bear, for a woman than a man; the burden ought to rest on the children rather than on the mother.

On the whole, the most sensible disposition of our property at death is, in my opinion, to let it be divided according to the custom of the country. The laws have considered the matter

* Probably the Maréchal de Montmorency, son of the Constable, whose mother survived his death in 1579 by a year.

better than we; and it is preferable to let them err in their decisions, than rashly to run the risk of erring in ours. The wealth is, properly speaking, not our own, since by a civil provision and independently of us, it is destined for particular successors. And, although we have some liberty to vary this, I hold that we should not, without a great and most manifest reason, deprive anyone of what is his by fortune, and what common justice entitles him to receive. And it is an unreasonable abuse of this liberty to make it serve our frivolous and personal whims. My fate has been so kind as not to present me with occasions that might have tempted me, or diverted my inclinations from the common and lawful course.

I know some on whom it is a waste of time to lavish a long succession of kindly services; one word taken amiss blots out the merit of ten years. He is a lucky man who finds a way of gratifying their desires at this final passing! The last action carries the day; not the best and most frequent services but the most recent and immediate do the work. There are people who juggle with their last wills as with apples or sticks, to reward or punish every action of those who claim an interest in them. A will is too far-reaching in its consequences, and too important to be thus brought out at every moment; sensible men settle it once and for all, in the light of reason and the general custom.

We attach rather too much importance to male substitutions,* and ridiculously design an eternity for our names. We also give too much weight to idle conjectures about the future, suggested to us by the minds of children. It might perhaps have been unjust to displace me as heir for being heavier and duller, slower, and more reluctant at my lessons, not only than any of my brothers, but than any boy in my province, whether in mental or physical exercises. It is folly to make special selections on the strength of these prognostications, which so often prove deceptive. If we may violate the usual custom, and correct the

* Male substitution was a method of nominating male heirs into the distant future, and thus avoiding the possibility of estates being alienated by later generations. Montaigne himself fell into this error, and by nominating the son of his daughter's second marriage as his heir, ran his family into two centuries of lawsuits.

choice which the fates have made of our heirs, we are more justified in doing so on the score of some marked and gross physical deformity, some persistent and incurable blemish, which with us, who are great admirers of beauty, may do a descendant serious harm.

The amusing dialogue between Plato's lawgiver and his fellow-citizens will illustrate this passage. 'What then,' they say, when they feel their end draw near, 'may we not dispose of what is ours to whom we please? Ye gods, how cruel that we should not be allowed to give more or less to our friends at our pleasure, according to the help they have given us in our sickness, our old age, and our affairs!' To which the lawgiver replies: 'My friends, who will doubtless die very soon, it is hard for you to know yourselves and to know what is yours, in accordance with the Delphic inscription. I who make the laws hold that neither you nor the goods of which you enjoy the use belong to yourselves. Both you and they belong to your family, past as well as future. Furthermore, both your family and your goods belong to society. Therefore, in case some flatterer, in your old age or sickness, or some passion of your own, may wrongfully urge you to make an unjust will, I will protect you from it. But out of regard for the general interest of the city and of your family, I will establish laws, and make you understand what is only reasonable, that private advantage must make way for public interest. Go then, peacefully and cheerfully, where human necessity calls you. It is for me, who look on all things equally, and who provide, in so far as I can, for the general interest, to take care of what you leave behind you.'

To return to my subject, it appears to me, I do not know why, that women ought not to possess any sort of authority over men, other than the natural authority of the mother, except a right to punish those who, by some amorous impulse, have voluntarily submitted to them. But that has nothing to do with old women, of whom we have been speaking. It is the obviousness of this consideration that has made us so ready to invent and give force to that law, which no man ever saw,* that bars

* The so-called Salic Law.

women from succession to the crown. There is hardly any realm in the world where it is not pleaded, as it is here, with a show of reasons to support it, but fortune has given it more credit in some places than in others.

It is dangerous to leave the disposal of our succession to women's judgement, and let them choose between our children, for their choice is always capricious and unfair. For those undisciplined appetites and perverse tastes that they display during their pregnancies are present in their hearts at all times. One commonly sees them devoted to the weakest and puniest of their children, or to those, if they have them, who are still hanging around their necks. Lacking strength of judgement to choose and embrace those who deserve it, they easily allow themselves to be carried away where the promptings of nature are simplest; like animals that only recognize their young while they are pulling at their teats.

Moreover, it is easy to see from experience that this natural affection to which we give such authority has very frail roots. Every day we snatch children from the arms of their mothers, and put our own in their charge for a very small payment. We force them to give theirs over to some wretched nurse, with whom we will not trust our own, or to a she-goat; forbidding the mothers, never mind at what risk to their children, either to give them suck or to do anything at all for them, so that they may devote themselves entirely to the service of ours. And we see that in most of these women habit soon gives rise to a bastard affection, stronger than the natural, and a greater concern for the well-being of others' children than of their own.

I have spoken of goats because it is an ordinary thing in my part of the world to see the village women who cannot feed their children at their own breasts calling in the aid of she-goats. And I have at present two men-servants who never sucked mother's milk for more than a week. These goats are quickly trained to come and suckle the little ones; they recognize their voices when they cry, and run up to them. If any but their nursling is brought to them, they refuse to feed it, and the child likewise will refuse a strange goat. I saw one the other day whose goat had been taken from him, because his father had only borrowed it from a neighbour; he could never get used to another that was brought to him and died, no doubt of starvation. Animals change and pervert their natural affections as easily as we do.

I think that there must be frequent mistakes in that district of Libya that is described by Herodotus,* in which he says that the men have intercourse with the women promiscuously, but that a child, as soon as it can walk, will find its father in the crowd, natural instinct guiding its first steps towards him.

Now if we consider this simple reason for loving our children, that we have begotten them, and therefore call them our other selves, there seems to me to be a very different kind of production coming from us which is no less worthy of consideration. For what we engender from the soul, the offspring of our mind, our heart, and our talents, springs from parts nobler than the corporeal, and more truly our own. In this act of generation we are father and mother at once; these cost us much dearer and, when there is anything good in them, bring us greater honour as well. For the merits of our other children are much more theirs than ours, the share we have in them being very slight; but all the beauty, all the grace, and all the value of these are our own. They therefore represent us and resemble us more vividly. Plato adds that they are immortal children, who immortalize their parents and even raise them to be gods, as they did Lycurgus, Solon, and Milnos.

Now, since history abounds in instances of the common affection of fathers for their children, it has seemed to me not inappropriate to pick out an example or two of this other kind. Heliodorus, that good bishop of Tricea, preferred to forfeit the dignity, profit, and reverence of his venerable prelacy, rather than sacrifice his daughter – a very charming daughter that still survives, but perhaps a little too curiously and wantonly

* This story is based on a misreading by Herodotus's French translator, Saliat, of IV, 180.

adorned, and rather too amorous for the daughter of a bishop and priest.*

There was also a certain Labienus at Rome, a personage of great worth and authority, who amongst eminent qualities excelled in all forms of literature. He was, I believe, a son of the great Labienus, chief of the captains who served under Caesar in the Gallic War, who afterwards joined the party of Pompey the Great, and conducted himself most valiantly until Caesar defeated him in Spain. The Labienus of whom I am speaking was envied by many for his great qualities; and it is likely that the imperial courtiers and favourites of his day disliked his independence and his antagonism towards tyranny: qualities inherited from his father, which most probably coloured his books and writings. His adversaries prosecuted him before the Roman magistrates, and succeeded in having several of his works, which were in circulation, condemned to the flames. He was the first to be sentenced to this new form of penalty, which was afterwards repeated on various others at Rome, whereby a man's writings and studies were punished with death. As if there were not enough opportunities or objects for cruelty without including things that nature has made immune from all feeling and suffering – such as reputation and the products of the mind – and without inflicting corporal punishment on the teachings and monuments of the Muses! Now Labienus could not bear this loss, nor to survive his most beloved progeny; he had himself taken to the tomb of his ancestors, and there shut up alive, thus providing for his death and burial in a single act. It would be difficult to show a stronger paternal affection than that. When his intimate friend Cassius Severus, a man of great eloquence, saw the burning of Labienus's books, he exclaimed that by the same sentence he should himself have been condemned to be burnt alive with them, since he carried their complete contents stored up in his memory.

* Heliodorus, the third-century Greek bishop who was said to have been given the choice between burning his *Ethiopian History*, a sensuous and romantic story, and resigning his bishopric. He chose the latter course. Modern scholarship has suggested that the story was not his, but was written by a Syrian layman of the same name.

A similar fate befell Cremutius Cordus, who was accused of having written in praise of Brutus and Cassius. That base, servile, and corrupt senate, which deserved a worse master than Tiberius, condemned his books to the flames; and he, content to accompany them in their death, killed himself by abstaining from food.

When the good Lucan, condemned to die by that scoundrel Nero, was breathing his last; when most of his blood had already flowed out of the veins of his arms which his physician had opened at his request, in order to bring on his death; and when coldness, having already seized his extremities, was approaching his vital organs, the last thing that came to his memory was a passage from his poem on the Battle of Pharsalia, which he then recited; and he died with those last words on his lips. What was this but a tender and paternal leavetaking from his children, the counterpart of those farewells and close embraces with which we at our death part from ours, and the effect of that natural affection which calls to our memory, in these last moments, the things that have been dearest to us in our lives?

Epicurus, when dying, as he tells us, in the torments of an acute colic, derived his sole consolation from the beauty of the teachings that he left to the world. Can we believe that he would have felt as much satisfaction in a family of well-born and well-reared children, had he had one, as he did in the authorship of his precious writings? Can we suppose that, if offered the choice between leaving behind him a deformed and low-born child and a foolish and pointless book, he would not have preferred – and not he alone, but any man of his genius – to incur the first misfortune rather than the second? It would probably have been an impiety in St Augustine, for example, if, confronted with the proposal that he should bury either his writings, from which our religion derives such great benefit, or his children, supposing that he had any,* he had not elected to bury his children. And I do not know whether I would not much rather have produced a perfectly formed child by intercourse with the

* He had an illegitimate son, Adeodatus, who was baptized with him. See *Confessions*, IX, 14.

Muses than by intercourse with my wife.

To this child, such as it is, what I give I give purely and irrevocably, as one does to the children of one's body. The little good that I have bestowed on it is no longer at my disposal. It may know many things that I know no longer, and may hold for me things that I have not myself retained, and that I should have to borrow from it, in case of need, as from a stranger. If I am wiser than it, it is richer than I.

There are few lovers of poetry who would not be prouder to be the father of the *Aeneid* than of the handsomest youth in Rome, and who would not more gladly endure the loss of the son than of the poem. For, according to Aristotle, of all craftsmen the poet is avowedly the greatest lover of his own work. It is hard to believe that Epaminondas, who boasted of leaving no other posterity but daughters who would one day do honour to their father – meaning the two noble victories that he gained over the Lacedaemonians – would willingly have agreed to exchange these for the most gorgeous beauties in the whole of Greece, or that Alexander and Caesar would ever have wished to forfeit the grandeur of their glorious deeds of war for the advantage of having heirs and offspring, however perfect and talented these might have been. Indeed, I very much doubt whether Phidias, or any other fine sculptor, would have been so anxious for the preservation and longevity of his human children, as for that of a beautiful statue which with long toil and study he had perfected according to his art. As for those wicked and violent passions that have sometimes made fathers lust for their daughters, or mothers for their sons, there are parallels to be found in this other kind of parenthood; as witness the tale that is told of Pygmalion who, having made a statue of a woman of singular beauty, fell so desperately and madly in love with his creation that the gods, in pity for his frenzy, were compelled to endow it with life.

> *Tentatum mollescit ebur, positoque rigore*
> *subsedit digitis.**

* 'The ivory grows soft at his touch; it loses hardness and yields to his fingers.' Ovid, *Metamorphoses*, x, 283.

On books

I HAVE no doubt that I often speak of things which are better treated by the masters of the craft, and with more truth. This is simply a trial* of my natural faculties, and not of my acquired ones. If anyone catches me in ignorance, he will score no triumph over me, since I can hardly be answerable to another for my reasonings, when I am not answerable for them to myself, and am never satisfied with them. Let the man who is in search of knowledge fish for it where it lies; there is nothing that I lay less claim to. These are my fancies, in which I make no attempt to convey information about things, only about myself. I may have some objective knowledge one day, or may perhaps have had it in the past when I happened to light on passages that explained things. But I have forgotten it all; for though I am a man of some reading, I am one who retains nothing.

So I can offer nothing certain except to recount the extent of my knowledge at the present moment. No attention should be paid to the matter, only to the shape that I give it. Let it be judged from what I borrow whether I have chosen the right means of exalting my theme. For I make others say what I cannot say so well myself, sometimes from poverty of expression, sometimes from lack of understanding. I do not count my borrowings, I weigh them; had I wished them to be valued by their number, I could have loaded myself with twice as many. They are all, or very nearly all, by names so famous and ancient that I think their authors reveal themselves without my mentioning them. In the case of arguments and ideas that I transplant on to my own soil and mix with my own, I have sometimes deliberately omitted to name my source, in order to check the rashness of those hasty critics who pounce on writings of every sort, especially on new books by men still living, written in the vulgar tongue: a practice which permits the whole world to comment, and seemingly to prove that their conception and design are

* The French word is again *essai*.

vulgar also. I will gladly take on my nose the tweak that is rightly Plutarch's, and receive on my head the rage that should be poured on Seneca's. For I must use these great men's virtues as a cloak for my weakness. But I will love anybody who can strip me of my feathers, by clarity of judgement, I mean, and merely by distinguishing the strength and beauty of the ancients' language. For though my memory is so faulty that I constantly fail to recognize their place of origin, I can very well tell, by measuring my own capacities, that my soil is quite incapable of producing any of the more precious flowers I find sown there, and that all the fruits of my own growing would never equal them in value.

If I get myself into a muddle, if there is something empty and faulty in my reasoning that I am unable to perceive for myself, or incapable of seeing when it is pointed out to me, then for this I may be held to account. Mistakes often escape our eyes, but it is the sign of a poor judgement if we are unable to see them when shown to us by another. Knowledge and truth may dwell in us without judgement, and judgement also without them; indeed to recognize one's ignorance is one of the best and surest signs of judgement that I know. I have no other drill-sergeant but chance to put order into my writings. As my thoughts come into my head, so I pile them up; sometimes they press on in crowds, sometimes they come dragging in single file. Even if I have strayed from the road I would have everyone see my natural and ordinary pace. I let myself go forward as I am. Besides, these are not matters about which it is wrong to be ignorant, or to speak casually and at random.

I could indeed wish to have a more perfect understanding of things, but I do not wish to pay the high price that it costs. My purpose is to pass the remainder of my life pleasantly and not laboriously. There is nothing for which I would care to rack my brains, not even the most precious of knowledge.

In books I only look for the pleasure of honest entertainment; or if I study, the only learning I look for is that which tells me how to know myself, and teaches me how to die well and to live well:

*Has meus ad metas sudet oportet equus.**

When I meet with difficulties in my reading, I do not bite my nails over them; after making one or two attempts I give them up. If I were to sit down to them, I should be wasting myself and my time; my mind works at the first leap. What I do not see immediately, I see even less by persisting. Without lightness I achieve nothing; application and over-serious effort confuse, depress, and weary my brain. My vision becomes blurred and confused. I must look away, and then repeatedly look back; just as in judging the brilliance of a scarlet cloth, we are told to pass the eye lightly over it, glancing at it several times in rapid succession. If one book bores me, I take up another; and I turn to reading only at such times as I begin to be tired of doing nothing. I do not easily take to the moderns, because the ancients seem to me fuller and more virile; nor to the Greeks, because my mind is not satisfied with my imperfect schoolboy's knowledge of the language.

Among books of simple entertainment, I find such moderns as Boccaccio's *Decameron*, Rabelais, and *The Kisses* of Johannes Secundus† – if they may be placed under this head – worthy of an idle hour. As for *Amadis*, and other such books, they had not the power of interesting me even in my boyhood. I will say further, boldly or recklessly perhaps, that my heavy old soul can no longer be tickled by Ariosto, or even by the excellent Ovid; his facility and inventiveness, which charmed me once, hardly hold my attention today.

I freely state my opinion about all things, even those which perhaps fall outside my capacity, and of which I do not for a moment suppose myself to be a judge. What I say about them, therefore, is meant to reveal the extent of my own vision, not the measure of the things themselves. When I feel a distaste for Plato's *Axiochus*,‡ as a work which, coming from such an

* 'This is the goal towards which my horse should strain.' Propertius, IV, i, 70.

† Latin poems in the style of Catullus, by Johannes Everaarts (1511–36), a Dutchman.

‡ This was an apocryphal work, and was already recognized as such in Montaigne's day. It is possible that he knew this.

author, seems lacking in power, my judgement will not trust itself. For it is not so foolish as to oppose the authority of so many other famous minds of antiquity, which it regards as its teachers and masters, and with whom it would be quite content to be wrong. It blames and condemns itself, either for stopping short at the surface, unable to penetrate to the heart, or for looking at things in a false light. It is satisfied if it has merely secured itself against confusion and disorder; that it is weak it clearly acknowledges and confesses. It thinks it is making a just interpretation of the picture presented to it by its understanding; but this is a weak and imperfect representation. The majority of Aesop's fables have several meanings and interpretations. Those who expound their symbolism pick some aspect that squares well with the fable, but generally it is only the first and superficial aspect; there are others more vital, more essential and deeper, to which they have been unable to penetrate; and so it is with me.

But, to pursue my path, it has always seemed to me that in poetry Virgil, Lucretius, Catullus, and Horace are far and away the first in rank; and particularly Virgil in his *Georgics*, which I regard as the most accomplished work in all poetry, in comparison with which one can easily see that there are passages in the *Aeneid* to which the author would have given a further polishing if he had had the time. And the fifth book of the *Aeneid* seems to me the most perfect. I like Lucan too, and turn to him with pleasure, not so much for his style as for his intrinsic worth and the truth of his opinions and judgements. As for good old Terence, who personifies the charm and grace of the Latin tongue, I am astounded by the lifelike way in which he depicts ways of thought and states of manners which are true of us today; at every turn our actions send me back to him. As often as I read him, I find some new charm and beauty in him.

Those who lived near Virgil's time protested if Lucretius was compared to him. I believe the comparison to be, in fact, unequal, but I find it difficult to confirm myself in my belief when I am caught up by one of Lucretius's fine passages. If the Romans were annoyed by this, however, what would they say

to the crass and barbarous stupidity of those who today place
Ariosto and Virgil side by side? And what would Ariosto himself say?

O seclum insipiens et infacetum!*

I think the ancients had still more reason to protest against
those who coupled Plautus with Terence – the latter is much
the more decent – than against those who compared Lucretius
with Virgil. It says much for the higher value set on Terence
that the father of Roman eloquence† quotes him so often, and
him alone of his kind; as does also the verdict which the first
critic among Roman poets passed on his fellow-dramatist.‡

It has often struck me that those who try to write comedies in
our day – including the Italians, who are quite successful at it –
use three or four plots from Terence or Plautus to make one of
their own; and they will crowd into a single play five or six
tales by Boccaccio. What makes them thus overburden themselves with material is a distrust of their power to support themselves on their own talents; they must find a body to lean on and,
not having enough substance of their own to hold our attention,
hope that the plot at least will amuse us. It is quite the opposite
with my author;§ the perfections and beauties of his style take
away all our appetite for his subject; his charm and delicacy hold
us throughout; everywhere he is so delightful,

liquidus puroque simillimus amni,‖

and so fills our mind with his charms that we forget those of his
plot.

This same consideration carries me further. I observe that
the good poets of antiquity avoided not only the far-fetched
affectations of the lofty and fantastic Spaniards and Petrarchists,
but even the milder and more restrained conceits which form
the ornaments of all the poetry of the ages after them. And yet
there is no good critic who regrets their absence in the ancients,
and who does not feel infinitely greater admiration for the

---

* 'Oh tasteless and ignorant age!' Catullus, xliii, 8.
† Cicero.   ‡ See Horace, *Ars Poetica*, 270.   § Terence.
‖ 'Flowing and like a pure stream.' Horace, *Epistles*, ii, ii, 120.

smooth polish, the continuous delight, and the flowering beauty of Catullus' epigrams than for all the barbs which Martial sets in the tails of his. This is for the reason that I gave a little while ago, and that Martial applied to himself; 'He had little need to labour his wits; his subject served instead.'*

Those early writers score their effects without exciting and spurring themselves on. They find something to laugh at everywhere; they do not have to tickle themselves. Later writers require help from without; they have less wit, they require more body. They ride on horseback because they have not enough strength in their legs. You will see the same thing at the ball, where those men of low condition who keep the dancing-schools try to win our applause by perilous leapings and other strange acrobatic feats because they cannot imitate the bearing and seemliness of the nobility. And the ladies too find it easier to show off in such dances as demand violent and abrupt bodily movements, than when treading those ceremonious measures in which they have only to move with a natural step, carrying themselves simply and with their ordinary grace.

I have seen very good clowns, also, in ordinary dress and with their ordinary faces, give us all the amusement that their art can provide, while beginners who are not so highly trained, have to flour their faces, dress themselves up, and assume wild gestures and grimaces in order to draw a laugh out of us. This idea of mine is nowhere more demonstrable than in a comparison between the *Aeneid* and the *Orlando furioso*. We see the former upon swift wings in strong and lofty flight, and always following its course, while the latter flutters and hops from tale to tale as if from branch to branch, never trusting its wings except for a very short flight, and coming down at every field's end for fear that its breath and strength may fail,

Excursusque breves tentat.†

These then are the authors that please me, on this sort of subject.

As for my other reading, in which a little more profit is mixed with the pleasure, and by which I learn how to order my

* Martial, Preface to Book VIII.
† 'He attempts only short flights.' Virgil, *Georgics*, IV, 194.

moods and character, the books that serve me are Plutarch, now that he has been put into French,* and Seneca. They both have this particular advantage for my temperament that the knowledge I seek is there treated in disconnected pieces that do not demand the bondage of prolonged labour, of which I am incapable. Such are the minor works of Plutarch and Seneca's *Letters*, which are the best things that he wrote, and the most profitable. It needs no great effort to settle down to them, and I leave them when I please. There is no continuity between one piece and the next.

These two authors agree in the majority of their true and useful opinions; and fortune brought them into the world at about the same time. Both were tutors of Roman emperors, both came from foreign countries, both were rich and powerful men. Their teaching is of the cream of philosophy, and is presented in a simple and pertinent fashion. Plutarch is the more uniform and consistent; Seneca the more uneven and various. He toils and strains every muscle and sinew to fortify virtue against weakness, fear, and evil appetites, which Plutarch seems to consider less dangerous, since he disdains to quicken his pace for them or to put himself on his guard against them. His opinions are Platonic, moderate, and suitable to a civilized society. Seneca's are Stoical and Epicurean, and much more unusual but, in my opinion, more suitable to the individual and more steadfast. In Seneca one seems to find some yielding to the tyranny of the emperors of his time, for I am sure that his judgement was forced when he condemned the cause of Caesar's noble-hearted murderers; but Plutarch is everywhere unconstrained. Seneca is full of wit and sallies, Plutarch of substance. The former stirs and excites us more; the latter gives us more satisfaction and profit. Plutarch guides us, while Seneca drives us on.

As for Cicero, the works of his which best serve my purpose are those that treat of philosophy, especially moral philosophy.

---

* Amyot's translation of the *Lives* appeared in 1559, and of the *Moralia* in 1572, the year of Montaigne's retirement. North's Plutarch of 1579, which had so important an influence on Elizabethan literature, was a translation of Amyot's, not of the original.

But to confess the truth boldly – for once one has leapt the barriers of audacity, one is quit of all restraint – this style of writing, and the style of others like him, strikes me as tiresome. His preambles, definitions, classifications, and etymologies take up the greater part of his work; such life and pith as it has is smothered by these long-drawn-out preliminaries. If I have spent an hour reading him, which is a long time for me, and consider what sap and substance I have drawn from him, I generally find nothing but wind, for he has not yet come to the arguments that support his case, or to the reasoning that properly applies to the problem I am concerned with. For me, who only want to become wiser, not more learned or more eloquent, these logical and Aristotelean orderings of the material are of no use; I should like him to begin with his conclusion. I know well enough what is meant by death and pleasure; there is no need to waste time in dissecting them. I look for good and solid reasons at the outset that will teach me to resist their power. Neither grammatical subtleties, nor the ingenious weaving of words and arguments help me there. I want discourses that plunge straight into the heart of the perplexity; his beat feebly about the bush. They are good for the school, the bar, and the pulpit, where we have leisure to doze, and are still in time a quarter of an hour later to pick up the thread of the argument. Cicero's way is right for addressing a judge whom one wishes to convince by fair means or foul, or for using on children, and the common people, with whom nothing must be left unsaid, in the hope that something will hit the mark. I do not want anyone to spend his time arousing my attention and shouting at me fifty times, 'Hark ye, hark!', as the heralds do. The Romans said in their religious services, 'Do this', as we in ours say 'lift up your hearts'. These are so many words wasted on me. I come from home fully prepared; I need no enticement or sauce; I can take my meat quite raw. Instead of my appetite being whetted by these preparations and preludes, it is merely jaded and dulled.

Will the licence of the age excuse my sacrilegious boldness in thinking that even Plato's dialogues drag, and stifle their meaning in a plethora of argument? Can I be forgiven for deploring the time that a man who had so many more valuable things to say spent on long and useless preliminary discussions? But my ignorance will serve as a better excuse, since I perceive none of the beauty of his language. In general, I want books that offer the results of learning, not those that set it out.

The first two* and Pliny, and their kind, are free from that 'Do this'; they write for readers who come with their attention prepared; or if they have a 'Do this', it is a substantial one with a body of its own.

I also like reading the *Letters to Atticus*, not only because they contain very ample information about the history and affairs of Cicero's time, but for the pleasure of discovering his personal humours. For I have a particular curiosity, as I have said elsewhere, to know the mind and natural opinions of my authors. From the display of their writings that they make on the world-stage, we may indeed judge their talents, but not their characters or themselves. I have a thousand times regretted that we have lost the book which Brutus wrote on virtue, for it is a fine thing to take lessons in theory from those who are so skilled in practice. But, in as much as the sermon is not the same as the preacher, I am just as glad to meet Brutus in Plutarch as I should be in his own book. I would rather have an exact report of the conversations he held with some of his close friends in his tent on the eve of a battle than the speech he delivered next day to his army. I had rather know what he did in his study and his chamber than what he did in the Forum and before the Senate.

As for Cicero, I am of the common opinion that, apart from his learning, he had no great excellence of mind; he was a good citizen, and easy-going by nature, as stout and jovial men† of his kind usually are; but he had, in all truth, a great deal of weakness and ambitious vanity about him. And I do not know how to excuse him for thinking his poetry fit to be published; it is no great failing to write bad verses, but it is a fault of judgement in him not to have seen how unworthy they were of the glory

* Plutarch and Seneca.
† Plutarch describes him, however, as lean and dyspeptic!

of his name. As for his eloquence, it is beyond all comparison; I believe that no man will ever be his equal. When Cicero the younger, who resembled his father in name alone, was commanding in Asia, there happened one day to be several strangers, Cestius among them, sitting at the lower end of his table, as men often do, unasked, at the tables of the great. Cicero asked one of his servants who the man was, and was told his name. But as one whose thoughts are elsewhere and who has forgotten an answer, he asked two or three times more. To save himself the trouble of repeating the same thing so many times, and to make Cicero recognize the man by some particular circumstance, the servant said: 'It is that man Cestius, about whom they told you that he has no high opinion of your father's eloquence compared with his own.' Cicero was suddenly stung by this. He ordered the unfortunate Cestius to be seized, and had him soundly whipped in his presence – a most discourteous host!

Even among those who, all things considered, have reckoned that Cicero's eloquence was incomparable, there have been some who have not failed to find faults with it, his friend the great Brutus among them, who said it was a broken and emasculated eloquence – *fractam et elumbem*. The orators around his own day also blamed him for his careful striving after a particular long cadence at the end of his periods, and especially noted the words *esse videatur** that he so often places there. For myself, I prefer a cadence that ends more abruptly on a sequence of iambics. Also, he sometimes, though not often, mixes his rhythms very roughly. One particular instance has struck my ear: '*ego vero me minus diu senem esse mallem, quam esse senem, antequam essem.*'†

Historians give me a fairer service; they are easy and entertaining; and at the same time the man as a whole, whom it is my object to know, is more vividly and completely presented in their works than anywhere else. In them I find the diversity of

* May be seen to be.

† 'For my part, I should prefer to have a shorter old age than to be old before my time.' Cicero, *De Senectute*, x.

his inner qualities truly portrayed, in the large and in detail, also the various traits that make up his character, and the accidents that threaten him. Now those of them that write separate lives, being concerned rather with motives than with events, more with what arises from within than with what arrives from without, suit me best of all. That is why in every way Plutarch is my man. I am very sorry that we have not a dozen Laertiuses,* or that he is not in wider circulation or better understood. For I am no less anxious for knowledge of the lives and fortunes of those great world teachers, than to know their different doctrines and speculations.

In this study of history one must run through all sorts of authors, both old and new, in French and in gibberish, without distinction, to learn from them the various things they teach. But, in my opinion, Caesar is deserving of particular study, not for the knowledge of history alone, but for himself; so much more perfect and excellent is he than all the rest, even including Sallust. Indeed, I read him with a little more reverence and respect than one pays to human works; sometimes considering the man himself in his actions and his miraculous greatness, sometimes the purity and inimitable polish of his language, in which he excels not only all other historians, as Cicero says, but perhaps even Cicero himself. And so sincere are his judgements, when he speaks of his enemies, that if it were not for the false colours in which he endeavours to cloak the wrongness of his cause, and the vileness of his pestilent ambition, I think that one could find only one fault with which to chide him: that he speaks too sparingly about himself. For he could not have achieved so many great exploits unless he had played a much greater part in them than he records.

I like historians who are either very simple or of the first rank. The simple, lacking the ability to add anything of their own, merely apply themselves with care and attention to the task of collecting every detail that comes to their knowledge, and faithfully record everything, without sifting or choice, leaving it entirely to our judgement to discern the truth. Such, for

* Diogenes Laertius, author of *The Lives of the Philosophers.*

example, among others, is the good Froissart, who pursued his task with such candid simplicity that when he made a mistake he was not afraid to acknowledge it and set it right as soon as it was pointed out to him. He even reports the various rumours that were current, and the different accounts of events that were given to him. This is the stuff of history, and naked unshaped; each man may profit from it according to his understanding.

Really eminent historians have the ability to select what deserves to be known; they can decide which of two reports is the more probable. From the characters and humours of princes they deduce their motives, and put appropriate words into their mouths. They have a right to assume the authority for moulding our beliefs on theirs; but this right certainly belongs to few.

Those between the two classes – which are the commonest sort – spoil everything. They want to chew our food for us. They take it upon themselves to judge, and consequently to fashion history to their own ideas. For once their judgement leans to one side, they avoid turning and twisting the narrative in that direction. They undertake to select what is worthy of mention, and often conceal from us some speech or secret action which might give us better information. They omit as incredible whatever they do not understand, and sometimes even pass a thing over because they cannot describe it in good Latin or French. Let them boldly display their eloquence and their reasonings, and judge in their own way. But they should at the same time leave us the chance to judge after them. They should not, by their selections and their abridgements, alter or arrange any part of the material substance, but should hand it on to us, complete and unalloyed, in all its aspects.

The men chosen as historiographers are, for the most part, and especially in our present age, drawn from the common people, their only qualification being a mastery of language – as if we wanted them to teach us grammar! And they are right, having been hired for this alone, and having nothing to sell but their tattle, to make this side of things their chief concern. So, with an abundance of grand words they compose a fine medley of the rumours they pick up at the corners of the city streets.

The only good histories are those written by men who were themselves at the head of affairs, or took a share in the conduct of them, or at least had the good fortune to direct others of a similar nature. Of this kind are almost all the Greek and Roman histories. For when several eye-witnesses have written of the same events – as used to be the case in those days when eminence and learning were commonly combined – if there is any mistake, it must be an extremely slight one concerning a most unimportant incident. What can one expect of a physician writing of war, or a scholar dealing with the plans of princes? Should we wish to observe how scrupulous the Romans were in this respect, a single example will suffice. Asinius Pollio found in the histories of Caesar himself a mistake into which he had fallen, either because he had been unable to keep an eye on every part of his army, and had taken the word of some persons whose reports to him were often insufficiently verified, or perhaps because he had not been fully enough informed by his lieutenants of what they had done in his absence. One can tell from this example what a delicate business this search for the truth is, when one cannot rely, in the case of a battle, on the knowledge of the man who commanded in it, or on its soldiers for what happened close beside them unless, after the manner of a judicial inquiry, we confront the witnesses and hear the objections before admitting the details of each incident as proved. But all this has been sufficiently treated by Bodin,* whose way of thinking is like my own.

To compensate a little for the treacheries and deficiencies of my memory, which are so extreme that more than once I have picked up, thinking it new and unknown to me, some book that I had carefully read some years before, and scribbled all over with my notes, I have adopted the habit for some time now of noting at the end of every book – I mean of those that I do not intend to read again – the date when I finished it and the opinion

* Jean Bodin, author of a Latin treatise on the understanding of history, which was published in 1566. Montaigne refers to him again in Chapter 32 of this book.

I had formed of it as a whole, my purpose being at least to remind myself of the character and general impression of the
author that I had conceived when reading it. Some of these
notes I will transcribe here.

This is what I put down about ten years ago in my Guicciardini* – for whatever language my books speak to me, I speak
to them in mine: He is a careful historian and, in my opinion, a
man may learn the truth about the affairs of his time as accurately from him as from any other. In the majority of them, he
was himself an actor, and played a distinguished part. There is
no indication of his having disguised anything out of hatred,
favour, or vanity; as is proved by the freedom with which he
judges the great, and especially those who advanced him and
employed him, among them Pope Clement the Seventh. As to
that part in which he seems to take the greatest pride – I mean
his digressions and discourses – some of these are good, and
embellished with fine details, but he was too fond of them. For,
wishing to leave nothing unsaid, and having so full, broad, and
almost boundless a subject, he here becomes weak; they smell of
pedantic garrulity. I have also noticed that in all the many characters, actions, motives, and designs that he judges, he never
attributes anything to virtue, religion, or conscience; it is as if
these factors were entirely extinct in the world. However noble
an action may seem in itself, he always traces it to some vicious
motive or to the hope of gain. It is impossible to imagine that
among the infinite number of actions on which he passes judgement, not a single one was inspired by motives of reason. Corruption can never have affected men so universally that someone did not escape the infection. This makes me fear that he had
a certain taste for wickedness, and that perhaps he came to judge
others according to himself.

In my Philippe de Commines there is this: You will find the
language smooth and agreeable, and of a natural simplicity. The
narrative is clear, and the author's good faith shines plainly
through it. He is free from vanity when speaking of himself, and

* Francesco Guicciardini (1483–1540), a contemporary of Machiavelli,
and the author of a history of contemporary Italy.

from partiality and malice when speaking of others. His speeches and exhortations show honest zeal and regard for truth, rather than any rare talent; and he displays an authority and seriousness throughout which proclaim him a man of good birth, brought up amidst great affairs.

In the *Memoirs* of Monsieur du Bellay: It is always a pleasure to see things reported by men with experience of how they should be done. But there is no denying that in these two noblemen* one can plainly see a great falling-off from the frankness and freedom of writing that shine out from the older historians of their kind, such as the Sire de Joinville, St Louis' intimate friend, Eginhard, Charlemagne's chancellor, and Philippe de Commines, of more recent memory. This is a plea for King Francis against the Emperor Charles V, rather than a history. I will not believe that they have falsified any general facts, but they have made it a general practice to twist the verdict on events, often against all reason, to our advantage, and to omit any awkward moments in the life of their master: as witness the disgrace of Messieurs de Montmorency and de Brion, which they pass over, while Madame d'Estampes'† name is not even mentioned.

Secret actions may be concealed, but to keep silent about what all the world knows, and about things that have led to public consequences of such importance, is an inexcusable defect. In short, for a complete knowledge of King Francis the First and the events of his time, one must, in my opinion, look elsewhere. The useful parts of these *Memoirs* are the detailed accounts of the battles and other exploits of war at which these two gentlemen were present; also the reports of some private speeches and actions of certain princes of their time, and of the intrigues and negotiations conducted by the Seigneur de Langey,‡ in which there is a great deal that is noteworthy and many reflections above the common level.

* Guillaume and Martin du Bellay, the first of whom was Rabelais' patron. The *Memoirs* are in ten books, seven of which are by Martin, and three by Guillaume.
† Mistress of Francis I.
‡ Guillaume de Bellay himself.

BOOK TWO: Chapter 11

On cruelty

I IMAGINE virtue to be both something else and something nobler than the propensity towards goodness that is born in us. The well-disposed and naturally well-controlled mind follows the same course as the virtuous, and presents the same appearance in its actions. But virtue sounds like some greater and more active thing than merely to let oneself be led by a happy disposition quietly and peaceably along the path of reason. One who out of natural mildness and good-nature overlooks injuries received performs a very fine and praiseworthy action; but another who, though provoked and stung to anger by an insult, takes up the weapons of reason against his furious desire for revenge, and after a hard battle finally masters it, is undoubtedly doing a great deal more. The first man is behaving well, the second virtuously; the first action might be called goodness, the second virtue. For the word virtue, I think, presupposes difficulty and struggle, and something that cannot be practised without an adversary. This is perhaps why we call God good, mighty, liberal, and just, but do not call Him virtuous; His workings are all natural and effortless.

Of the philosophers, not only the Stoics but the Epicureans also – and in ranking the former higher than the latter I am following the common opinion; and this, in spite of Arcesilaus' subtle answer to the taunt that many went over from his school to the Epicureans but never the reverse, is a false one. 'I can well believe you,' he said to his taunter, 'cocks can easily be made into capons, but you cannot make a capon into a cock.' For truly, in steadfastness and strictness of opinions and precepts, the Epicurean sect yields nothing to the Stoic. There was one Stoic, indeed, who showed more honesty than the common run of disputants who, to combat Epicurus and load the dice in their favour, made him say things that he never thought, twisting his words, and using the rules of grammar to extract from his language a meaning and belief contrary to the one which they knew he had in mind and showed in his conduct; and that Stoic said that he had left the Epicurean sect for this reason among others: that he found their way too high and inaccessible; 'and they who are called lovers of pleasure are in fact lovers of beauty and justice. They cultivate and practise all the virtues.'*

Among the Stoic and Epicurean philosophers, I say, there are several who have thought it not enough to have the soul in a good state, under firm control and well disposed to virtue, and not enough to keep our thoughts and resolutions high above the assaults of fortune, but that we must also seek opportunities of putting ourselves to the proof. They would have us go in quest of pain, poverty, and scorn, in order to combat them and keep our souls exercised, since 'virtue assailed is greatly strengthened'.† This is one of the reasons why Epaminondas, who was of yet a third sect, refused the riches which fortune put into his hands in an entirely lawful way, in order, as he said, that he might fight a battle with poverty – a condition in which he remained to the end. Socrates, I think, tried himself even more severely by keeping the shrewishness of his wife to practise on: a battle against a sharpened sword.

Metellus, alone of all the Roman senators, undertook by the power of his virtue to withstand the violence of Saturninus, Tribune of the people at Rome, who was trying by main force to pass an unjust law in favour of the plebeians. Having thus incurred the dire penalties that Saturninus had provided for all dissentients, Metellus addressed those who, in this extremity, were leading him to execution, in words to this effect: that it was too easy and too base a thing to do a bad action, and that good actions involving no danger were quite common; but to act well when it was dangerous to do so was the proper duty of a virtuous man.

These words of Metellus very clearly state the case that I was trying to prove: that virtue refuses facility as a companion, and that the easy, smooth, and gentle slope down which we are guided by the even steps of a naturally good disposition is not the path of true virtue. Virtue demands a harsh and thorny road;

* Cicero, *Letters*, xv, xix.   † Seneca, *Letters*, xiii.

it desires either external difficulties, like those of Metellus, to contend with, by means of which fortune is pleased to interrupt its headlong career, or internal difficulties, created by the disorderly appetites and the imperfections of our natural state.

I have come so far with great ease. But as I conclude my reflections, it occurs to me that the mind of Socrates, the most perfect of which I have any knowledge, would, by this reckoning, have little to commend it. For I cannot imagine that man ever to have been prompted by evil desires. I can conceive of no difficulty or constraint in the way of his virtue; I know his reason to have been so powerful and so absolute a mistress over him, that it can never have permitted a wicked desire even to arise in him. I have nothing to set against a virtue as lofty as his. I seem to see it marching with victorious and triumphant steps, in state and at ease, without hindrance or obstacle. If virtue can only shine in battle with opposing desires, must we therefore say that it cannot dispense with the assistance of vice, and that it is to vice that it owes the reputation and honour in which it is held? What should we say then of that noble and generous Epicurean pleasure that prides itself on nourishing virtue tenderly in its bosom, and letting it frolic there, giving it disgrace, fever, poverty, death, and tortures as toys to play with?

If I assume that perfect virtue shows itself in the struggle with and the patient endurance of pain, in suffering the assaults of gout without being shaken from its place; if I allow hardships and difficulties to be its necessary aim, what shall we say of a virtue which has climbed to such a height that it not only despises pain but rejoices in it, and is tickled by the pangs of a severe colic? For such is the virtue established by the Epicureans, of which several of them, by their actions, have left us manifest proofs; as have many others, also, who have, I find, actually surpassed even their teaching. Witness the younger Cato. When I see him die, tearing out his own entrails, I cannot be content simply to believe that his mind was then wholly free from disturbance and terror. I cannot believe that he merely maintained that attitude which the rules of the Stoic sect prescribed, calm, unperturbed, and impassive. There was, it seems to me, in that man's virtue, too much joyousness and vigour to stop there. I am quite certain that he felt delight and pleasure in that noble act, and that he took more satisfaction in it than in any other that he ever performed: 'He thus quitted life, rejoicing that he had found a reason for dying.'*

So thoroughly do I believe this that I begin to wonder whether he would have wished the opportunity for this heroic achievement to be denied him. And were it not for the goodness which made him put the public interest before his own I could easily fall into the opinion that he was grateful to fortune for putting his virtue to so noble a proof, and helping that villain† to trample the ancient liberty of his country underfoot. As I read of Cato's action, I seem to see a strange rejoicing in his soul, and with it a feeling of extraordinary pleasure and manly delight as he considered the noble sublimity of his deed:

Deliberata morte ferocior,‡

not spurred on by any hope of glory, as the vulgar and weak judgements of some have supposed, for that is too mean a consideration to touch a heart so generous, so proud, and so unbending, but for the inherent beauty of the deed itself, which he, who controlled its springs, saw much more clearly in all its perfection than we can.

I am pleased by philosophy's decision that so brave an action would have been out of keeping with any other life but Cato's, and that his alone was fitted to end in this way. Therefore he rightly ordered his son and the senators who attended him to provide otherwise for themselves. 'But Cato had been endowed by nature with an incredible strength of soul, which he had reinforced by his unremitting constancy; and he remained true to his fixed resolve that it was better to die than to look upon the face of a tyrant.'§

Every man's death should correspond to his life. We do not change to die. I always interpret the death by the life;‖ and if I

---

* Cicero, *Tusculans*, I, xxx.   † Julius Caesar.
‡ 'More courageous after resolving to die.' Horace, *Odes*, I, xxxvii, 29.
§ Cicero, *De Officiis*, I, 31.
‖ Cf. the last sentence of Book One, Chapter 29.

am told of an apparently brave death joined to a feeble life, I hold that it is the product of some feeble cause in keeping with that life.

Must we say therefore that the simplicity of Cato's end, and the ease that he had acquired by strength of soul, should in any way detract from the splendour of his virtue? And what man whose brain is at all imbued with the true philosophy can be content to think of Socrates as merely free from fear and disturbances when prison fetters and condemnation fell to his lot! Who does not recognize in him not only courage and constancy – the former was natural to him – but also a certain new contentment, a delightful gaiety, in his last words and actions? In that thrill of pleasure that he felt when scratching his leg after the fetters had been removed, does he not reveal a like joy and relief in his soul at being released from past discomforts and about to enter into the knowledge of things to come? May Cato forgive me if he please; his death is more tragic and more violent, but that of Socrates is in some way still more beautiful. 'May the Gods send me one like it!' said Aristippus to those who were lamenting it.

We see in the souls of these two men and their imitators – for I very much doubt whether they had equals – so perfect a habit of virtue that it has become their common complexion. It is no longer a painful virtue, nor one dictated by reason, for the maintenance of which the soul needs to brace itself; it is the very essence of the soul, it is its natural and habitual way. They have made it so by long practice of the precepts of philosophy, exercised upon a rich and fine nature. The wicked passions that spring up in us can find no entrance into them; the strength and firmness of their souls stifle and extinguish the lusts as soon as they begin to stir.

Now I think there can be no doubt that it is finer by a lofty and divine resolution to prevent the birth of temptations, and so to shape oneself to virtue that the very seeds of vice are rooted out, than to arrest their growth by main force and, after being surprised by the first onset of the passions, to arm and brace oneself to stay their advance and conquer them. Nor can one doubt that this second course is still finer than simply to be endowed with an easy and tractable nature which has an instinctive distaste for debauchery and vice. For this third and last way seems indeed to make a man innocent, but not virtuous; free from evil-doing, but not sufficiently apt to do well. Moreover, it is a condition so close to imperfection and weakness that I am uncertain how to draw the frontiers and distinguish them. The very words goodness and innocence have for this reason become in some sort terms of contempt. I can see that several virtues, among them chastity, sobriety, and temperance, may come to us from bodily defects. Firmness in the face of danger – if firmness is the proper word – contempt for death and patience in misfortunes, may arise in men – and often does – from an inability to judge events correctly and realize their actual nature. Thus failure of apprehension and stupidity sometimes disguise themselves as valorous actions; and I have often seen it happen that men have been praised for deeds that really deserved blame.

An Italian gentleman once said in my presence, to the discredit of his nation, that their subtlety and the brilliance of their imaginations were such that they foresaw the accidents and dangers which might befall them when they were still far off; that it must not appear strange, therefore, if in war they were often seen to provide for their safety even before they had clearly perceived the danger; that we French and the Spaniards, who were not so acute, would advance further, and had actually to see the danger with our eyes and feel it with our hands before it alarmed us, at which point we lost all control; but the Germans and the Swiss, who are coarser and heavier-witted, have hardly enough sense to change their minds even when the blows are raining on their bodies. This was, perhaps, only a jest. Yet it is very true that, in the business of war, raw soldiers often rush into dangers more recklessly than they do after once being scalded:

> *Haud ignarus quantum nova gloria in armis,*
> *et praedulce decus primo certamine possit.* *

That is why, in judging a particular action, we must take many

* 'Knowing how potent is a new-born pride in arms, and the hope of winning glory in the first battle.' Virgil, *Aeneid*, XI, 154.

179

circumstances into account, and consider the whole man who performed it, before we give it a name.

To say a word about myself; I have sometimes heard my friends credit my prudence with what was really the product of good fortune, and attribute to my courage and patience what was in fact achieved by my reason and judgement, thus endowing me with one quality instead of another, sometimes to my advantage and sometimes to my detriment. Meanwhile, I am so far from having attained that first and most perfect degree of excellence, in which virtue becomes a habit, that I have hardly given proof even of the second. I have not made any great efforts to curb the desires by which I have found myself assailed. My virtue is a virtue that could be more properly called a casual and fortuitous innocence. If I had been born with a more unruly temperament, I fear that I should have been in a most pitiable way. For I have never observed any great firmness in my soul that would be capable of resisting even the mildest of passions. I am unable to cherish quarrels and contentions in my breast; and so I can give myself no great thanks for happening to be free from several vices;

> *si vitiis mediocribus et mea paucis*
> *mendosa est natura, alioqui recta, velut si*
> *egregio inspersos reprehendas corpore naevos,**

I owe it rather to my fortune than my reason. Fortune caused me to be born of a race famous for its integrity, and of an excellent father. I do not know whether he passed some part of his character on to me or whether family example and my good upbringing in childhood insensibly contributed to it, or whether I was, on the other hand born so,

> *Seu Libra, seu me Scorpius aspicit*
> *formidolosus, pars violentior*
> *natalis horae, seu tyrannus*
> *Hesperiae Capricornus undae;*†

* 'If my nature, otherwise good, is marred by a few slight faults, like the spots that you will wish away when scattered over a lovely body.' Horace, *Satires*, 1, vi, 65.

† 'Whether the Scales or the dread Scorpion, the most powerful influence over the hour of birth, or Capricorn, lord of the western wave, controls me.' Horace, *Odes*, 1, xvii, 17.

But it so happens that for most vices I have an instinctive abhorrence. Antisthenes' reply to the men who asked him what was the best training seems to be rooted in this idea; he said it was to unlearn evil. I hold them in abhorrence, I say, from so natural and inborn a conviction that I still retain the same instinctive attitude to them that I imbibed at the breast. No circumstances have ever had the power to alter it, not even my own reasonings, which have in many ways departed from the common road, and so might easily have given me licence for actions which these natural inclinations make me hate. I will tell you something extraordinary, but I will tell it just the same: in many matters I find more order and restraint in my morals than in my opinions, and my appetites less depraved than my reason.

Aristippus put forward such bold arguments in favour of pleasure and riches, that he stirred up all philosophy to oppose him. But as for his morals, when the tyrant Dionysius offered him three pretty girls to choose from, he replied that he chose all three, since Paris had got into trouble for preferring one beauty to her two companions. After taking them home, however, he sent them back untouched. Once too, on a journey, when his servant complained at the weight of the money he was carrying, Aristippus ordered him to throw out so much as he found too heavy and leave it behind.

And Epicurus, who taught irreligion and luxury, was most scrupulous and laborious in his way of life. He wrote to a friend that he lived on nothing but coarse brown bread and water, and asked him to send a little cheese in case he might want to make a sumptuous meal. Can it perhaps be true that if we are to be absolutely good, it must be by an occult, natural, and universal quality, without rules, without reason, and without examples?

The excesses which I have happened to commit are not, thank God, of the worst kind. I have condemned them in myself, for my judgement has not been infected by them. On the contrary, it blames them more severely in me than in another. But that is all. For the rest, I put up insufficient resistance to them, and let myself too easily incline to the other side of the scales, except that I keep them under control and prevent their mingling with other vices. For vices generally cling together and become interlocked in anyone who is not on his guard. I have cut mine down, and forced them to be as single and as simple as I could.

> *nec ultra*
> *errorem foveo.**

Now as for the opinion of the Stoics, who say that the wise man acts, when he does act, with all the virtues together, although one may be more in evidence according to the nature of the action – and here a comparison with the human body might to some extent support them, for the action of anger cannot work unless all the humours assist it, even though anger may predominate – if they wish to draw a parallel deduction, that when the sinner sins he sins with all the vices together, I cannot believe them so simply; or else I do not understand them, for in effect I feel the contrary. These are ingenious, unsubstantial subtleties, with which philosophy sometimes amuses itself. I am addicted to some vices, but I avoid others as thoroughly as any saint could do.

The Peripatetics, likewise, reject this indissoluble link and union; and Aristotle holds that a wise and just man may be intemperate and incontinent. Socrates admitted to those who recognized some inclination to vice in his face, that it was indeed his natural propensity, but that he had corrected it by discipline. And the philosopher Stilpo's intimates used to say that, though naturally given to wine and women, he had by efforts made himself most abstinent in respect to both. Such good as is in me I owe, on the contrary, to the chance of my birth. I owe it neither to law, nor to precept, nor to any other schooling. The innocence that is in me is a native innocence: I have little strength and no art.

Among other vices, I cruelly hate cruelty, both by nature and judgement, as the worst of all vices. But here my weakness extends so far that I cannot see a chicken's neck twisted without

---

* 'And I do not indulge my faults further.' Juvenal, VIII, 164.

distress, or bear to hear the squealing of a hare in my hounds' jaws, though hunting is a very great pleasure to me.

Those who set out to combat sensual desires are fond of using the following argument to prove that they are wholly vicious and contrary to reason: that when pleasure is at its extreme height, it so masters us that reason can have no access. And they instance our experience of it in intercourse with women,

cum iam praesagit gaudia corpus,
*atque in eo est Venus ut muliebria conserat arva.**

Here they think pleasure so transports us that our reason cannot perform its function, being benumbed by the ecstasy of pleasure. I know that it may be otherwise, and that one can sometimes, by force of will, successfully direct one's mind at that very instant to other thoughts. But one must prepare and brace it deliberately. I know that it is possible to curb the violence of this pleasure, and I know it by experience. For I have never found Venus so imperious a goddess as many who are chaster than I consider her to be. I do not, as the Queen of Navarre does in one of the tales in her *Heptameron* – which is a pleasant book for its matter – consider it miraculous, or extremely difficult, for a man to pass whole nights with every opportunity and in all freedom beside a long-desired mistress, in fulfilment of a promise he has made to her to be satisfied with kisses and simple caresses.

I think that the example of the chase would be more appropriate. Though the pleasure is less, there is more excitement and surprise, and so our reason, taken unawares, has no time to prepare and brace itself for the encounter, when after a long quest, the quarry suddenly starts up, appearing, perhaps, in the place where we least expected it. This shock and the violence of the hue and cry strike us so hard that it would be difficult for anyone who loves this kind of sport to turn his thoughts elsewhere at *that* moment. And the poets make Diana victorious over Cupid's torch and arrows:

* 'When the body has a foretaste of pleasure, and man is about to sow the field of woman.' Lucretius, IV, 1106.

Quis non malarum, quas amor curas habet,
*Haec inter obliviscitur?**

To return to my subject, I am most tenderly sympathetic towards the afflictions of others, and would readily weep for company if I were able to weep on any occasion. There is nothing that moves me to tears except tears, and not only real ones but tears of any sort, feigned or painted. I hardly pity the dead, I rather envy them; but I feel great pity for the dying. I am not so shocked by savages who roast and eat the bodies of their dead as by those who torture and persecute the living. I cannot even look on legal executions, however just they may be, with a steadfast eye. Someone who had occasion to testify to the clemency of Julius Caesar observed: 'He was mild in his vengeance. Having forced some pirates to surrender who had previously captured him and held him to ransom, since he had threatened them with the cross, he condemned them to be crucified. But he had them strangled first. His secretary, Philemon, who had tried to poison him, he punished no more harshly than by a simple death.' Without naming this Latin author† who dares to advance as evidence of clemency a mere putting to death of those by whom one has been wronged, it is easy to guess that he was affected by the horrible and villainous examples of cruelty practised by the Roman tyrants.

For my part, even in judicial matters, anything that goes beyond a plain execution seems to me pure cruelty, and especially in us who ought to take care that souls should be sent to heaven in a state of grace; which cannot be, if they have been shaken and driven to despair by insufferable tortures.

Not long ago, a soldier, having observed from the tower in which he was imprisoned some carpenters busy erecting a scaffold and people gathering in the market-place, concluded that the preparations were for him. In his despair, having nothing else to kill himself with, he picked up an old rusty cart-nail which chance had put in his way, and gave himself two serious wounds

* 'Who does not forget among these delights all the pangs that love brings with it?' Horace, *Epodes*, II, 37.
† Suetonius, *Life of Julius Caesar*.

in the throat. Then seeing that this had not been enough to despatch him, he soon afterwards dealt himself another wound in the belly, from which he became insensible. In this condition he was found by the first of his gaolers who came in to see him. They brought him round and, to fill the time until he expired, they quickly read him his sentence, which was that he was to be beheaded. This delighted him immeasurably, and he consented to take a draught of wine which he had previously refused. Then after thanking the judges for the unexpected leniency of their sentence, he said that his resolve to kill himself was due to the dread of some more cruel punishment, which had been increased by the sight of the preparations. He had taken his life in this way to avoid a more unbearable fate.

I should advise that such examples of severity, the purpose of which is to keep people in awe, be practised on the dead bodies of criminals. For to see them refused burial, to see them boiled and quartered, would affect the common herd almost as much as do the pains inflicted on the living; although in reality all this amounts to little or nothing, since God says: Be not afraid of them that kill the body, and after that have no more that they can do.* But the poets particularly dwell upon the horror of this picture as something worse than death:

> Heu! relliquias semiassi regis, denudatis ossibus,
> per terram sanie delibutas foede divaxarier.†

One day in Rome I happened to be present at the moment when they were executing Catena, a notorious robber. There was no excitement among the spectators at the strangling. But when it came to quartering his body, every single stroke that the executioner made was greeted by the people with doleful cries and exclamations, as if everyone had lent his own sense of feeling to the carrion.

These inhuman excesses should be exercised against the skin, not the flesh. Thus Artaxerxes, in a somewhat similar case,

* Luke, XII, 4.

† 'Alas, that remains of a half-burnt king, with the bones bare, should be dragged along the ground, besmeared with foul dirt.' Ennius, quoted by Cicero, *Tusculans*, I, xlv.

mitigated the harshness of Persia's ancient laws, by ordaining that nobles who had failed in their duties should not be given the customary scourging; but should be stripped and have their garments scourged in their stead; and that, whereas the custom was that they should have their hair torn out, they should now merely be deprived of their tall headdresses. The Egyptians, who were so devout, thought that they sufficiently satisfied divine justice by sacrificing effigies and representations of pigs: a bold idea, to try with shadowy imitations to make payment to God, the essential substance!

I live in an epoch when, owing to the licence of our civil wars, we abound in incredible examples of this vice: there is nothing to be found in ancient histories more extreme than what we witness every day. But this has by no means reconciled me to it. I could hardly persuade myself, before I had actual evidence, that there exist any souls so unnatural as to commit murder for the mere pleasure of doing so; as to hack and chop off men's limbs, as to sharpen their wits for the invention of unusual tortures and new forms of death; and all this without enmity or gain, but merely for the enjoyment of the pleasing spectacle afforded by the pitiful gestures and motions, the lamentable groans and cries, of a man dying in anguish. This is the extreme limit to which cruelty can attain, 'that one man should kill another, not in anger or in fear, but solely to enjoy the sight'.*

For my part, I have never been able to watch without distress even the pursuit and slaughter of an innocent animal, which has no defence and has done us no harm. And when, as will commonly happen, a weak and panting stag is reduced to surrender, and casts itself with tears in its eyes on the mercy of us, its pursuers,

> *quaestuque cruentus*
> *atque imploranti similis,*†

this has always seemed to me a most unpleasant sight.

I hardly ever capture an animal alive that I do not set it free

---

* Seneca, *Letters*, xc.

† 'Bloodstained and groaning, like one imploring mercy.' Virgil, *Aeneid*, vii, 501.

in the fields. Pythagoras would buy them from fishermen and fowlers, to do the same:

> primoque a caede ferarum
> incaluisse puto maculatum sanguine ferrum.*

Natures that are bloodthirsty towards animals show a native propensity towards cruelty. At Rome after the people had inured themselves to watching the slaughter of animals, they went on to men and gladiators. Nature herself, I fear, implants in men some instinct towards inhumanity. No one enjoys the sight of animals playing together and fondling one another, but the spectacle of them rending and dismembering one another is a universal entertainment.

And let no one mock me for this sympathy of mine, since theology itself commands us to treat them with some kindness. Considering that one and the same Master has lodged us in this place to serve Him, and that they as well as we are of His family, it is justified in enjoining us to show them some regard and affection. Pythagoras borrowed the doctrine of metempsychosis from the Egyptians, but it has since been accepted by many nations, and notably by our Druids:

> Morte carent animae; semperque, priore relicta
> sede, novis domibus vivunt, habitantque receptae.†

The religion of our ancient Gauls maintained that souls, being eternal, never cease to move and change their lodging from one body to another; and they mixed with this conception some ideas about divine justice. For according to a soul's conduct when it was in Alexander, God, they said, assigned it another body to inhabit, more or less disagreeable, and suitable to its condition:

> muta ferarum
> cogit vincla pati, truculentos ingerit ursis,
> praedonesque lupis, fallaces volpibus addit;

* 'I think the blood of animals was the first to stain our weapons.' Ovid, *Metamorphoses*, xv, 106.

† 'Souls are exempt from death; always when they have left their first body, they go to new homes, are received there, and there dwell.' Ovid, *Metamorphoses*, xv, 158.

atque ubi per varios annos, per mille figuras
egit, lethaeo purgatos flumine, tandem
*rursus ad humanae revocat primordia formae.**

If it had been courageous, it was lodged in the body of a lion, if licentious in a hog's, if cowardly in a stag's or a hare's, if crafty in a fox's, and so on, until, purified by this punishment, it took on the body of some other man.

Ipse ego nam memini, Troiani tempore belli
Panthoides Euphorb 's eram.†

As for this relationship between us and the beasts, I do not set much store by it; nor by the fact that many nations, and notably some of the most ancient and noble, not only admitted beasts as their friends and companions, but ranked them far above themselves, regarding them sometimes as familiars and favourites of their gods, and holding them in superhuman respect and reverence. And others recognized no other god or divinity but them: 'Beasts were treated as sacred by the barbarians, because of the benefits they bestowed.'‡

Crocodilon adorat
pars haec, illa pavet saturam serpentibus Ibin,
effigies sacri hic nitet aurea cercopitheci: ...
... hic piscem fluminis, illic
oppida tota canem venerantur.§

And even Plutarch's interpretation of this error, which is very well reasoned, still does them honour. For he says that it was not the cat or the ox, for example, that the Egyptians adored, but that in those beasts they worshipped some image of the divine attributes; in the latter patience and usefulness; and in the

* 'He throws them into prison in the bodies of dumb beasts, the cruel into bears, robbers into wolves, and the cunning into foxes. And when after many years, they have passed through a thousand forms, they are purged by the river Lethe, and at last return to their primordial human forms.' Claudian, *Against Rufinus*, II, 482.

† 'I myself, as I remember, in the days of the Trojan war, was Euphorbus, son of Panthous.' Ovid, *Metamorphoses*, xv, 160.

‡ Cicero, *On the Nature of the Gods*, I, xxxvi.

§ 'This land adores the crocodile, that trembles before a snake-gorged ibis. Here gleams the golden image of a sacred long-tailed monkey: here a river-fish, there a dog, are gods for a whole city.' Juvenal, xv, 2.

former activity, or an impatience at being confined (like that of our neighbours the Burgundians, and the rest of the Germans), that they thought of the cat as a symbol of liberty, which they loved and worshipped above every other divine attribute; and so on for the rest.

But when, among the most moderate opinions, I meet with arguments that set out to prove how closely we resemble the animals, how largely they share in our greatest privileges, and how feasible are the comparisons between us and them, I certainly forswear a great deal of our presumption, and willingly resign that imaginary sovereignty over other creatures which we are supposed to have.

But if all this were untrue, yet there is a certain consideration, and a general duty of humanity, that binds us not only to the animals, which have life and feeling, but even to the trees and plants. We owe justice to men, and kindness and benevolence to all other creatures who may be susceptible of it. There is some intercourse between them and us, and some mutual obligation. I am not ashamed to admit to so childishly tender a nature that I cannot easily refuse my dog when he offers to play with me or asks me to play with him at an inopportune moment.

The Turks have alms-houses and hospitals for animals. The Romans made the feeding of geese a public charge, since it was their vigilance that had saved the Capitol. The Athenians decreed that the mules, great and small, which had served in the building of the temple called Hecatompedon should be set at liberty and allowed to graze wherever they pleased, without hindrance. The Agrigentines had the common custom of solemnly burying animals that they had loved, such as horses of particular excellence, dogs and domestic birds, or even birds that had been kept for their children's pleasure. And the magnificence which was characteristic of them in all other things was also singularly apparent in the number and costliness of the monuments which they erected to that end, and which survived in all their splendour for many centuries.

The Egyptians buried wolves, bears, crocodiles, dogs, and cats in holy places, embalming their bodies and wearing mourn-

ing at their death. Cimon gave burial with honour to the mares
with which he had three times won the prize for the race at the
Olympic games. Xanthippus of old had his dog buried on a
headland of that seacoast which has been called after it ever
since. And Plutarch tells us that it was a matter of conscience
with him not to sell and send to the slaughter-house, for some
trifling sum, an ox that had given him long service.

BOOK TWO: Chapter 17

On presumption

THERE is another kind of glory,* which is to have too good
an opinion of our own worth. It is an unthinking affection
with which we flatter ourselves, and which presents us to ourselves as other than we are; just as the passion of love lends
beauties and charms to the object it embraces in such a way
that the lover's judgement is troubled and distracted, and he
finds the lady he loves other and more perfect than she is. Yet I
would not wish a man to be mistaken about himself out of fear
of erring in this way, or think himself less than he is. The judgement should maintain its rights always and in all places; and it
is reasonable that, here as elsewhere, he should see what the
truth sets before it. If he be a Caesar, let him boldly consider
himself the greatest captain in the world.

We are all convention; convention carries us away, and we
neglect the substance of things. We hold on to the branches,
and let go of the trunk and the body. We have taught ladies to
blush at the mere mention of things they are not in the least
afraid to do. We dare not call our parts by their right names, but
are not afraid to use them for every sort of debauchery. Convention forbids us to express in words things that are lawful and
natural; and we obey it. Reason forbids us to do what is unlaw-
ful or wicked, and no one obeys it. Here I find myself fettered
by the laws of convention, for it forbids a man to speak either
well or ill of himself. We will set it aside for the moment.

* The previous essay has been on the subject of martial glory.

Those whom fortune – call it good or bad, as you please – has made to pass their lives in some eminent position, may by their public actions show what they are. But those whom it has only employed in the crowd, and of whom no one will speak unless they speak of themselves, may be excused if they are so bold as to do so, especially to those who are interested to know them. Take Lucilius as an example:

> *Ille velut fidis arcana sodalibus olim*
> *credebat libris, neque, si male cesserat, usquam*
> *decurrens alio, neque si bene: quo fit ut omnis*
> *votiva pateat veluti descripta tabella*
> *vita senis.**

He committed his actions and thoughts to paper, and depicted himself there as he felt himself to be. 'Nor were Rutilius and Scaurus disbelieved or blamed for so doing.'†

I remember, then, that from my tenderest childhood a certain bodily carriage and certain gestures were observed in me which revealed a vain and foolish pride. I should like to say first of all that there is no harm in having qualities and propensities so individual and so much a part of us that we have no means of perceiving and recognizing them. And from such innate tendencies the body may readily retain some bent, without our knowledge or consent. It was an affectation‡ which chimed with his beauty that made Alexander carry his head a little on one side, and Alcibiades speak with an effeminate lisp. Julius Caesar used to scratch his head with one finger, which is characteristic of a man full of troublesome thoughts; and Cicero, I believe, had the habit of wrinkling up his nose, which indicates a scornful disposition. Such movements may arise in us unnoticed. There are others of an intentional kind, of which I do not speak, like our salutations and bowings, by which a man acquires, wrongly for the most part, the reputation of being

---

* 'He used to confide his secrets to his books as to good friends, and never had any other confidant in good or evil fortune. So it is that the old man's whole life is to be seen in his writings, as on a votive tablet.' Horace, *Satires*, II, i, 30. † Tacitus, *Agricola*, I.
‡ Actually it was an arrow wound.

most humble and courteous: one may be humble out of pride. I am prodigal enough of cap-raisings, particularly in summer, and never receive a salute without returning it, whatever the person's rank may be, unless he is in my service. I could wish that some princes whom I know would be more sparing and judicious in bestowing that courtesy; for when lavished indiscriminately it is thrown away; if given without respect of persons, it has no effect.

Amongst instances of extravagant behaviour, let us not forget the haughty bearing of the Emperor Constantius who, in public, always looked straight in front of him, without turning or bending his head this way and that, even to look at those who saluted him from the side. He would keep his body stiff, and never sway with the motion of his carriage, and he would never dare to spit, or blow his nose, or wipe his face, before the people.

I do not know whether these gestures that were observed in me were of the first sort, or if I had any secret propensity to this vice, as may well have been the case. And I cannot answer for the movements of my body; but as for the movements of the soul, I will here set down my feelings about them.

This vainglory has two sides: the over-estimation of ourselves, and the under-estimation of others. As to the first, I think that these considerations should be taken into primary account: I feel myself oppressed by an error of the mind which displeases me as being unjust, and still more as being tiresome. I try to correct, but I cannot uproot it. It is that I undervalue the things that I possess, just because I possess them, and attach a higher value to things that are not mine, but belong to another and are beyond my reach. This habit of mind is very widespread. As the prerogative of authority causes husbands to view their wives, and many fathers to view their children, with an unjust disdain, so it is with me; judging between two equal works, I should always incline against my own. It is not so much that desire for my progress and improvement disturbs my judgement and prevents my being satisfied with myself, as that mastery itself breeds contempt for what we hold and control.

The governments, the manners, and the languages of distant

lands charm me, and I see Latin cheating me, by its dignity, into giving it more than its due favour, as it cheats children and the common people. My neighbour's domestic economy, his house, and his horse, though no better than mine, are more valuable in my eyes because they are not mine and because, in addition, I know very little about my own affairs. I admire the assurance and confidence that everyone has in himself, while there is hardly anything that I am sure of knowing, or that I dare answer to myself that I can do. I never have my means marshalled and at my service, and am only aware of them after the event. I am as doubtful of myself as of everything else. So it comes about that, if I happen to do well in any enterprise, I ascribe it more to fortune than to my ability, since in my planning I am slapdash and diffident.

I have this general characteristic too, that of all the opinions held by ancient writers of man in the mass, those that I most readily accept and most strongly adhere to are those which are most contemptuous, most vilifying, and most annihilating. Philosophy seems to me never to have so easy a game as when it is attacking our presumption and vanity, and when honestly admitting its own indecision, weakness, and ignorance. It is my opinion that the nurse and mother of the falsest opinions, both public and private, is the excessive opinion that man has of himself.

Those people who bestraddle the epicycle of Mercury and see so far into the heavens make me grind my teeth. For in my studies, the subject of which is man, I find an extreme variety of opinions, an intricate labyrinth of difficulties, one on top of another, and a very great uncertainty and diversity in the school of wisdom itself. Seeing therefore that these people have been unable to agree on their knowledge of themselves and of their condition, which is constantly before their eyes, and is within themselves; seeing that they do not know how these things move that they themselves set in motion, nor how to describe and explain to us the springs that they themselves hold and manage, you may judge how little I can believe them when they set out the causes of the rise and fall of the Nile. The curiosity to know things has been given to man for a scourge, says Holy Writ.

But, to come to my own case, I think it would be difficult for any man to have a poorer opinion of himself, or indeed to have a poorer opinion of me, than I have of myself. I regard myself as one of the common sort in all save this, that I do so regard myself. I plead guilty to the meanest and most ordinary failings; I neither disown nor excuse them; and I value myself for nothing except that I know my own value. If I have any vainglory in me, it is but superficially infused by the treachery of my nature; it has no body visible to the eyes of my judgement. I am sprinkled with it, not thoroughly dyed.

For, truly, as to intellectual achievement, I have never produced anything whatever that has satisfied me; and other people's approval is no compensation. My taste is delicate and hard to please, especially in regard to myself; I constantly repudiate myself, and feel myself wavering and yielding through weakness. I have nothing of my own that satisfies my judgement. My perception is clear and normal enough, but when at work, it becomes blurred. Of this I have the plainest evidence in the matter of poetry. I love it infinitely, and can form a fair judgement of other men's work. But when I try to set my own hand to it, I am indeed like a child; I have no patience with myself. One can play the fool everywhere else, but not in poetry,

> *mediocribus esse poetis*
> *non di, non homines, non concessere columnae.**

Would to God that this sentence were inscribed above the doors of all our printers' shops, to forbid the entry of so many versifiers!

> *verum*
> *nil securius est malo poeta.†*

What numbers we have of that tribe! Dionysius the elder valued nothing in himself so much as his poetry. At the time of

* 'Mediocrity in poets is not allowed by gods or men, or by the columns' (on which they hang their verses). Horace, *Ars Poetica*, 372.

† 'But really there is no one more confident than a bad poet.' Martial, XII, lxiii, 13.

the Olympic games, when his chariots surpassed all others in magnificence, he also sent poets and musicians to present his verses, with tents and pavilions royally gilded and hung with tapestry. When they began to recite these compositions, the charm and excellence of their delivery at first attracted the people's attention; but when, later, they came to weigh up the inanity of the work, they first became contemptuous, and then, growing more and more exasperated, flew into a fury and rushed, in their resentment, to pull down his tents and tear every one of them in pieces. And when his chariots did no good in the race, and the ship bringing his men back failed to make Sicily, and was driven before the gale and wrecked on the coast at Tarentum, the people were quite certain that it was the wrath of the gods, who were incensed, like themselves, by his bad poem. And even the sailors who escaped from the wreck supported the popular opinion, with which the oracle that predicted his death seemed in some sort to agree. For it declared that Dionysius would be near his end when he had overcome men who were better than himself. He interpreted this as meaning the Carthaginians, whose forces were greater than his; and when he was fighting them, he frequently avoided victory, or made it less complete, in order not to incur the fate promised by this prediction. But he misunderstood it; for the god was referring to the time when, by favour and injustice, he triumphed at Athens over the tragic poets who were better than he, and had his play, *The Leneians** acted in competition with theirs. He died immediately after this victory, partly from excessive joy at his success.

What I find tolerable in my own work is not so really and in itself, but only in comparison with other worse productions that I see well received. I envy the happiness of those who are able to delight and find satisfaction in their own work. This is an easy way of giving ourselves pleasure, since the source is in ourselves, especially if we are somewhat strong in our self-

* This was actually the name of the festival; his play was called *The Ransom of Hector*. Montaigne was led into this error by a slip of Amyot's in his translation of Plutarch.

conceit. I know a poet against whom the powerful and the weak, in public and in private, and heaven and earth themselves, cry out that he has hardly the slightest notion of his art. But for all that, he does not abate one inch of the stature that he has conferred upon himself. He is always beginning afresh, always persisting, and always reconsidering; and is all the firmer and more inflexible in his opinion for being the only man interested in maintaining it. My works are so far from pleasing me, that every time I look at them they annoy me:

> *Cum relego, scripsisse pudet, quia plurima cerno,*
> *me quoque qui feci judice, digna lini.**

I have always an idea in my mind, a certain confused picture, which shows me, as in a dream, a better form than I have used; but I cannot grasp it and develop it. And even this idea is only on a middling plane. From this I conclude that the works of those rich and great minds of ancient days are very far beyond the utmost stretch of my hopes and imagination. Their writings not only satisfy me to the full, but astound me and strike me with wonder. I appreciate their beauty; I see, if not the whole, at least so much that I cannot possibly aspire to equal it. Whatever I undertake, I owe a sacrifice to the Graces, as Plutarch says of someone, to obtain their favour,

> *si quid enim placet,*
> *si quid dulce hominum sensibus influit,*
> *debentur lepidis omnia Gratiis.†*

But they always leave me in the lurch. With me everything is rough; there is a lack of grace, charm, and beauty. I am incapable of making things show for all that they are; my style adds nothing to the matter. That is why my subject must be a solid one, with plenty to grip, and one that shines with its own lustre. When I attempt some popular and lighter theme, it is to follow my own inclination – since I do not care for a formal and gloomy wisdom, as the world does – and to enliven myself, not

---

* 'When I re-read them, I am ashamed of having written them, because I see many things that I, as their author, think should be bundled away.' Ovid, *Ex Ponto*, I, v, 15.

† 'For, if anything pleases, if anything sweetly influences the mortal senses, all is due to the charming Graces.' Source unknown.

my style, which is better suited to a grave and serious theme; always supposing that I can give the name of style to a formless and irregular utterance, a popular jargon that runs on without definitions, without divisions, without conclusions, and is as vague as that of Amafanius and Rabirius.

I do not know how to please or to delight, or to amuse; the best story in the world becomes dry and withers in my hands. I can only speak seriously and am altogether without that easy knack, which I see in many of my friends, of entertaining chance comers and keeping a whole company amused, or of holding the attention of a prince with all kinds of small talk, and never boring him. Such men never lack a subject, thanks to their gift of knowing how to use the first that comes, and to adapt it to the humour and understanding of anyone they may have to do with. Princes are not very fond of serious discourse, nor am I of telling stories. I do not know how to use the first and simplest arguments, which are generally the best received; I am a poor preacher to the people. On all subjects I am prone to say everything that I know. Cicero holds that in a philosophical treatise, the most difficult part is the introduction. If this is so, I confine myself to the conclusion. And yet we must tune the string to every kind of note; and the sharpest is the one that is most rarely touched.

It needs at least as much accomplishment to develop an empty theme as to sustain a weighty one. Sometimes one must treat things superficially, and sometimes go deeply into them. I am well aware that most men remain on this lower level, because they have no conception of things except from the outer shell. But I also know that the greatest masters, both Xenophon and Plato, are often seen to relax into this low and popular manner of speech and treatment, enhancing it, however, with that charm which never fails them.

Now my language has no ease or grace; it is rough and contemptuous, free and irregular in its arrangement; and my inclination, if not my judgement, likes it so. But I am well aware that sometimes I let myself go too far, and that by trying to avoid art and affectation, I fall into them on the other side:

brevis esse laboro,
*obscurus fio.**

Plato says that length and brevity are qualities that neither detract from nor enhance the value of language.

If I tried to imitate the smooth, even, and regular style of other writers, I should never achieve it; though the breaks and cadences of Sallust make a more natural appeal to me, yet I find Caesar both greater, and harder to copy; and if my bent leads me rather to imitate Seneca's style, I nevertheless have much more admiration for Plutarch's. As in deeds, so in words, I simply follow my natural way; which is perhaps why I speak better than I write. Movement and action put life into words, especially with those who move briskly, as I do, and get heated. The bearing, the expression, the voice, the gown, the attitude, may give some weight to things that, like idle chatter, have hardly any of their own. Messala, in Tacitus, complains of the tightness of certain garments in his day, and of the arrangement of the benches from which orators had to speak, as hampering their eloquence.

My French is distorted, both in pronunciation and otherwise, by the barbarisms of my native place. I have never met a man of these southern parts whose speech did not smack of his origins, and did not offend a pure French ear. It is not that I am so much at home in my Périgordin, for I can speak it no better than I can German, and do not much care for it. It is like the other dialects around me on either side – Poitevin, Saintongeois, Limousin, and Auvergnat – a soft, drawling, and prolix tongue. There is, certainly, above us, towards the mountains, a Gascon dialect that I find singularly beautiful, blunt, brief, expressive, and indeed a more virile and soldierly language than any I know; it is as vigorous, forcible, and direct as French is graceful, precise, and fluent.

As for Latin, which was given me as my mother-tongue, I have by disuse lost my facility for speaking it; and for writing it too, at which I used to be reckoned a master. So I am not worth much on that score either.

* 'I want to be brief, but I become obscure.' Horace, *Ars Poetica*, 25.

Good looks are a possession of great value in human relations; they are the first means of establishing goodwill between men, and no one can be so barbarous or so surly as not to feel their attraction in some degree. The body enjoys a great share in our being, and has an eminent place in it. Its structure and composition, therefore, are worthy of proper consideration.

Those who would divide our two principal parts, and isolate one from the other, are in the wrong. On the contrary, we must reunite them and bring them together. We must command the soul not to draw aside and hold herself apart, not to scorn and abandon the body – which she can only do by some false pretence – but to ally herself with it, help, control, advise, and correct it, and bring it back when it goes astray; in short, marry it and become its partner, so that their actions may not appear diverse and opposed, but harmonious and uniform. Christians have some particular instruction concerning this bond. For they know that divine justice embraces the union and fellowship of body and soul, to the extent of making the body capable of eternal rewards; and that God regards the actions of the whole man, and wills him to receive as a whole his punishment or reward according to his deserts.

The Peripatetic school, of all sects the best adapted to society, assigns to wisdom this sole task, to provide for and procure the common welfare of these two associated halves. And it points out how by paying insufficient attention to the existence of this bond, other schools have taken sides, some for the body and some for the soul, with equal error on both sides; and that they have lost sight of their subject, which is man, and of their guide, which they generally admit to be nature.

The first distinction that ever existed among men, and the first consideration that gave some pre-eminence over others, was in all likelihood that of beauty:

> *agros divisere atque dedere*
> *pro facie cuiusque et viribus ingenioque:*
> *nam facies multum valuit viresque vigebant.**

* 'They divided the land and gave to each man in proportion to his beauty, strength, and intellect; for they prized beauty and esteemed strength.' Lucretius, v, 1110.

Now, I am a little below middle stature, and this defect is not only ugly, but a disadvantage too, especially in those who hold commands and offices. For the authority conferred by a fine presence and dignity of body is lacking. Caius Marius was unwilling to accept soldiers less than six foot in height. The Courtier* is indeed right to desire for the gentleman he is educating the common stature, rather than any other, and to object to any peculiarity that causes him to be noticeable. But if a soldier fails to be of the proper medium height, I should prefer him to be above it, rather than below it.

Small men, said Aristotle, are very pretty, but not beautiful; and as a great soul can be recognized by outward greatness, so a large and tall body connotes beauty. The Ethiopians and Indians, he says, in electing their kings and magistrates, took their bodily looks and height into consideration. They were right; for to see a captain of fine and ample stature marching at the head of his troops excites respect in his followers, and strikes dread into the enemy:

> *Ipse inter primos praestanti corpore Turnus*
> *vertitur, arma tenens, et toto vertice supra est.*†

Our great, divine, and heavenly King, about whom every detail should be carefully, religiously, and reverently noticed, did not despise bodily superiority, for He was 'fairer than the children of men'.‡ And Plato desires beauty, as well as temperance and courage, in the guardians of his Republic.

It is most vexing if you are standing among your servants, to be asked the question: 'Where is the master?', and to receive only the fag-end of a salute made to your barber or your secretary, as happened to poor Philopoemen. When he arrived, ahead of his company, at an inn where he was expected, the landlady failed to recognize him and, observing that he was a plain-looking fellow, gave him the job of helping her maids to draw the water and kindle the fire, in preparation for his own

---

* *Il Cortegiano*, Castiglione's book on the ideal courtier.

† 'Turnus, outstanding in appearance, and a whole head higher than the rest, marches in the lead, his weapons in his hands.' Virgil, *Aeneid*, VII, 783.

‡ Psalms, 45, 2.

coming. When the gentlemen of his suite arrived, and found him engaged in this fine occupation – for he had dutifully obeyed the orders given him – they asked him what he was doing there. 'I am paying the penalty for my ugliness,' he answered.

Other kinds of beauty are for the women; beauty of stature is the sole masculine beauty. When the body is small, neither a broad and domed brow, nor a clear and soft eye, nor a regular nose, nor small ears and mouth, nor white and regular teeth, nor a thick, smooth beard, the colour of chestnut husks, nor curly hair, nor a well-shaped head, nor a fresh complexion, nor a pleasing face, nor an odourless body, nor limbs of good proportion, will make a handsome man.*

For the rest, I have a strong and thick-set body, my face is full but not fat, and my temperament between jovial and melancholy, moderately sanguine and fiery,

Unde rigent setis mihi crura, et pectora villis:†

My health was sound and vigorous until I was well on in years, and I was rarely troubled by illness. Such I was; for I am not portraying myself as I am now that I have entered the avenues of old age, having long since passed my fortieth year:

*minutatim, vires et robur adultum
frangit, et in partem peiorem liquitur aetas.*‡

What I shall be henceforth will be only half a man, and myself no longer. I slide and steal away from myself every day,

Singula de nobis anni praedantur euntes.§

Skill and agility were never mine; and yet I am the son of a very active father, who remained agile into extreme old age. He could hardly find a man in his station who was his equal in all physical exercises, while I have seldom met anyone who did not excel me in any but running, at which I was moderately good. In music, either for the voice – for which mine is very ill-suited –

* This is a portrait of Montaigne himself.

† 'Whence the rough hair that is stiff upon my legs and breast.' Martial, II, xxxvi, 5.

‡ 'Little by little age destroys our powers and adult strength, and drags us down to decay.' Lucretius, II, 1131.

§ 'The years, as they run, steal one thing after another from us.' Horace, *Epistles*, II, ii, 55.

or instrumental, they were never able to teach me anything. In dancing, tennis, or wrestling, I was never able to acquire more than a very slight and ordinary competence; in swimming, fencing, vaulting, and leaping, none at all. My hands are so awkward that what I write is illegible even to me; and so, when I have scribbled something down I would rather work it all out again than give myself the trouble of deciphering it. And I do not read much better. I feel that I weary my hearers. Otherwise, a fair scholar. I cannot fold a letter properly, and have never been able to cut a pen, or carve well at table, or saddle and bridle a horse, or carry a hawk on my fist and cast her off, or control dogs, birds, or horses.

In short, my physical qualities are much on a par with those of my mind. There is nothing sprightly about them; there is only a full, firm vigour. I can stand hard work, but only when it is voluntary, and for so long as my desire prompts me.

Molliter austerum studio fallente laborem.*

Otherwise, unless I am allured to it by some pleasure, and have no other guide than pure free will, I am of no use at all. For I have come to the point where there is nothing I will bite my nails over except life and health, nothing that I am willing to purchase at the price of mental torment and constraint,

tanti mihi non sint opaci
omnis arena Tagi, quodque in mare volvitur aurum.†

I am extremely idle and extremely independent both by nature and by intention. I would as willingly lend my blood as my pains.

I have a mind that belongs wholly to itself, and is accustomed to go its own way. Having never until this hour had a master or governor imposed on me, I have advanced as far as I pleased, and at my own pace. This has made me slack and unfit for the service of others; it has made me useless to any but myself.

And, in my own interest, there has been no need to put press-

* 'With eagerness deceptively lightening hard work.' Horace, *Satires*, II, ii, 12.
† 'I would not buy all Tagus's dark sands at such a price, nor all the gold it washes into the sea.' Juvenal, III, 54 (adapted).

ure on this heavy, indolent, and inactive nature. For having enjoyed from birth such a degree of fortune that I have had reason to be content with it, and as much intelligence as I have felt I had occasion for, I have sought for nothing and taken nothing:

> *Non agimur tumidis velis Aquilone secundo;*
> *non tamen adversis aetatem ducimus austris:*
> *viribus, ingenio, specie, virtute, loco, re,*
> *extremi primorum, extremis usque priores.**

It has taken only a sufficiency to content me. But this implies, if properly understood, a disciplined mind, which is hard to attain in any walk of life, and which, in practice, we find to exist more easily with want than with abundance; since, as with our other passions, the appetite for riches is perhaps made sharper by their enjoyment than by their scarcity, and the virtue of moderation is rarer than that of patience. All that I have needed has been quietly to enjoy the good things that God, in His bounty, has put into my hands.

I have never had a taste for any sort of tiresome labour. I have hardly ever managed any business but my own; or if I have, it has been on condition that I did things in my own time and in my own way. And I have only acted for people who trusted me, and did not bother me, and knew me well. For expert riders will get some service even from a restive and broken-winded horse.

Even my childish upbringing was gentle and free, and subject to no rigorous discipline. All this bred in me a sensitive disposition, incapable of bearing worries; to such a degree that I like to have any losses or troubles that concern me concealed from my knowledge. I enter under the head of expenses the sum that it costs me to keep my negligence fed and maintained.

> *haec nempe supersunt,*
> *quae dominum fallant, quae prosint furibus.†*

* 'My sails are not filled by the favouring north winds nor is my voyage troubled by the hostile south winds. In strength, intelligence, looks, in virtue, place, and possessions, although the last of the great, I am among the first of the last.' Horace, *Epistles*, II, ii, 201.

† 'These are superfluities, that slip from the master's hands for the profit of thieves.' Horace, *Epistles*, I, vi, 45.

I prefer to have no inventory of my possessions, so that I may be the less sensible of a loss. I beg those who live with me, if they lack affection and honesty, at least to pay me the tribute of outward decency when they cheat me. Since I have not the steadfastness to bear the annoyance of those unfortunate accidents to which we are subject, and cannot endure the strain of regulating and managing my affairs, I leave myself entirely in fortune's hands, encouraging myself, to the best of my ability, to the idea that everything will be for the worst, and resolving to bear that worst with meekness and patience. For this alone do I strive; it is the aim to which I direct all my thoughts.

When in danger, I do not consider so much how I shall escape as how little it matters whether I escape or not. If I were to succumb to it, what would that amount to? Not being able to control events, I control myself, and adapt myself to them if they do not adapt themselves to me. I have hardly the skill to circumvent fortune, or to escape and overcome it, or wisely to arrange and incline things to serve my purpose. Still less have I the patience to resist the sharp and painful anxieties that such action entails. And the most painful situation for me is to be in suspense about urgent matters, and tossed between fear and hope.

Deliberation, even in the most trivial affairs, is irksome to me; and my mind is more put about when suffering the shocks and trepidations of uncertainty and doubt than in settling down and accepting whatever happens, once the die is cast. My sleep has been broken by few passions; but the slightest suspense will break it. When travelling, I prefer to avoid steep and slippery slopes, and to follow the beaten track, however deep the mud, for though I may sink in, that is the lowest I can fall, and I choose it as a measure of safety. Similarly, I prefer a disaster unalloyed, in which I am no longer tormented by the possibility that things may improve. I prefer to be plunged straight into suffering at the first blow,

*dubia plus torquent mala.**

When the thing has happened I behave like a man; when I have

* 'Uncertain evils torture us more.' Seneca, *Agamemnon*, III, i, 29.

204

to manage it, like a child. Fear of a fall makes me more feverish than the fall itself. The game is not worth the candle. A miser suffers worse from his passion than a poor man, a jealous man than a cuckold. And often there is less harm in losing one's vineyard than in going to law for it. The lowest step is the firmest. It is the seat of constancy. There you have need of no one but yourself. It has its own foundation, and rests solely on itself.

Is there not a touch of philosophy in the case of a certain gentleman once known to many? He married when well on in years, after spending his youth in riotous company; and he was a great talker and wag. Remembering how often the subject of cuckoldry had given him occasion to gossip and mock at others, he decided to protect himself. So he chose a woman from a place where a man may have what he wants for money, and made a match of it with her. 'Good morning, harlot.' 'Good morning, cuckold.' And there was nothing that he discussed more freely and openly with those who came to see him than this arrangement of his, by which he stopped the secret prattlings of mockers and blunted the point of their taunts.

As for ambition, which is a neighbour – or rather a daughter – of presumption, if fortune had wished to advance me, she would have had to come and lead me by the hand. For to give myself trouble for an uncertain hope, and to submit myself to all the difficulties that attend men endeavouring to force themselves into favour at the beginning of their career, that I could never have done:

*spem pretio non emo.**

I cling to what I see and hold, and do not go far from port,

Alter remus aquas, alter tibi radat arenas.†

Besides, a man rarely attains these advantages without first risking what he already has; and it is my opinion that if one has enough to keep one in the condition in which one was born and

* 'I do not buy hope for ready cash.' Terence, *Adelphi*, II, ii, 11.
† 'One oar sweeps the water, the other the sands.' Propertius, III, iii, 23.

brought up, it is foolish to let it out of one's hand in the uncertain hope of increasing it. The man to whom fortune has
denied a place where he can set his foot and establish a quiet and
peaceful existence is to be forgiven if he hazards what he has,
since in any case necessity is sending him to seek his living.

*Capienda rebus in malis praeceps via est.**

And I more readily forgive a younger brother for exposing his
inheritance to the winds than a man who has the honour of his
house in his keeping, and cannot fall into want except through
his own fault.

Following the advice of my good friends of early days, I have
discovered a much shorter and easier way of giving up such
ambitions and sitting still,

Cui sit conditio dulcis sine pulvere palmae;†

at the same time making a sound assessment of my powers, that
they are incapable of great things, and remembering the words
of the late Chancellor Olivier, that the French are like monkeys,
which go clambering up a tree, from branch to branch till they
get to the top, and display their backsides when they get there.

Turpe est, quod nequeas, capiti committere pondus,
et pressum inflexo mox dare terga genu.‡

Even those qualities in me that are irreproachable I would
have found useless in this age. My easy-going habits would
have been called laxity and weakness; my loyalty and con-
scientiousness would have appeared excessive and superstitious; my frankness and independence, tiresome, rash, and
inconsiderate. Misfortune has its uses. It is good to be born in
very depraved times; for, compared with others, you gain a
reputation for virtue at a small cost. In our days a man who is

* 'In misfortune one must take a headlong course.' Seneca, *Agamemnon*,
II, i, 47.
† 'Whose agreeable lot it is to receive the palm without the dust (of the
race).' Horace, *Epistles*, I, i, 51.
‡ 'It is unseemly to put too great a burden on one's head, when soon
one's knees will bend and one's back give way.' Propertius, III, ix, 5.

only guilty of parricide and sacrilege is a man of worth and
honour:

> *Nunc, si depositum non inficiatur amicus,*
> *si reddat veterem cum tota aerugine follem,*
> *prodigiosa fides et Tuscis digna libellis,*
> *quaeque coronata lustrari debeat agna.**

Never was there a time or place in which a prince could count
on a surer or greater reward for goodness and justice. I shall be
much surprised if the first who decides to push himself into
favour and credit by this road does not easily outstrip his fellows. Power and violence can do something, but not always
everything.

We see merchants, country justices, and craftsmen competing
with the nobility in valour and the martial arts. They behave
honourably both in public and private combat; they fight, they
defend towns in our wars. A prince's special virtue is stifled in
this crowd. Let him excel in humanity, truth, loyalty, moderation, and, particularly, in justice: traits now rare, unknown, and
exiled. It is solely by the will of the people that he can perform
his function; and no other qualities can gain their good will as
well as these, which are most beneficial to them. 'Nothing is as
popular as goodness.'†

Judged by this standard I might seem both great and rare,
whereas I look like a commonplace pygmy when the standard
is that of certain past ages when, even if no other stronger qualities were present, it was usual to find a man moderate in his
vengeance, slow in resenting insults, scrupulous in keeping
his word, neither double-faced nor pliable, nor prone to make
his faith conform to the will of others or the turn of the times.
I would rather let an affair run to ruin than twist my words to
further it. As for this new virtue of pretence and dissimulation
which is so highly thought of at present, I hate it mortally. Of
all the vices, I know none that testifies to such a mean and

* 'Now if your friend does not deny his trust, and returns an old purse
with all its verdigrised coins, this is prodigious probity, worthy to be
recorded in the Tuscan annals, and celebrated with the sacrifice of a
crowned lamb.' Juvenal, XIII, 60.

† Cicero, *Pro Ligario*, 12.

craven spirit. It is a cowardly and servile characteristic, to go about in disguise, concealed behind a mask, without the courage to show oneself as one is. Thus the men of today train themselves in perfidy; becoming accustomed to twist their words, they do not scruple to break them. A generous heart should never disguise its thoughts, but willingly reveal its inmost depths. It is either all good, or at least all human.

Aristotle thinks it the duty of a great soul to hate and love openly, to judge and speak with entire freedom and, in the cause of truth, to take no account of other men's approval or disapproval. Apollonius said that it was for slaves to lie and for free men to speak the truth.

Truth is the principal and fundamental part of virtue. It must be loved for its own sake. A man who speaks the truth because he is in some way compelled or for his own advantage, and who is not afraid to tell a lie when it is of no importance to anyone, is not truthful enough. My soul naturally shuns a lie, and hates even the thought of one. I feel an inward shame and a sharp remorse if an untruth happens to escape me – as sometimes it does if the occasion is unexpected, and I am taken unawares.

It is not necessary always to say everything, for that would be foolish; but what we say should be what we think, the contrary is wicked. I do not know what advantage men expect from their eternal pretences and deceits, unless it is to be disbelieved when they do tell the truth. Such conduct may deceive men once or twice, but to make a profession of concealment, and to brag, as some of our princes have done,* that they would throw a shirt on the fire if it were aware of their real intentions – which was a saying of Metellus of Macedon of old – and that one who cannot dissemble does not know how to rule,† is to give warning to those who have dealings with them that what they say is so much trickery and falsehood. 'The subtler and more astute a man is, the more he is hated and mistrusted once he has lost his reputation for honesty.'‡ Only a very simple man would let

* Charles VIII.
† A saying of Louis XI.
‡ Cicero, *De Officiis*, II, ix.

himself be taken in by the looks or words of someone who makes it his business always to be outwardly one thing and inwardly another, as Tiberius did. And I cannot imagine how such persons can take part in human society, seeing that they utter nothing which can be received as common coin. Anyone who is disloyal to truth is disloyal to falsehood also.

Those who in our day, in defining the duties of a prince, have considered the success of his rule alone, putting it before all regard for his faith and conscience, might be of some service to one whose affairs have been so arranged by fortune that he can settle them once and for all by a single breach of his pledged word. But that is not how things happen. He is always making similar bargains; he concludes more than one peace, and more than one treaty, in his life. It is gain that tempts him to his first breach of faith – and gain is almost always the motive, as it is in every other kind of crime; sacrilege, murder, rebellion, treason are all undertaken for profit of some kind – but this initial gain is followed by endless losses, and the prince is debarred by this instance of faithlessness from all chance of amity and negotiation. When, during my boyhood, Soliman of the Ottoman race – a race not very careful in the keeping of their promises and agreements – had made a military raid on Otranto, he was informed that, contrary to the terms of capitulation arranged with his people, Mercurino de' Gratinare and the inhabitants of Castro had been kept prisoner after the surrender of the place. Thereupon he ordered their release, since he had other great enterprises under way in that country; and such a breach of his word, although it might appear to be an immediate gain, would bring him into future distrust and discredit, which would be infinitely prejudicial to him.

Now, for my part, I would rather be tiresome and tactless than a flatterer and a dissembler. I admit that there may be some touch of pride and self-will in my maintaining such candour and integrity as I do, without any consideration of others. It seems that I am growing a little more outspoken where I should be less so, and that the more respect I owe to my opponent the hotter I grow in my opposition. It may also be that through lack

of art, I let my nature have its way. Employing towards the
great the same liberty of speech and demeanour that I have
brought from home, I am conscious that it greatly inclines me
to be tactless and impolite. I was born like this, but in addition
I am not quick-witted enough to evade a sudden question and
escape by some shift, or to invent a truth; nor have I a good
enough memory to remember it when invented, and I certainly
lack the assurance to maintain it. So I brave things out, from
weakness. That is why I take refuge in candour, and always say
what I think, both naturally and intentionally, leaving it to
fortune to decide the issue. Aristippus used to say that the
principal advantage he had derived from philosophy was that
he spoke freely and openly to everyone.

The memory is an instrument of wonderful utility, and without it the judgement can hardly perform its duties; I am almost
completely without it. Anything that is put before me must be
presented piecemeal. For it is beyond my powers to reply to a
proposition with several heads. I cannot take a message if I have
not put it down in my notebook; and when I have an important
speech to make that is of any length, I am reduced to the mean
and miserable necessity of learning by heart, word for word,
what I am going to say. Otherwise, I should have neither power
nor assurance, but should always be afraid that my memory was
going to play me a trick. But this method is just as difficult for
me. It takes me three hours to learn three lines; and then, if I have
composed it myself, the freedom and authority with which I
change the order, or alter a word, and my constant variations of
matter, make it more difficult to keep in mind. Now, the more I
distrust my memory, the more confused it becomes; it serves me
best by accident, I have to woo it unconcernedly. For if I press
it, it becomes bewildered; and once it has begun to waver, the
more I sound it the more perplexed and embarrassed it grows; it
serves me at its own hours, not at mine.

This same defect that I find in my memory, I find also in
several other places. I avoid commands, obligations, and constraint. What I do easily and naturally, I can no longer do if I
command myself to do it by an express and definite injunction.

In the case of my body too, those organs that have some liberty and special jurisdiction over themselves at times refuse to obey me, when I fix and bind them to a particular place and hour for the service I need of them. This compulsive and tyrannical prescription offends them; either from fear or spite, they shrink and grow numb.

Once, long ago, I was in a place where it is considered a barbarous discourtesy not to respond to those who pledge you a toast; and, though I was allowed complete freedom, I tried to be convivial, according to the custom of the country, in order to please the ladies of the party. But there was an amusing result. For this threat, and my preparations forcibly to make myself violate my natural habits, so choked my throat that I could not swallow a single drop, and I was unable to drink even the amount I needed for my meal. I found myself full, and my thirst was quenched by the quantity of drink that I had consumed in my thoughts.

This defect is most apparent in those who have the strongest and most active imaginations; yet it is natural, and there is no one who does not feel it in some degree. An excellent archer, who had been condemned to death, was offered his life if he would give some noteworthy proof of his skill. But he refused to try, fearing that the excessive strain on his will might cause him to miss his aim, and that far from saving his life, he would also forfeit the reputation he had acquired as a marksman. A man whose thoughts are elsewhere will not fail to take the same number and length of steps almost to an inch, every time that he walks in a particular place. But if he applies his attention to measuring and counting them, he will find that what he did naturally and by chance, he will not do as accurately by design.

My library, which is a fine one for a country library, is situated at one corner of my house. But if anything occurs to me that I want to look up or write down there, I have to entrust it to some other person for fear that it will escape me merely as I cross my courtyard. If I venture in speaking to wander ever so little from my argument, I never fail to lose it; which is the reason why I keep myself short, concise, and terse in my conversation.

I am obliged to call the men who serve me by the names of their offices or their provinces, for I find it very hard to remember a name. I can tell, to be sure, that it has three syllables, that it sounds harsh, and that it begins or ends with a certain letter. And, if I live long enough, I am not sure that I shall not forget my own name, as others have done.

Messala Corvinus was for two years without any trace of memory, and the same is said of George of Trebizond. I often wonder, in my own interest, what kind of life theirs was, and whether, without that faculty, I shall have enough left to support me in some comfort. And when I look closely into it, I fear that this failing, if complete, will destroy all the functions of the soul. 'Memory is, beyond a doubt, the sole receptacle not only of philosophy, but of all that appertains to living and of all the arts.'*

Plenus rimarum sum, hac atque illac effluo.†

It has happened to me more than once that I have forgotten the password which three hours ago I had given to, or received from another, or that I have been unable – whatever Cicero may say‡ – to remember where I have hidden my purse. If I lock up anything with particular care, I am helping myself to lose it.

Memory is the receptacle and container of learning; mine being so defective, I have no great cause to complain that I know so little. In general, I know the names of the arts and the subjects they treat, but nothing more. I turn over the pages of books; I do not study them. What I retain from them is something that I no longer recognize as another's. All the profit that my mind has made has been from the arguments and ideas that it has imbibed from them. The author, the place, the words, and other facts I immediately forget.

I am so good at forgetting that I forget my own jottings and compositions no less than everything else. People are always quoting me to myself without my noticing it. Anyone who wanted to know where the verses and examples come from that

* Cicero, *Academica*, II, 7.

† 'I am full of cracks. I leak on every side.' Terence, *Eunuchus*, I, ii, 25.

‡ 'I have certainly never heard of an old man who forgot where he had buried a treasure.' *De Senectute*, VII.

I have accumulated here would leave me at a loss for an answer; and yet I have begged them only at familiar and famous doors, and have not been content with their being rich unless they also came from rich and honourable hands; authority and reason are present in equal quantity. It is no great wonder if my book incurs the same fate as other books, and if my memory loses hold of what I write as it does of what I read, of what I give as of what I receive.

Besides my defect of memory, I have other defects that greatly contribute to my ignorance. I have a slow and lazy mind, whose point is dulled by the slightest cloud, so that I have never, for instance, put any puzzle before it that has been easy enough for it to solve. The smallest, silliest subtlety will perplex me. In those games in which the mind takes a part – chess, cards, draughts, and the like – I understand only the simplest play. My intellect is slow and muddled, but what it once grasps, it grasps thoroughly and understands very completely, both in depth and in detail, for so long as it retains it. My sight is long, sound, and perfect, but it is soon tired by work and becomes blurred; which is why I cannot spend a long time with books except by the help of others.* The younger Pliny can inform those without experience of their own, how grievous this impediment is to those addicted to reading.

No mind is so feeble and brutish that some special faculty cannot be seen to shine in it; there is none so completely buried that it does not light up at some point. And how it happens that a soul which is blind and asleep to everything else is found to be quick, clear-sighted, and excellent in some one particular, is a question we must ask of the masters. But fine minds are those which are universal, open, prepared for everything, and if not educated, at least capable of education. When I say this, I condemn my own. For whether out of feebleness or indifference – and to be indifferent to what is at our feet, to what we hold in our hands, and to what most closely concerns the conduct of our lives, is very far from my purpose – there is no mind so inept as mine, or so ignorant of many common things of which a man

* Who would read aloud to him.

cannot be ignorant without shame. I must give a few examples of this.

I was born and bred in the country, among tillers of the soil. I have had the business of estate management to deal with ever since my predecessors in the possession of the property I enjoy left it to me. Yet I still cannot reckon either with counters or with a pen. I am unfamiliar with most of our current coins. I do not know the difference between one grain and another, either in the field or in the granary, unless it is quite obvious, and I can hardly distinguish between the cabbages and the lettuces in my garden. I do not even know the names of the commonest farm implements, or the plainest principles of agriculture, which are familiar to boys; and I know even less of the mechanical arts, of trade and merchandise, of the nature and variety of fruit, wines, and food, of training a hawk, or physicking a horse or a dog. And since I must make full show of my shame, it is only a month ago that I was caught in ignorance of the fact that leaven is used in bread-making, and of the purpose of putting wine into vats. In Athens of old, they supposed anyone who was seen stacking and binding a load of brushwood deftly to have an aptitude for mathematics. One would certainly draw quite the contrary conclusion from me; for give me the whole equipment of a kitchen, and still I shall go hungry.

From these articles of my confession you can imagine others to my discredit. But whatever I make myself out to be, provided that I show myself as I am, I am fulfilling my purpose. So I will not apologize for daring to put in writing such mean and frivolous things as these. The meanness of my subject compels me to do so. You may condemn my project if you will, but not my way of carrying it out. However that may be, I see well enough, without anyone pointing it out, how little weight and value all this has, and how foolish my plan is. It is sufficient if my judgement, of which these essays are the proof, has not gone lame.

> *Nasutus sis usque licet, sis denique nasus,*
> *quantum noluerit ferre rogatus Atlas,*
> *et possis ipsum tu deridere Latinum,*
> *non potes in nugas dicere plura meas,*

ipse ego quam dixi: quid dentem dente iuvabit
rodere? carne opus est, si satur esse velis.
Ne perdas operam: qui si mirantur, in illos
virus habe; nos haec novimus esse nihil.*

I am not obliged to refrain from saying foolish things, provided I do not deceive myself, and know them to be so. And to err consciously is so common with me that I hardly ever err in any other way; I never make chance mistakes. It is no great accusation to attribute my stupidities to a temperamental heedlessness, since I cannot deny that I generally blame my wicked actions on the same defect.

I was present one day at Bar-le-duc, when a portrait of René, King of Sicily, painted by himself, was presented to King Francis II, to recall him to his memory. Why should not everyone be allowed to draw himself with a pen, as King René did with his pencil? I will therefore not pass over another blemish, though it is most unfit for public presentation; and this is my irresolution, a very serious defect when worldly business has to be transacted:

Nè sì, nè no, nel cor mi suona intero.†

I am quite capable of defending an opinion, but I cannot choose one.

For, in human affairs, whichever way one inclines, many probabilities present themselves to confirm one's opinion – and the philosopher Chrysippus said that he wanted to learn from his masters Zeno and Cleanthes only their dogmas; as for proofs and arguments, he could supply enough for himself – so to whichever side I turn I can always provide myself with enough reasons and probabilities to keep me there. Therefore I retain my doubt and liberty of choice until the occasion presses. And

* 'Let your nose be as keen as it will, let it be so big that Atlas would refuse if asked to carry it, and beat Latinus, if you can, at scoffing, still you cannot say worse of my trifles than I have said myself. What pleasure is there in grinding your teeth together? To satisfy your hunger, you must have food. Do not waste your labour. Keep your venom for those who admire themselves. I know that these things of mine are valueless.' Martial, XIII, ii, 1.

† 'Neither yes nor no rings clearly in my heart.' Petrarch, cxxxv.

then, to confess the truth, I generally throw a feather into the wind, as the saying goes, and commit myself to the mercy of fortune; a very slight inclination, and circumstances carry me with them, 'when the mind is in doubt, the slightest weight pulls it this way or that'.*

The uncertainty of my judgement is so evenly balanced in most cases that I would willingly refer the decision to a throw of the dice; and, after giving much thought to our human weakness, I observe that even sacred history has left us examples of this custom of leaving chance and fortune to make the decision in matters of doubt: 'and the lot fell upon Matthias'.† Human reason is a two-edged and dangerous sword. Even in the hands of Socrates, its closest and most familiar friend, see what a many-ended stick it is! So I am only fitted for following, and easily allow myself to be carried along by the crowd. I have not sufficient confidence in my own abilities to set up as a commander or a guide; I am very pleased to find my path marked out by others. If I must run the risk of a dubious choice, I prefer to do so under someone who is more certain of his opinions and more closely wedded to them than I. For I find the ground and foundation of mine to be very slippery.

Yet I do not change my opinions too easily, since I see a similar weakness on the other side. 'The very habit of agreeing seems to be dangerous and chancy.'‡

In political matters especially, there is a wide field open for wavering and dispute:

> *Iusta pari premitur veluti cum pondera libra*
> *prona, nec hac plus parte sedet, nec surgit ab illa.*§

Machiavelli's arguments, for example, were substantial enough for their subject, yet they were quite easy to contest; and his opponents have left their own just as open to confutation. In that kind of argument there will always be matter for answers

---

* Terence, *Andria*, 1, vi, 32.   † Acts, 1, 26.
‡ Cicero, *Academica*, 11, 21.
§ 'As when a true balance is charged with equal weights, its scales do not fall on one side or rise on the other.' Tibullus, 1v, i, 40.

and rejoinders, double, triple, and quadruple, and for that endless fabric of debates which our lawyers drag out to the uttermost in the making of their pleas:

> *Caedimur, et totidem plagis consumimus hostem;**

for our arguments have little foundation except that of experience, and the variety of human events furnishes us with infinite examples of every possible kind. A shrewd man of our own times says that if when our almanacks say cold, you say hot, and when they say dry you say wet, and always put down the opposite of what they predict, were he to lay a wager on the outcome he would not mind which side he took, except in matters where there can be no uncertainty: on the promise of extreme heat at Christmas, for example, or severe cold at midsummer.

I should say the same about these political controversies; whatever part you are set to play, you have just as good a chance as your opponent, provided that you do not go counter to principles that are too solid and obvious. And so, in my view, there is, in public affairs, no state so bad, provided it has age and continuity on its side, that is not preferable to change and disturbance. Our morals are extremely corrupt, and have a remarkable tendency to grow worse; many of our laws and customs are monstrous and barbarous: nevertheless, because of the difficulty of improving our state, and the danger of a collapse, if I could put a drag on our wheel and stop it at this point, I would gladly do so:

> *nunquam adeo foedis adeoque pudendis*
> *utimur exemplis ut non peiora supersint.*†

The worst thing I find about our state is its instability, and that our laws are no more capable than our clothes of settling into a fixed shape. It is very easy to accuse a government of imperfection, for all mortal things are full of it. It is very easy to arouse people to a contempt for their ancient observances: no man has ever attempted this without succeeding. But to establish

---

* 'We are beaten, and rain as many blows on the enemy.' Horace, *Epistles*, ii, ii, 97.

† 'The examples we cite are never so shameful or so foul that there are not others still worse.' Juvenal, viii, 183.

a better state of things in place of what he has destroyed – many a man has failed in his endeavours to do that.

I let prudence play only a very small part in my conduct; I generally allow myself to be guided by the general way of the common world. Happy the people who do what they are commanded better than their commanders, and do not worry themselves as to causes; who let themselves gently revolve with the revolutions of the heavens! Obedience is never pure or simple in one who reasons and disputes.

In fine, to return to myself, the sole feature for which I hold myself in some esteem is that in which no man has ever thought himself defective. My self-approbation is common, and shared by all. For who has ever considered himself lacking in sense? That would be a self-contradictory proposition. Lack of sense is a disease that never exists when it is seen; it is most tenacious and strong, yet the first glance from the patient's eye pierces it through and disperses it, as a dense mist is dispersed by the sun's beams. To accuse oneself would amount to self-absolution. There never was a street-porter or a silly woman who was not sure of having as much sense as was necessary. We readily recognize in others a superiority in courage, physical strength, experience, agility, or beauty. But a superior judgement we concede to nobody. And we think that we could ourselves have discovered the reasons which occur naturally to others, if only we had looked in the same direction.

We are soon aware when the learning, the style, and suchlike qualities that we find in the works of others, surpass our own: but with the simple products of the understanding, everyone thinks that it was in him to discover the same things, and is scarcely aware of the effort and difficulty involved, unless they are at an extreme and incomparable distance from him; and he hardly does so even then. So this is a kind of exercise for which I must expect very little esteem or praise, a kind of composition which gains small repute.

Well, then, for whom are you writing? The scholars, to whom right of judgement over books belongs, recognize no other value but that of learning, and approve no other mental processes than those of erudition and philosophy. If you have mistaken one of the Scipios for the other, what can be the value of anything else you have to say? According to the learned whoever is ignorant of Aristotle is at the same time ignorant of himself. Vulgar and commonplace minds cannot see the grace and dignity of a fine and elevated style. Now these two classes of men make up the world. The third, among whom it is your lot to fall,* that of men with firm minds under strong control, is so small that it has neither name nor standing amongst us; one is wasting half one's time if one aspires and endeavours to please it.

It is commonly said that the fairest division of her favours that nature has bestowed on us is that of sense. For there is no one who is discontented with the portion she has granted him. Is not this reasonable? Anyone who saw further would see beyond vision. I think my opinions are good and sound. But who does not think the same of his? One of the best proofs I have that they are right is the smallness of my self-esteem. For if they had not been well-founded, they might easily have let themselves be swayed by my singular self-regard. For I centre my affection almost entirely on myself, bestowing only very little on others. All that others divide among an infinite number of friends and acquaintances, to their glory and to their grandeur, I devote entirely to my mind's repose and to my own person. What escapes from me into other channels, does not really do so with my deliberate consent,

mihi nempe valere et vivere doctus.†

Now I find my opinions extremely bold and persistent in condemning my own insufficiency. Indeed, this is a subject which occupies my mind as much as any other. The world always looks outward, I turn my gaze inward; there I fix it, and there I keep it busy. Everyone looks before him; I look within. I have no business but with myself, I unceasingly consider, examine, and analyse myself. Others, if they will but see, are always going

* Montaigne seems here to be referring to his writings. But the identity of the *you* is not quite clear. He might still be addressing himself.

† 'Trained, indeed, to consider and live for myself.' Lucretius, v, 961, slightly altered.

elsewhere; they are always going forward,

*nemo in sese tendat descendere.**

But I revolve within myself.

This faculty which I have – whatever its value to me – for sifting the truth, and my independence in not easily subjecting my beliefs to those of others, I owe principally to myself. For the strongest and most general ideas that I possess are those which, in a manner of speaking, were born with me; they are natural, and wholly my own. I brought them forth crude and simple; at their birth they were bold and vigorous, though a little confused and imperfect. Since then I have established and fortified them with the authority of others and the sound reasonings of the ancients, with whose judgements I have found myself to agree. They have given me a firmer grasp on my ideas, and have enabled me to possess and enjoy them more fully.

Where others seek the reputation for an active and ready mind, I would be praised for my steadiness; what others aspire to gain by some brilliant and noteworthy deed, I claim for the uniformity, consistency, and moderation of my opinions and conduct. 'If there is one quality truly admirable, it is a uniform consistency in our whole lives and in our several acts; and this cannot be maintained by imitating the natures of others and neglecting our own.'†

Here then is the extent to which I feel myself guilty of what I called the first part of the vice of presumption. As to the second, which consists in not valuing others highly enough, I do not know whether I can excuse myself so well. For, whatever it may cost me, I am determined to speak of things as they are.

Whether it is that the constant intercourse I have with ancient ways of thought, and the conception I have formed of those gifted minds of olden times, disgust me both with others and with myself, or whether we really live in an age that produces only very mediocre things, the fact is that I see nothing today worthy of great admiration. What is more, I know few men

* 'No man attempts to descend into himself.' Persius, IV, 23.
† Cicero, *De Officiis*, I, 31.

intimately enough to be able to judge them; those with whom my social position brings me into closest touch are, for the most part, men who pay very little attention to the cultivation of their minds, and to whom honour is the greatest of all blessings, valour the height of all perfection. Such fine qualities as I see in others, I am very ready to praise and esteem; indeed, I often overstate my real opinion, permitting myself to that extent to lie. But I cannot invent anything entirely false. I gladly bear witness to any quality in my friends that I find praiseworthy; and where a foot is due I cheerfully make it a foot and a half. But I cannot lend them qualities that are not in them, or openly defend them for the imperfections that are.

Even to my enemies I frankly concede the honour that is their due. My feelings change; my judgement does not. And I do not confuse my quarrel with other circumstances that have nothing to do with it. For so jealous am I of my independence of judgement that I can hardly give it up for any passion whatever. I do more harm to myself by lying than I do to the man about whom I lie. One praiseworthy and generous custom has been observed in the Persian people, that they speak of their mortal enemies, even while they are at war to the death with them, as honourably and justly as their valour deserves.

I know plenty of men who have various fine qualities: one has wit, another courage, another resource, another conscience, another eloquence; one has some branch of learning, another a different one. But a man wholly great, one who has all these fine qualities together, or any one of them to such a degree of excellence as to arouse admiration, or to challenge comparison with those whom we honour in the past; such a man I have never had the good fortune to meet. The greatest man I have known in person – I mean for natural qualities of soul and noble disposition – was Étienne de la Boétie. His was a full mind indeed, which appeared beautiful from every point of view, a soul of the old stamp, which would have produced great deeds if his fortune had so willed, for he had added much to his rich nature by learning and study.

I do not know why it is, and yet it is undoubtedly the case that there is as much vanity and as little intelligence in those who lay claim to the highest abilities, and who follow learned pursuits and literary occupations, as in any other sort of people: whether it is because more is required and expected of them, and in them common faults cannot be excused; or perhaps because the opinion they have of their own learning emboldens them to display and obtrude themselves too far, with the result that they betray themselves and work their own undoing. Just as an artist reveals his lack of skill much more completely when working a rich material if he handles it in a muddled and stupid way, contrary to the rules of his craft, than when using a poor one; and as one is more shocked by a defect in a gold statue than in a plaster model; so is it with these men when they put forward ideas which would be good in themselves and in their proper place. For they serve them up without discretion, vaunting their memories at the expense of their intelligence; they honour Cicero, Galen, Ulpian, and St Jerome, but they make themselves ridiculous.

I readily relapse into my reflections on the uselessness of our education.* Its aim has been to make us not good and wise, but learned; and in this it has succeeded. It has not taught us to follow and embrace virtue and wisdom, but has imprinted their derivations and etymologies on our minds. We are able to decline *virtue*, even if we are unable to love it; if we do not know what wisdom is in fact and by experience, we are familiar with it as a jargon learned by heart. We are not content to know the origins, kindred, and alliances of our neighbours; we wish to be friends with them, and to enter into some relations and understanding with them. But our education has taught us the definitions, divisions, and subdivisions of virtue, as we know the surnames and branches of a family-tree, without taking the further trouble to put us on familiar and intimate terms with it. It has chosen for our instruction, not those books which contain the soundest and truest opinions, but those which speak the best Latin and Greek; and along with all its fine words has poured into our minds the idlest fancies of antiquity.

* See Book One, Chapter 26, 'On the education of children.'

A good education alters the judgement and character, as it did for Polemon, that dissolute young Greek, who went by chance to hear a lecture by Xenocrates. He was not only struck by the lecturer's eloquence and learning; he did not bring home only knowledge of some noble subject, but a more visible and substantial fruit, which was the sudden change and reformation of his former life. Who has ever been affected in this way by our education?

> *faciasne quod olim*
> *mutatus Polemon? ponas insignia morbi,*
> *fasciolas, cubital, focalia, potus ut ille*
> *dicitur ex collo furtim carpsisse coronas,*
> *postquam est impransi correptus voce magistri?**

The least contemptible sort of man seems to me to be one who, because of his simplicity, stands on the lowest rung; with him, I think, equable relations are most possible. I generally find the behaviour and conversation of peasants more accordant with the rules of true philosophy than those of philosophers. 'The common people are wiser because they are no wiser than they need to be.'† The most remarkable men, to judge by external appearances – for to judge them in my way, it would be necessary to see them in a closer light – have been, for the conduct of war and military qualities, the Duke of Guise, who died at Orléans, and the late Marshal Strozzi; and for great ability and uncommon virtue, Olivier and l'Hôpital, chancellors of France. Poetry too, in my opinion, has flourished in our times. We have had plenty of good workmen in this craft: Dorat, Bèze, Buchanan, l'Hôpital, Montdoré, and Turnebus.‡ As for writers in French, I think they have raised our poetry to the highest point that it will ever reach; and in those branches in which Ronsard and du Bellay excel, they seem to me scarcely to fall

---

* 'Will you do what Polemon did when reformed? Will you not put aside the tokens of your disease, the garters, the elbow-cushions, and the neck-cloths, as he is said to have slipped the wreaths from his neck, stealthily, after being reproached when drunk by a master who was fasting?' Horace, *Satires*, II, iii, 253.

† Lactantius, *The Divine Institutions*, III, v.

‡ All writers in Latin.

short of the ancients' perfection. Adrianus Turnebus knew more, and knew what he did know better than any man of his time, or long before his time.

The lives of the lately deceased Duke of Alva and of our Constable de Montmorency were noble lives, and in several respects their fortunes were strangely alike. But the beauty and glory of the latter's death, beneath the gaze of Paris and his king, fighting in their service against his closest kindred, at the head of an army victorious through his leadership, seems to me, coming as it did so suddenly in his extreme old age, to deserve a place among the most remarkable events of my time. The same may be said of the constant goodness, gentleness of character, and conscientious kindness of Monsieur de la Noue, amidst all the injustices of armed faction: a true school of treason, inhumanity, and brigandage, in which he had been brought up from birth. He was a great and most experienced soldier.

I have proclaimed with very great pleasure in several places the hopes I have of Marie de Gournay le Jars, my daughter by adoption, for whom I certainly feel much more than a paternal love and whom, in my solitary retreat, I cherish as one of the best parts of my own being. She is now my sole concern in the world. If youth can offer any predictions, her soul will one day be capable of the greatest achievements, among them perfection in that sacred bond of friendship, to which her sex has, according to what we have read, never yet attained. The sincerity and steadfastness of her character are quite sufficient for it, and her affection for me is more than superabundant. It is such, in fact, that it would leave nothing to be desired were she less cruelly exercised by fears of my death, since I was already 55 when we first met. The opinion that she formed of my first essays, though a woman of our times, and so young, and without friends in her district; and the remarkable strength of her love and desire to make my acquaintance, solely because of her admiration for me as their writer, before ever she saw my face; these are matters that deserve the highest consideration.

Other virtues have been little, if at all prized in this age. But bravery has become general through our civil wars, and we have among us souls that in this respect are steadfast to perfection, and so numerous that to choose among them is impossible.

These are all that I have met with up to now of extraordinary and uncommon greatness.

BOOK TWO: Chapter 28

All things have their season

THOSE who compare Cato the Censor with the younger Cato, who took his own life, compare two noble natures of kindred character. The former displayed his in more ways, and was the superior both in military exploits and the usefulness of his public services. But the Younger's virtue – apart from its being blasphemy to compare any other man's with it for strength – was far freer from blemish. For who could acquit the Censor of envy and ambition, in having dared to attack the honour of Scipio, a man far and away richer in goodness and all other finer qualities than he or any man of his time?

One of the stories told of him, that in extreme old age he set about learning Greek with the eagerness of one quenching a long thirst, does not seem to me much to his credit. It is really what we should call falling into a second childhood. All things have their season, the good as well as the rest, and I may say the Lord's Prayer at the wrong moment. T. Quintius Flaminius was blamed, indeed, for being seen to stand apart and waste his time praying to God, at the onset of a battle in which he commanded the victorious army:

*Imponit finem sapiens et rebus honestis.**

When Eudaemonidas saw Xenocrates, as a very old man busy over the lessons of his school, he asked: 'When will this man have knowledge, if he is still learning?' And Philopoemen remarked to those who were extolling King Ptolemy for toughening his body every day in the practice of arms: 'There is nothing praiseworthy in a king of his years taking such

* 'The wise man puts limits even to his good actions.' Juvenal, VI, 444.

exercise. Now he ought really to be using his weapons.'

The young should make the preparations, the old should enjoy the fruits, say the sages. And the greatest fault they observe in our nature is that our desires constantly renew their youth. We are always beginning our lives afresh. Our studies and ambitions ought sometimes to have a feeling of age. We have one foot in the grave, and our appetites and pursuits are only just born:

> Tu secanda marmora
> locas sub ipsum funus, et sepulchri
> immemor, struis domos.*

The most far-reaching of my plans have no more than a year in view; henceforth I think of nothing but an ending. I put aside all new hopes and enterprises, and take my last farewell of all the places I leave. Every day I dispossess myself of what I have. 'For a long time I have made no losses or gains. I have more than enough provisions for my journey.'†

> Vixi, et quem dederat cursum fortuna peregi.‡

It is indeed the only comfort I find in my old age, that it deadens in me many desires and preoccupations that are disturbers of life: care for how the world goes, care for riches, rank, knowledge, and health, and for myself. Here is a man learning to talk, when he should be learning to be silent for ever. One may always continue to study, but not to go to school. How ridiculous is an old man learning his A B C!

> Diversos diversa iuvant, non omnibus annis
> omnia conveniunt.§

If we must study, let us choose a subject suitable to our condition, so that we may answer like the man who, when asked why he was learning in his old age, replied: 'In order to leave

* 'You have marble cut when you are on the brink of death, and you build houses, forgetful of the tomb.' Horace, *Odes*, II, xviii, 17.

† Seneca, *Letters*, LXXVII.

‡ 'I have lived, and covered the course allotted me by fortune.' Virgil, *Aeneid*, IV, 653.

§ 'Different things please different men; not all things are appropriate to all ages.' Pseudo-Gallus, I, 104.

the world a better and more contented man.' This was the aim
of the younger Cato who, when he felt that his end was near,
turned to Plato's discourse on the eternity of the soul. It was
not, as we may well believe, because he had not, for a long time,
been furnished with all provisions for such a departure. He had
more confidence, resolution, and instruction than Plato has in
all his writings; his learning and courage were, in this respect,
superior to philosophy. He resorted to Plato to help him in his
death, but, like a man who does not allow the importance of
such a problem even to disturb his sleep, he continued his
studies, without choice or change, alongside the other habitual
actions of his life. The night that he was refused the praetorship
he spent in play; that on which he was to die, he spent in reading.
Loss of life or loss of office were all one to him.

BOOK TWO: Chapter 32

A defence of Seneca and Plutarch

MY familiarity with these great persons, and the help they
give to my old age,* and to my book, which is constructed
wholly of spoils taken from them, compel me to champion
their reputations.

As for Seneca, among the thousands of little books that those
of the so-called Reformed religion circulate in defence of their
cause – which sometimes proceed from such good hands that
it is a great pity they were not employed on a better subject – I
once saw one in which, to extend and amplify the parallel which
the writer was pleased to see between the government of our
poor late king Charles IX and that of Nero, he compared the
dead Cardinal of Lorraine to Seneca; in their fortunes, in that
they were both heads of their prince's governments, and also
in their characters, their situations, and their conduct. Here, in
my opinion, he does the said Cardinal very great honour. For
though I am one of those who think most highly of his intelligence, his eloquence, his zeal for his religion and the service of

* Montaigne was not 46 yet when he wrote this.

his king, and his good fortune in being born at a time when it was so novel and rare a thing, as well as so necessary for the public good, to have an ecclesiastic of his high birth and dignity able and competent to exercise such an office, yet, to confess the truth, I do not reckon his capacity as nearly equal to Seneca's, or his virtue so strong and pure, or so solid.

Now this book I am speaking of, to justify its case, gives a most damaging description of Seneca, borrowing its strictures from the historian Dion, in whose testimony I put no trust whatever. For apart from his inconsistency – in some places he calls Seneca very wise, and again a mortal enemy to Nero's vices, but elsewhere makes him out to be avaricious, usurious, ambitious, cowardly, sensual, and a false pretender to the title of philosopher – Seneca's virtues appear so lively and vigorous in his writings, and his defence against some of these imputations – those of wealth and lavish expenditure for instance – is there so clear, that I would accept no evidence to the contrary. Besides, it is much more reasonable, in such matters, to believe the Roman historians than Greeks and foreigners. Now Tacitus and the others speak very honourably of his life and death, and portray him as in every way a most excellent and virtuous person. And I will level no other reproach against Dion's judgement than this, which is irrefutable: that his views on Roman affairs are so unsound that he dares to defend Julius Caesar's cause against Pompey's, and Antony's against Cicero's.

Let us turn to Plutarch. Jean Bodin is a good author of our day, endowed with much more judgement than the crowd of contemporary scribblers, and he therefore deserves attentive consideration. I find him somewhat bold in that passage of his *Guide to History*,* in which he not only accuses Plutarch of ignorance – on which I should have let him have his say, since it is outside my scope – but also remarks that this author often writes 'things incredible and entirely fabulous' – these are his words. If he had simply said 'things otherwise than they are', it would have been no great reproach; for what we have not

* His *Methodus ad facilem historiarum cognitionem,* already referred to in Chapter 10.

A DEFENCE OF SENECA AND PLUTARCH

seen, we accept on trust from others, and I observe that Plutarch sometimes knowingly reports different versions of the same story; as, for instance, Hannibal's opinion as to the three greatest generals that ever lived, which he gives in one way in his Life of Flaminius, and in another in that of Pyrrhus. But to accuse him of having taken incredible and impossible things for current coin is to accuse the most judicious author in the world of lack of judgement.

As his example Bodin quotes the tale that Plutarch tells about the Lacedaemonian boy who let all his bowels be torn out by a fox-cub he had stolen, and kept it hidden under his clothes till he fell down dead, rather than betray his theft. In the first place, I find the example ill-chosen, inasmuch as it is very difficult to define the power of the mental faculties, whereas in the case of the physical powers we have far more right to assume how far they will go. And for this reason, if I had been in his place I would rather have chosen an example of this second kind; and here Plutarch selects some that are even less credible, as for instance the story he tells of Pyrrhus, that 'wounded as he was, he dealt one of the enemy, who was armed at all points, so great a stroke that he cleft him from his head to his seat, leaving his body divided into two parts.'

In Bodin's example I see no great miracle, nor do I admit the excuse with which he shields Plutarch, that he added the words 'as it was told', as a warning to us that we must put a curb on our credulity. For except in matters received on authority, or out of reverence for antiquity or religion, Plutarch would never have been willing himself to accept, or to ask us to believe, things intrinsically incredible. And it can easily be seen that here he is not using the words 'as it is told' for that purpose, for he tells us elsewhere, in connexion with the endurance of Spartan boys, of contemporary examples which are much harder to believe; the one, for instance, to which Cicero testified before him – as having been, so he said, on the spot – that down to their own time there were boys who, in a test of endurance to which they were subjected before Diana's altar, allowed themselves to be whipped till the blood ran all over their bodies, not only without crying out, but without even groaning, and some to the point of voluntarily giving up their lives.

There is the tale too that Plutarch relates, with a hundred other witnesses, that when, at a sacrifice, a burning coal fell into the sleeve of a Lacedaemonian boy, as he was serving the incense, he allowed his whole arm to be burned until the smell of scorching flesh was noticed by the bystanders.

Now by their customs, there was nothing that so much affected the reputation, or which would cause a lad to be so blamed and despised, as to be caught in the act of theft. Not only does Plutarch's story not seem incredible to me therefore, as it does to Bodin, but so convinced am I of this people's greatness that I do not even find it rare and strange. Spartan history is full of countless crueller and stranger examples; in this respect it is all miracle.

Marcellinus* reports, on this subject of theft, that in his day no torture had yet been discovered that could compel an Egyptian caught in the act, which was very common among them, to confess so much as his name.

A Spanish peasant, who was racked to make him betray the names of his accomplices in the murder of the praetor, Lucius Piso, cried out in the midst of the torture that his friends need not stir, but could look on in perfect security, for pain had no power to wrest a word of confession from him. And that was all they could get on the first day. On the next, as they were leading him back to resume the torture, he tore himself violently from the hands of his guards, and dashed his head against a wall, thus killing himself. Epicharis, having satiated and exhausted the cruelty of Nero's henchmen, by enduring their fire, their beatings, and their instruments for a whole day, without betraying her conspiracy even by a word, on the next day, as she was being carried to the torture with all her limbs broken, slipped one of the laces of her gown over the arm of her chair in a running knot and, thrusting her head into it, strangled herself by the weight of her body. Since she had the courage to die like

* Ammianus Marcellinus, 330–c. 390, author of a history of the Roman Empire.

this, and so could have avoided her previous tortures, does it not seem as if she deliberately submitted herself to this test of her endurance in order to mock the tyrant and encourage others to make similar attempts against his life?

And if anyone asks our musketeers for their experiences in these civil wars, he will be told of acts of endurance, persistence, and stubbornness in this miserable age of ours, and among this rabble that is even softer and more effeminate than the Egyptians, which will bear comparison with those we have just related of Spartan courage.

There have been, to my knowledge, simple peasants who have allowed the soles of their feet to be scorched, their finger-ends to be crushed with the hammer of a pistol, and their bleeding eyes to be squeezed out of their heads by a thick cord twisted round their foreheads, before they would so much as agree to a ransom. I have seen one left for dead, stark naked in a ditch, with his neck all bruised and swollen by a halter that still hung round it, with which he had been dragged all night at a horse's tail. His body had been wounded in a hundred places by dagger-blows, which had been dealt him, not to kill him, but to cause him pain and terror. But he had endured all this, even to the point of losing speech and consciousness, resolved, as he told me, to die a thousand deaths – and, indeed, so far as suffering goes, he had already died one – rather than make any promise; and yet he was one of the richest farmers in the whole district. How many have been seen patiently suffering themselves to be burnt and roasted for opinions borrowed from others, of which they had neither knowledge nor understanding!

I have known hundreds of women – for they say that Gascon heads have a certain prerogative in this – who would rather bite into red-hot iron than abandon an opinion that they had conceived in anger. Blows and constraint only make them wilder. And whoever made up the story of the women whom no threats or beatings could persuade to stop calling her husband 'lousy', devised an example of women's obstinacy that we can see repeated every day. All correction was in vain; when plunged into a pond, she raised her hands above her head even as she was drowning, and made the gesture of cracking lice. And obstinacy is sister to constancy, at least in its strength and firmness.

We must not decide what is possible and what is not, as I have said elsewhere,* by what is credible or incredible to our senses. It is a great fault, into which, however, most men fall – I do not apply this to Bodin – to have difficulty in crediting others with what they could not – or would not – do themselves. Everyone thinks himself the master pattern of human nature; and by this, as on a touchstone, he tests all others. Behaviour that does not square with his is false and artificial. What brutish stupidity! For my part, I consider some men, particularly among the ancients, greatly superior to me; and though I clearly recognize my inability to follow in their footsteps, still I follow them with my eyes, and observe the force that lifts them so high. I detect some seeds of it in myself, as I do also of an extreme spiritual baseness, which I find neither astonishing nor incredible. I clearly see to what contrivances these others resort in order to ascend, and I admire them for their greatness. I understand those upward flights that I find so beautiful; and if my strength does not reach to them, at least my mind most gladly applies itself to them.

The other example adduced by Bodin of things related to Plutarch which were incredible and wholly fabulous is that Agesilaus was fined by the Ephors for having drawn the hearts and goodwill of his fellow-citizens to himself alone. I do not know what mark of falsehood he finds in that. Now surely Plutarch is here speaking of things that must have been much better known to him than to us; and it was no new thing in Greece to see men punished and exiled solely for being too popular with their fellow-citizens, as witness ostracism and petalism.†

There is also in this same book another accusation which

* See Book One, Chapter 27, 'That it is folly to measure truth and error by our own capacity.'

† Forms of banishment at Athens and at Syracuse; in the former the exile's name was written on a potsherd, in the latter on an olive leaf.

annoys me on Plutarch's behalf. Bodin says that he was fair in his parallels between Roman and Roman, and between Greek and Greek, but not in those between Roman and Greek, and he cites as evidence the cases of Demosthenes and Cicero, Cato and Aristides, Sulla and Lysander, Marcellus and Pelopidas, Pompey and Agesilaus, claiming that Plutarch favoured the Greeks by giving them such unequal companions. This is really to attack the most excellent and commendable thing in Plutarch. For in his parallels – which are the most admirable part of his works and, in my opinion, the part in which he took most pleasure – the truth and sincerity of his judgements are equal to their depth and weight. He is a philosopher who teaches us virtue. Let us see if we cannot defend him from this reproach of prevarication and falsity.

What I think may have given occasion to this censure is the great and dazzling brilliance which falls on the Roman names in our imagination. It seems to us unlikely that Demosthenes could be equal in glory to one who was a consul, proconsul, and quaestor of that great Republic. But if, as was Plutarch's principal aim, one considers the truth of the matter, and the men in themselves, and weighs up their characters, their natures, and their abilities rather than their fortunes, I think, contrary to Bodin, that Cicero and Cato the elder fall short of the men to whom Plutarch compares them. In Bodin's place I should have taken as my example the comparison between Cato the younger and Phocion; for in this couple there would have been a more plausible disparity in favour of the Roman. As for Marcellus, Sulla, and Pompey, I clearly see that their martial exploits are greater, grander, and more glorious than those of the Greeks beside whom Plutarch places them. But, in war as elsewhere, the noblest and bravest actions are not always the most famous. I often see the names of commanders eclipsed by the brightness of less meritorious names; witness Labienus, Ventidius, Telesinus, and many others.

Looking at it from Bodin's point of view, if I had to complain on behalf of the Greeks, could I not say that Camillus is no fair match for Themistocles, or the Gracchi for Agis and

Cleomenes, or Numa for Lycurgus? But it is folly to attempt with one stroke of the pen to pronounce on things that have so many aspects. When Plutarch makes a comparison, he does not, on that account, put his two characters on an equality. Who could set down their differences more eloquently and conscientiously? When he comes to compare the victories, the martial exploits, the military strength, and the triumphs of Pompey with those of Agesilaus, he says: 'I do not believe that Xenophon himself, were he living, though allowed to write whatever he liked to Agesilaus's advantage, would dare to institute a comparison.' On the subject of Lysander and Sulla also, he observes: 'There is no comparison either in the number of victories or in hazards of war; for Lysander won only two naval battles, etc.'

This is to steal no glory from the Romans; by simply putting them beside the Greeks, he can have done them no wrong, whatever the disparity may have been. And Plutarch does not weigh them up as a whole; he shows no general preference. He compares details and circumstances, one after another, and judges them separately. Therefore, should we wish to convict him of partiality, we should have to pick some particular judgement to pieces, or to say broadly that he was wrong in matching a certain Greek with a certain Roman, because there were others who could more suitably have been compared with him, and who resembled him more closely.

BOOK THREE

BOOK THREE: Chapter 2

On repentance

OTHERS shape the man; I portray him, and offer to the view one in particular, who is ill-shaped enough, and whom, could I refashion him, I should certainly make very different from what he is. But there is no chance of that.

Now the lines of my portrait are never at fault, although they change and vary. The world is but a perpetual see-saw. Everything goes incessantly up and down – the earth, the rocks of Caucasus, the pyramids of Egypt – both with the universal motion and with their own. Constancy itself is nothing but a more sluggish movement. I cannot fix my subject. He is always restless, and reels with a natural intoxication. I catch him here, as he is at the moment when I turn my attention to him. I do not portray his being; I portray his passage; not a passage from one age to another or, as the common people say, from seven years to seven years, but from day to day, from minute to minute. I must suit my story to the hour, for soon I may change, not only by chance but also by intention. It is a record of various and variable occurrences, an account of thoughts that are unsettled and, as chance will have it, at times contradictory, either because I am then another self, or because I approach my subject under different circumstances and with other considerations. Hence it is that I may well contradict myself, but the truth, as Demades said, I do not contradict. Could my mind find a firm footing, I should not be making essays, but coming to conclusions; it is, however, always in its apprenticeship and on trial.

I present a humble life, without distinction; but that is no matter. Moral philosophy, as a whole, can be just as well applied to a common and private existence as to one of richer stuff. Every man carries in himself the complete pattern of human nature.

Authors communicate with the world in some special and peculiar capacity; I am the first to do so with my whole being, as Michel de Montaigne, not as a grammarian, a poet, or a lawyer. If people complain that I speak too much of myself, I complain that they do not think of themselves at all.

But is it reasonable that, being so private in my way of life, I should set out to make myself known to the public? Is it reasonable either that I should present to the world, in which style and artifice receive so much credit and authority, the crude and simple products of nature, and of a weakish nature at that? Is it not like building a wall without stone or some similar material, to construct books without learning or art? Musical compositions are the product of skill, mine of chance.

To this extent, at least, I have conformed to the rules: that no man ever came to a project with better knowledge and understanding than I have of this matter, in regard to which I am the most learned man alive; and secondly that no man ever went more deeply into his subject, or more thoroughly examined its elements and effects, or more exactly and completely achieved the purpose he set out to work for. To perfect it I need only bring fidelity to my task; and that is here, the purest and sincerest that is to be found anywhere. I speak the truth, not to the full, but as much as I dare; and as I grow older I become a little more daring, for custom seems to allow age greater freedom to be garrulous and indiscreet in speaking of itself. It cannot happen here, as I often see it elsewhere, that the craftsman and his work are in contradiction. Can a man so sensible in his conversation, they ask, have written so foolish a book? Or can such learned writings proceed from one so poor in conversation?

If a man's talk is commonplace and his writing distinguished, it means that his talent lies in the place from which he borrows, and not in himself. A learned person is not learned in all things, but a man of talent is accomplished in every respect, even in his ignorance.

Here my book and I proceed in agreement, and at the same pace. In other cases, the work may be praised or blamed apart from the workman; but here it cannot be. Who touches one, touches the other. The reader who passes judgement on the book without knowing the man will do himself more wrong than he does me. But anyone who comes to know the man will give me complete satisfaction. It will be more than I deserve if I win only so much public approbation as to make intelligent men realize that I could have profited by learning, had I possessed it, and that I deserved better assistance from my memory.

Let me here excuse myself for saying what I often repeat, that I rarely repent, and that my conscience is content with itself, not as the conscience of an angel or a horse, but as the conscience of a man; though always with the addition of this refrain – which is no formal refrain but a true and sincere confession – that I speak as one who questions and does not know, referring the decision purely and simply to common and authorized belief. I do not teach, I relate.

There is no vice that is absolutely a vice which does not offend, and which is not detected by a sound judgement. For its ugliness and impropriety are so apparent that those who say it arises chiefly from stupidity and ignorance are probably in the right; so hard is it to imagine that a man could recognize it without loathing. Malice sucks up the greater part of its venom, and so poisons itself. Vice leaves in the soul, like an ulcer in the flesh, a remorse which is always scratching itself and drawing blood. For reason obliterates other grief or sorrow, but it engenders that of remorse, which is harder to bear because it springs from within, as the cold and heat of fever are sharper than those in the outer air. I regard as vices – but each in its degree – not only those that reason and nature condemn, but those that are the creation of human opinion, false and erroneous though it may be, so long as they are confirmed as such by law and custom.

There is likewise no goodness in which a noble nature does

237

not delight. There is indeed a certain sense of gratification when we do a good deed that gives us inward satisfaction, and a generous pride that accompanies a good conscience. A resolutely wicked soul may perhaps arm itself with some assurance, but it cannot provide itself with this contentment and satisfaction. It is no slight pleasure to feel oneself preserved from the contagion of so corrupt an age, and to say to oneself: 'A man might look into my very soul, and yet he would not find me guilty of anyone's affliction or ruin, or of revenge or envy, or of offending against the public laws, or of innovation and disturbance, or of failing to keep my word. And whatever the licence of the age may permit or suggest to any man, I have never laid my hands on any Frenchman's goods, or put my fingers into his purse. I have lived only on what is my own, in war as in peace, and have never used another man's labour without paying him.' These testimonies of a good conscience are pleasant; and such a natural pleasure is very beneficial to us; it is the only payment that can never fail.

To base the reward for virtuous actions on other men's approval is to rely on too uncertain and shaky a foundation. Especially in so corrupt and ignorant an age as this, the good opinion of the crowd is injurious. Whom are you trusting to see what is praiseworthy? God preserve me from being an honest man according to the criterion that I daily see every man apply to himself, to his own advantage! 'What were once vices have now become customs.'*

Some of my friends have at times taken it upon themselves to school and lecture me most outspokenly, either of their own accord or at my invitation: a service which, to a healthy mind, surpasses, not only in utility but in kindness, every other office of friendship. I have always welcomed it with the most open arms both of courtesy and gratitude. But to speak of it now in all honesty, I have often found both in their blame and their praise so much false measure that I should not have been much amiss if I had done what according to their notions was wrong, instead of what they considered right. Those of us, especially,

* Seneca, *Letters*, xxxix.

who live retired lives, exposed only to our own gaze, should have a fixed pattern within us by which to test our actions and, according to this, sometimes hug and sometimes correct ourselves. I have my own laws and my own court to judge me, and I refer to these rather than elsewhere. I certainly restrain my actions out of deference to others, but I understand them only by my own light. None but you know whether you are cruel and cowardly, or loyal and dutiful. Others have no vision of you, but judge of you by uncertain conjectures; they see not so much your nature as your artifices. Do not rely on their opinions, therefore; rely on your own. 'You must use your own judgement about yourself.'* 'The inner conscience of virtue and vice exercises a great influence; take that away, and all is in ruins.'†

But the saying that repentance follows close on sin does not seem to apply to sin in all its array, when it lodges in us as if in its own home. We may disown and reject vices which take us by surprise, and into which we are impelled by our passions; but those which by long habit are rooted and anchored in a strong and vigorous will are not prone to be gainsaid. Repentance is simply a recanting of our will and an opposition to our fancies; it may shift us in any direction. It makes one man disavow his past virtue and continence:

> *Quae mens est hodie, cur eadem non puero fuit?*
> *vel cur his animis incolumes non redeunt genae?*‡

It is a rare life that remains orderly even in private. Everyone can play his part in the farce, and act an honest role on the stage. But to be disciplined within, in one's own breast, where all is permissible and all is concealed – that is the point! The next step, therefore, is to be orderly at home, in our common actions, for which we are accountable to no man, and in which there is no study or artifice. That is why Bias, describing an ideal household,§ says that it is one where the master is the

* Cicero, *Tusculans*, I, xxiii.
† Cicero, *De Natura Deorum*, III, xxxv.
‡ 'Why was my mind when a boy not the same as it is today? Or why, with my present mind, do my cheeks not become fresh as of old?' Horace, *Odes*, IV, x, 7. § See Plutarch, *Banquet of the Seven Sages*.

same alone in his house as abroad, where he is afraid of the law
and of what men will say. And it was a worthy answer that
Julius Drusus gave to the builders who offered for three thousand crowns so to alter his mansion that his neighbours could
no longer overlook him, as they then did. 'I will give you six
thousand,' he said, 'if you will make it possible for everyone
to see into it from every side.' It is observed to the honour of
Agesilaus that, when travelling, he would take up his lodgings
in temples, so that the people, and the gods themselves, might
witness his private actions. Many a man has been a wonder
to the world, whose wife and valet have seen nothing in him
that was even remarkable. Few have been admired by their servants.

No man was ever a prophet, not merely in his own house,
but in his own country, says the experience of history. It is the
same in trivial matters. And in this humble example you may
see a reflection of greater ones. In my region of Gascony, they
think it funny to see me in print. But the further from my own
haunts my reputation spreads, the higher I am rated. In Guienne
I pay the printers; elsewhere they pay me. It is on this accident
that men rely who conceal themselves whilst they are alive and
present, to gain a name when they are dead and gone. I am less
ambitious; I cast myself upon the world, solely for my present
advantage. When I leave it – that is that!

See, after a public function, how the admiring crowd escorts
a man to his door; with his robe he drops his part, and falls as
low as his ascent was high. Within himself, all is baseness and
confusion. Even if there were some order in him, it would take
a keen and perspicacious mind to perceive it in his humble and
private actions. Moreover, discipline is a dull and dismal virtue.
To storm a breach, conduct an embassy, govern a people, those
are brilliant actions. To scold, laugh, sell, pay, love, hate, and
deal gently and justly with one's family and oneself, not to
relax or contradict oneself: that is something rarer, more difficult and less noticed by the world. A life of retirement, therefore, whatever men may say, is subject to duties as harsh and
exacting as any other, if not more so. And private persons, says

Aristotle, do virtue a higher and more difficult service than men in authority. We prepare ourselves to meet outstanding occasions rather for glory than for conscience' sake. The shortest way to gain a great name, however, would be to do for conscience' sake what we now do for glory. And Alexander's virtue seems to me to show somewhat less strength on his great stage than that of Socrates in his humble and obscure activities. I can easily imagine Socrates in Alexander's place, but Alexander in that of Socrates, I cannot. If Alexander were asked what he could do, he would reply, 'Conquer the world'; but if the same question were put to Socrates, his answer would be, 'Lead a man's life according to its natural conditions': a much more general, more important, and more legitimate undertaking.

The worth of a soul does not consist in soaring to a height, but in a steady movement. Its greatness is not exercised in a mighty, but in an intermediate state. As those who judge and test our inner being attach no great importance to the brilliance of our public acts, and see that these are no more than jets and beads of clear water spurting from an otherwise thick and muddy bottom; so, under similar circumstances, those who judge us by our brave outward show come to a like conclusion about our inner character. They cannot reconcile common faculties, just like their own, with these other faculties, which astound them and are so far beyond their vision.

Therefore we endow demons with monstrous shapes. And who does not picture Tamburlaine with arched brows, open nostrils, a grim visage, and a prodigious stature, in accordance with the picture that the imagination has conceived of him from the report of his fame? If, years ago, I had been taken to see Erasmus, it would have been hard for me not to take as precepts and maxims every word that he said to his servant or his landlady. It suits our imagination better to think of a craftsman on the close-stool or on top of his wife, than of a Chief Justice, venerable for his bearing and his talents, in the same position. From such high thrones, it seems to us, men do not descend so low as to live.

As wicked souls are often driven by some external impulse to perform a good deed, so are virtuous souls to do wrong. They must be judged, therefore, by their settled state, when they are at home, supposing that they are sometimes there; or at least when they are nearest to repose and to their true situation. Natural inclinations are assisted and reinforced by education, but they are hardly ever altered or overcome. In my time, a bare thousand natures have escaped to virtue or to vice from a contrary education.

> *Sic ubi desuetae silvis in carcere clausae*
> *mansuevere ferae, et vultus posuere minaces,*
> *atque hominem didicere pati, si torrida parvus*
> *venit in ora cruor, redeunt rabiesque furorque,*
> *admonitaeque tument gustato sanguine fauces;*
> *fervet, et a trepido vix abstinet ira magistro.**

These original qualities are not to be extirpated; they are covered up, they are concealed. Latin is to me, as it were, my natural language; I understand it better than French. But for the last forty years I have had no practice in speaking or writing it. And yet on the two or three occasions in my life when I have been overwhelmed by extreme and sudden emotion – once when I saw my father, though in perfect health, fall towards me in a faint – the first words that have risen from the depths of my heart have always been in Latin. Nature has surged up and forcibly expressed herself, in spite of long disuse. And the same is said to have happened to many others.

Those who, in my time, have attempted to correct the morals of the world by new ideas, have reformed the surface vices; but the essential ones they have left unaffected, if not increased; and here one must fear an increase. We are apt to refrain from all other good deeds on the strength of these arbitrary and external improvements, which are less costly and earn greater honour. And by this means we beg a cheap exemption for our other

---

* 'So wild beasts in captivity may forget their forests, grow tame, lose their fierce habits, and learn to endure the control of man. But if a little blood touches their hot lips, their rage and ferocity return. Roused by the taste of blood, their jaws distend, and they hardly refrain from springing on their frightened master.' Lucan, IV, 237.

vices, natural, consubstantial, and internal. Consider for a moment how our experience of the matter stands. There is no man who, if he listens to himself, does not discover within him an individual principle, a ruling principle, that struggles against his education, and against the tempestuous passions opposing it. For my part, I am seldom roused by sudden impulses; I find myself, like some heavy and cumbrous body, almost always in my place. If I am not at home, I am always very near. My excesses do not carry me far away. There is nothing extreme or odd about them. And I have strong and vigorous revulsions.

The true reproach, the one which applies to the common run of men, is that their very retraction is full of filth and corruption; their idea of reformation is blurred; their penitence is almost as faulty and diseased as their sin. Some are so wedded to vice by a natural bond, or from long habit, that they can no longer see its ugliness. Others, in whose ranks I belong, feel sin to be a burden, but counterbalance it with pleasure, or something else; they suffer it and give way to it for a certain price; but wickedly and basely, nevertheless. Yet it might perhaps be possible to imagine such a disproportion between the pleasure and the sin that the first might justly be said to excuse the second, as we say utility does; and this not only if the pleasure were accidental, and apart from it, as in theft, but also if it lay in the very commission of the sin, as in intercourse with women, where the provocation is violent and, so they say, sometimes irresistible.

The other day, when I was on the estate of a kinsman of mine in Armagnac, I saw a peasant whom everybody called *The Thief*. He told us his story, which was like this: Born a beggar, and realizing that if he were to earn his living by the work of his hands, he would never succeed in securing himself against want, he decided to become a thief; and thanks to his physical strength, he practised his trade quite safely throughout his youth. He gathered his harvest and his vintage from other men's lands, but at such great distances and in such great stacks that no one could conceive how one man could carry away so much on his shoulders in a single night. And he took care, besides, to equalize and distribute the damage that he caused, so as to minimize the loss to each individual. Now, in his old age, he is rich for a man of his condition, thanks to his trade, which he openly confesses. And to reconcile God to his winnings, he has made it, he said, his daily task to compensate the heirs of the men he robbed by voluntary gifts. If he does not complete his task – for to do it all at once is beyond him – he will, he says, leave it as a charge to his heirs, to repay them according to the wrong he did to each, which is known to him alone. From his account, whether true or false, it seems that this man regards theft as a dishonest action, and hates it, though less than he hates poverty. He repents of it quite simply, but in so far as it was thus counterbalanced and compensated, he does not repent of it. This is not a case in which habit makes us one with our sin, and even conforms our understanding to it; nor is it a case of an impetuous gale whose gusts confuse and blind our souls, flinging us for the moment, judgement and all, into the power of vice.

Habitually, I do what I do with all my being, and keep step with myself; I seldom do anything that hides from and escapes my reason, and that is not guided more or less by the concurrence of all my faculties, without division and without internal rebellion. My judgement takes all the blame or all the praise for my actions. And once it takes the blame, it keeps it for good; for it has been the same almost since birth, with the same character, the same inclinations, the same strength. And in the matter of general opinions, I established myself in my youth in the position where I was to stay.

Some sins are impulsive, hasty, and sudden: let us leave them aside. But as regards those other sins which are so often repeated, meditated, and considered, whether they are temperamental sins, or arise from our profession and vocation, I cannot imagine their being implanted for so long in one and the same heart, unless the reason and conscience of the man who harbours them constantly wills them and intends them to be there. And I find it somewhat hard to call up a picture of that repentance which, according to this thief's boast, comes on him at a certain prescribed moment.

I do not agree with the Pythagorean sect, that men take on a new soul when they approach the images of the gods, to receive their oracles. Unless what he meant to say was that it must be a strange, new soul, borrowed for the occasion, since their own show so little sign of the purification and cleansing needed for this ceremony.

The actions of these habitual sinners are quite contrary to the precepts of the Stoics, which command us to correct the imperfections and vices that we recognize in ourselves, but forbid us to be troubled and disturbed by them. They give us to believe that they feel great inward grief and remorse: but of amendment and correction, or of ceasing to sin, they show us no sign. Yet if the disease is not thrown off there is no cure. If repentance were laid on one dish of the scales it would outweigh the sin. I know of no quality so easy to counterfeit as godliness, when the life and morals do not conform to it. Its essence is abstruse and secret; its externals are easy and ostentatious.

For myself, I may wish, on the whole, to be otherwise; I may condemn and dislike my general character, and implore God to reform me throughout, and to excuse my natural weakness. But I should not, I think, give the name of repentance to this, any more than I should to my dissatisfaction at not being an angel or a Cato. My actions are controlled and shaped to what I am, and to my condition of life. I can do no better. And repentance does not properly apply to things that are not in our power, though regret certainly does. I can imagine numberless loftier and better disciplined natures than mine; but this does not make me amend my character, any more than my arm or my mind grows stronger by my conceiving some other man's to be so. If to imagine and desire a nobler way of conduct than ours were to make us repent of our own, we should have to repent of our most innocent actions, in as much as we may rightly suppose that a more excellent nature would have performed them more perfectly and with more nobility; and we should wish to do likewise.

When I look back on the conduct of my youth, I find that I generally behaved in an orderly manner, according to my lights;

that is as much as my powers of control can manage. I do not flatter myself; in similar circumstances I should always be the same. It is not a single spot, but rather a general stain that dyes me. I know of no superficial, middling, or formal repentance. It must touch me in every part before I can call it so. It must pierce my bowels and pain them as deeply and as completely as God sees into me.

As for business, many good chances have escaped me for lack of good management. Yet my plans have been well-chosen, according to the opportunities that I had, my habit being always to take the easiest and safest course. I find that in my past decisions I have, by my own rules, acted wisely, taking into account the state of the matter confronting me; and I should do the same a thousand years hence in the same situations. I am not thinking of conditions as they are at present, but as they were when I was considering them.

The importance of any decision depends on the hour; circumstances and things are always moving and changing. I have committed some serious and grievous errors in my life, not for lack of good judgement but for lack of good fortune. In what we have to deal with, there are hidden elements, at which we cannot guess, particularly in human nature: silent states that make no show and are sometimes unknown to their very possessors, but that are roused and brought out by circumstances as they arise. If my foresight has been unable to fathom and predict them, I have no complaint against it; its functions are limited. If the event goes against me; and if it favours the side I have rejected, there is no remedy. I do not reproach myself for this; I blame my fortune, not my performance; and this cannot be called repentance.

Phocion had given the Athenians some advice which was not followed. When, however, contrary to his expectation, the affair turned out happily, someone said to him: 'Tell me, Phocion, are you glad things are going so well?' 'Yes, I am very glad things have turned out like this,' he answered, 'but I am not sorry that I gave the advice I did.' When my friends come to me for an opinion, I give it freely and frankly, without being deterred, as most people are, by the fact that, the matter being risky, it may turn out contrary to my expectations, and I may then be blamed for my advice. That does not trouble me in the least. For though they will prove to be wrong, I should not have been right to refuse them the service.

I have generally only myself to blame for my errors or mishaps. For, as a matter of fact, I rarely ask others for advice, except out of formal courtesy, unless I have need of learned instruction or factual knowledge. In matters where I have only to exercise my judgement, others' opinions may serve me as confirmation, but do not often deter me. I listen to them all politely and gravely; but I do not remember ever, to this day, having trusted any but my own. In my view they are just flies and specks that distract my will. I do not much value my own opinions, but I value those of others no more. Fortune pays me as I deserve. If I take no advice, I give still less. I am very seldom consulted, and even more seldom heeded; and I know of no undertaking, public or private, that my advice has advanced and improved. Even those who, by chance, have come to depend on it, have in the end preferred to be guided by any other brain than mine. And as one who is quite as jealous of his right to leisure as of his right to authority, I would rather have it so. By leaving me alone, they follow my declared wish, which is to be wholly self-reliant and self-contained. It pleases me not to be interested in the affairs of others, and to be free from responsibility for them.

Once any business is over, I have few regrets, whatever the result. For my grief is soothed by the reflection that things were bound to happen as they did. I see them as part of the great stream of the universe, in the Stoics' chain of cause and effect. Your mind cannot, by wish or thought, alter the smallest part without upsetting the whole order of things, both past and future.

Moreover, I hate that repentance which is incidental to old age. I do not agree with that man of old* who said that he was grateful to the years for having rid him of sensuality; I can never

* A saying attributed to Sophocles in Plato's *Republic*.

give thanks to impotence for any good it may do me. 'Providence will never appear so hostile to its own work that weakness will rank among the blessings.'* Our passions are rare in old age; and a deep satiety overcomes us after the act. I can see no sign of conscience in that. Vexation and weakness impose a sluggish rheumatic virtue upon us. We must not let ourselves be so wholly carried away by our natural changes as to let them warp our judgement. Youth and pleasure did not prevent me, of old, from recognizing in sensuality the face of vice; nor does the distaste which the years have brought me make me fail to see in vice the face of sensuality. Now that I am no longer in it, I judge it as if I were. When I give my mind a jolt and observe it, I find that it is the same as it was in my most licentious days, except, perhaps, that it has weakened and deteriorated as it has grown old. And I find that though it refuses to embroil me in these pleasures out of regard for my physical health, it would be no more likely than it was of old to do so for my spiritual good. I do not regard it as more valiant for being out of the battle. My temptations are so broken and mortified that they are not worth a fight. By merely stretching out my hands, I exorcize them. But should my reason be faced again with my old lust, I am afraid it would have less strength of resistance than it had of old. I do not see that of itself it judges otherwise than it did then; nor that it has received any new light. Therefore, if there is an improvement, it is a sickly one. It is a poor kind of remedy, to owe one's health to a disease!

It is not the business of our misfortunes to work us a remedy; a sound judgement must do that. Ills and afflictions cannot make me do more than curse them; they are good enough for people who can only be roused by the whip. My mind runs a freer course in prosperity. It is much more distracted and occupied when digesting pains than pleasures. I see much more clearly in fine weather. Health gives me more cheerful and more effective admonishment than sickness. I came as near as is possible for me to a reformed and disciplined life when I had the health to enjoy it. I should be angry and ashamed if my sad and

* Quintilian, v, xii, 19.

wretched decrepitude should seem preferable to my good healthy, active, and vigorous years. I should hate to be valued not for what I have been, but for what I have ceased to be.

In my opinion it is in a happy life, not, as Antisthenes said, in a happy death, that human felicity consists. I never looked forward to becoming that monstrosity, a philosopher's tail tied to the head and body of a libertine; nor to having this miserable remainder renounce and belie the fairest, fullest, and longest part of my life. I wish to present and exhibit myself uniformly, in every part. If I had my life to live again, I should live as I have lived; I neither deplore the past, nor fear the future. And if I am not mistaken, I have been much the same inwardly as on the surface. One of my principal debts to fortune is that the course of my physical life has brought each thing in its season. I have seen the leaves and the flowers and the fruit; and now I see the withering. And this is fortunate because it is natural. I bear the infirmities that I suffer much more patiently because they have come at the proper time, and also because they make me remember more kindly the long happiness of my past life. So also my wisdom may well be of the same proportions now as in former years. But it was more capable and attractive when it was fresh, gay, and natural than it is in its present worn, peevish, and heavy condition. I will have nothing to do, therefore, with these fortuitous and tearful reformations.

God must touch our hearts. Our conscience must amend itself by the strengthening of our reason, not by the weakening of our appetites. Sensual pleasures are neither pale nor colourless in themselves because they seem so to dull and bleary eyes. Temperance should be loved for its own sake, and out of reverence for God, who has enjoined both it and chastity upon us; what chills impose on us, and what I owe to the good offices of my colic, is neither chastity nor temperance. One cannot boast of despising and combating sensual desires if one does not see them, if one does not know them, their charms, their power, and their most alluring beauty. I know it all, and have the right to speak. But it seems to me that in old age our souls are subject to more troublesome ailments and weaknesses than in youth. I said this when I was young, and they scoffed at me for my beardless chin. I repeat it now that my grey hairs give me authority. We call the queasiness of our tastes and our dislike of present-day things by the name of wisdom. But the truth is that we do not so much give up our vices as change them, and in my opinion for the worse. Besides a foolish and tottering pride, a tedious garrulity, prickly and unsociable moods, superstition, and an absurd preoccupation with money after we have lost the use for it, I find in old age an increase of envy, injustice, and malice. It stamps more wrinkles on our minds than on our faces; and seldom, or very rarely, does one find souls that do not acquire, as they age, a sour and musty smell. Man moves onward as a whole towards his growth and towards his decay.

When I consider the wisdom of Socrates, and several details of his condemnation, I venture to believe that he in some degree deliberately lent himself to it by prevarication, since, at the age of 70, he was so soon due to suffer the benumbing of his mind's rich activities, and the dimming of its accustomed clarity.

What metamorphoses do I see old age working every day in many of my acquaintances! It is a powerful disease, which makes natural and imperceptible advances. It requires a great store of study and great precautions, if we are to avoid the infirmities that it lays upon us, or at least to retard their progress. Despite all my entrenchments, I feel it gaining on me foot by foot. I resist for as long as I can, but I do not myself know to what it will reduce me at last. But come what may, I am glad that the world will know the height from which I shall have fallen.

BOOK THREE: Chapter 3

On three kinds of relationships

A MAN should not rivet himself too fast to his own humours and temperament. Our chief talent is the power of suiting ourselves to different ways of life. To be tied and bound of necessity to one single way is not to live but to exist. The best minds are those that are most various and most supple. Here is an honourable testimony to the elder Cato: 'His versatile genius was so equally adapted to everything that, whatever he happened to be doing, you would say he was born to do that thing alone.'* If it were in my power to mould myself as I would, there is no form, however good, in which I should wish to be so fixed that I could not depart from it.

Life is an unequal, irregular, and multiform movement. Incessantly to follow one's own track, to be so close a prisoner to one's own inclinations that one cannot stray from them, or give them a twist, is to be no friend to oneself, still less to be one's master; it is to be one's own slave. I say this at the present moment because I cannot easily shake off the tyranny of my mind, which is ordinarily unable to take up anything without becoming absorbed, or to work at anything without devoting all its powers to it. However trifling the subject presented, it is prone to magnify it and expand it to such a point as to require its utmost strength. Mental idleness is therefore to me a troublesome state. and detrimental to my health. Most minds have need of some foreign matter to quicken and exercise them; mine needs it rather in order to relax and compose itself – 'the vice of leisure must be shaken off by occupation'† – for its chief and most laborious study is the study of itself. Books are the sort of employment that distracts it from this study. At the first thoughts that come to it, the mind bestirs itself and makes trial of its strength in all directions, exercising its power of handling a subject sometimes forcibly, sometimes in an orderly and graceful way; it steadies, moderates, and strengthens itself. It has its own powers of rousing its faculties. Nature has given to it, as to all other minds, enough material of its own for its use, and enough subjects for its imagination and judgement.

Meditation is a rich and powerful method of study for anyone who knows how to examine his mind, and to employ it vigorously. I would rather shape my soul than furnish it. There is no exercise that is either feebler or more strenuous, according to the nature of the mind concerned, than that of conversing

* Livy, xxxix, xl.   † Seneca, *Letters*, LVI.

with one's own thoughts. The greatest men make it their vocation, 'those for whom to live is to think'.* Moreover, nature
has favoured it with this privilege, that there is nothing we can
do for so long at a time, nor any action to which we can apply
ourselves more frequently and easily. It is the occupation of
the gods, says Aristotle, the source from which comes their
beatitude and ours.

Reading does me the special service of awakening my reasoning powers by presenting different objects for their consideration; it puts my judgement to work, not my memory.

Few conversations, therefore, hold my interest unless they
are vigorous and forcible. It is true that charm and beauty hold
me and satisfy me no less, or even more, than weight and pro-
fundity. And since I doze through all other kinds of conversation and only lend them the surface of my attention, it often
happens during such languid and feeble talk – mere talk for
talking's sake – that I either make meaningless remarks and
answers so stupid as to be unworthy of a child or, even more
foolishly and discourteously, maintain an obstinate silence. I
have a dreamy way of retiring into myself and, on the other
hand, a gross and puerile ignorance of many common matters.
These two qualities have given rise to five or six stories that are
told of me, as silly as any that can be told of any man on earth.

Now, to proceed with my argument, this difficult disposition
of mine makes me fastidious in my dealings with men; it causes
me to sift and pick them over, and makes me unfit for ordinary
concerns. We live and have our dealings with the people. If
their conversation wearies us, if we scorn to adapt ourselves to
humble and common minds, and the humble and common are
often well-tempered as the most refined – and all wisdom is
foolish that does not accommodate itself to the common ignorance – we must give up meddling with our own and other
men's business; for both public and private affairs have to be
conducted with such people.

The least strained and most natural movements of the soul
are the most beautiful; the least laborious occupations are the

* Cicero, *Tusculans*, v, xxxviii.

best. O God, what a good service wisdom performs when she suits a man's desires to his powers! There is no knowledge more useful. 'According to one's ability,' was Socrates' motto and favourite saying, a saying of great substance. We should direct and fix our desires on those objects that are nearest and easiest. Is it not a foolish humour in me to be out of sympathy with the thousand people to whom my destiny has joined me, and whom I cannot do without, in order to attach myself to one or two who are outside my circle, or rather to pursue a fantastic desire for something I cannot obtain? My easy nature, averse from all bitterness and asperity, may well have saved me from envies and enmities; no man ever gave others more cause, I will not say for loving him, but for not hating him. But my coldness in company has justifiably deprived me of the good-will of many, who have every excuse for interpreting it in a different and worse sense.

I have a great aptitude for acquiring and retaining rare and admirable friendships. Since I grasp very eagerly at any acquaintance that is to my liking, I make such advances, and rush so eagerly forward, that I rarely fail to attach myself and to make an impression where I strike. I have often had happy proof of this. In common relationships I am somewhat dry and cold, for my movement is not natural if I am not under full sail. Moreover, fortune, by accustoming me in my youth to the delicacy of a single and perfect friendship, has in fact given me a certain distaste for other kinds, and has too strongly impressed on my mind that it is a creature for companionship, not for the herd, as the ancient writer put it.* Also, I find an innate difficulty in giving myself by halves and with reservations, and with that slavish and suspicious prudence that is required of us in the conduct of our numerous and imperfect friendships. And this is particularly enjoined upon us at the present time, when we cannot speak truthfully of the world without risk.

I clearly see, however, that one who, like myself, has the comforts of life in view – the essential comforts I mean – ought to avoid like the plague these difficulties and delicacies of humour.

* See Plutarch, *On the Plurality of Friends*.

I should admire a mind of various levels, capable of rising and descending, and comfortable wherever fortune may take it, a mind able to converse with a neighbour about his building, his hunting, and his quarrels, and to enjoy talking to a carpenter or a gardener. I envy those who know how to be familiar with the meanest of their retinue, and to start a conversation among their own domestics. And Plato's advice does not please me, that one should always use the language of a master to one's servants, both male and female, without jests or familiarity. For, besides the reasons I have given, it is inhuman and unjust to lay so much stress on this chance prerogative of fortune; and those societies in which there is least disparity between servants and masters seem to me the most equitable.

Others study to launch their minds forward and elevate them; I seek to humble and lower mine. It is only refractory when overstretched.

> *Narras, et genus Aeaci,*
> > *et pugnata sacro bella sub Ilio:*
> *quo Chium pretio cadum*
> > *mercemur, quis aquam temperet ignibus,*
> *quo praebente domum, et quota,*
> > *Pelignis caream frigoribus, taces.**

Thus, as the Spartan valour stood in need of moderation, and of the sweet and pleasing music of flutes to soothe it in battle, for fear it might turn to recklessness and fury, whereas all other nations generally make use of shrill and loud music and shouting to kindle their soldiers' courage and fan it to a flame, so it seems to me, contrary to the common idea, that in the use of our minds we have usually more need of lead than of wings, of coolness and composure than of ardour and agitation. It is especially foolish, to my mind, always to speak formally, *'favellar in punta di forchetta'*.† You should come down to the

---

* 'You tell of the descent of Aeacus, and of the battles fought under the walls of sacred Troy. But you are silent about the price of a barrel of Chian wine; you do not tell who will heat the water for my bath, or when and where I shall be offered shelter from the Pelignian frosts.' Horace, *Odes*, III, xix, 3.

† 'Speak on the point of a fork': that is, in carefully chosen words.

level of those in whose company you are, and sometimes feign ignorance. Lay aside your strength and subtlety; in common conversation it is enough to preserve coherence. For the rest, keep close to the ground, if that is what they like.

The learned generally trip over this stone. They are always parading their pedantry, and quoting their books right and left. They have in recent days poured so much of this out in the ladies' drawing-rooms and into their ears, that if these ladies have not retained the substance of it, they at least make out they have done so. On every subject and in every conversation, however shallow and commonplace it may be, they use a new and learned style of speaking and writing,

> *Hoc sermone pavent, hoc iram, gaudia, curas,*
> *hoc cuncta effundunt animi secreta; quid ultra?*
> *Concumbunt docte;**

and they quote Plato and Aquinas when the first comer would serve for a witness just as well. The learning that could not penetrate to their minds has remained on the tips of their tongues. If they will take my advice, these well-bred ladies will be satisfied to make the most of their own natural riches. They hide and cover their beauties beneath those of others. It is very foolish to stifle one's own brilliance in order to shine with a borrowed light. They are buried and entombed in artifice, 'fresh from the bandbox'.†

The fact is that they do not know themselves well enough. The world has nothing fairer in it. It is for them to honour the arts, and beautify what is beautiful. What else do they need but to live beloved and honoured? They have and know more than enough for that. They need only waken a little and rekindle the faculties that are in them. When I see them intent on rhetoric, horoscopes, logic, and suchlike nonsense, quite vain and useless for their needs, I begin to fear that the men who put them up to this do so in order to domineer over them. What other excuse can I find for them?

* 'In this style they express their fear, anger, joy, and anxiety. In it they confess their secrets; and what is more they sleep with you in a learned fashion.' Juvenal, VI, 189. † Seneca, *Letters*, CXV.

It is enough that women can, without our aid, train their charming eyes to be gay, to be severe or soft, can season a 'no' with cruelty, hesitation, or kindness, and that they require no interpreter for the speeches we make in wooing them. With this knowledge they have the whip-hand over us, and can master their teachers and the school.

If, nevertheless, it vexes them to yield to us in anything at all, and if, out of curiosity, they wish to have their share in book-learning, poetry is a diversion suited to their needs. It is a wanton and subtle art, ornate and verbose, all pleasure and all show, like themselves. They will also derive various benefits from history. From that part of philosophy that is an aid to living, they can choose the dissertations that will teach them to judge of our humours and characteristics, to protect themselves from our treacheries, to control their own impetuous desires, to make proper use of freedom, to prolong the pleasures of life, and to bear with patience a lover's inconstancies, a husband's gruffness, the importunities of age and wrinkles, and other things of that sort. This is the utmost share that I should allow them in the matter of learning.

There are some peculiar natures that are retiring and self-absorbed. My essential disposition is to communicate and come forward; I am all on the outside, for everyone to see, born for society and friendship. The solitude that I love and advocate is chiefly a matter of drawing my feelings and thoughts back into myself; of restraining and checking, not my steps but my desires and anxieties; of avoiding all solicitude about outside things; of shunning like death all subjection and obligation, and not so much the press of men as the press of affairs. Solitude of place, in fact, expands me rather and sets me at outward liberty; I throw myself more freely into affairs of state and of the world when I am alone. At the Louvre and in the throng, I withdraw and shrink into my skin. The crowd thrusts me back upon myself, and I never indulge in such wild, licentious, and private imagination as in places that call for formality and cere-monious discretion. It is not our follies that make me laugh, but our wisdom. By nature I am no enemy to the bustle of courts. I have spent a part of my life in them, and am accustomed to behave cheerfully in great company, provided that it is only occasionally and when I am in the mood.

But that nice judgement, of which I was speaking, forcibly binds me to solitude, even at home, amidst a numerous household, in a house that receives more visitors than most. Here I see enough people, but rarely those whose conversation I enjoy; and I reserve, at home, an unusual liberty, both for myself and others. Here there is a truce to ceremony, to waiting on people when they arrive and ushering them out when they depart, and to other such painful behests of our courtesy – slavish and tiresome customs! Here everyone behaves as he pleases, and communes with his thoughts if he likes. I remain silent, dreamy, and withdrawn without offence to my guests.

The men whose society and intimacy I seek are those who are called well-bred and talented men; and the thought of these gives me a distaste for others. Their kind is, rightly considered, the rarest that we have, a kind that owes almost everything to nature. The purpose of our intercourse is simply intimacy, familiarity, and talk; the exercise of the mind is our sole gain. In our conversations all subjects are alike to me. I do not care if there is no depth or weight in them; they always possess charm, and they always keep to the point. All is coloured by a ripe and steady judgement, blended with kindness, candour, gaiety, and friendship. It is not only on questions of succession and the affairs of kings that our wit displays its strength and beauty; it displays it just as much in intimate chat. I know my kind even by their silences and their smiles, and discover them more easily, perhaps, at the dining-table than in the council room. Hippomachus said truly that he knew a good wrestler simply by seeing him walk in the street.

If learning be pleased to take part in our talk, it will never be refused, so long as it is not schoolmasterly, imperious, and tiresome, as it usually is, but meek and ready to take a lesson. We are only seeking to pass the time; when the hour comes to be instructed and preached to, we will go to seek learning on its throne. Let it descend to our level for the moment, if it will.

For, however useful and desirable it may be, I take it that we can, at a pinch, easily dispense with its presence, and manage our affairs without it. The mind of a well-bred person, familiar with the world of men, can be sufficiently agreeable in itself. Art is nothing else but the register and record of the works of such minds.

The companionship of beautiful and virtuous women is also pleasing to me: 'for we too have eyes learned in such matters'.* If the mind derives less enjoyment from such company than from that of men, the bodily senses, besides having a greater share in it, also succeed in raising it to a level almost as high, although, in my opinion, it still falls a little short. But this is a relationship in which men have to remain slightly on their guard, especially those, like myself, over whom the body exercises great sway. I scalded myself in my youth, and suffered all the torments that poets say come upon those who abandon themselves to it without sense or discipline. It is true that this whipping has since been a lesson to me,

> *Quicunque Argolica de classe Capharea fugit,*
> *semper ab Euboicis vela retorquet aquis.†*

It is folly to fix all one's thoughts upon relationship with a woman, and to become involved in a furious and reckless passion. But, on the other hand, to enter into it without any love or bond of affection; to play, as actors do, the common and customary role of the age, and to put in nothing of oneself but the words: that is indeed to keep on the safe side, but in a very cowardly fashion, like a man who forswears his honour, his profit, or his pleasure for fear of danger. For those who enter into it in this way can never expect it to bring any result capable of moving or satisfying a noble mind.

One must have desired a thing in all seriousness, if one wishes to take serious pleasure in it. This I say even though fortune may undeservedly favour our play-acting, as often happens, since

* Cicero, *Paradoxes*, v, ii.
† 'Anyone in the Argolid fleet who has escaped the Capharean rocks will always turn his sails away from the Euboean seas.' Ovid, *Tristia*, 1, i, 83.

there is no woman, however ill-favoured, who does not think herself quite attractive, and who has not something to recommend her, her youth, her smile, or her graceful bearing. For there is no absolutely plain woman any more than there are any absolutely beautiful; Brahmin girls who lack any other attractions go into the market-place, where the people have been expressly assembled by the public crier, and display their connubial parts, to see if these at least will not serve to get them a husband.

Consequently, there is no woman who does not easily let herself be persuaded by the first vow that a man swears to be her slave. Now the necessary result of those betrayals that are the common and ordinary practice of present-day men is, as experience has already shown us, either that women unite and fall back on themselves, banding together to avoid us, or that they conform to the example which we set them, play their part in the farce, and lend themselves to the business without passion, without concern or love. 'Untouched by passion, either in themselves or in another'* they think that, as Lysias argued in Plato,† the less we love them the more profitably and advantageously they may surrender to us. The result will be the same as in the theatre; the public will take as much or more pleasure in the play than the actors.

For my part, I can no more recognize Venus without Cupid than motherhood without offspring; these are things that lend and owe their essential character to one another. So this deception recoils on the man who practises it. It costs him little, but he gains nothing of value by it. Those who made Venus a goddess observed that her chief beauty was incorporeal and spiritual; but the desires that such men pursue are not only subhuman, they are not even animal.

The animals will not have things so crude and so earthy. We see that imagination and desire often inflame and invite them before the body does. We observe that in the herd both sexes pick and choose the object of their affection, and that they maintain long and kindly companionship together. Even those to whom old age denies bodily vigour still tremble, neigh, and

* Tacitus, *Annals*, XIII, 45.   † In the *Phaedrus*.

quiver with love. We see them before the act full of hope and ardour; and when the body has had its sport, they are still gratified by the sweetness of recollection. Some even swell with pride as they walk away, and, weary and sated as they are, give voice to their joy and triumph. A creature who has only to relieve the body of a natural urge has no reason to trouble others with such elaborate preparations; love is no meat for a coarse and greedy appetite.

As I do not ask to be taken for any better than I am, I will say this of the errors of my youth. Not only because of the danger to my health – and yet I could not contrive so well as not to have had a couple of touches, though both slight and transitory – but also out of contempt for the practice, I have seldom had recourse to venal and public intimacies. I preferred to enhance my pleasure by difficulty, by desire, and by some measure of glory. I shared the taste of the Emperor Tiberius who, in his love-affairs, was as much captivated by modesty and noble birth as by any other quality; and the whim of the courtesan Flora, who never gave herself to anyone below the rank of dictator, consul, or censor, and took delight in the dignity of her lovers. Doubtless pearls and brocade contribute something in such cases, as well as titles and retinue.

For the rest, I used to set great store by the mind, but only on condition that there were no defects in the body. Indeed, to speak in all conscience, if one or the other of these attractions must perforce be lacking, I would rather have renounced the spiritual; since it can be employed on better things. For in the business of love, which is principally a matter of sight and touch, one can do something without the charms of the mind, nothing without the charms of the body. The true advantage of the ladies lies in their beauty; and beauty is so peculiarly their property that ours, though it demands somewhat different features, is at its best when, boyish and beardless, it can be confused with theirs. They say that at the court of the Grand Turk, those youths who are chosen for his service on the score of beauty, and the number is enormous, are dismissed at the age of 22, at the latest.

Reason, wisdom, and the offices of friendship are more easily found among men; that is why they govern the affairs of the world.

These two kinds of relationship are fortuitous and depend upon others. The first is disappointingly rare; the second withers with age. So they have been incapable of providing adequately for the needs of my life. The companionship of books, which is the third, is much more certain and more our own. It yields all other advantages to the first two, but it has on its side the constancy and facility with which it serves us. It has accompanied me all along my way, and assists me everywhere. It comforts me in my old age and solitude. It frees me from the weight of a tedious idleness, and releases me at any moment from disagreeable company. It dulls the pangs of any grief that is not intense and overmastering. To distract myself from tiresome thoughts, I have only to resort to books; they easily draw my mind to themselves and away from other things. And yet they show no resentment when they see that I only turn to them through lack of those other more real, lively, and natural satisfactions; they always receive me with the same welcome.

A man may well go on foot, as the saying is, if he is leading his horse by the bridle; and our contemporary James, King of Naples and Sicily, who, though handsome, young, and sound in health, had himself carried about the country on a stretcher, lying on a wretched feather pillow, dressed in a grey cloth coat with a cap to match, but followed nevertheless by a great regal train, by litters, by led horses of all kinds, and by gentlemen and officers, presented a picture of an austerity still tender and wavering. A sick man is not to be pitied if he has a cure in his sleeve. In the experience and application of this maxim, which is a very true one, lies all the profit that I have derived from books. As a matter of fact, I hardly make more use of them than those who do not know them. I enjoy them as misers do their treasures, by knowing that I can enjoy them when I please; my mind is fully satisfied and contented by this right of possession.

I never travel without books either in peace or in war. Yet

many days or months will go by without my using them. Very soon, I say to myself, or tomorrow, or when I feel like it. Meanwhile time runs by and is gone, and I am none the worse. For you cannot imagine how much ease and comfort I draw from the thought that they are beside me, to give me pleasure when I choose, and from the feeling that they bring great help to me in my life. They are the best provision I have found for this human journey, and I am extremely sorry for any intelligent man who is without them. I am the readier to accept any other sort of entertainment, however trivial, for knowing that this one can never fail me.

When at home, I turn a little more often to my library, from which I can easily overlook my whole household. There I am above the gateway, and can see below me my garden, my farm-yard, my courtyard, and most parts of my house. There I turn the pages now of one book, now of another, without order and without plan, reading by snatches. Sometimes I reflect, and sometimes I compose and dictate my reflections, walking up and down, as at present.

My library is in the third story of a tower; on the first is my chapel, on the second a bedroom with ante-chambers, where I often lie to be alone; and above it there is a great wardrobe. Formerly, this was the most useless part of the house. But now I spend most of the days of my life there, and most of the hours of the day. I am never there at night. Adjoining my library is a very neat little room, in which a fire can be laid in winter, and which is pleasantly lighted by a window. And if I were not more afraid of the trouble than of the cost – trouble which deters me from every kind of business – I could easily join to each side a gallery a hundred paces long and twelve paces wide on the same level. For I have found the necessary walls built for another purpose to the requisite height. Every place of retire-ment requires a room for walking. My thoughts go to sleep if I sit still. My mind does not work if my legs do not shake it up. Those who study without books are all in this plight.

My library is circular in shape, with no flat wall except that taken up by my table and chair; and, being rounded, it presents me with all my books at once, arranged about me on five tiers of shelves. From this room I have three open views, and its free space is sixteen paces across. In winter I am there less continually, for my house is perched on a hill, as its name implies, and there is no room more exposed to the winds than this. It is a little difficult of access and out of the way, but this I like, both for the benefit of the exercise and for its keeping people away from me. It is my throne, and I try to rule here absolutely, reserving this one corner from all society, conjugal, filial, and social. Everywhere else I have just a verbal authority, which is essentially doubtful. Miserable, to my mind, is the man who has no place in his house where he can be alone, where he can privately attend to his needs, where he can conceal himself! Ambition fitly requites her servants by keeping them always on show, like a statue in a market-place; 'a great fortune means great bondage'.* They can have no privacy even in the privy. I consider nothing so harsh in the life of austerity followed by our religious orders, as the rule which I found in one of their communities, by which they are required perpetually to be in company, and to have numerous persons with them whatever they do. I find it rather more bearable always to be alone than never to have the power to be so.

If anyone tells me that it is degrading to the Muses to use them only as a plaything and a pastime, he does not know, as I do, how valuable pleasure, sport, and amusement are. I am almost prepared to say that any other aim is ridiculous. I live from day to day and, with reverence be it said, live only for myself; my purposes go no further. In my youth I studied out of ostentation; later a little to gain wisdom; now for pleasure; but never for the sake of learning. The idle and extravagant hobby I once had of collecting books as a kind of furniture, not merely enough to fill my needs but rather more for decoration and wall-lining, I gave up long ago.

Books have many pleasing qualities for those who know how to choose them. But nothing good is without its evil side; this pleasure is no purer or more unmixed than any other. It has its

* Seneca, *Consolation to Polybius*, xxvi.

disadvantages, and very grave ones. Books exercise the mind, but the body, whose interests I have never neglected either, remains meanwhile inactive, and grows heavy and dull. I know of no excess that does me more harm, or that I should avoid more strictly in these my declining years.

These are my three favourite and especial occupations. I say nothing of those which the world compels me to follow as a civic duty.

BOOK THREE: Chapter 6

On vehicles

IT may easily be verified that when great authors write of causes, they make use not only of those they think true, but also of some in which they do not believe, providing there is some originality and beauty in them. They speak truly and profitably enough if they speak judiciously. We cannot make sure of the fundamental cause; we pile up many, to see if by chance it is to be found among them,

> *namque unam dicere causam*
> *non satis est, verum plures, unde una tamen sit.**

Do you ask me whence comes the custom of saying 'Bless you' when a man sneezes? We produce three sorts of wind; that which issues from below is too foul; that which comes from the mouth carries some reproach of over-eating; the third is sneezing, and because it comes from the head and is irreproachable, we give it this honourable greeting. Do not laugh at this subtle reasoning; it is said to be Aristotle's.

I think that it was in Plutarch – who, of all the authors I know is the best at combining art with nature, and judgement with knowledge – that I read an explanation of that heaving of the stomach in those who travel by sea. He says that the cause is fear, he having discovered some reasons to prove that fear

* 'For it is not sufficient to state a cause. We should state many, of which one will prove to be true.' Lucretius, VI, 703.

may produce some such effect. I, who am very subject to sea-sickness, know quite well that this cause does not affect me; and I know it not by reasoning, but by necessary experience. Not to mention what I have been told, that the same thing frequently happens to animals, and particularly to hogs, who have no apprehension of danger, or to repeat what an acquaintance of mine said about himself that, though he was very subject to it, on two or three occasions when he was in great fear during heavy storms, the desire to vomit passed away, as it did from that ancient writer who said: 'I was too sick to think of danger.'* I have never been afraid on the water, or indeed anywhere else – and if death is to be feared I have often enough had good cause – at least not so afraid as to be disturbed or bewildered. Fear sometimes arises from deficient judgement as much as from deficient courage. All the dangers I have seen, I have looked at with open eyes, and with clear, sound, and perfect vision. Besides, it needs courage to be afraid. Mine once stood me in such good stead as to contrive that my flight should be orderly compared with the rest, and that I should get away, if not without fear, at least without terror and dismay. I was excited, but not distraught or bewildered.†

Great souls go much further; they give us examples of escapes that are not only steady and composed, but even proud. Let me quote what Alcibiades says of Socrates, his comrade in arms. 'I found him,' he says, 'after the rout of our army, with Laches, among the last of the fugitives. I watched him at my leisure, and from a safe place, for I was on a good horse and he on foot, as we had been in the battle. I noticed first what discretion and resolution he showed in comparison with Laches, and then how boldly he marched, his step never faster than his ordinary pace; how firm and steady was his gaze, as he observed and took in the situation, glancing first on one, then on another, on friends and enemies, in such a way as to encourage the former, and to inform the latter that he was ready to sell his life and his blood very dearly to anyone who might try to take them.

* Seneca, *Letters*, LIII.
† Montaigne may be referring to his flight from the plague.

And so they escaped. For no one willingly attacks men like that; they pursue the frightened ones.'*

There we have this great captain's testimony, which teaches us what we may learn any day by experience, that nothing is so likely to throw us into danger as a frantic eagerness to avoid it. 'The less fear there is, the less is the danger.'† Our common people are wrong to say of a man that he is afraid of death when they mean that he is thinking about it and foresees it. Foresight is equally proper in all that concerns us, whether for good or ill. To consider and estimate the danger is in a way the reverse of being daunted by it.

I do not feel myself strong enough to withstand the impetuous onset of this passion of fear, or of any other violent passion. If I were once conquered and beaten to the ground by it, I should never rise again quite whole. If anyone caused my soul to lose its foothold, he would never be able to set it upright again. It probes and searches itself too keenly and deeply, and so would never let the wound that had pierced it close up and heal. Fortunately for me no sickness has yet unsettled it. Each time an attack is made on me, I step forward and defend myself in all my armour. But the first charge that bowled me over would leave me without resources. I have no second defence; if the flood broke down my dykes at any point, I should be exposed and irremediably drowned.

Epicurus says that a wise man can never pass over to a contrary state. The opinion that I hold is quite the reverse, that a man who has once been a fool will never afterwards be wise.

God sends the cold according to the cloak, and gives me passions proportionate to my means of resistance. Nature has exposed me on one side, but covered me on the other; having disarmed me of strength, she has armed me with insensibility, and with limited or dull powers of apprehension.

Now I cannot stand for long – and found it even more difficult to stand in my youth – either a coach, a litter, or a boat, and I detest every means of travel except a horse, either in the town

* Plato, *Symposium*.   † Livy, XXII, 5.

or country. But I can endure a litter less than a coach and, for the same reason, prefer a rough tossing on the water, which is generally alarming, than the motion we feel in calm weather. The slight shock given by the oars, as they slide the boat forward beneath us, somehow upsets both my head and my stomach in the same way as a shaky seat, which is something that I cannot bear. When the sail or the current carries us smoothly on, or when we are towed, the uniform motion causes me no discomfort at all. It is a broken movement that upsets me, especially when it is slow. I cannot describe it in any other way. Physicians have recommended me to swathe and bind my belly tightly with a towel as a remedy for this state. But I have never tried this, being accustomed to combat my weaknesses and overcome them by myself.

If my memory were well enough stored, I should think it no waste of time to set down here the infinitely various ways, recorded by history, in which vehicles have been used for purposes of war, ways that vary according to the nation and the century. They have, in my opinion, been most effective and most necessary; and it is a marvel to me that we have lost all knowledge of them. I will merely say here that quite recently, in our fathers' time, the Hungarians made very advantageous use of them against the Turks, each of them carrying a man with a buckler and a musketeer, together with a number of muskets, arranged and ready loaded, the whole covered with a screen of shields like a galley. They formed their battle-front of three thousand such vehicles; and after the cannon had played, they were made to rush forward and send a volley down the enemy's throat before he tasted the rest, which was no slight advantage. Alternatively, they drove them into the enemy's squadrons, to break them up and open a way; and besides this, they used them for flanking, at dangerous spots, troops advancing across the fields, or as a hasty cover and fortification for a camp.

In my time, a gentleman living on one of our frontiers, who was personally weak and could find no horse strong enough to bear his weight, being engaged in a feud, used to go about the district in a conveyance of this description, and found it very convenient. But let us leave these vehicles of war. The kings of our first dynasty used to travel the country in a cart drawn by four oxen.

Mark Antony was the first man to have himself drawn through Rome, by lions harnessed to a chariot, with a girl musician beside him. Heliogabalus afterwards did the same thing, calling himself Cybele, the mother of the gods; and he was also drawn by tigers,* after the fashion of the god Bacchus. On one occasion, he harnessed two stags to his chariot, and on another four dogs, and again four naked girls, being drawn by them in state, himself also stark naked. The emperor Firmus had his chariot pulled by ostriches of marvellous size, so that he seemed to fly rather than to bowl along.

The strangeness of these inventions brings another idea into my head: that it is a kind of mean-spiritedness in monarchs, and a proof that they are insufficiently conscious of what they are, when they labour to make themselves honoured and conspicuous by excessive expenditure. It might be excusable in a foreign country; but among their own subjects, where they are all-powerful, their dignity itself confers on them the highest degree of honour to which they can attain. In the case of a nobleman too, it seems to me superfluous for him to dress exquisitely in his own home; his house, his retinue, his table sufficiently proclaim his quality. The advice that Isocrates gave to his king seems to me not unreasonable: to be sumptuous in his expenditure on furniture and plate, since these were durable possessions that would pass on to his successors, but to avoid all such magnificence as would quickly drop out of use and memory.

When I was young, having no other attraction, I was fond of adornment, and it suited me well. There are some on whom fine clothes look miserable. We have marvellous stories of the frugality of our kings in regard to their own persons and in their gifts – of kings great in fame, in valour, and in fortune. Demosthenes vigorously opposed the law of his city which allotted public money to be spent on ostentatious games and feasts; he

* More properly, by panthers.

wanted its greatness to be shown by squadrons of well-equipped ships and good, well-furnished armies. And Theophrastus was justly condemned for having, in his book on riches, advanced a contrary opinion, maintaining that expenditure of this sort was the true fruit of opulence. These are pleasures, says Aristotle, that only appeal to the very lowest classes; and that vanish from their memory once they are sated with them. In his opinion, no serious or sensible person can value them.

The outlay would, I think, be far more royally, and usefully, properly, and durably, devoted to ports, harbours, fortifications, and walls, to fine buildings, churches, hospitals, colleges, and the improvement of streets and roads, for which in modern times, Pope Gregory the Thirteenth won a commendable reputation, and by which our Queen Catherine would, for long years, leave evidence of her natural liberality and munificence, if her means were equal to her desires. Fortune has done me a bad turn by interrupting the noble construction of the new bridge in our great city,* and depriving me of the hope of seeing it in use before I die.

Moreover, to a monarch's subjects, who are the spectators of these triumphs, it appears that they are being given a display of their own wealth, and being feasted at their own expense. For people generally assume of their kings, as we do of our servants, that they should make it their business to provide us abundantly with all we need, but that they ought not to touch any part of it themselves. And this is why, when the Emperor Galba was pleased with a musician who had played to him during supper, he sent for his money-box, fished out a fist-full of crowns, and put them into his hands, with the words: 'This is not out of the public purse, but my own.' Nevertheless, it most often happens that the people are right, and that their eyes are feasted with what should go to feed their stomachs.

Liberality itself does not shine brightest in the hands of a sovereign; private persons have a better right to be liberal. For, to look at the matter closely, a king has nothing that is properly his; he owes even himself to others. Justice is administered not

* The Pont-Neuf in Paris.

for the benefit of the administrator, but of those who are judged. A superior is never appointed for his own advantage, but for that of the inferior, and a physician for his patient, not for himself. All authority, like all art, has a purpose outside itself: 'no art is an end in itself'.* The tutors of young princes, therefore, who make a point of instilling into them this virtue of liberality and tell them never to refuse anything, and to think nothing so well spent as what they give away – a lesson that I have known to be highly commended in my day – are either more intent on their own profit than their master's, or do not quite realize to whom they are preaching. It is too easy to inculcate liberality in one who has unlimited means of practising it at others' expense. And since its value is reckoned not by the gifts, but by the resources of the giver, it becomes an empty thing in such powerful hands. Kings become prodigal before they are liberal.

Liberality, therefore, is not very commendable when compared with other royal virtues; it is the only one, as Dionysius the tyrant said, that goes well with tyranny itself. I would rather teach a pupil this verse of the ancient farmer:

$$T\tilde{\eta} \ \chi\epsilon\iota\rho\grave{\iota} \ \delta\epsilon\tilde{\iota} \ \sigma\pi\epsilon\acute{\iota}\rho\epsilon\iota\nu, \ \grave{\alpha}\lambda\lambda\acute{\alpha} \ \mu\grave{\eta} \ \acute{o}\lambda\omega \ \theta\upsilon\lambda\acute{\alpha}\kappa\omega\dagger$$

that if one wants a good crop one should sow with the hand, and not pour out of the sack. The seed should be scattered not spilt; and since he has to give – or, to put it better, to pay and reward – so many people according to their deserts, he must be a fair and careful dispenser. If a prince's liberality lacks measure and moderation, I would rather have him mean.

Kingly virtue seems to lie chiefly in justice; and of all the divisions of justice, that which best stamps a king is one that is accompanied by liberality. For this kings have especially reserved to themselves, whereas they generally administer other forms of justice by deputy. Immoderate bounty is for them a feeble means of acquiring goodwill, for it alienates more people than it wins. 'The more you use it, the less you can use it. What is more foolish, if you want to do something, than to make

* Cicero, *De Finibus*, v, 6.
† A verse of Corinna, quoted by Plutarch and translated in the text.

yourself incapable of doing it for long?'* And if it is bestowed without regard for merit, it puts the recipient to shame, and is received without gratitude. Tyrants have been sacrificed to popular hatred by the hands of the very men whom they have unjustly advanced. For people of that kind think they are securing themselves in the possession of their ill-gotten gains by showing contempt and hatred for the man from whom they came. And so they adhere to the judgements and opinions of the crowd.

The subjects of a prince who is excessive in his gifts grow lavish in their demands; they take not reason but precedent for their standard. Indeed, we have often cause to blush at our shamelessness; from the standpoint of justice, we are overpaid when our reward equals our service. For do we owe our prince nothing by natural obligation? If he makes good our expenses, he does too much; it is enough if he contributes to them. More than that must be called beneficence, and it cannot be exacted; for the very word liberality suggests liberty. As we behave, there is no end to it; what has been received no longer counts. We love only the liberality to come. Therefore the more a prince exhausts himself in giving, the poorer he grows in friends. How shall he satisfy desires that increase as quickly as they are fulfilled? The man whose thoughts are on taking no longer remembers what he has taken. Nothing goes so naturally with greed as ingratitude.

The example of Cyrus will not be out of place here, to serve the kings of today as a touchstone by which they may know whether their gifts are well or ill bestowed, and see how much more successfully that emperor disposed his gifts than they do. For they are reduced by their bounty to borrowing from unknown subjects, and more often from those they have wronged than from those they have benefited. They receive aids that are only gratuitous in name. Croesus reproached Cyrus for his extravagance, and calculated what his wealth would have amounted to if he had been closer-fisted. But Cyrus, wishing to justify his liberality, sent messengers in all directions to the

* Cicero, *De Officiis*, II, 15.

great men of his realm whom he had especially favoured, asking each one of them to assist him with as much money as he could, to meet an urgent need, and to send him a statement of the amount. When all the notes were brought to him, he found that every one of his friends had thought it insufficient to offer only so much as he had received out of the royal munificence, and had added a great deal more of his own: and the total was found to be very much greater than the sum that Croesus reckoned could have been saved. Whereupon Cyrus said: 'I have no less love of riches than other princes, but I am rather more careful with them. You see at what small expense I have acquired the inestimable treasure of so many friends, and how much more loyal treasurers they are to me than mercenary men would be who owed me nothing and felt no affection for me. And my wealth is better stored than in strong-boxes, which would call down on me the hatred, envy, and contempt of other princes.'

The emperors excused the extravagance of their games and public spectacles, on the ground that their authority in some sort – at least in appearance – depended on the goodwill of the Roman people, who had from time out of mind acquired the habit of being flattered by that sort of lavish spectacle. But it was private individuals who had built up this custom of entertaining their friends and fellow-citizens, chiefly out of their own purses, with such profusion and magnificence. It had quite another flavour when their masters came to imitate them. 'The conveyance of money from its rightful owners to others without claim on it should not be viewed as generosity.'* When Philip saw his son trying to purchase the Macedonians' goodwill with gifts, he taunted him in a letter to this effect: 'Tell me, do you want to have your subjects look on you as their purse-bearer, not as their king? If you want to bribe them, do so with the benefits of your virtue, not with the contents of your strong-box.'

It was a fine thing, however, to bring and plant in the amphitheatre a great number of tall trees, with all their branches covered with leaves, to represent a large, shady forest, arranged

* Cicero, *De Officiis*, I, 14.

in perfect symmetry; and, on the first day to let loose in it a thousand ostriches, a thousand stags, a thousand boars, and a thousand fallow-deer, and to leave them to be picked up and destroyed by the common people; then, on the next day, to have a hundred great lions, a hundred leopards, and three hundred bears slaughtered in their presence; and on the third to stage a fight to the death between three hundred pairs of gladiators, as was done by the Emperor Probus. It was also a fine thing to see those great amphitheatres faced with marble outside, adorned with carvings and statues, and sparkling on the inside with many rich ornaments,

*Baltheus in gemmis, en illita porticus auro;**

all the sides of this great space completely filled from top to bottom with sixty or eighty tiers of seats, also of marble, covered with cushions,

exeat, inquit,
si pudor est, et de pulvino surgat equestri,
cuius res legi non suffit;†

where a hundred thousand men might find room, and sit at their ease.

The arena in which the games took place would be made by some mechanism to open and split into chasms, representing caverns that vomited forth the beasts intended for the spectacle. Then, secondly, it would be filled with deep water, in which swam many sea-monsters, and on which floated armed ships, to represent a naval battle. Thirdly, it would be drained and levelled for the fight of the gladiators; and, for the fourth show, it was strewn with red earth and storax instead of sand, to provide a stage for a solemn banquet for all that infinite number of people: the final event of one single day;

quoties nos descendentis arenae
vidimus in partes, ruptaque voragine terrae
emersisse feras, et iisdem saepte saepe latebris
durea cum croceo creverunt arbuta libro.

* 'Behold, a circumference of gems, a portico overlaid with gold.' Calpurnius, *Eclogues*, VII, 47.

† 'Let him depart, he says, if he has any shame, and leave the knight's cushioned seat, if he has not paid the lawful tax.' Juvenal, III, 153.

*Nec solum nobis silvestria cernere monstra
contigit, aequoreos ego cum certantibus ursis
spectavi vitulos, et equorum nomine dignum,
sed deforme pecus.* *

Sometimes they constructed a high hill, covered with fruit and other trees in full leaf, and from the summit flowed a rivulet, as from the mouth of a living spring. Sometimes they sailed a great ship on it, which opened and divided of itself and, after disgorging from its belly four or five hundred fighting beasts, closed up again and vanished without assistance. On other occasions, they made jets and spouts of water shoot up into the air from the arena floor, and from an infinite height sprinkle and perfume that infinite multitude. For protection against bad weather, they had this immense area covered with embroidered purple awnings, or with silk of one colour or another; and these they spread or pulled back in a moment, just as it pleased them:

*Quamvis non modico caleant spectacula sole,
vela reducuntur, cum venit Hermogenes.* †

The nets too, that were hung in front of the people to protect them from attack by the animals, when they were released, were woven of gold:

*auro quoque torta refulgent
retia.* ‡

If there is anything excusable in these extravagances, it is where the conception and the novelty, not the expense, arouse men's wonder. §

Even in these vanities we discover how productive those ages were of minds that differed from ours. It is the same with this

* 'How often we have seen one part of the arena sink, and wild beasts come out from the chasm cleft in the floor, and often from the same dark place a grove of gilded trees with saffron bark has grown. Nor was it only the monsters of the forest that we saw; I have seen sea-calves fighting with bears, and hideous flocks of real sea-horses.' Calpurnius, *Eclogues*, VII, 64.

† 'Though the amphitheatre scorches under a grilling sun, the awnings are drawn back when Hermogenes appears.' Martial, VII, xxix, 15.

‡ 'The nets gleam too, being woven of gold,' Calpurnius, *Eclogues*, VII, 53.

§ This whole passage on spectacles was inspired by Justus Lipsius, *On the Amphitheatre*.

kind of fertility as with all other natural phenomena. That is not to say that nature then exhausted all her powers. We do not move forwards, but rather wander, turning this way and that. We return over our tracks. I am afraid that our knowledge is weak in every direction; we do not see far ahead or far behind us. It embraces little, and its life is short both in extent of time and extent of matter:

> *Vixere fortes ante Agamemnona*
> *multi, sed omnes illachrimabiles*
> *urgentur ignotique longa*
> *nocte.**

> *Et supera bellum Troianum et funera Troiae,*
> *Multi alias alii quoque res cecinere poetae.†*

Solon's account, too, of what he learnt from the Egyptian priests about the long persistence of their state, and their method of learning and preserving the history of other nations, seems to me a testimony that should not be slighted in this connexion.‡ 'If we could see the whole boundless extent of space and time, in which the resolute and exploring mind travels far and wide without finding any ultimate limit to arrest its journey, we should in that immensity discover an infinite multitude of forms.'§

Even if all the reports that have come down to us concerning the past, up to our own time, were true and were known by some one person, it would be less than nothing in comparison with what is unknown. And of the present face of the world, which slips away while we live on it, how wretched and restricted is the knowledge even of the most inquiring! Not only regarding particular events, which chance often renders exemplary and important, but regarding the state of great govern-

---

* 'Many heroes lived before Agamemnon, but no one weeps for them; they all lie forgotten in darkness.' Horace, *Odes*, IV, ix, 25.

† 'Before the Trojan war and the destruction of Troy, other exploits were celebrated by many other poets.' Lucretius, V, 326, misquoted.

‡ Plato, *Timaeus*.

§ Cicero, *De Natura Deorum*, I, xx, much modified to suit Montaigne's argument.

ments and nations, a hundred times more escapes us than comes to our knowledge. We exclaim at our miraculous invention of artillery and of printing; but other men, at the other end of the earth, in China, used them a thousand years before us. If we saw as much of the world as we do not see, we should be aware, in all probability, of a perpetual multiplication and variation of forms.

There is nothing single and rare from nature's point of view, but only from the point of view of our knowledge, which is a poor foundation for the rules we make, and which is apt to give us a very false picture of things. Just as today we vainly infer the decline and decrepitude of the world from arguments based on our own weakness and decay,

> *Iamque adeo affecta est aetas, affectaque tellus;* *

so, just as vainly, did Lucretius conclude its recent birth and youth from the vigour that he saw in the minds of his day, which were fertile in inventions and novelties in all the arts.

> *Verum, ut opinor, habet novitatem summa, recensque*
> *natura est mundi, neque pridem exordia coepit:*
> *quare etiam quaedam nunc artes expoliuntur,*
> *nunc etiam augescunt, nunc addita navigiis sunt*
> *multa.* †

Our world has lately discovered another – and who can assure us that it is the last of its brethren, since the Daemons, the Sibyls, and ourselves have known nothing of this one till now? – another, no less large, populous, and manifold than itself, but so new and so infantile that it is still being taught its A B C. It is not fifty years ago that it knew neither letters, nor weights and measures, nor clothes, nor corn, nor vines. It was still naked in its mother's lap, and lived only on the milk that it sucked from her.

If we are right about the approaching end of our world, and

---

* 'So now our age is affected, and the earth with it.' Lucretius, II, 1150.

† 'Indeed, the universe, as I believe, is new. The world is quite fresh, and came into being not long ago. So some arts are still being perfected, and are even now advancing, and many things are now being discovered about the art of navigation.' Lucretius, V, 330.

the poet was right about the youth of his age, this new world will only be coming into the light as ours is leaving it. The universe will fall into a paralysis; one limb will be numbed while the other is full of vigour. I very much fear that we shall have greatly hastened the decline and ruin of this other hemisphere by our contact, and that we shall have made it pay very dearly for our arts. It was an infant world, and yet, with all our advantages in valour and natural strength, we have not whipped it into subjection to our teaching; we have not won its favour by our justice and goodness, or subdued it by our magnanimity. As most of their responses in our negotiations with them testify, its people were in no sense our inferiors in natural clarity of understanding and cogency. The astonishing magnificence of the cities of Cuzco and Mexico and, among many similar things, that king's garden in which all the trees and fruit, and all the plants were exquisitely fashioned of gold to the same size and in the same order as they would have in any ordinary garden; also the animals in his private apartments, which were modelled after every kind that lived in his land or his seas; and, in addition, the beauty of their workmanship in precious stones, feathers, cotton, and painting; all these things show that they were in no way inferior to us in industry either. But as to religious conduct, obedience to the law, goodness, liberality, loyalty, and honest dealing, it was greatly to our advantage that we had not as much as they. By excelling us in these virtues, they ruined, sold, and betrayed themselves.

As for hardiness and courage, as for firmness, constancy, and resolute endurance of pain, hunger, and death, I should not fear to compare examples that I could find among them with the most famous examples of old, of which we read in the records of our hemisphere. For take away from their conquerors the tricks and stratagems which they used for deception, and the natural astonishment that overcame those peoples on seeing the unexpected arrival of men with beards, of strange language, religion, shape, and appearance, from a distant part of the world which they had imagined to be quite uninhabited. Consider that these strangers were mounted on great, unfamiliar monsters, and opposed to men who had never seen a horse, or indeed any animal trained to carry a man or bear any other burden; that they were furnished with hard and shining skin, and sharp and glittering weapons, and were opposed to men who would barter a great pile of gold and pearls for the marvel of a gleaming mirror or a knife, and who had neither the knowledge nor the means with which they could have pierced our steel, even if they had had the time. Add the thunder and lightning of our cannon and musketry – enough to frighten even Caesar, if he had been surprised at that hour and with so little experience – against people who were naked, except in so far as they had risen to the invention of some cotton fabric; that they had no other arms, at best, but bows, stones, sticks, and wooden shields; that these peoples were taken at a disadvantage, under the pretence of friendship and good faith, and betrayed by their curiosity to see new and unknown things. Place to the account of the conquerors, I say, this disparity, and you deprive them of the entire credit for all their victories.

When I reflect on the indomitable courage with which so many thousands of men, women, and children so often advanced and flung themselves against certain dangers, in defence of their gods and their liberty; and on their noble persistence in withstanding every ordeal and hardship, even death, rather than submit to the domination of the men who had so shamefully deceived them – some, when captured, preferring to pine away from hunger and fasting rather than accept food from the hands of their enemies, who had won by such foul means – I can see that if anyone had attacked them with equality of arms, experience, and numbers, it would have been as perilous a war as any that we know of, or even more perilous.

Why did not so noble a conquest fall to Alexander, or to the ancient Greeks and Romans! Why did not this vast change and transformation of so many empires and peoples fall to the lot of men who would have gently refined and cleared away all that was barbarous, and stimulated and strengthened the good seeds that nature had sown there, not only applying to the cultivation of the land and the adornment of cities the arts of this hemisphere, in so far as they were necessary, but also blending the Greek and Roman virtues with those native to the country?

What a compensation it would have been, and what an improvement to this whole earthly globe, if the first examples of our behaviour offered to these peoples had caused them to admire and imitate our virtue, and had established between them and us a brotherly intercourse and understanding! How easy it would have been to turn to good account minds so innocent and so eager to learn, which had, for the most part, made such good natural beginnings! On the contrary, we have taken advantage of their ignorance and inexperience to bend them more easily to treachery, lust, covetousness, and to every kind of inhumanity and cruelty, on the model and after the example of our own manners. Who ever valued the benefits of trade and commerce at so high a price? So many towns razed to the ground, so many nations exterminated, so many millions put to the sword, and the richest and fairest part of the world turned upside down for the benefit of the pearl and pepper trades! Mere commercial victories! Never did ambition, never did public hatreds drive men, one against another, to such terrible acts of hostility, and to such miserable disasters.

Coasting the shore in search of their mines, certain Spaniards landed in a fertile, pleasant, and well-populated country, and made their accustomed professions to the inhabitants; that they were peaceable men who had sailed from far away, and were sent by the King of Castile, the greatest prince of the habitable world, to whom the Pope, God's representative on earth, had given dominion over all the Indies; and that if these people would become his tributaries, they would be most kindly treated. The Spaniards demanded provisions for their sustenance, and some gold to use for some kind of medicine. In addition, they urged on them a belief in one God and the truth of our religion, which they advised them to embrace, adding a few threats into the bargain.

The answer was this: that, as to their being peaceable, they had not that appearance even if they were; as to their king, since he begged he must be poor and needy; and that whoever had parcelled things out to them must be a man who loved quarrels, to give another person something that was not his, in order to set him at odds with its ancient possessors. As to the provisions, they would supply them. Of gold they had little, it being a thing to which they attached no value since it did not help them in their daily life, which they were only anxious to spend in a happy and pleasant way. But their visitors might boldly take as much as they could find, except what was used in the service of their gods. As to the one God, what had been said about him had given them pleasure, but they had no wish to change their religion, having followed it happily for so long; and it was their custom to take counsel only from their friends and acquaintances.

As for their threats, it was the sign of a faulty judgement to go threatening men whose character and resources were unknown to them. So they had better make haste to quit the land, for they, its inhabitants, did not usually take in good part the civilities and professions of armed strangers; if they did not, they would be dealt with like these others – and here they pointed to the heads of some executed men around the city.

There is an example of the babbling of these children! But it is to be noticed that neither here nor in several other places where they did not find the merchandise they were seeking, did the Spaniards make any stay or attempt any violence, whatever other advantages they found there; witness my Cannibals.*

The Spaniards drove out the last representatives of the two most powerful monarchies in that world – and perhaps in the whole world – who were kings over so many kings. One was the king of Peru, whom they took in battle and for whom they demanded a ransom so exorbitant that it passes all belief. But when this was duly paid, and the king had given proof in his negotiations of a frank, generous, and steadfast spirit, also of a clear and orderly mind, the conquerors took it into their heads, after extorting one million, three hundred and twenty-five thousand, five hundred weight of gold, besides silver and other things no less in value, so that their horses were never shod with anything but solid gold, to find out, by any treacher-

* See Book One, Chapter 31.

ous means they could think of, what the rest of this king's treasures might amount to, and then to get possession of all that he
had in reserve. They trumped up a false charge against him, and
advanced false proofs that he was plotting to raise an insur-
rection in the provinces to restore him to liberty. Thereupon,
by a nice judgement pronounced by those very men who had
contrived this treachery, he was condemned to be publicly
hanged and strangled, after being forced to purchase remission
from the torment of being burnt alive by accepting baptism,
which was given to him at the moment of execution. He endured
this horrible and monstrous fate without betraying himself by
look or word and with a truly royal gravity of demeanour. Then,
to pacify the people, who were dazed and dumbfounded by
these strange events, the Spaniards made a show of being
greatly grieved at his death, and ordered him a magnificent
funeral.

The other, the king of Mexico, after putting up a long defence of his besieged city, during which he and his people
showed the utmost that endurance and perseverance can do if
ever a prince and a nation did so, had the misfortune to fall alive
into the hands of the enemy, the condition of surrender being
that he should be treated as a king – and nothing about his conduct as a prisoner showed him to be unworthy of the title. After
their victory, however, the Spaniards did not find all the gold
they had promised themselves. So, after first ransacking and
rifling everything, they set about obtaining information by inflicting the severest tortures they could devise upon the prisoners in their hands. But they found their victims' hearts stronger
than their torments, and gained nothing by this; which so enraged them that, in violation of their pledged word and of the
law of nations, they condemned the king himself and one of his
chief nobles to be tortured in each other's presence.

The nobleman, who was surrounded by red-hot braziers,
found himself overcome by pain, and at last turned his eyes
piteously on his master, as if to ask his pardon for being unable
to hold out any longer. The king, fixing his gaze proudly and
sternly upon him in reproof of his cowardly weakness, spoke

these words only, in a harsh and unfaltering voice: 'And I, am I in a cold bath? Am I any more comfortable than you?' The nobleman soon afterwards succumbed to his pain, and died on the spot. The king, half roasted, was taken away, not so much out of pity – for what pity ever touched the soul of a man who, for some dubious information about a golden vessel to be pillaged, would have a man grilled before his eyes; even worse a king of such great fortune and merit? – but because his firmness made their cruelty more and more shameful. They hanged him afterwards, when he had courageously attempted to deliver himself by arms from his long captivity and subjection; and he made an end worthy of a great-hearted prince.

On another occasion, they burned alive in the same fire four hundred and sixty living men, the four hundred being of the common people, and the sixty principal lords of a province, who were simple prisoners of war. We have these narratives from themselves, for they not only acknowledge these things, but boast of them and proclaim them abroad. Can it be as testimony to their justice or to their religious fervour? No, these methods are too much opposed and too detrimental to this holy cause. If their purpose had been to extend our faith, they would have considered that it is not by possession of territories that it spreads, but by the possession of men; and they would have been more than satisfied with the slaughter which war demands without adding an indiscriminate butchery, as of so many wild beasts, and as universal as fire and sword would permit. For they deliberately kept alive only so many as they wanted to make into miserable slaves for labour and service in their mines.

As a result of these hideous crimes, several of the Spanish captains were put to death on the scene of their conquests by order of the Kings of Castile, who were justly outraged; and almost all of them were loathed and despised. God deservedly ordained that the whole of this vast booty should be swallowed up by the sea in course of transport, or by the internal wars in which they destroyed one another; and the majority of the conquerors were buried in that country, without enjoying the fruits of their victory.

As for the revenue, even in the hands of a thrifty and careful prince* it is far from corresponding to the expectations held out to his predecessors, or to that abundance of riches which they found on their first landing in these new countries – for though a great deal is brought over, this is plainly nothing compared with what we should expect – this is because, the use of coin being entirely unknown to them, their gold was all found in one place, since it served only as an object for show and parade. It was, in fact, a piece of furniture that had been preserved from father to son by many powerful kings, who were always exhausting their mines in order to create this vast pile of vessels and statues for the adornment of their palaces and temples, instead of keeping their gold, as we do, in circulation and for commerce. We divide and convert it into a thousand shapes, we spread it abroad and disperse it. Imagine our kings amassing all the gold they could find for several centuries, and keeping it in idleness!

The inhabitants of the kingdom of Mexico were rather more civilized and more advanced in the arts than the other nations in those parts. They thought, as we do, that the world was near to its end, and they took the desolation that we brought upon them as a sign of this. They believed that the existence of the world is divided into five ages, corresponding to the lives of five successive suns, of which four had already completed their time, and that the one which then lighted them was the fifth. The first perished with all other creatures in a universal flood; the second by the falling of the sky on the earth, which stifled every living thing; to this age they assigned the giants; and they showed the Spaniards bones, according to the proportions of which the stature of men once amounted to about seven feet. The third ended by fire, which burned and consumed everything; the fourth by a movement of the air and wind, which even levelled many mountains; human beings did not die of this, but were transformed into apes. What ideas does not man accept in his credulous weakness! After the death of this fourth sun, the world was for twenty-five years in perpetual darkness, in the

* King Philip II.

fifteenth of which a man and woman were made who restored the human race. Ten years later, on a certain date in their calendar, the sun appeared newly created, and the reckoning of their years starts from that day. On the third day after this creation, the old gods died; and the new ones were born afterwards, one by one. In what way they expect this last sun to perish, my author* had not discovered. But their computation of this fourth cataclysm coincides with the great conjunction of the stars which, some eight hundred years ago, according to the astrologers' calculations, produced many great alterations and new conditions in the world.

As for pomp and magnificence, which were the cause of my entering on this discourse, neither Greece, nor Rome, nor Egypt has any work to compare, either for utility, or difficulty, or grandeur, with that road, to be seen in Peru, which was constructed by the kings of the country and led from the city of Quito as far as Cuzco – a distance of nine hundred miles. It was twenty-five yards wide, straight, level, and paved; and it was enclosed on either side by fine, high walls, parallel with which, on the inside, ran two perennial streams, bordered by fine trees of the kind that they call molles.† Where they met with mountains and rocks, they cut and levelled them, and they filled in the valleys with stone and chalk. At daily stages on the road were fine palaces stocked with provisions, garments, and weapons, both for travellers and for any armies that have to pass that way.

In estimating this work, I have taken into account the difficulties, which are particularly severe in that place. They did not use any stones smaller than ten feet square, and they had no other means of transporting them but to drag their loads by sheer strength of arm; they had not even the art of scaffolding, and could do nothing instead except pile earth against a building

* Francisco López de Gómara, a priest and a member of Cortés' household, whose *History of the Indies* Montaigne would have read in a French translation. That this is an accurate account of the Aztecs' beliefs can be seen in *Burning Water*, by Laurette Séjourné (Thames and Hudson, 1957).

† The molle (*Schinus molle*) was the sacred tree of the Incas. The name was taken into Spanish from the Quechua language.

as it went up, and take it away afterwards.

Let us return to our vehicles. In place of chariots or any other kind of conveyance, they had themselves carried by men, and on their shoulders. This last king of Peru, on the day that he was captured, was thus carried on golden poles, seated in a chair of gold, into the midst of his battle array. As fast as they killed these bearers of his, in order to bring him down – for they wished to take him alive – as many others struggled to take the places of the dead. So they could never upset him, whatever slaughter they made of these people, until a horseman seized him round the body and pulled him to the ground.

BOOK THREE: Chapter 8

On the art of conversation

IT is a practice of our justice to condemn some as a warning to others. To condemn them because they have done wrong would, as Plato says, be stupid, for what is done cannot be undone. It is in order that they may not err again in the same way, or that others may avoid following their example. We do not correct the man we hang; we correct others through him. I do the same. My errors are sometimes natural and incorrigible. But just as honest men do the public a service by setting them a model to imitate, I shall perhaps do likewise by showing them what to avoid:

> Nonne vides Albi ut male vivat filius, utque
> Barrus inops? magnum documentum, ne patriam rem
> perdere quis velit.*

If I publish and admit my imperfections, someone will learn to fear them. The qualities that I most value in myself derive more honour from self-censure than from any self-praise. That is why I so frequently fall into this strain and remain in it. But when all is told, a man never speaks of himself without losing

* 'Do you not see what an evil life Albus' son lives, and how needy is Barrus? They are a striking lesson, to warn us against squandering a patrimony.' Horace, Satires, I, iv, 109.

something. What he says in his disfavour is always believed, but when he commends himself, he arouses mistrust.

There may be some persons of my temperament who learn more by avoidance than by imitation, and by shunning than by following. It was this sort of teaching that the elder Cato had in mind when he said that wise men have more to learn from fools than fools from wise men; and that ancient player on the lyre also, who, according to Pausanias's story, was in the habit of making his pupils go and listen to a wretched strummer who lived across the way, where they might learn to hate his discords and false measures. Horror of cruelty impels me more strongly towards clemency than any example of clemency could attract me to it. A good horseman does not correct my seat as well as a lawyer or a Venetian on horseback; and a bad style of speaking improves mine more than a good one. Every day another's foolish behaviour gives me warning and admonishment; a sting touches and arouses us better than something pleasant. These times are not fitted to reform us except by reaction, by disagreement more than by agreement, by difference rather than by accord. Having learnt little from good examples, I make use of bad ones, which offer me everyday lessons. I have endeavoured to make myself as agreeable as I find others rude, as firm as I find others pliable, as mild as I have seen them harsh. But I set myself unattainable standards.

The most fruitful and natural exercise for our minds is, in my opinion, conversation. I find the practice of it pleasanter than anything else in life; and that is the reason why, if I were at this moment forced to choose, I would, I believe, rather consent to lose my sight than my hearing or speech. The Athenians, and the Romans still more, held this exercise in great honour in their Academies. In our time, the Italians preserve some traces of the art, to their great profit, as can be seen by a comparison between their intelligence and ours. The study of books is a languid and feeble process that gives no heat,* whereas conversation teaches and exercises us at the same time. If I talk with a man of strong mind and a tough jouster, he presses on my

* See Book Three, Chapter 3.

flanks, he pricks me right and left, his ideas stimulate mine. Rivalry, vanity, and the struggle urge me on, and raise me above myself. And agreement is an altogether tiresome constituent of conversation.

Just as our mind is strengthened by communication with vigorous and orderly intellects, it is impossible to say how much it loses and is debased by our constant intercourse and association with mean and feeble intellects. There is no contagion which spreads like that. I know from plentiful experience how much a yard it costs! I like to dispute and discuss, but in a small company only and for my own pleasure. For to serve as a spectacle to the great, and to make a competitive display of one's wit and chatter is an occupation that ill becomes a man of honour.

Stupidity is a bad quality; but to be unable to bear it, to be vexed and fretted by it, as is the case with me, is another kind of disease that is hardly less troublesome; and of this I am now going to accuse myself.

I enter into conversation and argument with great freedom and facility, since opinions find in me a soil into which they cannot easily penetrate or strike deep roots. No proposition astounds me, no belief offends me, however much opposed it may be to my own. There is no fantasy so frivolous or extravagant that it does not seem to me a natural product of the human mind. Those of us who deny our judgement the right of making final decisions, look mildly on ideas that differ from our own; if we do not give them credence, we can at least offer them a ready hearing. Where one scale of the balance is quite empty, I let the other swing up and down under a load of old wives' superstitions. And it seems to me excusable if I accept an odd number rather than an even, Thursday in preference to Wednesday; if I had rather make a twelfth or fourteenth than be thirteenth at table; if I am gladder to see a hare running alongside my path than crossing it when I am on a journey, and put out my left foot to be booted before my right. All such fantastic notions, which enjoy credit around us, deserve at least a hearing. For me they do no more than balance a vacuum, but they have weight. Common and chance opinions are in their nature still a little heavier than nothing. And a man who takes no account of them may perhaps fall into the vice of obstinacy in avoiding that of superstition.

Contradictions of opinion, therefore, neither offend nor estrange me; they only arouse and exercise my mind. We run away from correction; we ought to court it and expose ourselves to it, especially when it comes in the shape of discussion, not of a school lesson. Each time we meet with opposition, we consider not whether it is just, but how, wrongly or rightly, we can rebut it. Instead of opening our arms to it, we greet it with our claws. I could stand a rough shaking from my friends: 'You are a fool, you're talking nonsense.' In good company, I like expression to be bold, and men to say what they think. We must strengthen our ears and harden them against any weakness for the ceremonious use of words. I like strong and manly acquaintanceships and society, a friendship that prides itself on the sharpness and vigour of its dealings. I like love that bites and scratches till the blood comes. It is not vigorous and free enough if it is not quarrelsome, if it is polite and artificial, if it is afraid of shocks, and is constrained in its ways: 'for there can be no discussion without contradiction'.*

When I am opposed, my attention is roused, not my anger. I go out to meet the man who contradicts me and corrects me. The cause of truth ought to be a cause common to us both. How will he reply? The passion of anger has already struck down his judgement; confusion has usurped the place of reason. It would be useful if a wager were to hang on the result of our disputes, if there could be some material mark of our losses, so that we might keep a record of them. My man could then say to me: 'Your ignorance and stubbornness on some twenty occasions last year cost you a hundred crowns.'

I welcome and embrace the truth in whosoever hands I find it. I cheerfully surrender to it, and offer it my vanquished arms as soon as I see it approaching in the distance. And provided that I am not treated with too imperious and magisterial a frown, I am

* Cicero, *De Finibus*, I, viii.

glad of any criticisms upon my writings. Indeed I have often made changes in them, more out of politeness than because they were improved by it. For I like, by yielding easily, to gratify and foster the freedom to find fault with me, even at some cost to myself. It is, however, difficult to induce men of my time to do this; they have not the courage to correct because they have not the courage to stand correction; and they never speak frankly in one another's presence. I take so much pleasure in being judged and known that it is almost indifferent to me whether I am admired or criticized. My mind so frequently contradicts and condemns itself that it is all one to me if someone else does so, especially as I only give his criticism such authority as I choose. But I quarrel with the man who behaves like someone that I know, who regrets having offered advice if it is not taken on trust, and is affronted when one does not follow it immediately.

Socrates' invariable and smiling acceptance of any contradictions advanced against his arguments might be attributed to his strength; in the certainty that the advantage would be his, he welcomed all criticisms as so many opportunities for fresh triumphs. We, on the other hand, see that nothing so sharpens our delicate sensibilities as the feeling of our adversary's superiority and of his scorn for us; and that, in all reason the weaker party ought gratefully to accept all opposition that corrects him and sets him right. In fact, I seek the company of those who buffet me rather than of those who fear me. It is a poor and harmful pleasure to consort with people who admire and give way to us. Antisthenes commanded his children never to show gratitude or favour to men who praised them. I feel much prouder of the victory I win over myself when, in the very heats of the battle, I make myself bow to the strength of my adversary's argument, than I feel gratified by a victory gained over him through his weakness.

In short, I accept and admit any kind of attack that is directed in the proper way, however feeble it may be, but I am far too intolerant of those that are not made in due order. I care little about the subject; all opinions are alike to me; and I am almost indifferent as to who wins. I will argue peaceably all day, so long as the discussion is conducted according to the rules. It is not so much force and subtlety that I demand as order, such order as we see every day in the altercations of peasants and shopboys, but never amongst ourselves. If they go wrong, it is from lack of breeding; and so it is with us. But their brawling and impatience never deflects them from their theme; their argument keeps its course. If they interrupt one another, if they do not pause for one another, at least they understand one another. I regard any answer as only too good so long as it is to the point. When the argument becomes confused and disorderly, I foresake the matter and, losing my temper and my head, fasten on to the manner. I fall into a headstrong, malicious, and domineering style of debate, for which I have afterwards to blush.

It is impossible to hold a straight argument with a fool. Not only my judgement but my conscience suffers at the hands of so impetuous a master. Our wranglings ought to be forbidden and punished, like other verbal crimes. What vice do they not provoke and multiply, being always ruled and governed by anger! We quarrel first with the reasons, and then with the man. We only learn to debate in order to contradict and, everyone contradicting and being contradicted, it follows that the fruit of disputation is a loss and destruction of the truth. Therefore Plato, in his *Republic*, forbids debates among fools and ill-bred people.

What is the good of setting out in pursuit of the truth in the company of a man whose pace and walking-power are inadequate? We do a subject no harm when we leave it in order to look for a better way of handling it; I do not mean the artificial and scholastic way; I mean the natural method of any sound intelligence. What will be the end of it all? One will go east, the other west; they lose the main theme, and wander off into a multitude of incidentals. At the end of a stormy hour, they do not know what they are after; one is below, one is above, and the other beside the mark. One catches hold of a word or a simile. Another forgets his opponent's point, so intent is he on following his own course; his mind is only on his own argument, not on yours. Another, finding himself weak in the spine, takes fright and refuses to debate. He either mixes and muddles the issues from the very outset or, at the height of the discussion, sulks and stops dead, affecting in malicious ignorance to give up the struggle on grounds of lordly disdain or foolish modesty. One man does not mind how much he exposes himself, provided he gets in his blow. Another counts his words and weighs them as if they were so many arguments. Yet another uses nothing but his superior voice and lungs. Here is one who concludes against himself, and another who deafens you with useless preambles and digressions. There is one who arms himself with sheer abuse, and seeks a Dutch quarrel, in order to rid himself of the company and conversation of a mind that presses his too hard. This last man can see nothing in reason, but hems you into the enclosure of his logical clauses and the formulas of his art.

Now who does not begin to distrust knowledge and to doubt whether he can derive any solid benefit from it for the purposes of his life, when he considers the use we put it to: 'learning that cures nothing'?* Who has ever acquired understanding from logic? Where are its fine promises? 'Neither for living better, nor for reasoning more effectively.'† Do we hear any worse jumble in the gabblings of fish-wives than in the public disputations of these professional logicians? I would rather my son learnt to speak in the taverns than in the talking-schools. Take a Master of Arts, and converse with him. Why does he not make us feel the excellence of his training? Why does he not strike women and ignorant people like ourselves with admiration for the soundness of his reasoning, and the beauty of his ordered argument? Why does he not conquer us and persuade us of what he will? Why is a man with such advantages in matter and method unable to fence without losing his head and his temper, and insulting his opponent? Let him drop his hood, his gown, and his Latin, let him stop battering our ears with his quite raw and undigested Aristotle, and you will take him for one of us, or worse.

Those complications and convolutions of language with

* Seneca, *Letters*, LIX.   † Cicero, *De Finibus*, I, xix.

which the scholars drive us into a corner seem to me like so much jugglery: their dexterity imposes on our senses, and overcomes them, but it does not in any way shake our belief. Apart from these tricks, all that they do is common and worthless. They may be more learned than we, but they are none the less foolish.

I love and honour knowledge as much as those who possess it; put to its proper use, it is the noblest and most powerful acquisition of man. But in those – and there is an endless number of them – who make it the ground of their worth and excellence, who appeal from their understanding to their memory, 'hiding themselves beneath another's shadow',* and who are powerless without their book, I hate it, if I may venture to say so, a little more than I do stupidity.

In my country and in my time, learning often enough mends the purse, but seldom the mind. When the intelligence it lights on is heavy its effect is to make it heavier and to choke it; and fine-spun intelligences it purges, clarifies, and subtilizes to the point of inanition. It is a thing of almost indeterminate quality; a very useful adjunct to a well-endowed mind, but pernicious and harmful to any other; or rather, it is a thing of very precious use, which will not let itself be purchased cheaply. In one man's hands it is a sceptre, in another's a fool's bauble. But let us proceed.

What greater victory do you expect than to teach your enemy that he cannot withstand you? When you win the advantage by the substance of your argument, it is truth that wins; when you do so by your method and handling, you alone are the victor. I conclude from Plato and Xenophon that Socrates argued rather for the sake of the debater than for the debate; to make Euthydemus and Protagoras realize their own irrelevance rather than the irrelevance of their art. He seizes hold of the first subject to hand, like one who has a more useful aim than to clear it up: namely, to clear up the minds that he has undertaken to train and exercise.

The active pursuit of truth is our proper business. We have

* Seneca, *Letters*, XXXIII.

no excuse for conducting it badly or unfittingly. But failure to capture our prey is another matter. For we are born to quest after it; to possess it belongs to a greater power. Truth is not, as Democritus said, hidden in the depths of the abyss, but situated rather at an infinite height in the divine understanding. The world is but a school of inquiry. It does not matter who hits the ring, but who runs the best course. The man who says what is true may be as foolish as the man who utters falsities, for we are concerned with the manner of speaking, not with the matter. It is my nature to consider the form as much as the substance, the advocate as much as the cause; as Alcibiades ordained that we should. And every day I entertain myself by browsing among books without a thought for their learning; and examining their authors' style, not their subject. In the same way, I seek the company of some famous mind, not so that he may teach me, but that I may know him.

Any man may speak truly; but to speak methodically, prudently, and ably, that few men can do. So it is not the errors which arise from ignorance that offend me, but people's sheer foolishness. I have broken off several bargains that would have been to my profit, because of the pointless protestations of the men with whom I was dealing. I am not annoyed once in a year by the faults of those over whom I am in authority, but the stupid obstinacy of their asinine and brutish assertions, excuses, and justifications sets us at each other's throats every day. They understand neither what is said to them nor why, and answer accordingly; it drives one to despair. My head is never hurt except when it collides with another's, and I am readier to put up with my servants' faults than with their thoughtlessness, pig-headedness, and stupidity. Let them do less, provided that they are capable of doing something. Then you live in hope of stimulating their will, but from a log there is nothing to be hoped for, and nothing of any value to be had.

But what if I take things as other than they are? Perhaps I do; and for this I blame my impatience, which I firmly believe to be just as great a fault in one who is right as in one who is wrong. For it is only a sour and arbitrary nature that cannot tolerate an

attitude different from its own; and besides there is really no
greater or more persistent folly, nor anything more anomalous,
than to be excited and annoyed by the fatuities of the world. For
it irritates us chiefly against ourselves, and that philosopher of
old* would never have lacked an occasion for his tears so long
as he had himself to meditate upon. Miso, one of the seven sages,
was a man of Timon's or Democritus' kind. When asked what
he was laughing at, all to himself, he answered: 'At myself
laughing to myself.'

How many times a day do I make remarks or answers that
appear foolish to myself; and how much more commonly and
often, therefore, must they appear foolish to others. If I bite
my own lips over them, what must they do? In short, we must
live with the living, and let the river flow under the bridge without heeding it, or at least, without being disturbed by it. Why
indeed are we unmoved when we meet a man with a twisted
and misshapen body, yet cannot restrain our annoyance on
meeting with an ill-ordered mind? Such cruel harshness is to be
blamed on the judge rather than on the fault.

Let us always have this saying of Plato's on our lips: 'If I find
a thing unsound, is it not because I am myself unsound? Am I
not myself at fault? May not my observations reflect on myself?'
A wise and divine saying which lashes the most common and
widespread error of mankind! Not only the blame we cast at another, but also our reasonings, our arguments, and our subjects
of dispute may generally be turned against us; we stab ourselves
with our own weapons; and of this antiquity has left enough
weighty examples. It was wittily and very aptly said by the man
who first thought of it: 'Every man's filth smells sweet to him.'†
Our eyes can see nothing behind us. A hundred times a day,
when laughing at our neighbours, we are laughing at ourselves.
We detest in others defects which are much more glaring in us,
and, with surprising impudence and thoughtlessness, express
our surprise at them.

* Heraclitus.
† An old proverb, adapted in a slightly different form by Erasmus,
Adages, III, 4, 2.

Only yesterday, I happened to overhear an intelligent and well-bred man mocking, both wittily and justly, at the foolish habits of another, who wearies everyone with his genealogies and alliances, which are more than half false – for the readiest to seize on this silly subject are those whose quality is most doubtful and least established. But if the mocker had turned his attention on himself, he would have found that he was no less extravagant and tiresome in publishing and extolling the prerogatives of his wife's family. Oh, the grievous presumption with which a wife sees herself endowed by the hands of her own husband! If these men understood Latin, they should be told:

*Age! si haec non insanit satis sua sponte, instiga.**

I do not say that no man should judge who is not blameless, for then there would be no judges; nor do I even say that he should be free from the same sort of fault. But I mean that our judgement, in laying a charge against another who is open to it, does not exempt us from an inward examination. It is a deed of charity that one who cannot eradicate a fault in himself shall nevertheless attempt to eradicate it in another, in whom it may be less deeply and stubbornly rooted. And I do not think it an appropriate reply to one who points out a fault in me, to say that he has it also. What of that? The warning is still true and useful. If we had good noses our dung would smell the worse to us for being ours. And it was Socrates' opinion that should a man find himself, his son, and a stranger to be guilty of some violence or wrong, he ought first to offer himself for judicial condemnation, and implore for his purgation the help of the killer's hand; then do the same for his son, and lastly for the stranger. Though this precept may take rather too high a tone, a man should at least present himself first to the punishment of his own conscience.

The senses, which are our proper and principal judges, perceive things only by their external circumstances; and it is no wonder that in every department of our social life there is such a perpetual and universal mixture of ceremonies and superficial

* 'Come, if she is not mad enough of herself, spur her on!' Terence, *Andria*, IV, ii, 9.

shows; so much so that the best and most effective part of our government is made up of them. It is always man that we are dealing with, whose state is surprisingly corporeal.

Let those who wished to construct for us, in these past years, so contemplative and immaterial a religious practice,* not be surprised if there are some who think that it would have vanished and melted between their fingers had it not maintained itself among us more as a mark, title, and instrument of division and faction than by its own power.

So in conversation, the gravity, gown, and fortune of the speaker often lend weight to vain and foolish utterances. No one will presume that so formidable a gentleman, with such a following, has not within him more than a common ability; and that a man who is trusted with so many commissions and offices, and who is so disdainful and overbearing, is not more able than a fellow who salutes him from a distance and to whom no one gives employment. Not only the words, but also the grimaces of these people, are pondered and weighed, everyone striving to give them some fine and solid interpretation. If they stoop to common conversation, and you show them anything but approbation and reverence, they floor you with the authority of their experience; they have heard this, they have seen that, they have done the other; you are overwhelmed with instances. I should like to tell them that the fruit of a surgeon's experience is not the history of his patients and his memory of having cured four cases of plague and three of gout, unless he can draw from that experience conclusions with which to form a judgement and can convince us that he has become wiser in the practice of his art. So in a concert of instruments, we do not hear the lute, the spinet, and the flute; we hear a full harmony, made up of the blending of them all.

If a gentleman's travels and experience in office have improved him, it is for the product of his mind to make this apparent. It is not enough to recount experiences; they must be weighed and sorted; they must be digested and distilled, so that they may yield the reasonings and conclusions they contain.

* Montaigne is referring to Protestantism.

There have never been so many historians. It is always good and useful to listen to them, for they provide us with an abundance of excellent and praiseworthy lessons from the store-house of their memory: a great thing, certainly, as an aid in the conduct of life. But that is not what we are looking for at present; we are looking to see whether these narrators and collectors are praiseworthy in themselves.

I hate any kind of tyranny, whether of words or deeds. I set up a ready resistance against those idle circumstances that delude our judgement through our senses; and when I carefully observe those who have risen to particular eminence, I generally find that they are men like the rest,

> *Rarus enim ferme sensus communis in illa*
> *fortuna.**

Perhaps they appear smaller in our estimation than they really are, because they attempt more and display themselves more; they are not equal to the load they have taken up. There must be more strength and power in the porter than in the burden. A man who has not exerted all his strength leaves you guessing whether he has not some left, or has been tried to the uttermost. But one who sinks beneath his load reveals his capacity and the weakness of his shoulders. That is why we see so many inadequate minds among scholars; more, in fact, than of the other kind. They would have made good farmers, good tradesmen, good craftsmen; their natural strength was cut to that measure.

Learning is a thing of great weight, and they collapse under it; their understanding is not powerful or adroit enough to display and distribute that rich and potent material, to make use of it and get help from it. Learning can only exist in a strong nature, and such natures are very rare. And the weak, says Socrates, by their handling impair the dignity of philosophy. It appears both useless and harmful when in a poor receptacle. See how they waste and befool themselves,

* 'For common sense is seldom found in men of such fortune.' Juvenal, VIII, 73.

Humani qualis simulator simius oris,
quem puer arridens pretioso stamine serum
velavit, nudasque nates ac terga reliquit,
*ludibrium mensis.**

So too it is not enough for those who rule and command us,
and who hold the world in their hands, to have merely a common understanding, to be able to do what we can all do. They
are very far beneath us if they are not very far above us. As they
promise more, so they are under a greater obligation. And therefore silence is in them not only a matter of gravity and decorum,
but often of policy and profit as well. When Megabysus came
to see Apelles in his workshop, he stood for some time without
saying a word. Then he began to give his opinion of the artist's
works, and received this sharp snub: 'So long as you kept quiet
your honour and your fine clothes made me think you a grand
person. But now that I have heard you speak, there is no one
down to the boys in my shop who does not despise you.' His
gorgeous robes and his great state were no excuse for his being
ignorant with a common ignorance, and speaking unintelli-
gently of painting. He should have preserved his outward and
presumed abilities behind a mask of silence. How many foolish
souls, in my time, have made a cold and taciturn expression
serve as evidence of their sound sense and capability!

Dignities and offices are necessarily conferred more by fortune than by merit; and it is often a mistake to lay the blame on
kings. On the contrary, it is marvellous that, having so little
skill, they have so much luck:

Principis est virtus maxima nosse suos.†

For nature has not given them a vision that can extend over so
many peoples, to discover peculiar excellence, and penetrate our
bosoms, where lies the secret of our intentions and our highest
worth. They have to choose us by guesswork and experiment,

* 'Like a monkey, whose face has the look of a man's, and whom a
sportive boy dresses in a rich silk garment, leaving his buttocks and back
bare, to set the table laughing.' Claudian, *In Eutropium*, I, 303.

† 'The greatest virtue in a prince is to know his subjects.' Martial, VIII,
XV.

by family, wealth, learning, and popular reputation; which is very weak evidence. If anyone could find a way of judging men justly and selecting them by standards of reason, he would by that single stroke establish a perfect form of government.

'Yes, but he managed that great affair most successfully.' That says something, but it does not say enough. For it is a rightly approved maxim that we must not judge the plan by the results. The Carthaginians punished their captains for their bad planning, even when it was rectified by a fortunate issue; and the people of Rome often refused a triumph for some great and very profitable victory, because the commander's conduct did not correspond with his good fortune. We commonly observe in the affairs of the world that fortune, to teach us her power over all things, and being pleased to humble our presumption, since she cannot make the incompetent wise, makes them lucky, to spite the virtuous; she is fond of interfering in favour of those actions that she has had the greatest hand in prompting. Hence it is that every day we see the simplest among us carrying through the most important business, both public and private. When certain men expressed surprise that the affairs of Siramnes turned out so badly, seeing that his plans were so wise, the Persian king replied that he was sole master of his plans, but the success of his affairs was in fortune's hands. And simple men can make the same answer, but from the contrary point of view.

The majority of things in the world go of their own accord,

*Fata viam inveniunt.**

The result often justifies a most foolish procedure. Our intervention is hardly more than a routine, and is most commonly based on usage and example rather than on reason. Being once amazed by some very great business, I inquired of the men who had carried it through what their motives and methods had been, and learned that their ideas had been no more than commonplace. And the most commonplace and threadbare are, perhaps the surest and most suitable in practice, if not in appearance.

* 'The Fates find a way.' Virgil, *Aeneid*, III, 395.

299

What if the shallowest reasons are the best grounded, if the lowest and loosest and most threadbare are the most applicable to public business? If the authority of the king's council is to be preserved, outsiders should not be allowed to join in it, or see into it any more closely than from the outer barrier. It must be respected on trust, and as a whole, if it is to keep its reputation.

In deliberating a matter, I give it some shape, and consider it superficially in its immediate aspects; the main and principal part of it I usually leave to heaven:

*Permitte divis caetera.**

Good and bad fortune are, in my opinion, two sovereign powers. It is unwise to think that human wisdom can fill fortune's role; and vain is the endeavour of the man who presumes to cover both cause and consequences, and to lead the progress of his affair by the hand – vain above all in the planning of war. There was never greater prudence and circumspection in military matters than is sometimes seen amongst ourselves. Can it be that, in our anxiety to preserve ourselves for the last scene of this play, we are afraid of getting lost on the way?

I will say more, that our very wisdom and deliberation generally follow the guidance of chance. My will and my reasoning are moved sometimes by one breeze, sometimes by another; and there are many such movements that are outside my control. My mind is subject to chance impulses and agitations that alter from day to day:

Vertuntur species animorum, et pectora motus
nunc alios, alios, dum nubila ventus agebat,
concipiunt.†

Only observe who have most power in the cities, and are most successful in their business, and you will generally find that they are the least talented. There have been cases in which women, children, or the feeble-witted have ruled great states just as well as the most capable princes. And Thucydides says

* 'Leave the rest to the gods.' Horace, *Odes*, 1, ix, 9.
† 'The aspects of the mind change; the heart follows first one feeling, then another, like clouds that are driven by the wind.' Virgil, *Georgics*, 1, 420.

that dull minds are generally more successful in this than the clever. We attribute the results of their good fortune to their wisdom.

> *Ut quisque fortuna utitur*
> *ita praecellet, atque exinde sapere illum omnes dicimus.**

Therefore I strongly affirm that, in every respect, results are poor evidence of our worth and capacity.

Now I was about to say that we have only to look at a man who has been raised to high rank and, although we knew him three days before to be an insignificant person, a picture of greatness and ability steals imperceptibly into our minds. We are persuaded that, having advanced in state and reputation, he has also advanced in merit. We judge of him not by his worth but, as with counters, by the marks of his value. Should his luck change again, should he fall and be lost in the crowd, every one will ask in amazement what it was that hoisted him so high. 'Is this the man?' they will say. 'Is this all that he knew when he was at the top? Are princes content with so little? We were in fine hands, indeed!' This is a thing that I have often seen in my time. Even the mask of greatness that actors put on in the theatre in some sort affects and deceives us. What I myself adore in kings is the crowd of their adorers. All deference and submission is due to them except that of the understanding. My reason was not formed to bow and stoop – that is for my knees.

When asked what he thought of Dionysius' tragedy, Melanthius answered: 'I could not see it; it was so obscured by words.' In the same way, most of those who judge the utterances of the great might say: 'I did not hear what he said; it was so obscured by solemnity, grandeur, and majesty.'

Antisthenes one day tried to persuade the Athenians that they should order their asses to be used for tilling the fields, as their horses were; and he was greeted with the answer that this animal was not born for such service. 'That does not matter,' he replied, 'you have only to give the order. The most ignorant and incapable men whom you appoint to a command in your

* 'When fortune raises a man to the top rank, we all conclude that he has wisdom.' Plautus, *Pseudolus*, II, iii, 15.

wars immediately and invariably become most worthy of their charge, just because you appoint them.'

This is akin to the custom of so many nations who canonize the king they have elected from among themselves, and are not content to honour him but must worship him as well. The Mexicans, once the ceremony of his consecration is performed, no longer dare to look him in the face. But, as if they had deified him by raising him to be king, make him swear, together with his oath to maintain their religion, their laws, and their liberties, and to be valiant, just, and gracious, that he will also make the sun move through the heavens with its accustomed light, the clouds drop their moisture in due season, the rivers run in their channels, and the earth bear all things necessary for his people.

I do not subscribe to this common fashion, and am inclined to doubt a man's ability when I find it accompanied by great fortune and popular acclaim. We must take care to observe how advantageous it is to a man to speak when he pleases, to choose his own subject, to break off or change the conversation with a magisterial authority, and to defend himself against the objections of others by a shake of the head, by a smile, or by silence, in front of an assembly that is tremulous with reverence and respect.

A man of prodigious fortune, throwing in his opinion on some slight matter that was being carelessly discussed around his table, began with these words: 'Nobody who was not a liar or an ignoramus could possibly deny that, etc.' Follow up this philosophical point with a dagger in your hand!

Here is another observation from which I derive great profit. It is that in discussions and debates we should not accept out of hand every remark that seems to us sound. The majority of men are rich in borrowed resources. It may happen that someone will bring out a fine point, a good answer, or a maxim, and put it forward without recognizing its force. That one does not possess all that one borrows, may perhaps be proved by my own case. We must not always grant it, whatever truth or beauty it contains. We must either seriously contest it, or retire under the pretext of not understanding it, to find out from every standpoint what it means to its author. It may be that we are running on his sword, and helping him to strike deeper than he can himself reach.

Sometimes when forced to it, in the stress of battle, I have used ripostes which have succeeded beyond my intention and hopes; I only employed them casually, but their effect was ponderous. When debating with a strong opponent, I like to anticipate his conclusions. I spare him the trouble of explaining himself, I try to forestall his idea while it is still unformed and hatching, the order and precision of his mind warning and threatening me from afar. But in dealing with these others I do quite the opposite; one must understand nothing except from their lips, and presume nothing. If they give judgement in general terms – this is good, that is not – and they happen to be right, see if it is not luck that hit the mark for them. Let them define and limit their judgement a little; why it is so; how it is so.

These universal judgements which I find to be so usual, mean nothing. They are like men who greet a great crowd as a whole and in the mass. Those who have a real acquaintance with people greet them and notice them individually, by name. But this is a hazardous undertaking. For I have seen it happen, more than once every day, that when a man of poor intellectual grounding is reading some book, and wants to display his cleverness by pointing out some fine passage, he will choose the piece he admires so badly that, instead of showing us the excellence of its author, he will only display his own ignorance. It is safe to exclaim, 'How fine that is!' after listening to a whole page of Virgil. That is how the wily ones save their faces. But as for attempting to follow a good author line by line, and to point out by choice and detailed judgements where he excels himself, where he touches the heights, weighing his words, his phrases, his ideas, one after another – keep clear of that! 'We have to discover not only what each person says, but also what he thinks, and even what his reasons are for thinking as he does.'* Every day I hear fools saying things that are not foolish.

When they say something good, let us find out how far they

* Cicero, *De Officiis*, I, 41.

understand it, let us see what hold they have on it. We then help
them to make use of this good expression and that argument,
which is not their own; they only have it in their keeping. They
will have brought it out tentatively and at a venture; it is we who
give it value and authority. You lend them a hand – but to what
purpose? They do not thank you for it, and become even sillier.
Do not back them up, but let them go on – then they will handle
the matter like men who are afraid of scalding themselves. They
dare not change its setting, or its light, or probe its meaning.
Give it the slightest shake, and it will escape them. However
strong or fine their point may be, they will surrender it to you.
Their weapons are good, but they are ill-hafted. How often I
have had experience of this!

Now if you set about enlightening them and corroborating
them, they will seize on you and incontinently rob you of the
advantage of your interpretation. 'That is just what I meant to
say. That is exactly my idea. If I did not put it like that, it was
merely for lack of words.' Nonsense! We must use even cunning
to correct such arrogant stupidity.

Hegesias' teaching, that we must neither hate nor condemn,
but instruct, is right in general; but here it is unjust and inhuman
to aid and set right a man who can make no use of your help and
is only the worse for it. I prefer to let them sink and get even
more bogged than they already are; so deeply indeed, if that is
possible, that they will finally recognize their mistake.

Stupidity and confusion of thought are not things that can be
cured by a piece of advice; and we may fitly say of such correction what Cyrus said in reply to the man who urged him to
exhort his men on the eve of a battle: that men are not suddenly
made brave and warlike by a fine harangue, any more than one
immediately becomes a musician by listening to a fine song. It
needs a preliminary apprenticeship, long and constant instruction. This attention, this care for their correction and guidance,
we owe to our own household, but to go preaching to the first
passer-by, and schoolmastering the ignorance or stupidity of
any chance comer, that is a thing that I very much dislike. I
seldom do it, even in private conversation, which I will break

off entirely rather than resort to elementary and pedantic instruction. I am no more fitted by nature to speak to beginners than to write for them. However false or absurd I may think what is said in company or in discussions between others, I never break out in protest, either by speech or gesture. For the rest, nothing annoys me so much in the stupid as that they are better pleased with themselves than any reasonable person has a right to be.

It is unfortunate that wisdom forbids you to be self-satisfied and trust in yourself, and always sends you away discontented and diffident, whereas an opinionated boldness fills its possessor with joy and assurance. It is the most empty-headed that view other men with scorn, and always return from the battle full of triumphant glee. What is more, their arrogant speech and cheerful looks most often give them the victory in the eyes of the bystanders, who are generally of a poor intelligence, incapable of judging and discerning where the advantage really lies. Obstinacy and heated argument are the surest proofs of stupidity. Is there anything so positive, immovable, disdainful, meditative, grave, and solemn as an ass?

May we not include under the heading of social conversation the brief and pointed repartees exchanged between friends under the influence of mirth and intimacy, when they briskly and pleasantly chaff and poke fun at one another? It is an exercise at which my natural gaiety makes me pretty apt; and if it is not as tense and serious as the other sort of which I have been speaking, it is no less keen and subtle; nor, in the opinion of Lycurgus, is it any less profitable. For my part, I bring more freedom than wit to it, and rely rather on my luck than my ingenuity. But in patience I am perfect, for I can bear retorts that are not only rude but impertinent without losing my temper. When an attack is made against me, and I have no brisk reply to hand, I do not waste my time pursuing the point with weak and tedious persistence that borders on obstinacy. I let it pass and, cheerfully bowing my head, put off my revenge to a better moment. There is no merchant who always makes a profit.

The voice and expression of most men change when their

strength gives out; they burst into untimely anger and, instead of getting their revenge, expose both their weakness and their impatience. In our frivolous moments, we sometimes pluck some secret string of each other's imperfections, which we cannot touch without offence when sober. Thus one points out the defects of another, to our mutual profit.

There are other kinds of rough play, both foolish and cruel, in the French style, which I mortally dislike. For I have a tender and sensitive skin. I have, in my lifetime, seen two princes of the blood royal brought to their graves by this means. It is an ugly thing to fight by way of sport.

For the rest, when I wish to size a man up, I ask him how far he is satisfied with himself, and how much what he says and does pleases him. I want to cut short such fine excuses as: 'I did it casually:

*Ablatum mediis opus est incudibus istud;** *

I did not spend an hour over it; I have not looked at it since.' 'Well, then,' I reply, 'let us put these pieces aside. Give me one that represents you fully, by which you would like to be judged.' And again: 'What do you think best in your work? Is it this feature or that? Its style, its matter, its originality, its judgement, or its learning?' For I notice that a man is usually as wide of the mark in judging his own work as in judging another's; not only because of the affection that creeps in, but out of an inability to know and distinguish it for what it is. The work, by its own power and fortune, may help the workman to transcend his own ideas and knowledge, and so outstrip him. For myself, I am no clearer in judging my own productions than another's: I place my essays now low, now high, with great fluctuations and uncertainties.

There are many books that are useful because of their subject, for which the author derives no praise; and there are good books, as well as good works, which shame the workman. I may describe the fashion of our banquets and our clothes, and write without charm; I may publish the edicts of my time, and

* 'It was taken half-finished from the anvil.' Ovid, *Tristia*, i, vii, 29.

the letters of princes that fall into public hands; I may make an abridgement of a good book – and every abridgement of a good book is a foolish abridgement – and the book itself may be lost, and so on. Posterity may derive singular benefit from such compositions. But what honour shall I get, except through my good fortune? A large proportion of famous books are of this kind.

When, many years ago, I read Philippe de Commines, certainly a very good writer, I noted this saying as an uncommon one: 'that a man must take care not to do his master so great a service that he will not be able to find a proper reward for it'.* I ought to have praised the saying, not the writer, for I met it again in Tacitus, not long ago: 'Benefactions are welcome so long as we feel we are able to return them. But if they pass far beyond that point, we requite them with hatred, not thanks.'† And Seneca vigorously remarks: 'The man who thinks it disgraceful not to repay a favour, would like to have no one to repay.'‡ And Quintus Cicero puts the same thing from a meaner point of view when he says: 'One who thinks he cannot pay you a debt can never be your friend.'§

A subject in itself may give a man the reputation for learning and a good memory; but to judge of those parts in him which are most valuable and most individual, the strength and beauty of his mind, one must know what is his and what is not; and with respect to what is not his, how much one owes him for the choice, arrangement, ornament, and style, which he has supplied. What if he has borrowed the matter and spoilt the form, as often happens? We who have little acquaintance with books are in this difficulty, that when we see some fine fancy in a new poet, some forcible argument in a preacher, we dare not praise him for it until we have been informed by some scholar whether it is his own or another's. Until then I always stand on my guard.

I have just read straight through Tacitus' histories – a thing that I seldom do; it is twenty years since I have given an hour on end to any book – and this I did at the persuasion of a gentle-

* Attributed by Commines to his master, Louis XI.
† Tacitus, *Annals*, IV, xviii.   ‡ *Letters*, LXXXI.
§ *De Petitione Consulatus*, IX.

man* who is greatly esteemed in France, both for his own worth and for an unfailing kind of ability and goodness that he shares with his many brothers. I know of no author who introduces into a public chronicle so many reflections on the natures of private men. And I believe, in total disagreement with his own opinion, that, his special purpose being to describe the lives of the emperors of his time, so strange and violent in every kind of way, and to tell of the many notable deeds to which their subjects were driven by their particular cruelty, he had richer and more attractive material with which to build his discourse and narrative than if he had had to tell of battles and general commotions. I often find him unprofitable, indeed, when he hurries over all those noble deaths† as if he were afraid of boring us with their length and number.

This form of history is by far the most useful. Public movements are more dependent on the guidance of fortune, private ones on our own. The *Annals* of Tacitus are an assessment, rather than an historical account: they contain more precepts than stories. This is not a book to read, but one to study and learn from; it is so full of maxims that they appear in and out of season. It is a nursery of ethical and political reflections for the equipment and adornment of those who play a part in the management of the world. Tacitus' pleading is always based on sound and forcible arguments, delivered in an acute and subtle fashion, that follows the affected style of his age. They were so fond of inflated language that when they found no fine point or subtlety in things, they made the words supply it. His way of writing is not much unlike Seneca's; he seems to me the wordier, and Seneca the more concise. The pen of Tacitus can bring more profit to a sick and disturbed state, such as ours is at present, you might often say that he is describing and stabbing at us.

Those who doubt Tacitus' sincerity plainly betray that they have some grudge against him on another account. He has sound opinions and leans to the right side in Roman politics. I blame him a little, however, for judging Pompey more harshly

* Louis de Foix, count de Gurson, or possibly one of his brothers.
† The deaths of the various emperors' victims.

than the opinion of honest men who lived with and had dealings with him would warrant, and for putting him on an exact par with Marius and Sulla, except that he was more secretive. In his aim of obtaining control of affairs, Pompey was not acquitted of ambition or vindictiveness; even his friends were afraid that victory might have carried him beyond the bounds of reason, but not to the unbridled extent of Marius or Sulla. There is nothing in his life to suggest their deliberate cruelty and tyranny. Besides, we must not treat suspicion as equal to evidence; so I do not believe Tacitus on this point. That his narrative is sincere and accurate may perhaps be argued from the fact that it does not always fit in with the deductions drawn by his judgement, which he follows along the bias he has taken often beyond the point that his material proves. But this he never deigned to distort even by a hair's breadth. He needs no excuse for having accepted the religion of his time, which was enjoined on him by law, and for his ignorance of the true one. That was his misfortune, not his fault.

I have chiefly considered his judgements, and I am not altogether clear about them in every instance. Take for example those words in the letter which Tiberius addressed to the Senate, when old and sick: 'What shall I write to you, sirs, or how shall I write to you, or what shall I not write to you at this time? If I know that, may the gods and goddesses cause me to perish in crueller torments than I now daily suffer.' I do not know why Tacitus ascribes them so surely to a stabbing remorse, tormenting Tiberius's conscience; at least, when I read the passage, I did not see it.

I find it a little mean also that, having occasion to state that he had filled a certain honourable office in Rome, he excuses himself by saying that he is not mentioning this out of ostentation. Such a remark seems to be shabby, coming from a mind like his. For a reluctance to speak directly of oneself argues some lack of spirit. A man of firm and lofty mind who is sound and certain in his judgements will unhesitatingly use himself as an example, as he would some other person; he will testify as frankly of his own experience as of another's.

One must waive these common rules of modesty for the sake of truth and liberty. I venture not only to speak of myself, but to speak of myself exclusively; I lose my way when I write of anything else, and wander from my subject. I am not so immoderately in love with myself, nor so attached to and bound up with myself as to be unable to distinguish and consider myself objectively as I do a neighbour or a tree. It is just as much a mistake not to see one's own value as to say more about oneself than one knows. We owe God more love than we owe ourselves, and we know Him less; and yet we talk our fill about Him.

If his writings reveal anything of his qualities, Tacitus was a great man, upright and fearless, and virtuous, not out of superstition, but out of philosophy and high-mindedness. We may think him somewhat rash in his statements, as when he says of a soldier who was carrying a load of wood, that his hands became so numb with cold that they stuck to his burden, and remained there fixed and dead, having broken off from his arms. In these matters, I am accustomed to bow to the authority of such great witnesses. When he says also of Vespasian that, by the grace of the god Serapis, he cured a blind woman in Alexandria by anointing her eyes with his spittle, and performed some other miracle, he is following the example and doing the duty of all good historians. They keep a record of important events; and among matters of public interest popular opinions and rumours have their place. It is the historian's task to set down the common beliefs, not to censor them. That is the business of theologians and philosophers, who are directors of consciences.

Therefore it was that his fellow-historian, a great man like himself, very wisely said: 'Truly I write down more than I believe, for I can never affirm what I doubt, nor suppress what I have heard';* and another† observes: 'It is not worth while either affirming or refuting these things. One must stick to the report.' And Tacitus, writing in an age when the belief in miracles was beginning to wane, says that, even so, he will not willingly fail to insert in his *Annals*, and give currency to, things accepted by so many worthy men, and regarded with such

* Quintus Curtius, IX, i.   † Livy, I, preface, and VIII, vi.

reverence in ancient times. That is a very good saying. Let them deliver history to us rather as they receive it than according to their beliefs.

I who am sole arbiter of the matter that I treat of, and am accountable for it to nobody, do not trust myself in all respects, all the same. I often risk some intellectual sallies of which I am suspicious, and certain verbal subtleties, which make me shake my head. But I let them go at a venture. I see that some are praised for such things; it is not for me alone to judge. I present myself standing and lying down, front and back, facing left and right, and in all my natural attitudes. Minds, though equal in strength, are not always alike in tastes and practice.

This is what my memory of Tacitus presents to me in a general way, and with no great certainty. All general judgements are weak and imperfect.

BOOK THREE: Chapter 12

On physiognomy

ALMOST all the opinions we hold are taken on authority and trust. There is no harm in this; we could not choose worse than by ourselves in so feeble an age. We approve of Socrates' discourses, as reflected in the works which his friends have left us, only out of respect for their general acceptance,* not from our own knowledge. They do not conform to our practice. If something of that kind should make an appearance today, there are few men who would value it.

We perceive no beauties that are not sharpened, prinked out, and inflated by artifice. Such as appear in their pure and natural simplicity easily escape a vision as coarse as ours. Theirs is a delicate and hidden beauty; it needs a clear and purified sight to discover their secret brightness. Is not simplicity, according to us, akin to foolishness and an object of scorn? Socrates sets his mind working with a natural and ordinary motion. A peasant says this, a woman says that. His talk is always of carters, joiners,

* By authors and critics in the past.

cobblers, and masons. His inductions and comparisons are drawn from the commonest and most familiar actions of men; everyone understands him. Under so humble a form we should never have recognized the nobility and splendour of his admirable ideas – we who regard as low and dull all that are not embellished by learning, and who recognize riches only in pomp and show. Our world is fashioned solely for ostentation; men only puff themselves up with wind, and leap here and there, like balls. Socrates' purpose was not vain and fanciful; it was to provide us with matter and precepts that are of real and very direct service to life,

> *servare modum, finemque tenere,*
> *naturamque sequi.* *

He was, moreover, always one and the same, and raised himself not spasmodically but by temperament to his highest efforts. Or, to put it better, he raised nothing, but rather brought down, reduced, and subjected all strength, obstacles, and difficulties to his own proper and natural level. In the case of Cato we can most clearly see that his pace is strained far beyond that of common men; in the brave exploits of his life and in his death, we always feel that he is mounted on a high horse. But Socrates moves close to the ground and, at a gentle and ordinary pace, discourses on the most useful subjects; and, when confronted with death and with the thorniest obstacles he could meet with, he follows the ordinary course of human life.

It is fortunate that the man who best deserves to be known and presented as an example to the world should be the one of whom we have the most certain knowledge. He has been revealed in a clear light by the most clear-sighted men who ever lived; the accounts that we have of him are admirable both for their fidelity and their fullness. What a great thing it is that he was able to impart such order to thoughts as simple as a child's; without straining or altering them, he drew from them the most beautiful effects possible to the human mind. He does not display this in a rich or elevated, but merely in a healthy state,

---

* 'To preserve the mean, pursue one's aim, and follow nature.' Lucan, II, 381.

yet assuredly its health is both sound and vigorous.

By these common and natural means, by these ordinary and familiar ideas, without exciting or pricking himself on, he expounded not only the most regular, but also the most exalted and vigorous beliefs, actions, and morals that ever were. It is he who brought human wisdom down again from the skies where it was wasting its labour, and restored it to man, with whom its most normal, its most toilsome, and its most useful business lies.

Hear him pleading before his judges. See with what reasons he rouses his courage in the hazards of war, with what arguments he strengthens his patience against calumny, tyranny, death, and against his wife's temper. There is nothing borrowed from art and learning; the simplest may here recognize their own powers and strength; it is impossible to mount higher or to drop lower. He has done human nature a great kindness by showing it how much it can do of itself.

We are each of us richer than we think; but we are trained to borrow and to beg; we are taught to make more use of what is another's than of our own. No man ever knows how to stop at the limit of his needs; of pleasure, riches, and power he grasps more than he can hold; his greed is incapable of moderation. I find that it is the same with his curiosity to know; he cuts out much more work for himself than he can do, and very much more than he has any need for, in the belief that the utility of knowledge is proportionate to the amount of its subject-matter. 'In learning, as in all other things, we are addicted to intemperance.'* And Tacitus is right in praising Agricola's mother for curbing in her son a too fervent appetite for books. Looked at with a steady eye, it is a good thing which, like all other human blessings, has a great deal of vanity and weakness proper and natural to it; and this costs it very dear.

The acquisition of learning is much more dangerous than that of any other food or drink. For with other things, we carry home what we have bought in some vessel; and there we have leisure to examine its value and decide how much of it we shall use, and when. But learning we cannot at the outset put in any

* Seneca, *Letters*, CVI.

other vessel but our minds; we swallow it as we buy it, and by the time we leave the market we are already either infected or improved. There is some that only obstructs and burdens us instead of nourishing us; and some too that, while pretending to cure us, gives us poison.

It once pleased me to see, in one place or another, men who had, in the name of religion, made vows of ignorance as well as of chastity, poverty, and penitence. This too is a gelding of our unruly appetites, a blunting of that cupidity which drives us on to the study of books, and a ridding the mind of that luxuriant complacency which tickles us with the belief in our learning. And it is a rich fulfilment of the view of worldly poverty to add to it poverty of mind. We need hardly any knowledge to live happily. And Socrates tells us that we have this within us; he teaches the way to find and make use of it. All these accomplishments of ours that are in excess of what is natural are more or less vain and superfluous. It is enough if they do not burden and disturb us more than they do us good. 'Little learning is needed to make a sound mind.'* They are feverish excesses of the intellect, a blundering and restless instrument. Collect yourself, and you will find within you nature's true arguments against death, which are the fittest to serve you in your need; it is they that make a peasant, and entire nations, die with the same constancy as a philosopher. Should I have done so less cheerfully before I had read the *Tusculans?* I think not; and when I come to the point, I feel that my tongue is the richer for them, but my heart not at all. It is just as nature fashioned it for me; and it arms for the battle in the common and ordinary way. Books have served me not so much for instruction as for mental exercise. What if learning, while trying to provide us with new defences against natural misfortunes, has rather impressed their weight and magnitude on our imaginations than furnished it with arguments and subtle reasonings to protect us against them? These are sophistries indeed with which it often alarms us to little purpose. Observe the wisest and most concise writers, and see how many frivolous arguments, which when

* Seneca, *Letters,* CVI.

we examine them closely appear quite bodiless, they will scatter around one good one. These are merely verbal tricks, which deceive us. But so long as the deception may be to our advantage, I do not care to examine them any further. There are enough arguments of this kind in different parts of my book, either borrowed or imitated. So we must be somewhat on our guard against taking for strength what is only nice phrasing, or for solid what is merely acute, or for good what is only beautiful: 'things that please the palate better than the stomach'.* Not everything that tastes good is nourishing, 'When it is a matter not of the mind but of the soul.'†

To see the efforts that Seneca takes to prepare himself for death, to see him sweating with the anguished effort to stiffen himself, and struggling for so long to keep a hold on his perch, would have shaken his reputation with me, had he not, in dying, most valiantly sustained it. His intense and frequent agitation shows that he was naturally a passionate and impetuous man. 'A great soul speaks more calmly and with more confidence.' 'A man's mind does not differ in colour from his soul.'‡ He has to be convinced at his own expense, and this in some sort shows that he was hard pressed by his enemy.

Plutarch's style, being more informal and less strained, is in my opinion the more virile and persuasive; I could easily believe that the workings of his soul were more assured and under better control. Seneca, being the sharper, pricks us and makes us jump; his effect is more on the spirit. Plutarch, the more sober, constantly instructs, sustains, and fortifies us; his effect is more on the understanding. The one sweeps our judgement away, the other convinces it.

I have seen other writings also, even more respected, which in depicting the struggle their authors maintain against the pricks of the flesh, represent them as so hot, so powerful, and so invincible that we who are of the commonest sort must wonder as much at the strangeness and unknown force of their temptations as at their resistance.

* Cicero, *Tusculans*, v, 5.   † Seneca, *Letters*, LXXV.
‡ ibid., CXV and XCV.

For what purpose do we subject ourselves to this laborious learning? Let us look down and see the poor people scattered about the fields, their heads bowed over their labour; they know nothing of Aristotle or Cato, nothing of example or precept. From them nature every day draws purer and stronger demonstrations of fortitude and patience than those that we study so attentively at school. How many do I commonly see who disregard poverty? How many who desire death, or who meet it without alarm and distress? That man who is digging my garden has this morning buried his father or his son. The very names by which they call their diseases soften and mitigate their harshness. Phthisis is for them a cough; dysentery a looseness of the bowels, pleurisy a cold; and as they give them gentle names, so they bear them gently. They must be very ill before they interrupt their daily labours; they only take to their beds to die. 'This simple virtue, which is within the reach of all, has been turned into an obscure and subtle science.'*

I was writing this at a time when a great load of our troubles had for some months been lying with all its weight on top of me.† I had, on the one hand, the enemy at my door; on the other, the marauders – a worse enemy: 'their weapons are not arms but crimes',‡ and I experienced every sort of military violence at once.

> *Hostis adest dextra levaque a parte timendus,*
> *vicinoque malo terret utrumque latus.*§

An unnatural war! Other wars act outwardly; this one acts inwardly also, gnawing and destroying itself with its own poison. It is of so malign and destructive a nature that it ruins itself together with everything else, and in its frenzy tears itself limb from limb. We more often see it dissolving of itself than from any lack of necessary resources or by the power of the enemy. All discipline flies from it. It comes to cure sedition, and is full

---

* Seneca, *Letters*, xcv.
  † In the latter part of 1585, during the Wars of Religion.
  ‡ Seneca, *Letters*, xcv.
  § 'The enemy threatens me from right and left, and terrifies me with imminent disaster from either side.' Ovid, *Ex Ponto*, i, iii, 57.

of it; it sets out to punish disobedience, and gives an example of it; and, though waged in defence of the laws, performs its share of rebellion against its own. What state have we come to? Our medicine spreads infection.

> *Notre mal s'empoisonne*
> *Du secours qu'on lui donne.**

> *Exuperat magis aegrescitque medendo.†*

> *Omnia fanda, nefanda, malo permista furore,*
> *iustificam nobis mentem avertere deorum.‡*

At the beginning of these general maladies we can distinguish the sound from the sick. But when they come to stay, as ours has, the whole body is infected from head to foot; no part is free from corruption. For there is no air that is inhaled so greedily, or that so spreads and penetrates as licence does. Our armies now are bound and held together only by foreign cement; it is no longer possible to form a steadfast and orderly body of Frenchmen. What a disgrace! The only discipline that exists is that displayed by the soldiers we have hired. As for ourselves, we follow our own judgement, not the leader's. Every man decides for himself; a commander has more to do internally than externally. It is his business to follow, wheedle, and give way. He alone has to obey; all the rest are free and disunited.

It pleases me to see ambition reduced to such weakness and cowardice, to such debasement and servility, in order to attain its end. But it gives me no pleasure to see honest natures, capable of just dealings, becoming daily corrupted by the management and command of this turmoil. Prolonged toleration engenders habit, habit engenders assent and imitation. We had enough ignoble souls without spoiling the good and generous. Indeed, if we continue like this, there will hardly be anyone left to whom we can entrust the health of this state, supposing that fortune should restore it.

* 'Our disease is aggravated by the aid we give it.'
† 'It mounts the higher and grows worse by treatment.' *Aeneid*, XII, 46.
‡ 'All things right and wrong, confused by our evil frenzy, have turned the just minds of the gods away from us.' Catullus, *Epithalamium*, 406.

Hunc saltem everso iuvenem succurrere saeclo
ne prohibete.*

What has become of that old precept that soldiers should
fear their commander more than the foe? And of that wonderful
example of the apple-tree that happened to be enclosed within
the precincts of the Roman army's camp, and was found on the
day after the soldiers moved off, with every one of its ripe and
delicious apples still hanging for its owner to pick? I could wish
that our youth, instead of spending their time in less profitable
travels and less honourable studies, would devote one half of
it to watching naval warfare under some good Captain-Com-
mander of Rhodes, and the other to observing the discipline of
the Turkish armies, which is very different from that of ours,
and greatly superior to it. One feature that distinguishes it is
that our soldiers become more licentious on active service,
whilst theirs grows more restrained and timid. For violences or
thefts committed against humble people, which are punished
by the bastinado in peacetime, are capital offences in time of
war. For an egg taken without payment, the penalty is fixed by
tariff at fifty strokes of the cane; for anything else however
trivial, except the theft of food, they are impaled or beheaded
without more ado. I was astonished to read in the history of
Selim, the cruellest conqueror that ever lived, that when he
subdued Egypt, the wonderful gardens around the city of
Damascus, with their abundance of luscious fruit, were left untouched by his soldiers' hands, open and unwalled though they
were.

But is there any political wrong so bad that it is worth fighting with so deadly a drug as civil war? Not even, said Favonius,
the usurpation of control over a state by a tyrant. Plato also will
not allow of a country's peace being disturbed in order to cure
it, and will accept no reform that is paid for by the blood and
ruin of its citizens. He declares that it is a good man's duty in

---

* 'Do not, at least, prevent this young man from coming to the rescue of
a ruined age.' Virgil, *Georgics*, 1, 500. Virgil was referring to Augustus,
Montaigne to Henry of Navarre, heir presumptive to the throne since 1584,
who was a leader on the Protestant side.

such a case to leave things as they are, only praying God to wield his wonder-working hand; and he seems to disapprove of his great friend Dion for having acted somewhat differently.

I was a Platonist in this respect before ever I knew there was a Plato in the world. And if this great man must be absolutely excluded from our fellowship* – one whose purity of conscience was rewarded with the divine favour of so deep a penetration towards the Christian light amidst the general darkness of the world in his time – I do not think it becomes us to be taught by a heathen how wicked it is not to look to God for help that can come only from Him, and without our cooperation.

I often doubt whether, among all the many participators in our wars, even one can be found of such feeble understanding as willingly to believe that he has come closer to reformation by such distorted paths; that he has moved towards salvation by the most certain means of damnation that we possess; that by overturning the government, the magistracy, and the laws, under whose guardianship God has placed him, by dismembering his mother and giving her limbs to be devoured by her oldest enemies, by filling his brothers' hearts with parricidal hate, by calling the devils and furies to his aid, he can have been supporting the most holy sweetness and justice of the divine word.

Ambition, avarice, cruelty, vengeance, have not enough natural fury in themselves; let us inflame them and stir them up with the high-sounding title of justice and devotion. It is impossible to imagine a worse outlook than when wickedness has become lawful, and by leave of the magistrate puts on the cloak of virtue. 'Nothing has a more deceptive face than a corrupt religion, in which the divine will acts as a screen for crimes.'† The extreme form of injustice, according to Plato, is one in which wrong passes for right.

* Montaigne seems to be pleading that Plato should be accepted as a forerunner of Christianity, since such lessons as he can give ought not to be accepted from a pagan.
† Livy, XXXIX, xvi.

The common people suffered greatly at that time, not present losses only,

> *undique totis*
> *usque adeo turbatur agris,**

but future losses also. The living had to suffer, and so had those who were as yet unborn. They robbed them, and consequently myself, even of hope, snatching from them all their means of providing for themselves for many years to come.

> *Quae nequeunt secum ferre aut abducere perdunt,*
> *et cremat insontes turba scelesta casas.*†

> *Muris nulla fides, squalent populatibus agri.*‡

This was not the only blow that I suffered. I incurred the penalties which accompany moderation in such diseases. I was belaboured from all sides; to the Ghibellines I was a Guelph, to the Guelphs a Ghibelline. One of my poets puts this very well, but I do not know where. The situation of my house and my relations with my neighbours§ made me look one thing, my life and actions another. No formal accusations were made, for there was nothing to lay hold of. I never infringe the laws; and if anyone had called me to account, he might have found himself worse incriminated than I. There were mute suspicions which circulated in private; and for these there is never a lack of plausibility under conditions of such confusion, any more than there is a lack of envious or foolish minds. I usually strengthen any injurious presumptions that fortune spreads against me by my way of always refraining from self-justification, excuses, and explanations, in the belief that to plead for my conscience is to compromise it. 'The clarity of the case is impaired by argu-

* 'With the whole countryside in such a state of turmoil.' Virgil, *Eclogues*, I, 11.

† 'What they cannot carry with them or remove, they destroy: the marauding rabble sets fire to inoffensive huts.' Ovid, *Tristia*, III, x, 65, adapted.

‡ 'There is no safety in walls, and the fields are laid waste by pillage.' Claudian, *Against Eutropius*, I, 244.

§ Who were mainly Protestants.

ments.'* And as if everyone saw as clearly into me as I do myself, instead of recoiling from an accusation, I go out to meet it. Indeed I tend to strengthen it by an ironical and scornful confession, if I do not keep quite silent on the subject, as something unworthy of an answer. But those who take this for overweening confidence feel scarcely less spite against me than those who mistake it for the weakness of an indefensible cause, especially those in high places, for whom lack of deference is the supreme fault, and who deal harshly with such self-conscious rectitude as does not feel submissive, humble, and suppliant. I have often run my head against that pillar.

However this may be, what I suffered then would have made an ambitious man hang himself, and an avaricious man too. I have not the least interest in gaining wealth.

> *Sit mihi quod nunc est, etiam minus, ut mihi vivam*
> *quod superest aevi, si quid superesse volent di.*†

But the losses that befall me through wrongs done me by another, whether by theft or violence, hurt me about as much as they would a man tortured by the disease of avarice. The wound is immeasurably more bitter than the loss.

A thousand different kinds of ills fell on me, one after another; I should have suffered them more cheerfully if they had fallen all together. I was already meditating to whom among my friends I could entrust an impoverished and unhappy old age; having cast my eyes in every direction, I found myself stripped to my shirt. When a man tumbles headlong and from such a height, it must be into the arms of a strong and firm affection that is favoured by fortune; such affections are rare, if they exist at all. Finally I realized that it was safest to rely on myself in my distress, and that if fortune should prove cold in her favours to me, I must the more earnestly see to my own protection, and more closely cling to and consider my own interest. In all matters, men throw themselves on external supports to spare their

---

* Cicero, *De Natura Deorum*, III, iv.

† 'May I keep what I now have, or even less: and may I live on it for the rest of my life, if the gods please that there shall be any left to me.' Horace, *Epistles*, I, xviii, 107.

own, which alone are certain and powerful, when one knows how to make use of them. Everyone turns elsewhere and to the future, since no one has discovered himself.

I decided that these were profitable disasters since, in the first place, bad pupils must be corrected by the rod when reasoning is not enough, even as we straighten a warped plank by heat and the force of wedges. For so long I have been urging myself to rely on myself and be independent of outside help, and yet I still keep casting glances to the side. A salutation, a gracious word from a great man, a pleasant smile, tempt me. God knows there is no dearth of them in these times, and how little they mean! I listen, moreover, without a frown to the blandishments that are offered me to lure me, into public life, and I protest so weakly that I appear quite willing to let myself be persuaded. Now a spirit so intractable needs a beating; it needs some good strokes of the mallet to knock together and tighten up this vessel, which is beginning to get loose and weak at the joints, to break up and fall to pieces.

In the second place, this misfortune would serve me as an exercise to prepare me for worse, since I, who had expected, by the kindness of fortune and my own natural qualities, to be among the last to be caught by this storm, had proved to be among the first. It would teach me to restrict my way of life in good time, and make it ready for a new condition. True freedom is to have complete power over one's own activities. 'He is most powerful who has power over himself.'*

In an ordinary time of tranquillity, we prepare for common and moderate mischances, but in the confusion in which we have been living for the last thirty years every Frenchman, whether as a private individual or a member of society, sees himself every hour on the edge of complete disaster to his fortune. Therefore our hearts must be the better supplied with strong and vigorous resources. Let us be grateful to fate for having made us live in an age that is neither soft, languid, nor idle. Many a man who could never have done so by other means will win fame by his misfortunes.

* Seneca, *Letters*, xc.

As I seldom read in histories of such disorders in other states without regretting that I could not be present to get a closer view of them, so my curiosity makes me in some way congratulate myself on being a witness of this noteworthy spectacle and seeing our society's death, its symptoms, and its nature. And since I am unable to delay it, I am content that I was destined to be a spectator of it and to get instruction from it. Thus we eagerly desire to see, even in pictures and the fictions of the theatre, the tragedies of human fortune, played out before our eyes.

It is not that what we hear does not excite our compassion, but we take pleasure in the pain that is aroused within us by these pitiable events, since they are so rare. Nothing tickles that does not prick; and a good historian skims over peaceful times, as over stagnant water or a still sea, to return to seditions and wars, to which he knows we beckon him. I doubt whether I am honest enough to confess at how small a cost to my peace and life's repose I have spent half my days amidst the ruin of my country. I pay rather too little for my tolerance of misfortunes which do not touch me personally; and when inclined to pity myself, consider not so much what is taken from me as what remains safe, both within and without.

There is some consolation in avoiding now one, now another of the ills that successively glance in our direction and then strike elsewhere, not far away. Also in this, that where public interest is concerned, the more widely my sympathy is dispersed, the weaker it is. And what is more, it is almost certainly true that 'we only feel public calamities in so far as they affect our private interests';* and that the state of health from which we declined was such as itself to weaken any regret we may feel for its loss. It was health, but only by comparison with the sickness that followed. We have not fallen from a very great height. The corruption and brigandage that is found in high places as part of the established order seems to me the least tolerable. We are less outraged at being robbed in a wood than in a place of safety. Our health was a general cohesion of individual

* Livy, xxx, xliv.

members, each one more diseased than the last, and afflicted for the most part with inveterate sores which no longer admitted of cure or asked for it.

This collapse, therefore, certainly inspirited me more than it depressed me, thanks to my conscience which bore itself not only peaceably but proudly; and I found no reason to complain of myself. Besides as God never sends wholly unmixed evil to man any more than unmixed good, my health at that time remained unusually sound; and as I can do nothing without health, there are few things that I cannot do with it. It afforded me the means of awakening all my powers, and of deflecting the stroke which might well have dealt me a deeper wound. And this patience of mine taught me that I had some power of resisting fortune, and that it would take a heavy blow to throw me out of my saddle. I do not say this to provoke her into making a more vigorous attack upon me. I am her servant, I hold out my hands to her; let her be satisfied in God's name!

Do I feel her assaults? Yes, I do. As one who is overwhelmed and possessed by grief will yet allow himself sometimes to be tickled by some joke, and break into a smile, I too have sufficient power over myself to keep my state of mind generally calm, and free from painful brooding. Yet, every now and then, I let myself be surprised by the stings of these unpleasant thoughts, which strike me even as I am putting on my armour to chase them away, or to struggle with them.

Here is a further aggravation of the evil, which came upon me in the wake of the rest. Both outside and inside my house I was greeted by a plague of the utmost severity. For, as healthy bodies are subject to grave maladies because they can be overcome by these alone, so our very healthy climate, in which no contagion had gained a foothold within living memory, though it had been in the vicinity, became poisoned, with the most unusual results.

Mista senum et iuvenum densantur funera, nullum
*saeva caput Proserpina fugit.**

* 'The obsequies of old and young crowd pell-mell together; no head is spared by cruel Proserpine.' Horace, *Odes*, I, XXVIII, 19.

I had to put up with this strange situation, that the sight of my house was frightful to me. Everything in it was unguarded, and at the mercy of anyone who might wish to take it. I, who am so hospitable, was engaged in a painful hunt for some refuge for my family: a family astray, alarming to their friends and to themselves, and spreading horror wherever they tried to settle. They had to change their abode as soon as any one of them began to feel so much as an ache in one finger-tip. Then every ailment is taken for the plague; no one gives himself time to investigate it. And the best of the joke is that, according to the rules of the profession, every time you go near any danger you have to spend forty days worrying about the disease, with your imagination working on you in its own way all that time, and making even your health into a fever.

All this would have affected me much less if I had not had to feel for the sufferings of others, and to spend six months miserably acting as guide to this caravan. For I carry in myself my own antidotes, which are resolution and endurance. Apprehension, which is especially dangerous in this disease, hardly affects me at all. And if I had been alone and allowed myself to catch it, it would have been a much more cheerful as well as a much more distant flight.* It is not, in my opinion, one of the worst kinds of death, it is generally quick, unconscious, and painless. One is consoled by sharing the general fate, and spared the ceremonial, the mourning, and the crowds of onlookers. But as for the people around us, not one soul in a hundred could escape:

> *videas desertaque regna*
> *pastorum, et longe saltus lateque vacantes.*†

In this place the best part of my revenue is from labour; the land that a hundred men had once worked for me lay a long time fallow.

* Montaigne's meaning seems to be that he would not have minded dying. But the sentence can also be translated: 'If I had been willing to run away alone, I should have gone further and have done so cheerfully.' The transition to the next sentence would, in that case, be rather abrupt.

† 'You see the realms of the shepherds deserted, and empty pastures far and wide.' Virgil, *Georgics*, III, 476, slightly altered.

But what an example of fortitude did we not then see in the simplicity of all these people? Each and everyone renounced all concern for life. The grapes, which are the principal wealth of the district, remained hanging on the vines; and all unconcernedly prepared themselves for a death which they expected that night or on the morrow; there was so little fear in their expressions or their voices that they seemed to have resigned themselves as to a necessity, and to regard it as a universal and inevitable doom.

Death is always inevitable. But on what small things depends our fortitude in dying! The difference of a few hours in our distance from it, the mere consideration of having company totally alters our feeling towards it. Look at these people. Because they are dying in the same month, children and the young and old, they cease to be appalled, they cease to lament. I saw some who were afraid of being left behind, as in some dreadful solitude, and I generally found them quite unconcerned except about their burial. It distressed them to see bodies scattered about the fields, at the mercy of the wild animals, which immediately infested them. How human ideas vary! The Neorites, a people conquered by Alexander, threw the bodies of the dead into the depths of their woods, to be devoured: the only method of disposal which they considered a happy one.

One man, while still healthy, was digging his grave; some others lay down in theirs while they were yet alive; and one of my labourers, as he was dying, shovelled the earth down over himself with his hands and feet. Was not this like getting under the covers to sleep more comfortably? – an action almost as sublime as that of the Roman soldiers who were found after the battle of Cannae, with their heads thrust into holes, which they had dug and filled up with their own hands as they stifled. In short, a whole nation was soon habituated by practice to a course of action in every way as firm as the most studied and premeditated fortitude.

Most of the instructions by which learning seeks to strengthen our courage have more show than force in them, and more style than effect. We have abandoned nature, and now wish to teach lessons to her who once guided us so happily and safely. And yet from the traces of her instruction and from such reflections of her image as still remain, by the favour of ignorance, imprinted on the lives of this unpolished crowd of rustics, learning is compelled to borrow every day patterns of constancy, innocence, and calm for the benefit of its disciples. It is good to see that they, though full of all their fine knowledge, have to imitate these foolish simpletons, and to do so in their elementary actions of virtue; and that our wisdom receives from the very animals instructions that are most useful in the concerns of our life. They teach us how to live and die, how to husband our wealth, love and bring up our children, and maintain justice – a singular testimony to human infirmity. They also teach us how the reason, which we use as it suits us, ever discovering something different and something novel, leaves in us no apparent trace of nature. Men have treated it as perfumers treat oil; they have refined it with so many arguments and far-fetched reasonings that it has become variable and individual to each person, and has lost its own constant and universal aspect. So if we want evidence of it, that is subject neither to partiality nor to corruption nor to differences of opinion, we must look for it in animals. It is indeed true that even animals do not always follow nature's path exactly, but their divergences from it are so slight that you can always perceive the track, just as horses that are led by hand do a great deal of prancing and leaping, but only to the length of their halters, and always follow the steps of the man who leads them; and as a hawk takes its flight, always under the restraint of its leash.

'Meditate upon exile, storms, war, sickness and shipwreck, so that no disaster will find you a novice.'* What good will it do us to anticipate so carefully all the disasters of human life, and prepare ourselves with such pains to meet just those which will probably never touch us? 'To be likely to suffer is as depressing as actually to have suffered.'† It is not only blows that alarm us, but also the wind and the noise. Why like a frenzied man –for this is certainly a frenzy – must you go and ask to be whipped,

* Seneca, *Letters,* XCI and CVII. † ibid., LXXIV.

because fortune may happen to have a whipping waiting for you in the future? Why put on your fur gown at midsummer because you will need it at Christmas?

'Make haste and try the evils that may befall you, the worst especially. Test yourself,' they say, 'and make sure you can bear them.' On the contrary, the easiest and most natural way would be to banish even the thought of them. They will not come soon enough, it is argued, their true duration is not long enough; the mind must extend and prolong them, must absorb them beforehand and cherish them, as if they did not sufficiently weigh on our senses. 'They will lie heavily enough when they come,' says one of the masters, not of some tender sect but of the most severe. In the meantime, be kind to yourself, believe what you like best. What good will it do you to rush ahead and welcome your misfortune, to lose the present out of fear for the future, to be miserable now because you are likely to be so in time?'* These are his words. Learning certainly does us a good service when it teaches us the exact extent of our evils,

Curis acuens mortalia corda.†

It would be a pity if any part of their greatness were to escape our perception and knowledge!

It is certain that to most men the preparation for death has been more tormenting than the pangs themselves. It was once said with truth, and by a writer of great intelligence, that 'the senses are less afflicted by physical suffering than by the thought of it'.‡

The feeling that death is at hand sometimes inspires us of itself with a quick resolve no longer to evade a thing that is quite inevitable. Many gladiators in times past, after some cowardly fighting, have been seen to swallow death bravely, offering their throats to their opponent's sword, and welcoming it. To contemplate death in the future calls for a courage that is slow, and consequently difficult to acquire. If you do not know how to die, never mind. Nature will give you full and adequate

* Seneca, *Letters*, XIII and XXIV, quoted by Montaigne in French.
† 'Sharpening men's wits with cares.' Virgil, *Georgics*, I, 123.
‡ Quintilian, *Inst. Orat.*, I, 12, slightly altered.

instruction on the spot. She will do this job for you neatly; do not worry yourself with the thought.

> *Incertam frustra, mortales, funeris horam*
> *quaeritis, et qua sit mors aditura via.**

> *Paene minor certam subito perferre ruinam,*
> *quod timeas gravius sustinuisse diu.†*

We trouble our life by thoughts about death, and our death by thoughts about life. The first saddens us, the second terrifies us. It is not for death that we are preparing; it is too momentary. A quarter of an hour's suffering, without any hurtful consequences, does not deserve special lessons. The truth is that we are preparing ourselves against the preparations for death. Philosophy commands us to have death always before our eyes, to foresee it and to reflect upon it in advance; and it then gives us rules and precautions to prevent this foresight and reflection from harming us. This is what physicians do who bring diseases upon us, so that they may have occasion to use their drugs and their art. If we have not known how to live, it is wrong to teach us how to die, and to give the end a different shape from the whole. If we have known how to live steadfastly and calmly, we shall know how to die in the same way. They may boast as much as they please, that 'a philosopher's whole life is a contemplation of death'.‡ It seems to me, however, that it is indeed the end but not the aim of life; it is its conclusion, its extreme point, yet not its object. Life should contain its own aim, its own purposes; its proper study is to regulate itself, guide itself, and endure itself. Among the many duties included under the general and principal head of knowing how to live, is this article of knowing how to die; and it would be one of the lightest if our fears did not weigh it down.

To judge them by their utility and by their natural truth, the

---

* 'In vain, mortals, do you seek to know the uncertain hour of your death, and the path by which it will come.' Propertius, II, xxvii, 1.

† 'It is less painful suddenly to undergo certain ruin than to suffer from a prolonged fear.' Pseudo-Gallus, I, 277.

‡ Cicero, *Tusculans*, I, xxx.

lessons of simplicity are hardly inferior to those which learning preaches in the contrary sense. Men differ in tastes and strength; they must be guided to what is good for them, according to their natures and by different roads.

*Quo me cumque rapit tempestas, deferor hospes.**

I have never found amongst my neighbours any peasant who deliberated on the bearing and assurance with which he would pass his final hours. Nature teaches him only to think of death when he is dying. And then it is with better grace than Aristotle, upon whom the end pressed with double weight, its own and that of a long anticipation. That is why Caesar thought that the death which was least premeditated was the happiest and the easiest. 'He grieves more than necessary who grieves before it is necessary.'†

The bitterness of these imaginings springs from our curiosity. So we are always bothering ourselves by trying to forestall and control nature's ordinances. It is only the learned who let these thoughts spoil their dinners while they are in good health, and who scowl at the image of death. The common man has no need of remedy or consolation till the blow strikes; and he dwells on it only at the moment when he feels it. Are we not right when we say that it is stolidity and lack of imagination that give the common man his patience under present evils, and his profound unconcern with unhappy events in the future; that since his mind is coarse and insensitive, it is less easily penetrated and shaken? If this be so, for God's sake let us set up a school of stupidity. For the best fruit that learning promises us is that to which stupidity leads its disciples so gently.

We shall not lack good teachers to interpret natural simplicity. Socrates will be one. For, to the best of my memory, he spoke in some such sense as this to the judges who were deliberating on his doom: 'I am afraid, sirs, that if I plead with you not to put me to death, I may convict myself of the charge I am accused of; which is that I pretend to be wiser than other men, as having some more hidden knowledge of the things that are

* 'Wherever the storm carries me, I land as a guest.' Horace, *Epistles*, I, i, 15.　　　　　　　　　　† Seneca, *Letters*, XCVIII.

above and below us. I know that I have had no dealings or acquaintance with death, nor have I met anyone who experienced it and can instruct me as to its nature. Those who fear it assume that they know it. For myself, I neither know what it is, nor what the other world is like. Perhaps death is an indifferent thing, perhaps it is desirable. We may believe, however, that if it is a migration from one place to another, there is some gain in going to live with so many great men who have departed, and in being excused from further dealings with wicked and corrupt judges. If it is an annihilation of our being, it is still a gain to enter upon a long and peaceful night. We have no sweeter sensation in life than quiet rest and deep dreamless sleep.

'The things I know to be evil, such as injuring one's neighbour and disobeying one's superior, whether God or man, I carefully avoid. But when I do not know whether a thing is good or evil, I cannot fear it. If I am to depart and leave you alive, the gods alone can see who will be the better off, you or I. Therefore, so far as I am concerned, you may decide as you will. But, if I am to follow my custom of advising what is just and profitable, I will certainly say that, for your conscience' sake, you will do better to set me free if you see no more deeply into my case than I do myself. And if you judge by my past actions, both public and private, by my intentions, by the profit that so many of our citizens, both young and old, derive every day from my conversation, and by the good that I have done you all, there is only one way in which you can requite my merits; and that is by decreeing that, in view of my poverty, I shall be maintained in the Prytaneum at the public expense: a privilege that I have frequently seen you grant to others with less reason.

'Do not take it for obstinacy or scorn that I do not follow the usual custom and try, by supplication, to excite your pity. I have friends and relations – not being, as Homer says, begotten of wood or stone, any more than other men – who might appear before you in tears and in mourning; and I have three disconsolate children who might move you to mercy. But I should bring shame upon our city if, at my age and with the reputation for wisdom that I stand here accused of, I were to descend to such abject devices. What would be said of the rest of Athens?

'I have always warned those who have listened to me never to purchase their lives by a dishonourable action; and in my country's wars, at Amphipolis, at Potidaea, at Delium, and at other battles in which I took part, I have shown in practice how far I was from securing my safety by shameful means. Besides, I should be influencing you in your duty and engaging you in unseemly conduct; for it is not my prayers that should persuade you, but pure and sound reasons of justice. You have sworn to the gods to maintain the law, and it would seem as if I suspected and accused you of not believing in their existence. Thus I should be testifying against myself that I do not believe in them as I ought, were I to distrust their guidance and not leave my case purely in their hands. I trust in them wholly, and entirely believe that they will do in this case what is most fitting for you and for me. Good men, whether in life or after death, have no cause to fear the gods.'*

Is not this a sound and sober pleading, but at the same time plain and natural? Is it not inconceivably lofty and frank, truthful and just beyond all example? And in what a critical need was it uttered! Truly Socrates had reason to prefer it to the speech which the great orator Lysias had written for him; which was admirably couched in the forensic style but unworthy of so noble an offender. Should words of supplication have issued from Socrates' mouth? Should that proud virtue have lowered sail when it was most fully displayed? Should his rich and powerful nature have committed its defence to artifice and, in its greatest trial, renounced truth and simplicity, the ornaments of his speech, to deck itself out in the tawdry figures and figments of an oration learned by heart? He acted very wisely, and was true to himself, in not corrupting the tenor of a righteous life, and spoiling so sacred a model of the human character, in order to prolong his old age by a year and to cheat us of the undying memory of his glorious end. He owed his life not to himself, but to the world, as an example. Would it not have been a public calamity if he had ended it in idleness and obscurity?

* This speech is a fairly free paraphrase from Plato's *Apology*.

Assuredly his own light and indifferent attitude to his death deserved that posterity should make more of it on his behalf; which it has done. And no verdict could be more just than that which fate pronounced in his honour. For the Athenians held those who had been the cause of his death in such abomination that they shunned them like men under excommunication. Anything they had touched was held to be polluted. No one washed with them at the baths; no one saluted them or spoke with them; until, at last, unable to bear this general hatred any longer, they hanged themselves.

If anyone should think that, among so many examples from the sayings of Socrates which I might have taken for the purpose of my argument, I did wrong in picking this one, and if this same person should consider this discourse to be far above the popular understanding, I may say that I have made my choice deliberately. For I judge otherwise, and hold that in its simplicity it falls far behind and beneath the popular understanding. In its artless and straightforward boldness, and in its childlike confidence, it embodies the pure and primitive ideas and the ignorance of nature herself. For it is to be believed that we have a natural fear of pain, but not of death, which is no less essential a part of our being than life. For what reason should nature have engendered in us a hatred and horror of it, since it performs the very useful and natural function of maintaining the succession and alternation of its works, and that in this universal commonwealth it conduces to birth and increase more than to loss or destruction?

> *Sic rerum summa novatur.** \
> *Mille animas una necata dedit.*†

The failure of one life is the passage to a thousand others. Nature has implanted in animals an instinct for their own preservation. This extends so far as to make them afraid of their own injury, of hurting and wounding themselves, and of our chaining them up or beating them: accidents known to their senses and experience. But that we should kill them, this they

* 'Thus is the universe renewed.' Lucretius, II, 75.

† 'One soul destroyed gives birth to a thousand.' Ovid, *Fasti*, I, 380.

BOOK THREE: CHAPTER 12

cannot fear; nor have they any faculty for imagining or inferring such a thing as death. So it is also said that they have been observed not only to suffer it cheerfully – most horses neigh when they are dying, and swans sing – but even to seek it in their need, as many stories of elephants tend to show.

Besides, is not the method of argument that Socrates uses here admirable also for its vigour and its simplicity? Truly, it is much easier to talk like Aristotle and to live like Caesar than to speak and live like Socrates. There lies the ultimate perfection and greatest difficulty: it is beyond the reach of artifice. Our faculties are not trained to this pitch. We do not test them and we do not know them. We invest ourselves with those of others, and let our own lie idle.

It might well be said of me here that I have merely made up a bunch of other men's flowers, and have provided nothing of my own but the string to bind them. Certainly I have yielded to public opinion in wearing these borrowed decorations. But I do not intend them to cover and hide me; that is the reverse of my design. For I only want to display what is mine, and what is mine by nature; and had I followed my own inclinations, I should at all hazards have spoken purely in my own person. Every day I load myself more heavily with these borrowings, following the fashion of the age and other people's advice against my intentions and my original plan. If this sits ill upon me, as I believe it does, no matter; it may be useful to someone else.*

Some men quote Plato and Homer who have never read them, and I myself have taken passages enough from places other than their source. Having a thousand volumes around me in the room where I am writing, I could at this moment, if I pleased, borrow without trouble and without learning from a dozen of these scrap-collectors, fellows whose books I seldom open, the wherewithal to embellish this treatise on physiognomy. I only need some German's introductory epistle to stuff me with quotations; and it is thus that we set out in pursuit of a nice reputation, and cheat the foolish world.

* Montaigne is excusing himself for including so many additional quotations in the later editions of the essays.

334

These concoctions of commonplaces, with which so many men eke out their learning, are of little use except for commonplace subjects. They help us to display ourselves, but not to guide our thoughts. They are a ridiculous fruit of learning, which Socrates amusingly satirizes in his argument with Euthydemus. I have seen books made up of things neither studied nor understood, the author asking various of his learned friends to look up this or that matter for him to build with, and being content, for his own part, to work out the plan and industriously pile up this stack of material unknown to him. But at least the ink and paper are his. This, in all conscience, is to buy or borrow a book, not to write one. It proves to all men not that you can create a literary work – in case they have doubts on this score – but that you cannot. A chief magistrate boasted in my hearing that he had packed two-hundred-odd quotations into one of his addresses to the court. In proclaiming this to all and sundry, he seemed to me to throw away such glory as he had won by it. A small-minded and ridiculous boast, in my opinion, for such a feat and from such a person!

I do the contrary.* Amongst so many borrowings, I am glad if I can occasionally steal something to disguise and adapt for a new service. At the risk of its being said that I have failed to understand its original application, I give it a particular twist with my hand, so as to make it less purely another man's property. These others parade their thefts and take credit for them, and so they keep on better terms with the law than I. We who follow nature reckon that the honour of invention is greatly – indeed incomparably – preferable to the honour of quotation.

If I had wished to speak learnedly, I should have spoken sooner. I should have written at a time closer to my studies, when I had more wit and memory; and had I wished to make writing a profession, I should have trusted more to my vigour at that time of life than at this. Moreover, such kindly favours as fortune may have offered me through the mediation of this

* This sentence is present in the 1595 edition alone. It seems necessary to the sense.

work would then have come at a more propitious time.*

Two of my acquaintances, great men of learning, have in my opinion lost half their advantage by refusing to publish at 40, in order to wait until they were sixty. Maturity has as many drawbacks as immaturity, and worse. And old age is as unsuitable for this kind of work as for any other. A man who puts his decrepitude under pressure is committing a folly, if he hopes to squeeze any juices from it that do not taste of misfortune, dreaminess, and doting. Our mind becomes costive and sluggish as it grows old. I dispense my ignorance grandly and lavishly, my knowledge in a weak and pitiable way; the latter as accessory and incidental, the former expressly and as of the first importance. And the only things I treat of adequately are nothing, the only knowledge I deal with is no-knowledge. I have chosen a time when my life, which I have to portray, lies complete before me; what remains of it has more to do with death. And even of death, if I should find it talkative, as some do, I should probably give an account to the world as I departed.

It grieves me that Socrates, who was a perfect pattern of all great qualities, should, as reports say, have had so ugly a face and body, so out of keeping with the beauty of his soul, seeing how deeply he was enamoured of beauty, how infatuated by it! Nature did him an injustice.

There is nothing more probable than that the body conforms and is related to the soul. 'It matters greatly to the soul in what sort of body it is placed; for there are many conditions of body that sharpen the mind, and many that blunt it.'† Cicero is speaking of an unnatural ugliness and deformity of the limbs. But we give the name of ugliness also to an unsightliness visible at first glance, which is chiefly a matter of face, and often repels us for quite trivial reasons – a bad complexion, a blemish, a rugged countenance – or for some entirely inexplicable reason when the limbs are otherwise perfect and well-proportioned. The ugliness which clothed a very beautiful soul in la Boétie was of

* Montaigne is probably alluding to the friendship of Mlle de Gournay.
† Cicero, *Tusculans*, I, xxxii.

this kind. This superficial ugliness, though making a strong impression, affects the state of mind less seriously, and has a less certain influence on men's opinions. The other sort, for which deformity is a better name, is more substantial, and is more likely to strike inwards. It is not the shoe made of polished leather, but the well-made shoe that reveals the shape of the foot within. So Socrates said of his ugliness, that it would have betrayed an equal ugliness of soul if he had not corrected it by schooling. But in saying this, I believe that he was joking in his usual fashion. A soul as excellent as his never fashioned itself.

I cannot say often enough how much I value beauty as a quality that gives power and advantage. Socrates called it 'a brief tyranny' and Plato 'nature's privilege'. We have nothing that gives a man better credit. It takes first place in human relations; it appears in the foreground, seduces and prepossesses our judgements, exercises great authority and is marvellously impressive. Phryne would have lost her case, though she had an excellent advocate, if she had not opened her robe, and corrupted her judges with the splendour of her beauty. And I note that Cyrus, Alexander, and Caesar, those three masters of the world, were not oblivious to it when performing their great deeds; nor was the first Scipio. One and the same Greek word covers both beauty and goodness; and the Holy Ghost often calls people good when the meaning is that they are beautiful. I would gladly defend the order in which the good things of life are set out in that song, taken from some old poet, which Plato said was current in his day: health, beauty, riches. Aristotle says that to the beautiful belongs the right to command, and that if there are any whose beauty approaches that of our idea of the gods, veneration is their due also. When asked why men spent longer in the company of the beautiful than with others, and visited them more often, he answered: 'No one that is not blind could ask that question.' Most philosophers, and the greatest of them, paid for their schooling and acquired their wisdom by means and by favour of their beauty.

Not only in my servants but in animals also, I regard it as only an inch short of goodness. Yet it seems to me that the face's shape and features, and those characteristics by which men infer a certain inward disposition and foretell our future fortunes, are things that cannot be quite directly and simply classified under the heading of beauty and ugliness. Nor can we say in times of plague that every good odour and clear atmosphere promises health, or that all heavy and fetid air threatens infection. Those who accuse the ladies of belying their beauty by their conduct do not always hit the mark: for in none too shapely a face there may dwell an air of honesty that inspires trust and, on the contrary, I have sometimes read between two lovely eyes menacing signs of a malign and dangerous nature. There are propitious physiognomies; and in a crowd of victorious enemies all unknown to you, you will immediately pick out one rather than another to whom you will surrender, and to whom you will entrust your life; and not precisely from considerations of beauty.

A face is a poor guarantee; nevertheless, it deserves some consideration. And had I the scourging of sinners, I should deal hardest with those who belie and betray the promises that nature has planted on their brows; I should inflict sharper punishment on wickedness when in a meek disguise. It would seem that some faces are lucky, some unlucky. And I think it requires some skill to distinguish the gentle from the silly, the stern from the rugged, the malicious from the sad, the scornful from the melancholy, and between other such closely related qualities. There is a beauty that is not only haughty but sour; there is another that is gentle but insipid too. As to prophesying men's future destinies from them, that is a matter I leave undecided.

I have, as I have said elsewhere, quite simply and crudely adopted for my own use the ancient rule that we cannot go wrong in following nature, and that the sovereign precept is to conform to her. I have not, like Socrates, corrected my natural disposition by force of reason, nor used any art to interfere with my native inclinations. I let myself go as I came; I struggle against nothing; my two dominant parts live, of their own accord, in peace and amity. But my nurse's milk, thanks be to

God, was tolerably healthy and temperate.

May I say this in passing, that I find we attach more value than it deserves to a certain idea of scholarly integrity, almost the only one in vogue amongst us, which makes learning a slave to precept and fetters it with hope and fear? I would have it not formed, but perfected and justified, by laws and religions, conscious of being able to sustain itself without help, springing up within us with its own roots from a seed of universal reason, which is implanted in every man who is not corrupt by nature. This reason, which cured Socrates of his vicious bent, made him obedient to the men and gods who ruled in his city, and courageous in his death, not because his soul was immortal, but because he was a mortal man. It is a doctrine ruinous to every society, and far more harmful than clever or subtle, which persuades people that religious belief alone, without morality, is sufficient to satisfy divine justice. Practice shows us an enormous difference between piety and conscience.

My bearing is prepossessing both in itself and by the impression it makes,

> *Quid dixi habere me? Imo habui, Chreme!**
>
> *Heu tantum attriti corporis ossa vides;†*

which is the very opposite of that made by Socrates. It has often happened to me that, solely on the strength of my presence and my looks, people who had no knowledge of me have placed great confidence in me, either in regard to their own affairs or to mine; and in foreign countries this has brought me rare and unusual kindness. But the two following experiences perhaps deserve relating in detail.

A certain person decided to make a surprise attack on my household and myself. His plan was to arrive at my gate alone, and rather importunately to demand admission. I knew him by name, and had reason to trust him as a neighbour and distant connexion. I admitted him as I do everyone. There he was, in a terrible fright, with his horse panting and worn out. This is the

---

* 'Did I say that I have? No, I had, Chremus!' Terence, *Heautontimoroumenos*, I, i, 42.

† 'Alas, you only see the bones of a wasted body.' Pseudo-Gallus, I, 238.

story he told me: that he had been set upon a mile or so away
by an enemy of his, whom I also knew – and I had heard about
their feud; that his enemy had made him clap on his spurs to
some purpose; that having been caught in disarray and out-
numbered, he had fled to my gates for safety; and that he was
very anxious about his men, whom he supposed to be either
dead or prisoners. In my innocence I tried to comfort, reassure,
and hearten him.

Presently there came four or five of his soldiers, with the
same appearance of terror, and demanded entrance. They were
followed by more, and by still more, well equipped and well
armed, to the number of twenty-five or thirty, all pretending
that the enemy was at their heels. This mystery began to rouse
my suspicions. I was not unaware of the times I was living in,
or that my house might be an object of great envy; and I had
several examples of others of my acquaintance who had had
similar misadventures. However, seeing that there was nothing
to be gained by beginning to show them courtesy if I did not
continue in the same way, and not being able to get rid of my
visitors without a complete breach, I took the most natural and
the simplest course, as I always do, and had them all admitted.

Besides, the truth is that I am naturally not much given to
mistrust and suspicions. My readiest inclination is to admit excuses and to accept the most favourable interpretation. I take
men much as they are, and do not believe in their wicked and
unnatural intentions unless I am forced to by weight of evidence, any more than I do in prodigies and miracles. I am a man,
moreover, who readily trusts to fortune, and I throw myself
headlong into her arms. And hitherto I have more reason to
commend than to blame myself for this. I have found fortune
both wiser and more favourable to my welfare than I am myself.

There have been some actions in my life, the conduct of which
might fairly be called painstaking or, if you like, cautious; but
even for these, supposing that a third part of the credit is mine,
two-thirds is most abundantly fortune's. We err, I think, in not
trusting ourselves sufficiently to heaven, and in claiming more
for our management than rightly belongs to it. That is why our

plans so often go wrong. Heaven is jealous of the scope we assign to the claims of human wisdom, to the prejudice of its own, and the more we extend them the more it cuts them down.

These men remained mounted in my courtyard, while their chief was with me in my hall. He had declined to have his horse stabled, saying that he would have to depart as soon as he had news of his men. He saw that he was master of the situation, and nothing now remained but to carry out his plan. He has often said since – for he has not been ashamed to tell the story – that my face and my open-heartedness had removed his treacherous intentions. He remounted his horse; and his men, whose eyes were constantly fixed on him, to see what signal he would give them, were amazed to see him ride away and abandon his advantage.

On another occasion, relying on some truce that had just been proclaimed between our armies, I started on a journey through a particularly tricky part of the country. No sooner did they get wind of my departure than three or four bands of horsemen set out from different places to capture me. One of them caught up with me on the third day, when I was attacked by fifteen or twenty masked gentlemen, followed by a swarm of troopers. There I was, seized and made prisoner, taken off into the depths of a near-by forest, dismounted, and robbed. My coffers were rifled, my strong-box taken, my horses and equipment divided among new owners. We spent a long time in this thicket, arguing about the amount of my ransom, which they set so high that it was quite clear they knew very little about me. They entered into a lively dispute on the subject of taking my life. Indeed there were many circumstances to warn me of the danger I was in.

*Tunc animis opus, Aenea, tunc pectore firmo.**

I kept insisting, on the strength of the truce, that I would yield them only the value of their plunderings, which was not to be despised, and would promise them no further ransom. After we had been at this for two or three hours, they mounted me on a

* 'Then you had need of courage, Aeneas, and of a stout heart.' Virgil, *Aeneid*, VI, 261, slightly altered.

horse that was not likely to get away, and put me under a special guard of fifteen or twenty musketeers, distributing my servants among the rest, with orders that we should be led as prisoners by different routes. When I was already two or three musket-shots on my way,

*Iam prece Pollucis, iam Castoris implorata,**

a sudden and altogether unexpected change came over them. I saw the leader return to me with milder words, and then go to the trouble of searching among the troopers for my scattered possessions, of which he restored to me as many as he could find, even to my strong-box. The best present that they made me was, after all, my liberty; the rest did not affect me much at that particular moment.

Really, I do not know even now the true cause of this sudden change of mind and of conduct, due to no apparent motive, and of this miraculous repentance, at such a time, in an enterprise that had been deliberately planned, and was such as had become sanctified by custom. For I had frankly told them at the outset to what party I belonged, and where it was I was going. The most prominent among them, who took off his mask and told me his name, repeated to me several times that I owed this deliverance to my face, to my freedom and firmness of speech, which showed me to be undeserving of such a misadventure. He asked me for an assurance that he would be similarly treated in a like case. It is possible that the divine goodness chose to use this insignificant instrument† for my preservation; it saved me again the next day from still worse ambushes, of which these men themselves had warned me.

The latter of these two gentlemen is still alive to tell the tale; the first was killed not long ago.

If my face did not answer for me, if men did not read the innocence of my intentions in my eyes and my voice, I should not have lived so long without quarrels and without hurt, in view of the foolish freedom with which I express, whether right or wrong, whatever comes into my mind, and of the bold-

* 'Having besought now Pollux and now Castor in prayer.' Catullus, LVXI, 65.   † Montaigne is referring to his appearance and his bearing.

ness with which I speak on all subjects. This habit may reasonably be thought impolite, and out of keeping with our customs. But I have never met anyone who considered it insulting and malicious, or who has been stung by my candour, if he heard it from my own mouth. When words are repeated, they sound differently and carry a different sense.

Besides, I hate nobody, and am so loath to hurt anyone that I cannot do so even if reason demands it. When circumstances required me to condemn criminals, I have preferred to sin against justice. 'I wish that no more crimes would be committed, since I have not the courage to punish them.'* Someone, it is said, reproached Aristotle for having been too merciful to a wicked man. 'I have indeed been merciful to the man,' he answered, 'but not to his wickedness.'† Common minds are incited to vengeance by their horror of the crime. It is this feeling that cools my judgement; horror of a first murder makes me afraid of a second, and hatred of the initial cruelty inspires me with fear of any repetition. To me, one of the humble cards in the pack, those words can be applied which were said of Charillus, king of Sparta: 'He cannot be good, since he is not hard on the wicked.'‡ Or these rather, for Plutarch reports it, as he does a thousand other things, in two different and contrary ways: 'He must certainly be good, since he is so even to the wicked.' As I dislike proceeding even lawfully against a man who will resent what I do, so, I confess, I have not the conscience to refrain from illegal actions when they are pleasing to those whom they affect.

BOOK THREE: Chapter 13

On experience

THERE is no desire more natural than the desire for knowledge. We try every means that may lead us to it. When reason fails us, we make use of experience,

---

* Livy, XXIX, 21.   † Diogenes Laertius, v, 17.
‡ Plutarch, *On Envy and Hatred*.

Per varios usus artem experientia fecit:
*exemplo monstrante viam.**

which is a feebler and less worthy means. But truth is so great a
thing that we ought not to despise any medium that will conduct us to it. Reason has so many shapes that we do not know
which to take hold of; experience has no fewer. The conclusions
that we seek to draw from the likeness of events are unreliable,
because events are always unlike. There is no quality so universal in the appearance of things as their diversity and variety.
The Greeks and Romans, as well as ourselves, use eggs as an
example of the perfect degree of similarity. Yet there have been
men, particularly one at Delphi,† who could detect marks of
difference between them, so that he never mistook one for another; and although he had many hens, he could always tell
which had laid a particular egg. Dissimilarity enters of itself into
our works; no art can achieve similarity. Neither Perrozet nor
any other can so carefully smooth and whiten the backs of his
cards that some gamblers do not distinguish between them on
merely seeing them pass through another man's hands. Resemblance does not make things as much alike as difference
makes them dissimilar. Nature has pledged herself to make no
second thing that is not unlike the first.

I hardly agree, therefore, with the opinion of that man‡ who
tried to curb the authority of his judges by a multitude of laws,
thus cutting their meat up for them. He did not understand that
there is as much liberty and latitude in the interpretation as in
the making of them. And those men who think they can lessen
and check our disputes by referring us to the actual words of
the Bible are deluding themselves, since our mind finds just as
wide a field for controverting other men's meanings as for
delivering its own. Could there be less spite and bitterness in
comment than in invention?

We can see how mistaken he was. For we have in France more

* 'By various experiments, experience has led to art, example showing
the way.' Manilius, 1, 59.
† Actually at Delos. See Cicero, *Academica*, 11, 18.
‡ Justinian, by his *Code* and his *Pandects*.

laws than the rest of the world put together, and more than would be necessary for all the worlds of Epicurus. 'As we once suffered from crimes, so now we are suffering from laws';* and yet we have left so much for judges to consider and decide, that there has never been such complete and uncontrolled freedom. What have our legislators gained by picking out a hundred thousand particular cases and deeds, and attaching to them a hundred thousand laws? This number bears no relation to the infinite diversity of human actions. The multiplication of our imaginary cases will never equal the variety of actual examples. Add to these a hundred times as many, and yet no future event will ever be found so to tally, so exactly to fit and match with one out of the many thousands selected and recorded, that there will not remain some circumstance or variation which requires separate consideration and judgement. There is little relation between our actions, which are perpetually changing, and fixed, immutable laws. The most desirable laws are those that are fewest, simplest, and most general; and I even think that it would be better to be without them altogether than to have them in such numbers as we have at present.

Nature always gives us happier laws than we give ourselves. Witness the Golden Age as described by the poets, and the condition in which we find those nations to be living that have no others. Some have no judges, but take the first traveller to pass through their mountains to decide their quarrels for them; and others, on their market-day, elect one of their own number to decide all their suits out of hand. What risk would there be if the wisest among us were to settle ours in the same way, according to the circumstances and at sight, without being bound by precedents and issues? For every foot its own shoe. When King Ferdinand sent out colonists to the Indies, he wisely provided that they should take no legal scholars with them, for fear that litigation might breed in that new world, jurisprudence being by nature a science productive of altercation and division. He agreed with Plato that lawyers and doctors are a bad provision for any country.

* Tacitus, *Annals*, III, xxv.

345

How is it that our ordinary language, so simple for any other use, becomes obscure and unintelligible in contracts and wills, and that a man who expresses himself very clearly in all that he says and writes, can find no way of declaring his meaning in these matters that does not fall into doubt and contradiction? It must be that the princes of this art, in applying themselves with particular attention to the selection of solemn words and the contriving of cunning phrases, have so weighed every syllable, and so minutely examined every sort of combination, that they finally become involved and entangled in their endless number of figures and very minute distinctions. These then cease to fall under any rule and prescription, or to convey any certain meaning. 'Anything that is divided into minute grains becomes confused.'*

Have you ever seen a child trying to divide a mass of quicksilver into a number of parts? The more he presses and squeezes it, and tries to bring it under control, the more he provokes the free-will of this noble metal. It eludes his skill, and keeps breaking and diversifying itself indefinitely. So it is here; for by the subdivision of these subtleties, we teach men to increase their doubts. We are put into a way of elaborating and diversifying our difficulties, of prolonging and dispersing them. By scattering and chopping their small questions, they make the world teem and fructify with uncertainties and disputes, even as the soil becomes more fertile the more it is broken and the deeper it is dug. 'Learning creates difficulties.'† We were puzzled by Ulpian, and we are still more puzzled by Bartolus and Baldus.‡ We ought to blot out all trace of this infinite diversity of opinions; not use them for display and stuff the heads of posterity with them.

I do not know how to explain it, but experience shows us that all these interpretations dissipate the truth and destroy it. Aristotle wrote to be understood. If he did not succeed, still less will another who is not so clever, or yet another who speaks from

* Seneca, *Letters*, LXXXIX.
† Quintilian, x, iii.
‡ Commentators on Ulpian.

his own imagination. We open a matter, and by diluting it make it expand. From one subject we turn it into a thousand, and by multiplying and subdividing arrive again at Epicurus's infinity of atoms. No two men ever judged alike of the same thing, and it is impossible to find two opinions exactly similar, not only in different men but in the same man at different times. I very often find doubtful points in passages that the commentary has not deigned to touch upon. I am most liable to trip up on flat ground, like certain horses I know that stumble most often on a level road.

Who would not say that commentaries increase doubt and ignorance, since there is no book to be found, human or divine, with which the world has any business, in which the difficulties are cleared up by the interpretation? The hundredth commentator passes it on to his successor in a thornier and more crabbed state than that in which the first discovered it. When did we ever agree in saying: 'This book has had enough. There is nothing more to be said about it?' This is best seen in the practice of law. We attribute binding authority to innumerable doctors, to innumerable decrees, and to as many interpretations. And yet do we find any end to the need for interpreting? Is there any progress to be seen, any advance towards peace? Do we need any fewer pleaders and judges than when this great mass of law was still in its infancy? On the contrary, we obscure and bury the meaning; we can no longer discover it without negotiating many fences and barriers. Men do not recognize the natural infirmity of the mind; it does nothing but ferret and search, and is all the time turning, contriving, and entangling itself in its own work, like a silk-worm; and there it suffocates, 'a mouse in pitch'.* It thinks it observes afar off some gleam of light and imaginary truth; but while it is running towards it, so many difficulties cross its path, so many obstacles and so many new quests, that it is driven astray and bewildered. Its case is much like that of Aesop's dogs who, seeing something like a dead body floating in the sea, and being unable to get near it, set about drinking up the water in order to make a dry passage, and

* Latin proverb. See Erasmus, *Adages*, II, iii, 68.

choked themselves.* Also apposite is the remark of a certain Crates about the writings of Heraclitus: that they required a reader who was a good swimmer, so that he would not be swallowed up and drowned by the depth and weight of their learning.

It is nothing but our personal weakness that makes us content with what others, or we ourselves, have discovered in this hunt for knowledge; a man of great ability will not be satisfied with it. There is always room for someone to improve on us; indeed, for us to improve on ourselves; and there is always a different road to follow. There is no end to our investigations; our end is in the other world. It is a sign of failing powers or of weariness when the mind is content. No generous spirit stays within itself; it constantly aspires and rises above its own strength. It leaps beyond its attainments. If it does not advance, and push forward, if it does not strengthen itself, and struggle with itself, it is only half alive. Its pursuits have no bounds or rules; its food is wonder, search, and ambiguity.

This was made clear enough by Apollo, who always spoke to us in a double, obscure, and oblique sense, not satisfying us but keeping us puzzled and busy. It is an irregular and perpetual motion, without model and without goal. Its inventions excite, pursue, and give birth one to another:

> *Ainsi voit l'on, en un ruisseau coulant,*
> *Sans fin l'une eau après l'autre roulant,*
> *Et tout de rang, d'un éternel conduict,*
> *L'une suit l'autre, et l'une l'autre fuyt.*
> *Par cette-cy celle-là est poussée*
> *Et cette-cy par l'autre est devancée:*
> *Toujours l'eau va dans l'eau, et toujours est-ce*
> *Mesme ruisseau, et toujours eau diverse.†*

* This is not from Aesop, but is taken from Amyot's translation of Plutarch's *Common Conceptions against the Stoics*, XIX. But even so, Montaigne has made his own version of the story.

† 'So we see, in a running stream, one ripple endlessly pursuing another; and all along, in never-ending sequence, one follows another, another flees from the one behind. That one is driven on by this, another goes ahead of that one. Water ever flows into water, and it is always the same stream, but always different water.' La Boétie, *Verses to Marguerite de Carles*, quoted inaccurately.

There is more trouble in interpreting interpretations than in interpreting the things themselves, and there are more books on books than on any other subject. We do nothing but write comments on one another. The whole world is swarming with commentaries; of authors there is a great dearth.

Is not the principal and most famous branch of modern learning that of learning to understand the learned? Is not this the common and final purpose of all studies? Our opinions are grafted one on another. The first serves as a stock for the second, the second for the third. We thus climb the ladder, step by step; and hence it is that the man who has mounted highest has often more honour than he deserves; for he has only raised himself by the height of one inch on the shoulders of the last but one.

How often, and perhaps foolishly, have I extended my book, to make it speak for itself? Foolishly, if only because I ought to remember what I say of other authors who do the same; that their frequent oglings of their work testify to a heart quivering with affection for it, and that even the contemptuous roughness with which they beat it is only the dandling and dissembling of maternal love. Here I follow Aristotle, according to whom self-esteem and self-disparagement often arise from one and the same arrogance. For, as to my excuse that I ought to be allowed more freedom than others in this respect, since I am writing specifically of myself, and of my writings as of my other actions, and that my theme turns upon itself, I do not know whether everyone will accept it.

I have observed in Germany that Luther has left behind him as many schisms and dissensions concerning the uncertainties in his beliefs as he raised about the Holy Scriptures.

Our disputes are about words. I ask what is Nature, Pleasure, a Circle, and Substitution. The question is couched in words, and is answered in the same coin. A stone is a body. But if you press the point: And what is a body? – A substance. – And what is a substance? and so on, you will end by driving the answerer to exhaust his dictionary. One substitutes one word for another that is often less well understood. I know what Man is better than I know the meaning of Animal or Mortal or

Rational. To resolve one doubt, they present me with three; it is the Hydra's head.

Socrates asked Memnon* what virtue is. 'There is,' replied Memnon, 'the virtue of a man and of a woman, of a magistrate and of a private citizen, of a child and of an old person.' 'This is fine!' exclaimed Socrates. 'We were looking for one virtue, and here are a swarm of them.' We put one question, and receive a hive full in return. As no event and no shape entirely resembles another, so none is wholly different from another. An ingenious mixture on nature's part! If our faces were not similar, we could not distinguish a man from a beast; if they were not dissimilar, we could not distinguish one man from another. All things hold together by some similarity; every example limps; and the comparison which is derived from experience is always weak and imperfect; yet comparisons always join at one corner or another. It is in this way that laws do their work; they are applied to each of our affairs by some far-fetched, forced, and oblique interpretation.

Since ethical laws, which are concerned with the individual duty of each man in himself, are so hard to establish as we see that they are, it is no wonder that those which rule so many individuals are even more so. Consider the form of this justice that governs us; it is a true testimony to human imbecility, so full is it of contradictions and errors. What we find to be favour and harshness in justice – and we find so much of each that I do not know whether the mean between them is to be met with as often – are the unhealthy parts and unsound limbs of justice's true body and essence.

Some peasants recently arrived in great haste to inform me that they had just left in a wood on my estate a man stabbed in a hundred places, but still breathing, who begged them for pity's sake to give them water and help him get up. They said that they dared not go near him, and ran away, for fear the officers of justice might catch them there and, as is usual with those found near a murdered man, that they would be held to account for this mischance; which would totally ruin them since

* Montaigne is referring to Meno, in the dialogue of that name.

they had neither the ability nor the money to defend their innocence. What should I have said to them? There is no doubt that an act of humanity would have brought them into trouble.

How many innocent people have we known who have been punished, through no fault, I will say, on the judge's part, and how many are there of whom we have never heard? Here is something that happened in my time: Certain men are condemned to death for a murder; their sentence, being agreed upon and determined, though not pronounced. At this point, the judges are informed by the officers of an inferior court in the neighbourhood that they are holding some prisoners who openly confess to this murder, and throw unquestionable light on the whole affair. And yet these judges deliberate whether they ought to interrupt or defer the execution of the sentence passed upon the first prisoners. They discuss the unusualness of the case, and the precedent it may set up for the reversal of judgements; for the sentence being juridically correct, the judges have no reason to change their minds. In short, these poor devils are sacrificed to the forms of justice.

Philip, or some other, dealt with a similar dilemma in this way: He had, in a considered judgement, condemned one man to pay heavy compensation to another. The true facts coming to light some time afterwards, it was found that his decision had been unfair. On one side were the rights of the case, on the other the claims of judicial formality. He satisfied both to some degree, by letting the sentence stand, and making good the condemned man's loss out of his own purse. But he was dealing with a mistake that could be rectified; my men were irreparably hanged. How many condemnations have I seen more criminal than the crime!

All this brings to my mind the ancient sayings: That a man must do wrong in detail if he wishes to do right on the whole and commit injustices in small matters if he hopes to deal out justice in great. That human justice is formed on the same model as medicine, in which all treatments that are useful are also just and proper. That, as the Stoics hold, nature herself in most of her works goes against justice. That, as the Cyrenaics contend, there is nothing inherently just; customs and laws make justice. That, according to the Theodorians, theft, sacrilege, and all sorts of crimes are lawful for the sage if he knows that they are profitable to him.

There is no remedy. I am like Alcibiades in this, that I will never appear in person, if I can avoid it, before a man who can decide my fate, when my honour and my life depend on the skill and care of my lawyer rather than on my innocence. I would trust myself to a form of justice which recognized my good deeds as well as my bad, in which case I should have as much to hope as to fear. Acquittal is no sufficient reward for a man who does better than just not doing wrong. Our justice offers us only one of its hands, and that the left. Let a man be who he may, he comes off with a loss.

In China, a kingdom in which government and the arts, though they have had no contact with or knowledge of ours, contain examples that surpass them in many excellent features, and whose history teaches me how much wider and more various the world is than either the ancients or ourselves have discovered, the officers deputed by the prince to inspect the state of his provinces, when punishing those guilty of abusing their office, also reward, out of pure liberality, any whose conduct has been above the common level of honesty, and who have done more than their obligatory duty. Men appear before them not only to defend themselves but to gain something; not simply to be paid but to receive a gift. No judge, thank God, has yet addressed me as a judge in any case whatever, either my own or another's, either criminal or civil. No prison has received me, even as a visitor. Imagination makes the sight of one, even from outside, unpleasant to me. I am so avid of freedom that were access to some corner of the Indies forbidden me, I should somehow live less comfortably. And so long as I can find open air and country elsewhere, I shall never lurk in a place where I must hide. Good God, how ill I should endure the condition in which I see so many people, tied to one corner of this kingdom, deprived of the right to enter the chief cities and courts, and to use the public roads, for having quarrelled with our laws! If those under which I live were even to threaten the tip of my finger, I should depart immediately to find others, no matter where. All my little prudence, in these present civil wars of ours, is employed in seeing that they do not interfere with the liberty of my comings and goings.

Now the laws maintain their credit, not because they are just, but because they are laws. This is the mystical basis of their authority; they have no other. And this serves them well. They are often made by fools, and more often by men who, out of hatred for equality, are lacking in equity, but always by men: vain and unstable creators. There is nothing so grossly and widely, nor so ordinarily faulty as the laws. Whoever obeys them because they are just is not, as he should be, obeying them for a just reason. Ours in France, by their lack of form and order, to some extent contribute to the disorder and corruption with which we see them being applied and executed. Their injunctions are so confused and inconsistent that there is some excuse both for disobedience and for faults of interpretation, administration, and observance. Whatever fruit, then, experience may yield us, the lessons we derive from the examples of others will hardly serve to instruct us, if we profit so little from those that come to us from ourselves. For these are more familiar to us, and certainly sufficient to instruct us in all that we need.

I study myself more than any other subject. This is my metaphysics, this is my physics.

> *Qua deus hanc mundi temperet arte domum*
> *qua venit exoriens, qua deficit, unde coactis*
> *cornibus in plenum menstrua luna redit;*
> *Unde salo superant venti, quid flamine captet*
> *Eurus, et in nubes unde perennis aqua.*
> *Sit ventura dies mundi quae subruat arces.**
> *Quaerite quos agitat mundi labor.†*

* 'By what art God rules this mansion, the universe; whence comes the rising moon and whither it sets, and how each month, joining its horns, it comes to the full: where the winds overwhelm the sea; what Eurus catches up with his blast; whence there gathers perpetual water to make the clouds; and if a day will come that will throw down the towers of the world.' Propertius, III, v, 26.

† 'Inquire, you whom the workings of the world perplex.' Lucan, I, 417

BOOK THREE: CHAPTER 13

In these universal matters I allow myself to be ignorantly and carelessly guided by the general law of the world. I shall know it well enough when I feel it. My learning cannot make it change its course; it will not modify itself for me. It is folly to have hope of this, and even greater folly to worry about it, since the law is necessarily uniform, manifest, and common to all. The goodness and capacity of a governor should discharge us wholly and absolutely from any concern about his government.

Philosophical inquiries and reflections serve only as food for our curiosity. The philosophers, very rightly, refer us to the laws of nature. But these have nothing to do with knowledge of this sublimity. The philosophers falsify them and present nature's face to us painted in over-bright colours and too sophisticated; whence spring so many different portraits of a subject so unchanging. As nature has provided us with feet for walking, so she has given us wisdom to guide us through life; a wisdom less subtle, robust, and spectacular than that of the philosophers' invention, but correspondingly easy and salutary, which actually performs very well what the other only promises, for anyone lucky enough to know how to use it plainly and properly, that is to say naturally. The more simply one entrusts oneself to nature, the more wisely one does so. Oh, how soft and pleasant and healthful a pillow, whereon to rest a prudent head, is ignorance and lack of curiosity!

I would rather understand myself well by self-study than by reading Cicero. In the experience that I have of myself I find enough to make me wise, if I were a good scholar. Anyone who recalls the violence of his past anger, and to what a pitch his excitement carried him, will see its ugliness better than in Aristotle, and will conceive a juster hatred for it. Anyone who remembers the ills he has undergone and those that have threatened him, and the trivial happenings that have brought him from one state to another, thereby prepares himself for future changes and for the understanding of his condition.

Caesar's life has no more examples for us than our own; whether an emperor's or a common man's, it is still a life subject to all human accidents. Let us but listen to it, and we will tell

354

ourselves all that we chiefly need to know. If a man remembers how very many times he has been wrong in his judgement, will it not be foolish of him not to mistrust it ever after? When I find myself convinced by another's argument that I have held a false opinion, I do not learn so much from the new fact he has taught me and from my ignorance on this particular point – this would be a small gain – as about my own weakness in general and the untrustworthiness of my understanding. From this I proceed to some reformation of the whole mass. With all my other errors I do the same, and find that my life greatly benefits by this rule. I do not look on the species and the individual as a stone over which I have stumbled; I learn to suspect my steps everywhere, and try to regulate them. To learn that one has said or done a foolish thing, that is nothing; one must learn that one is nothing but a fool, a much more comprehensive and important lesson.

The slips that my memory has so often made, even when it was most confident of itself, have not been wasted on me. In vain does it swear to me and assure me now; I just shake my head. The first contradiction offered to its testimony puts me in doubt; and I should not dare to rely on it for anything of importance, or stand security for it in someone else's business. And were it not that the faults I commit from want of memory others commit even more often from want of good faith, I should always, in matters of fact, accept the truth from another's mouth rather than from my own. If everyone were to watch closely the effects and circumstances of the passion that rules him, as I have watched those of the passions into whose realm I have fallen, he would see them coming, and would slightly slow up their headlong career. They do not always leap at our throats at one bound; there are threats and stages.

> *Fluctus uti primo coepit cum albescere ponto,*
> *paulatim sese tollit mare, et altius undas*
> *erigit, inde imo consurgit ad aethera fundo.**

* 'As when the waves begin to whiten beneath the mounting gale, and the sea rises little by little, throwing its waves higher, climbing from its lowest bed to assault the sky.' Virgil, *Aeneid*, VII, 528.

In me judgement sits in the magistrate's seat, or at least it endeavours to do so. It leaves my inclinations to take their course, both in hatred and friendship, and even in my own feelings for myself, without being changed or corrupted by them. If it cannot reform the other parts to its own liking, at least it does not allow them to deprave it; it plays its own game by itself.

The advice to everyone that he should know himself must be important in its results, since the god of learning and light* caused it to be inscribed on the front of his temple, as comprising all the counsel he had to offer us. Plato says too that wisdom is nothing else but the fulfilment of this command, and Socrates confirms him in detail, as Xenophon records.† The difficulties and obscurities in any branch of learning are perceived only by those who have entered into it. For it needs some degree of knowledge to observe that one does not know; and one has to push at a door before realizing that it is closed to one. Whence arises the Platonic paradox that those who know have no need to inquire because they know; and those who do not know have no need either, since in order to inquire one has to know what one is inquiring about. So, in this matter of self-knowledge, the fact that everyone appears so decided and self-satisfied, that everyone thinks he understands himself well enough, shows that nobody knows anything about himself, as Socrates pointed out to Euthydemus, in Xenophon's account. I, who pretend to nothing else, find in myself such an infinite depth and variety that the sole fruit of my study is to make me feel how much I have still to learn. To this weakness of mine, which I so often admit, I owe my tendency to be modest, to accept the beliefs laid down for me, and to be consistently cool and moderate in my opinions. I also owe to it my hatred for that tiresome and wrangling arrogance which believes and trusts entirely in itself, and is the chief enemy of learning and truth.

Listen to them laying down the law: the first stupidities they utter are in the style men use to proclaim religions and laws. 'Nothing is more discreditable than to assert and agree to some-

* Apollo.   † Xenophon, *Memorabilia*, IV, 2, 24, and 29.

thing before we know and understand it.'* Aristarchus said that in ancient times there were scarcely seven wise men to be found in the world, and that in his day one had difficulty in finding seven who were ignorant. Have we not even more reason to say this of our own? Assertion and dogmatism are positive signs of stupidity. One man will have tumbled on his nose a hundred times in the day, but will be at his arguments again, as positive and unshaken as before. You would imagine that some new soul and strength of understanding had been infused into him in the meantime, and that, like that old son of earth,† he had gained fresh courage and strength from each fall,

> *cui, cum tetigere parentem*
> *iam defecta vigent renovato robore membra.‡*

Does this stubborn blockhead think that he picks up new wits when he picks up a new argument? It is from experience of myself that I attack human ignorance; and the ignorant are, in my opinion, the most positive class in the world's school. Let those who refuse to acknowledge it in themselves from an example as trifling as mine or their own, recognize it from Socrates, the master of masters. For the philosopher Antisthenes said to his disciples: 'Let us go together to hear Socrates. There I shall be a learner like you.' And, in maintaining this doctrine of the Stoic sect, that virtue is enough to make a life completely happy and in need of nothing else, he would add, 'Excepting the strength of Socrates.'

This long attention that I give to self-study fits me to make very fair judgements of others; and there are few subjects of which I speak more happily and with better excuse. I am often able to see and distinguish my friends' natures more accurately than they do themselves. I have astonished some by the pertinency of my descriptions, and have warned them against themselves. From having, since childhood, trained myself to see my own life mirrored in that of others, I have acquired a propensity for this kind of observation; and when I give my mind to it, I

* Cicero, *Academica*, i, xii.   † Antaeus.
‡ 'Whose failing limbs gain fresh strength when they have touched their mother earth.' Lucan, iv, 599.

let few things around me, whether faces, humours, or speech, that have any bearing on the matter, escape me. I study everything: what I should avoid, what I should pursue. So from my friends' outward manifestations I discover their inward inclinations: not in order to arrange their infinite variety of actions, so diverse and disconnected, in definite orders and categories, or to distribute my apportionings and divisions under clearly recognized heads and classes,

> *Sed neque quam multae species, et nomina quae sint est numerus.**

The learned divide and define their ideas more specifically and in detail. I, who have no deeper insight into these things than unsystematic practice affords me, present mine tentatively and in general terms. As here, I deliver my thought disjointedly, article by article, as something that cannot be expressed all at once and as a whole. Connectedness and conformity are not to be found in low and commonplace minds, like ours. Wisdom is a solid and complete structure, every part of which has its place and bears its mark. 'Only wisdom is completely sufficient to itself.'† I leave it to artists – and I do not know whether they will succeed in so perplexed, so detailed, and so risky a task – to marshal this infinite variety of appearances into companies, to resolve our inconsistencies and reduce them to order. Not only do I find it difficult to connect our actions one with another, but I have trouble too in designating each one separately by some principal quality, so ambiguous and variegated do they appear in different lights.

What is noticed as remarkable in Perseus, king of Macedon, that his mind adhered to no one state, but wandered through every kind of existence, reflecting so flighty and erratic a character that he neither knew himself nor was known to anyone else, seems to me more or less true of all men. What is more, I have known another of the same type to whom I think this description could be even better applied: No intermediate

---

* 'It is impossible to count the number of their kinds and recount their names.' Virgil, *Georgics*, ii, 103.   † Cicero, *De Finibus*, iii, 7.

position, but always hurried from one extreme to another for reasons beyond any man's guess; no line of direction that is not interrupted by crossings and surprising changes; no simple quality; consequently the best conception that men will one day form of him will be that he studiously affected to make himself known by making himself unknowable.*

One needs very strong ears to hear oneself freely criticized; and since there are few who can stand it without being stung, those who venture to perform this service for us give us a remarkable proof of their friendship. For it is a healthy affection that dares to wound and offend us for our own good. I find it hard to pass judgement on a man whose bad qualities exceed his good. Plato demands three things of anyone who wishes to examine another's soul: knowledge, goodwill, and boldness.

I have sometimes been asked what service I should have thought myself fit for, if anyone had cared to employ me when I was still young enough,

> *Dum melior vires sanguis dabat, aemula necdum*
> *temporibus geminis canebat sparsa senectus.*†

'For none,' I have replied. And I generally give as my excuse that I can do nothing which makes me a slave to another. But I would have told my master the truth about himself, and would have criticized his conduct, if he had allowed me. Not as a whole, by schoolmasterly lectures, in which I have no skill – and I cannot see that those who have it can effect any real improvement – but by observing his behaviour step by step, at every opportunity, and judging it at a glance, simply and naturally; by showing him how he stood in the general opinion and opposing his flatterers. There is not one of us who would not be worse than any king if he were as continually corrupted as kings are by that sort of riff-raff. How can it be otherwise if Alexander, great both as king and as philosopher, could not resist them! I should have had loyalty, judgement, and candour

* This appears to be a portrait of Henry of Navarre, later Henry IV of France.
  † 'When my blood, richer than it is now, gave me strength, and before old age jealously sprinkled both temples with grey.' Virgil, *Aeneid*, v, 415.

enough for that purpose. It would have been an office without a title; otherwise it would have lost its efficacy and virtue. And such a role cannot be played indiscriminately by all men. For even truth is not privileged to be employed at all times and in all ways: its uses, noble though they be, are circumscribed and have their limits. It often happens, as the world is, that it is dropped into a prince's ear, not only to no purpose, but injuriously and even wrongfully. And no man will convince me that a righteous remonstrance may not be viciously applied, or that the nature of the statement ought not frequently to be subordinated to the nature of its delivery. I would choose for such a business a man content with his own lot,

*Quod sit esse velit, nihilique malit,**

and of middling rank; because then, on the one hand, he would not refrain from striking his master sharply and deeply to the heart out of fear that he would lose advancement thereby; and, on the other, his intermediate position would bring him into easier touch with all sorts of people. I would have this post given to one man alone, for to spread the privilege of such freedom and intimacy to many would breed a harmful lack of reverence. And of that one man I should require, above all things, a loyal silence.

A king is not to be believed when he boasts, for his fame's sake, of his firmness in resisting the enemy's attack, if he cannot, for the sake of his profit and improvement, suffer free speech from a friend, the sole effect of which can be to sting his ears, all further consequences being under his own control. Now, there is no class of men that stands in as great need of true and frank admonitions as kings. They lead a public life, and have to conform to the notions of so many onlookers that, as it is the custom to conceal from them anything that might divert them from their path, they insensibly come to incur the hatred and detestation of their people, often for reasons which they could have avoided without even the sacrifice of their pleas-

* 'Who is glad to be what he is, and wishes to be nothing else.' Martial, x, xlvii, 12.

ures, if they had been warned and set right in time. Commonly their favourites consider their own interests rather than their master's; and it suits them well to do so, for most offices of true friendship to a sovereign are difficult and dangerous to attempt. They require not only great affection and frankness, but great courage as well.

In fine, all this medley that I am scribbling here is but a record of my life's experiences,* which is sufficient for purposes of inward health, so long as my example is taken in reverse. But as to bodily health, no one can furnish more useful experience than I, who present it in all its purity, quite uncorrupted and unchanged by art and theory. In the realm of medicine, experience is at home on its own dunghill, where reason gives place to it entirely. Tiberius used to say that anyone who has lived twenty years ought to decide on his own responsibility what suits him and what does not, and be able to take care of himself without a doctor. And he might have learned this from Socrates who, in advising his pupils to make the preservation of their health a very special study, added that a sensible man who took care about his exercise, his drink, and his food would hardly fail to know what was good or bad for him better than any physician. And medicine itself always professes to make experience the test of its efficacy. So Plato was right when he said that, to be a true physician, anyone entering the profession should himself have suffered from all the maladies that he proposed to cure, and should have experience of all the accidents and circumstances on which he had to deliver judgement. They had better catch the pox themselves if they want to know how to treat it. Truly, I should trust myself to one who had. For the rest guide us like a man who paints seas, reefs, and harbours while sitting at his table, and then manoeuvres the model of a ship in perfect safety. Face him with the real thing, and he will not know where to begin. They describe our maladies as a town-crier does a lost horse or dog – of this colour, this height, and with this shape of ear – but show him the animal, and he will not recognize it at all.

* The French word is *essais*.

In heaven's name, let medicine one day give me some good and perceptible relief, and you shall hear me cry out sincerely enough:

*Tandem efficaci do manus scientiae!**

The arts which promise to keep our bodies and souls in health promise much; but at the same time there are none that keep their promises less. And today those among us who make profession of these arts show smaller results than any other men. The most that one can say of them is that they sell medicinal drugs; but that they are men of medicine, that one cannot say.

I have lived long enough to give an account of the way of life that has carried me so far. For anyone who has a mind to try it, I have, in the capacity of his wine-taster, made the test. Here are some features of it, as they spring to my memory. I have no habit that has not varied according to circumstances, but I record those that I have found most prevalent, those that have had the greatest mastery over me up to the present time.

My mode of living is the same in sickness and in health: the same bed, the same hours, the same food, and the same drink always serve me. I make no alteration at all, except in the amount, which I vary according to my strength and appetite. Health means to me the maintenance of our usual state without discomfort. If I find sickness deflecting me in one direction, I have only to trust the physicians and they will deflect me in the other. Then what with fate, and what with their art, I am properly off the road! There is nothing about which I have less doubt than this: That so long as I use things to which I have been long accustomed I can come to no harm. It is for habit to give such shape to our life as it pleases; here it is all powerful. It is Circe's draught which varies our nature according to its will. How many nations, and only three steps away from us, think fear of the night-dew, which seems so manifestly harmful to us, a ridiculous fancy! And our watermen and peasants laugh at it too. A German becomes ill if you give him a mattress to sleep on, an Italian if you put him on a feather-bed, and a Frenchman if

* 'At last I salute a science that gives results.' Horace, *Epodes*, xvii, 1, slightly altered.

he has to sleep without curtains and a fire. A Spaniard's stomach cannot stand our kind of food, nor can ours bear to drink like the Swiss.

I was amused by a German at Augsburg who attacked the discomforts of our fireplaces with the same arguments as we habitually use in criticizing their stoves. For indeed that airless heat, and the smell of the red-hot material of which they are made, give most people who are not used to them a headache; but not me. After all, their heat being even, constant, and generally diffused, without glare, without smoke, and without the draughts that blow down our open chimneys, their method can in other ways very well bear comparison with ours. Why do we not imitate the Roman practice? For it is said that, in ancient times, fires were not made inside the house, but outside and beneath, whence the heat was drawn through the whole dwelling by means of pipes, which were built in the thickness of the walls, and embraced the rooms that were to be warmed; as I have seen clearly described somewhere in Seneca.

This German, hearing me praise the amenities and beauties of his town, which are certainly praiseworthy, began to commiserate with me for having to go away; and among the first disadvantages that he mentioned was the heavy heads I should get from the fireplaces in other lands. He had heard someone make this complaint, and applied it to us, being by habit prevented from noticing the same thing in his own house. All heat coming from a fire weakens and oppresses me. And yet Evenus said that fire is the finest spice of life. I prefer any other way of protecting myself from the cold.

We are afraid of the wine at the bottom of the cask; in Portugal these lees are considered delicious, and are the drink of princes. In fact, each nation has many customs and habits that are not only unknown, but appear strange and surprising, to other nations.

What can we do with those people who accept no evidence that is not in print, who do not believe a man except from a book, or the truth if it is not of suitable age? We dignify our stupidities when we set them up in type. It carries much more weight with such people if you say, 'I have read it', than if you say, 'I have heard it said'. But I, who do not distrust a man's tongue any more than his pen, who know that men write as injudiciously as they speak, and think as much of this age as of one that is past, would as willingly quote one of my friends as Aulus Gellius or Macrobius, and what I have seen as what they have written. And as it is held that virtue is none the greater for being of long standing, so I hold that truth is none the wiser for being old. I often say that it is pure foolishness that makes us run after foreign and bookish examples. The present is just as fertile in them as the time of Homer and Plato. But are we not more anxious to gain credit by making a quotation than for the truth of what we quote? As if it were grander to borrow our proofs from Vascosan's office or Plantin's* than from what can be seen in our own village. Or is it not, indeed, that we lack the wit to examine and apply the events that happen before our eyes, or want the judgement to estimate their value as examples? For if we say that we have not the authority to make our testimony convincing, we are wide of the mark; since, in my opinion, the most familiar and commonplace events, could we but see them in their right light, would prove to be the greatest miracles in nature, and furnish us with the most marvellous examples, particularly in the matter of human actions.

Now, in this connexion – setting aside the examples that I know from books, and Aristotle's tale of Andron the Argive, who crossed the arid sands of Libya without drinking – a gentleman† who has acquitted himself most worthily in many offices once said in my presence that he had travelled from Madrid to Lisbon in the height of summer without drinking. He is in vigorous health for his age, and there is nothing extraordinary in his habits of life except that for two or three months, or even a year, as he told me, he will go without water. He feels some thirst, but he lets it pass, holding that it is a craving that easily wanes of itself. He drinks more from whim than from need or for pleasure.

* Two printers.
† The Marquis de Pisani, French ambassador to Spain from 1573 to 1583.

Here is another case. Not long ago I found one of the most learned men in France, a man of no mean fortune, studying in the corner of his hall, which had been partitioned off with hangings, whilst his servants were unrestrainedly creating a hubbub all around him. He told me – and Seneca says almost the same thing about himself – that he turned this hurly-burly to good account. For it would seem that, when stunned by the noise, he could the better collect his wits and retire into himself for contemplation, and that this tempest of voices drove his thoughts inwards. When a scholar at Padua, he had studied for so long in a room exposed to the clatter of coaches and the tumult of the market-place that he had trained himself not only to disregard the noise but to make use of it for the benefit of his studies. When Alcibiades asked in amazement how Socrates could put up with the continual din of his wife's nagging, the master replied: 'Like anyone who gets used to the common sound of the water-wheel.' It is quite the contrary with me; my mind is sensitive, and quick to take flight; when it is absorbed into itself, the slightest buzzing of a fly will torment it to death.

In his youth Seneca was so bitten by Sextius's example of eating nothing which had been killed* that he abstained from animal food for a year, and with pleasure as he says. He gave up the rule only because he did not want to be suspected of having borrowed it from certain new religions which were propagating it. At the same time, he adopted a precept from Attalus, never to sleep on any bedding that yielded under his weight; and he continued until his old age to sleep only on hard beds. What was regarded as a barbarous habit in his day could now be put down to effeminacy.†

Consider the difference between the manner of life of my farm-servants and myself. The Scythians and Indians are no more distant from me in habits and capabilities. I remember having taken children from beggary to serve me, who have almost immediately left my kitchen and abandoned their livery, simply to return to their old lives. And I found one of them afterwards picking up mussels from a garbage pile for his dinner,

* See Seneca, *Letters*, cv.   † ibid., cviii.

yet neither by entreaties nor threats could I make him abandon
the relish and charm that he found in indigence. Beggars have
their delights and sensual pleasures as well as the rich and, so
they say, their dignities and civil precedence as well.

These are the results of habit. Not only can it mould us into
whatever shape it pleases – wherefore, say the wise, we must
fix our minds on the best, and habit will soon make it easy for
us – but it can also accustom us to change and variety; which
is the noblest and most useful of its lessons. The best thing
about my physical constitution is that I am flexible and not at
all stubborn. Some of my inclinations are more personal and
usual, as well as being more agreeable, than others. But with
very little effort I can get myself out of them, and easily slip into
a contrary habit. A young man ought to break his rules in order
to stir up his energy, and keep it from getting mouldy and weak.
And there is no way of life so foolish as one that is carried out by
rule and discipline.

> *Ad primum lapidem vectari cum placet, hora*
> *sumitur ex libro; si prurit fructus ocelli*
> *angulus, inspecta genesi collyria quaerit.**

If he takes my advice, he will often plunge even into excesses;
otherwise the slightest over-indulgence will upset him, and he
will become difficult and disagreeable in company. The most
perverse quality in a well-bred man is fastidiousness and attachment to particular ways; and ways are particular if they are not
yielding and pliable. It is wrong for a man to refrain from what
he sees his companions doing, because he cannot or dare not
follow their example. Let such a man stay in his kitchen. It is
unbecoming in anyone; but in a soldier it is an intolerable vice.
For, as Philopoemen said, a soldier ought to accustom himself
to every change and vicissitude in life.†

Though I have been trained, as far as possible, to be free and

---

* 'When he wishes to be driven to the first mile-stone, he chooses the
hour from a book. If he rubs the corner of his eye and it itches, he consults
his horoscope before using the eye-salve.' Juvenal, VI, 577.

† Actually, this was not said by Philopoemen, but in conversation with
him. See Plutarch's *Life of Philopoemen*.

unconstrained, nevertheless, as I grow old, I have out of indifference become fixed in certain ways – at my age I am past instruction, and have now no other prospect but to remain where I am – and habit has already, unconsciously, so impressed its stamp upon me in certain things that I call any deviation from it an excess. And I am unable, without doing myself violence, to sleep in the daytime or to eat between meals, or to take breakfast, or to go to bed until a long time – three good hours or more – after supper; or to get children except before sleep, or standing; or to endure my own sweat, or quench my thirst with pure water or pure wine; or stay long bareheaded; or have my hair cut after dinner; and I should be as uncomfortable without my gloves as without my shirt; or without washing when I get up from table or on rising in the morning, or without a canopy and curtains for my bed: which are all quite essential to me.

I could dine without a tablecloth, but to dine in the German fashion, without a clean napkin, I should find very uncomfortable. I soil them more than the Germans or Italians, as I make little use of either spoon or fork. I am sorry that they did not keep up the custom which was introduced in my day, following the royal example, of changing napkins with each course as we do plates. We read that the hard-working soldier Marius, when he grew old, became so fastidious in his drinking that he would only use his own private cup. I have dropped into the habit of using a glass of a certain shape, and do not like drinking from a common glass or being served by a common hand. I dislike any metal cup, and prefer one made of a clear and transparent material, so that my eyes can taste the drink too, according to their capacity.

I am indebted to habit for several such weaknesses. But nature has also brought me her share of them, among which is my inability to take two full meals a day without overloading my stomach, or entirely to abstain from either without becoming filled with wind, dry in the mouth, and dull of appetite. Long exposure to the night air upsets me also. For of late years, when I am out all night on military duties, as frequently happens, my stomach begins to trouble me after five or six hours, my head aches violently, and I cannot hold out till daybreak without vomiting. When the others go to breakfast, I go to sleep, and after that I am as fresh as ever again.

I had always understood that the dew only rises early in the night, but of late I have been much in the close company of a gentleman who firmly believes that it is sharper and more dangerous as the sun is going down, an hour or two before it sets. He then carefully avoids it, but he does not mind the night air and he has almost persuaded me, if not to agree with him, at least to share his feeling.

What shall we say if a mere doubt or question concerning our health so strikes our imagination as to work a change in us? Those who suddenly yield to such impulses destroy themselves. And I am sorry for a number of gentlemen who, though still young and sound, have made themselves into prisoners through the folly of their physicians. It would, after all, be much better to put up with a chill than to lose for ever, by disuse, the ordinary pleasures of social life, by giving up so usual a habit as that of going out late. How mischievous is the science that discredits the pleasantest hours of the day! Let us extend what we possess to the utmost of our powers! For the most part, we become inured by stubborn persistence, and correct our constitutions, as Caesar did his epilepsy, by scorning and combating them. A man should put himself under the best rules, but not become a slave to them; except to such, if such there be, as it is profitable for him to observe and slavishly follow.

Both kings and philosophers defecate, and so do the ladies. The lives of public men owe an obligation to formality; mine, which is obscure and private, enjoys all the natural dispensations; to be a soldier and a Gascon, moreover, is to be somewhat subject to indiscretion. Therefore I shall say of this action that it should be relegated to certain prescribed hours of the night, and that one should compel and confine oneself to these by habit, after my example; but one should not enslave oneself, as I have done in my declining years, to the comfort of some particular place and seat for this purpose, or make the practice tire-

somely long or finicky. Yet, in the fouler offices, is it not to some
extent excusable to demand more care and cleanliness? 'Man is
by nature a clean and fastidious animal.'* Of all the functions of
nature, it is this that I can least bear to be put off. I have known
many soldiers to be bothered by the irregularity of their bowels:
I and mine never miss our punctual assignation at the moment
I leap out of bed, unless we are disturbed by some urgent
occupation or by serious illness.

I cannot think, therefore, as I was saying, of any way in which
a sick man can better protect himself than by quietly following
the way of life in which he has been bred and brought up.
Change of any sort is disturbing and harmful. Believe, if you
can, that chestnuts are injurious to a man of Périgord or Lucca,
or milk and cheese to a mountain dweller! Physicians are always
prescribing a diet that is not merely new but opposed to the
patient's usual one: a change that even a healthy man could not
stand. Order a 70-year-old Breton to drink water; confine a
seaman in a heated room; forbid a Basque footman to walk: you
deprive them of motion, and in the end of light and air.

> *An vivere tanti est? ...*

> *Cogimur a suetis animum suspendere rebus;*
> *atque, ut vivamus vivere desinimus.*

> *Hos superesse rear, quibus et spurabilis aer*
> *et lux qua regimur redditur ipsa gravis?*†

If they do no other good, they do this at least: they prepare
their patients in time for death by gradually sapping and
restricting their enjoyment of life.

Both in health and sickness, I generally give in to those
appetites that are insistent. I allow my desires and inclinations
great authority. I have no wish to cure one evil by another; I
hate remedies that are more troublesome than the disease. To

* Seneca, *Letters*, XCII.

† 'Is life then worth so much? ... We are compelled to wean our minds
of what we are accustomed to, and in order to preserve our lives we cease to
live. ... Shall I regard those as still living, for whom the air they breathe and
the light that guides them have become oppressive?' Maximianus, Pseudo-
Gallus, I, 155 and 247.

be a victim to the colic, and to subject oneself to abstinence from the pleasure of eating oysters, are two evils instead of one. The disease stabs us on one side, the diet on the other. Since there is the risk of a mistake let us take it, for preference, in the pursuit of pleasure. The world does the opposite, and considers nothing to be useful that is not painful; facility rouses its suspicions. My appetite, luckily enough, has in many ways accommodated itself of its own accord, and yielded to the health of my stomach. Tartness and pungency in sauces were agreeable to me when I was young; my stomach becoming intolerant of them since, my palate immediately following suit. Wine is bad for the sick; it is the first thing for which my mouth feels a distaste and the distaste is invincible. Whatever I take that is disagreeable to me harms me, and nothing harms me that I eat hungrily and gladly. I have never been harmed by doing anything that was a real pleasure to me. And so I have made all medical advice very largely give way to my pleasure. As a young man, I was one,

> *Quem circumcursans huc atque hic saepe Cupido*
> *fulgebat, crocina splendidus in tunica;**

and I yielded as licentiously and heedlessly as any man to the desire that had possession of me,

> *Et militavi non sine gloria†*

more in the length and endurance of my efforts than in the vigour of my assault:

> *Sex me vix memini sustinuisse vices.‡*

It is a sad and strange thing indeed to confess at how tender an age I first came to fall under its subjection. It was a mere chance, for it was long before the age of choice and knowledge. My memory does not go back so far; and my lot can be coupled with that of Quartilla,§ who could not remember when she was virgin.

* 'Around whom Love flew ceaselessly, and shone splendid in his saffron vest.' Catullus, LXVI, 133.

† 'And I fought, not without glory.' Horace, *Odes*, III, xxvi, 2.

‡ 'I scarcely remember having achieved six times.' Ovid, *Amores*, III, vii, 26. Ovid says not six but nine. § See Petronius, ch. xxv.

Inde tragus celeresque pili, mirandaque matri
barba meae.*

Physicians modify their rules, usually with advantage, according to the strength and sharpness of their patients' cravings; however strange or vicious we may imagine such a violent desire to be, we must still put it down to nature. And then, how much it takes to satisfy the imagination! In my opinion this faculty is all-important, or at least more important than any other. The most grievous and common evils are those that fancy loads upon us. This Spanish saying pleases me from many points of view: '*Defiéndame Dios de mi*'.† When I am sick, I am sorry not to have some desire that it would give me pleasure to satisfy; all the rules of physic would hardly restrain me. I feel the same when I am well; I see very little more to hope or wish for. It is pitiful to be languid and enfeebled even in one's desires.

The art of medicine is not so rigid that we cannot find an authority for anything that we may do. According to Farnel and l'Escale,‡ it changes according to climate and according to the phases of the moon. If your doctor does not think it good for you to sleep, to take wine or some particular meat, do not worry; I will find you another who will disagree with him. The diversity of medical arguments and opinions assumes all sorts of forms. I have seen a poor man fainting and perishing from thirst in pursuit of a cure, and afterwards laughed at by another physician, who condemned the first one's advice as harmful. Had the sick man tortured himself for nothing? There lately died of the stone a member of the faculty who had resorted to extreme abstinence to combat his disease. His colleagues say that, in fact, his fasting had dried him up and heated the gravel in his kidneys.

I have observed that, when I am wounded or ill, talking excites and harms me as much as any irregularity that I may commit. The use of my voice tries me and costs me dear, for it

* 'Hence goatish odours and quick growth of hair, and an early beard that astonished my mother.' Martial, XI, xxii, 7.

† God defend me from myself.   ‡ Two doctors of the day.

is loud and vehement. So much so that when I used to have private talks with great men about important matters, they would often anxiously entreat me to speak more quietly. This story is worth a digression. Someone* in a certain Greek school was talking in a loud voice, as I do. The master of ceremonies sent word to him to speak in a lower tone. 'Let him send me the tone then, in which he wishes me to speak,' said he. The master's reply was that he should suit his tone to the ears of the man to whom he was speaking. This was a good saying, provided that his meaning was: 'Speak according to the matter that you have to discuss with your listener.' For if he meant 'Let it be enough that he hears you', or 'Adapt your voice to his ear', I do not think the answer was good. The tone and inflection of my voice help to express the significance of my words; it is for me to regulate it in such a way as to make myself understood.

There is a voice for teaching, a voice for flattery, and a voice for scolding. I would have my voice not only reach my listener, but perhaps strike him and pierce him through. When I reprimand my footman in sharp and cutting tones, it would be a fine thing if he said to me: 'Speak more quietly, sir. I can hear you very well.' 'There is a kind of voice that accords with the ear, not so much by its volume as by its quality.'† A speech belongs half to the speaker, half to him who hears it. The hearer should let the form of its delivery prepare him for its reception; as, with tennis players, the man who takes the service shifts his position and makes ready according to the movements of the striker and to the nature of the stroke.

Experience has also taught me this, that we destroy ourselves by impatience. Evils have their life and limits, their sickness and their health.

The constitution of maladies follows the same pattern as that of living beings; their destiny and their length of days are limited for them from their birth. Anyone who attempts wilfully and forcibly to cut them short in the middle of their course, only lengthens and multiplies them, and incenses them instead of

* Carneades, the Sceptic philosopher.   † Quintilian, xi, iii.

appeasing them. I am of Crantor's* opinion, that we must neither obstinately and desperately oppose evils, nor softly succumb to them, but must yield to them naturally according to their nature and our own. We should give free access to illnesses; and I find that they stay a shorter time with me, who let them have their way. Some of those that are reckoned most obstinate and tenacious, have left me, dying of their own decay, without the help of medicine and in spite of its rules. Let us give nature some chance to work; she understands her business better than we. 'But so-and-so died of it!' So will you, if not of this disease, of another. And how many have died just the same though they had three doctors at their backs? Example is an uncertain mirror that reflects all things and from all angles. If the medicine is pleasant, take it; it is always so much present gain. I shall not be put off by its name or its colour, so long as it is tempting and delicious. Pleasure is one of the chief kinds of profit.

I have allowed colds, gouty discharges, looseness of the bowels, palpitations, headaches, and other ailments to grow old in me and die their natural death; they have left me when I have half enured myself to their company. One can exercise them better by courtesy than by defiance. We must quietly put up with the laws of our condition. We have to grow old, to become weak and to be ill, in spite of all medicine. That is the first lesson that the Mexicans teach their children. When they come forth from the mother's womb, their elders greet them with these words: 'Child, you have come into the world to endure. Endure, suffer, and be silent.'

It is wrong to complain because something has happened to one man which might happen to any; 'Complain if an unjust decree is made against you alone.'† See an old man who prays God to keep him in perfect and vigorous health, that is to say to restore his youth.

Stulte, quid haec frustra votis puerilibus optas.‡

* See Cicero, *Tusculans*, III, 6.   † Seneca, *Letters*, XCI.
‡ Fool, why do you vainly ask for these things in your childish prayers?'
Ovid, *Tristia*, III, vii, 11.

Is it not folly? His condition is incapable of it. Gout, the stone, and indigestion are symptoms of a long life as heat, rains, and wind are of a long journey. It is Plato's belief that Aesculapius did not trouble himself to treat a wasted and feeble body, or to prolong the life of one who was useless to his country, unequal to his occupation, and unable to beget sound and healthy children. He considers that such care would be inconsistent with divine justice and wisdom, which must direct all things according to their usefulness. My good friend, it is all up with you. No one can restore you; at best you can be plastered and propped up a little, and your wretchedness can be prolonged for a few hours.

> *Non secus instantem cupiens fulcire ruinam,*
> *diversis contra nititur obicibus,*
> *donec certa dies, omni compage soluta,*
> *ipsum cum rebus subruat auxilium.**

One must learn to endure what one cannot avoid. Our life, like the harmony of the world, is composed of contrarieties, also of varying tones, sweet and harsh, sharp and flat, soft and loud. If a musician liked one sort only, what effect would he make? He must be able to employ them together and blend them. And we too must accept the good and evil that are consubstantial with our life. Our existence is impossible without this mixture, and one side is no less necessary to us than the other. Any attempt to kick against natural necessity will be to copy the foolishness of Ctesiphon, who tried a kicking-match with his mule.†

I seldom consult physicians about the changes in my health, for these men take advantage of you when they have you at their mercy. They fill your ears with their prognostications. And formerly, when they took me unawares, weakened by my illness, they would come down on me with their dogmas and magisterial frowns, threatening me sometimes with severe pain,

* 'Thus if one wishes to shore up a tumbling building, one can place various props against it. But finally, on some fatal day, the whole structure will fall, dragging down the props with the rest.' Pseudo-Gallus, I, 171.
† See Plutarch, *On Anger*, viii.

and sometimes with approaching death. I was not upset or thrown off my balance, but I was battered and shaken. If my judgement was neither impaired nor disturbed, at least it was troubled; there is always agitation and conflict.

Now I treat my imagination as gently as I can, and would relieve it, if I could, of all distress and argument. It must be helped and flattered, and deceived if possible. My mind is well fitted for this service; it finds plenty of good reasons everywhere. If only it could persuade as well as it preaches, it would assist me most successfully.

Would you like an instance? It says that it is for my good that I have the stone, that structures of my age must necessarily suffer from some leakage. This is the time when they begin to loosen and decay. Such is the common lot. Would I have a new miracle performed in my favour? In this way I am paying the dues of old age, and I cannot expect to get off more cheaply. It says that the company I am in ought to console me, since I have succumbed to the ailment most common among men of my time. Everywhere I see victims to this sort of complaint, and I am honoured by their fellowship, since it attacks the great for preference: it is essentially a noble and dignified malady. My mind says, furthermore, that few of those who are attacked by it get off more cheaply; and then they pay the penalty of a tiresome diet and have every day to take unpleasant medicinal drugs, whereas I owe my recovery solely to good fortune. For some common decoctions of saxifrage or Turk's herb, which I have swallowed two or three times to oblige the ladies – who, with kindness greater than the sharpness of my pain, have presented me with half of theirs – have seemed to me as easy to take as they were ineffective in their results. Others must pay a thousand vows to Aesculapius, and as many crowns to their physician, for an easy and abundant discharge of gravel, which I frequently enjoy by the favour of nature. Even the correctness of my behaviour in ordinary company is not disturbed by my malady, and I can hold my water for ten hours, or as long as any man.

The prospect of this malady, says my mind, used to frighten

you once, when it was unknown to you. The despairing cries
of those who aggravate it by their impatience engendered a
horror of it in you. It is a malady that affects the organs with
which you have most transgressed. You are a man of conscience.

Quae venit indigne poena, dolenda venit. *

Consider this punishment; it is very mild by comparison with
others, and is inflicted with a paternal kindness. See how late it
has come; it attacks and incommodes only that season of your
life which will, in any case, be barren and wasted, having, as if
by agreement, given you time for the indulgences and pleasures
of your youth. The fear and pity that people feel at the sight of
this malady serve you as occasions for vainglory; for even
though you have purged your mind and cleansed your conversation of it, your friends can still recognize some traces of
this failing in your nature. It is gratifying to hear people say of
you: There is strength now! There's patience! They see you
sweating with anguish, growing pale, flushing, trembling,
vomiting your very blood, suffering strange contractions and
convulsions, and at times dropping great tears from your eyes.
You discharge thick, dark, and dreadful urine, or have it
stopped by a sharp rough-edged stone that cruelly pricks and
tears the neck of your penis; and all the time you are talking to
those around you with an ordinary expression, joking in the
intervals with your servants, taking your share in a sustained
conversation, apologizing for your pain and making light of
your suffering.

Do you remember those men of olden times who so avidly
sought out ills in order to keep their virtue in breath and exercise? Assume that nature is forcibly driving you into this glorious school, which you would never have entered of your own
free will. If you tell me that the disease is dangerous and mortal,
what diseases are not? It is trickery of the doctors to make some
exceptions, which they say do not lead directly to death. What
does it matter if they get there by accident, if they imperceptibly
slide and slip into the road that leads us there?

But you do not die because you are sick, you die because you

* It is undeserved suffering that is to be lamented.' Ovid, *Heroides*, v, 8.

are alive. Death can easily kill you without the help of the disease. And sickness has postponed death for some people who have lived longer because they thought they were dying. Moreover, there are maladies, as there are wounds, that are medicinal and salutary.

The stone has often no less life than we. We see men with whom it has lasted from their childhood to their extreme old age; and if they had not deserted it, it would have been prepared to accompany them still further. You kill it more often than it kills you, and even if it should present you with the image of approaching death, would it not be kindness to a man at that age to bring him to meditate upon his end? And, what is worse, you no longer have any motive for recovery. In any case, the common lot will call you at the first opportunity. Consider how skilfully and gently your illness disgusts you with life and detaches you from the world. It does not keep you in tyrannical subjection like so many other complaints that one sees in old men, which hold them continuously fettered, with no relief from their weakness and pain. It proceeds by warnings and instructions repeated at intervals, and interrupts them with long spells of peace, as if to afford you an opportunity of thinking over and repeating its lesson at your leisure. So that you may have the means of making a sound judgement and taking up your stand like a brave man, it puts before you the whole picture of your situation, at its best and at its worst, and on the same day offers you life in its most delightful and most unbearable forms. If you do not embrace death, at least you shake hands with it once a month; and this gives you greater reason to expect that one day it will catch you without warning. Then, after being led so often to the place of embarkation, still trusting that you are on the accustomed terms, you will find, one fine morning, that you and your confidence have unexpectedly been carried across the water. No one has reason to complain of a disease that honourably divides the time with good health.

I am grateful to fortune for attacking me so often with the same kind of weapons. She adopts me and trains me to resist them by use; she inures and habituates me to them. I now know more or less what it will cost me to be rid of them. For lack of a natural memory, I make one on paper, and as some new symptom appears in my disease, I write it down. So it is that now, having been acquainted with almost every kind, whenever some fresh alarm threatens me I turn over these little disconnected notes. In thus referring to my Sibylline leaves, I never fail to find in my past experience some favourable prognostic to comfort me. Familiarity also serves to give me better hopes for the future. For this passing of gravel having so long continued, it is probable that nature will not change her course, and that nothing worse will happen than what I have endured already. Besides, the character of this illness is not ill-suited to my hasty and vehement disposition. When it attacks me mildly, I am frightened because then its stay will be long. But normally its attacks are sharp and violent; it shakes me to the roots for a day or two.

My kidneys held out for an age without deterioration, and it is nearly another age since their condition changed. Evil things have their periods as well as good; perhaps this trouble is drawing to an end. Age reduces the heat of my stomach; the digestion, therefore, being less perfect, it sends this crude matter to my kidneys. Why then, at a certain fixed period, will not the heat of my kidneys also have abated so that they can no longer petrify my phlegm, and nature find some other way of purging me? Years have evidently caused some juices to dry up in me. Why not also the waste products that furnish material for the gravel?

But is there any delight comparable to that sudden change when by the passing of a stone, I come at a flash from extreme pain into the fair light of health, fully and freely restored, as happens in our sudden and most violent attacks of colic? Is there anything in the torment endured that can be balanced against the pleasure of this instantaneous recovery? How much more beautiful health appears to me after sickness, when the two are so close together that I can view each in the other's presence in full armour; when they stand as deadly rivals defying and battling with one another!

Just as the Stoics say that vices are introduced for our profit, to give value and assistance to virtue, we can say with better reason and less rashness, that nature has given us pain so that we may appreciate and be thankful for comfort and the absence of pain. When Socrates was relieved of his fetters he felt agreeably stimulated by the tingling which the weight of them had set up in his legs, and took pleasure in reflecting how closely pleasure and pain are allied, being linked together by a necessary bond, so that they follow and engender one another by turns. And he exclaimed that this thought might have given the excellent Aesop a theme for a fine fable.

The worst thing that I see in other diseases is that their immediate effects are less serious than their consequences. A man takes a year to recover, and is all the time full of weakness and dread. There are so many risks and so many stages on the road back to health that it is quite endless. Before they have unmuffled you first of a head-shawl and then of your skull-cap, before you are allowed fresh air, and wine, and your wife, and melons again, it is a wonder if you have not relapsed into some new trouble. The stone has this advantage, that it goes right away, whereas other maladies always leave some traces, and some deterioration, which leaves the body susceptible to fresh complaints; and they lend a hand to one another.

One can pardon those diseases that are content with their hold on us, without extending it and introducing their followers. But courteous and gracious are those whose visits bring us some beneficial results. Since I have had the stone, I find myself free from other ailments, more so I think than I was before; and I have had no fever since then. I argue that the severe and frequent vomitings to which I am subject purge me, and that, on the other hand, my loss of appetite and the unusual fasts that I keep digest my peccant humours, while nature ejects whatever is superfluous and harmful in me in these stones.

Let no one tell me this medicine is too dearly bought. What about all those stinking draughts, cauteries, incisions, sweatings, setons, dietings, and all those methods of cure that often bring us to our graves, being harsher and more violent than we can endure? So when I have an attack, I take it as a medicine; and when I am exempt I think of it as a lasting and absolute deliverance.

Here is another benefit peculiar to my disease: that it almost plays its game by itself, and lets me play mine – or if I do not, it is only from lack of courage. I have ridden a horse for ten hours when it was at its most severe. Only endure it, and you need follow no other rule. Play, dine, run, do this, and do that, if you can; your dissipation will do you more good than harm. You cannot say that to a man with pox, or with gout, or a hernia. Other maladies impose more general restrictions, and constrain our actions in a very different way. They disturb the whole order of our life, making our entire being subordinate to them. Mine only pricks the skin; it leaves the brain and the will wholly at a man's disposal, also the tongue, the feet, and the hands. It rouses rather than stupefies one. The mind is affected by the heat of a fever, struck down by an epilepsy, put out of joint by a severe sick-headache and, in fact, paralysed by all the maladies that hurt the main frame and the nobler organs. Here the mind is not attacked. If it sustains any harm, it is by its own fault; it has betrayed, abandoned, and disabled itself.

Only fools let themselves be persuaded that this hard and solid substance which forms in the kidneys can be dissolved by potions. Therefore, once it is shaken up there is nothing for it but to give it passage; and it will take it, anyhow.

I note this particular advantage also, that it is a disease which leaves us little scope for speculation. We are spared the uneasiness into which other maladies throw us by reason of our uncertainty as to their causes, states, and progress: an uneasiness that is extremely distressing. We have no need of medical consultation and diagnosis; our senses tell us what it is, and where it is.

By such arguments, both strong and weak, I try to lull and divert my imagination, and to salve its wounds, as Cicero did the infirmity of his old age. If things get worse next day, next day we will devise other stratagems.

Here is the proof of what I say. Since I last wrote, this new development has taken place, that the slightest movement draws the pure blood from my kidneys. What of it? I do not for all that give up moving about as before, and I gallop after my hounds with a youthful ardour that is unusual in me. And I find that I gain a great advantage by this serious affliction, which costs me no more than a dull heaviness and discomfort in that region. It is some large stone crushing and consuming the substance of my kidneys and it is my life that I am draining out little by little, not without some natural pleasure, as a waste substance henceforth troublesome and superfluous.

Now if I feel some disturbance, do not expect me to waste my time consulting my pulse and examining my urine in order to take some tedious precautions. I shall feel the pain soon enough without prolonging it by the pain of fear. He who is afraid of suffering already suffers from his own fears. What is more, the doubts and ignorance of those who take it upon themselves to interpret nature's workings and her internal progressions, and to explain away the many false prognostics of their art, should make us realize that its ways are utterly unknown. There is great uncertainty, variety, and obscurity both in its promises and its threats. Except for old age, which is an indubitable symptom of death's approach, I can see few signs in any of our other ills on which we can ground our divinations of the future.

I judge of myself only by actual sensations, not by reasoning. What would be the good of reasoning, since I intend to do nothing but wait patiently? Do you wish to know how much I gain by this? Observe those who do otherwise, and follow so many different arguments and opinions. See how often the imagination plagues them when the body is sound! Many a time, when comfortable and free from these dangerous attacks, I have taken a malicious pleasure in describing them to physicians as if they were just coming upon me. I have most cheerfully sustained the verdict of their terrible conclusions, which has made me the more grateful to God for His grace, and the more convinced of the worthlessness of their art.

There is nothing that should be so recommended to young people as activity and alertness. Our life is all movement, I bestir myself with difficulty, and am slow in everything: in getting up, in going to bed, and at my meals. Seven o'clock is early for me, and where I am master I neither dine before eleven nor sup till after six. Once I used to attribute the fevers and sicknesses that attacked me to the heaviness and sluggishness brought on by long sleep, and I have always been sorry if I have dozed off again in the morning. Plato condemns excessive sleep more than excessive drinking.

I like to lie hard and alone, yes without my wife, in royal fashion, and rather well covered up. My bed is never warmed, but since I have grown old they give me cloths, when I need them, to warm my feet and stomach. The great Scipio used to be reproached for his addiction to sleep; for no other reason, in my opinion, than because it annoyed men that he was the only person in whom they could find no fault. If I am particular about one detail in my life more than another, it is about my sleeping; but I generally accommodate myself to necessity as well as any other man. Sleeping has filled a great part of my life, and I continue at my present age to sleep for eight or nine hours at a stretch. I am breaking myself, to advantage, of this propensity to sloth, and am visibly the better for it. I feel the change a little difficult, but it is done in three days; and I know few who manage with less sleep when the need arises, or who take steadier exercise, or who are less affected by prolonged hard work.

My body is capable of sustained, but not of extreme or sudden exertion. Nowadays I avoid violent exercise and efforts that put me into a sweat; my limbs tire before they grow hot. I can keep on my feet all day long, and walking does not weary me; but on paved streets, ever since my youth, I have never cared to go except on a horse. On foot, I get splashed with mud up to the waist; in our streets a little man is liable to be elbowed and jostled for want of presence. And I have always liked to rest, whether lying or sitting, with my legs as high as my seat, or higher.

There is no calling so pleasant as a soldier's, a calling both noble in the performance – for the strongest, most generous and proudest of all virtues is valour – and noble in its cause. There is no service more justifiable or more universal than the defence of one's country's peace and greatness. You take pleasure in the company of so many noble and active young men, in the familiar sight of so many tragic spectacles, in the freedom of unaffected relationships, in the virile and unceremonious way of life, in the many and various military actions, in the brave harmony of martial music which delights the ears and excites the soul, in the honour of your employment, and even in its hardships and difficulties, of which Plato thought so little that in his *Republic* he makes the women and boys share in them. As a voluntary soldier, you take on particular duties and risks according to your judgement of their brilliance and importance, and you may see when life itself is staked in it with good reason,

pulchrumque mori succurrit in armis.*

To fear dangers that are shared in common with such a multitude, not to dare what is dared by so many kinds of souls, is to show a heart mean and debased beyond all measure. Company gives confidence even to children. If others excel you in knowledge, in charm, in strength, in fortune, you can blame external causes for it; but if you fall behind them in stoutness of spirit, you have only yourself to blame. Death is more inglorious, more lingering, and painful, in a bed than in battle; fevers and catarrhs are as distressing and as fatal as a musket-shot. Anyone who is capable of bravely bearing the mischances of ordinary life would have no need to increase his courage, to become a soldier. 'To live, my dear Lucilius, is to fight.'†

I do not remember that I ever had the itch. Yet scratching is one of nature's sweetest pleasures, and one of her readiest. But repentance follows too closely on its heels. I practise it particularly on my ears, the insides of which irritate me at times.

I came into the world with all my senses sound, and almost perfect. My digestion is reasonably good, and so is my head; and they generally remain so in my attacks of fever, as does my

* 'How the thought comes that it is a fine death to die in arms.' Virgil, *Aeneid*, II, 317.

† Seneca, *Letters*, XCVI.

breathing also. I shall soon have passed my fifty-sixth year, an age which some nations, not without reason, fixed as so proper a limit to life that they allowed no one to exceed it. Yet I still have occasional though uncertain and brief returns to health, so bright that they hardly differ from the sound and painless state of my youth. I do not mean vigour and activity; there is no reason why youth should follow me beyond its limits:

> *Non haec amplius est liminis, aut aquae*
> *coelestis, patiens latus.**

My face and eyes immediately reveal my state of health; all its changes begin with them, and they look a little worse than they really are. My friends often commiserate with me before I am aware of the cause. My mirror does not frighten me, for even in my youth it happened more than once that I had a bad colour and an appearance that boded ill, without any serious results occurring. The physicians, in fact, finding no inward causes to account for this outward change, attributed it to my mind, and spoke of some secret passion that devoured me within. They were wrong. If my body were as much under my control as my mind, we should get along a little more comfortably. My mind was then not only free from trouble, but full of enjoyment and content, as it usually is, half by its nature, half by design:

> *Nec vitiant artus aegrae contagia mentis.*†

I am of the opinion that this moderate tenor of mind has many a time raised the body after it has fallen. It is often downcast when my mind, if not gay, is at least calm and at rest. I had a quartan fever for four or five months which made me look quite wretched; my mind all the time went not only peacefully, but cheerfully on its way. If the pain is external, the weakness and languor hardly depress me. I know some bodily infirmities, dreadful even to name, that I should fear less than the thousand passions and agitations of the mind that I see around me. I have

---

* 'I càn no longer stand on the threshold, and expose myself to the rain from heaven.' Horace, *Odes*, III, x, 19 (adapted).

† 'My body is not affected by contagion from my sick mind.' Ovid, *Tristia*, III, viii, 25 (adapted).

made up my mind that I can no longer run; it is enough that I can crawl, and I do not complain of the natural decay that has taken hold of me,

Quis tumidum guttur miratur in Alpibus?*

any more than I regret that my life is not as long or as sound as an oak's.

I have no reason to complain of my imagination. I have had few thoughts in my life that have so much as interrupted my sleep, except those of desire, which have woken me without distressing me. I seldom dream; and then it is of fantastic and grotesque things, the product of thoughts that are amusing and absurd rather than melancholy. And I believe it to be true that dreams are faithful interpreters of our inclinations; but there is an art in sorting and understanding them.

Res quae in vita usurpant homines, cogitant, curat, vident,
quaeque agunt vigilantes, agitantque, ea sicut in somno accidunt,
minus mirandum est.†

Plato, moreover, says that it is a wise precaution to draw from them prophetic instructions for the future. I could see nothing in this were it not for the marvellous incidents related on this subject by Socrates, Xenophon, and Aristotle, men of unimpeachable authority. Histories say that the Atlanteans never dreamed, also that they never ate anything that had been killed. I add this fact, since it may be the reason for the first. For Pythagoras prescribed certain methods of preparing food to stimulate the right dreams. My dreams are very light, and neither disturb me physically nor make me talk in my sleep. I have known men in my time very much disturbed by them. Theon the philosopher walked in his sleep, as did Pericles' slave also on the very roof and tiles of the house.

I exercise little choice at table, but take the first and nearest thing, and am very reluctant to change from one flavour to an-

---

* 'Who is surprised to find a goitre in the Alps?' Juvenal, XIII, 162.

† 'What men commonly use in life, and think about, and look after, and see and do when they are awake, and what they pursue, comes to them in their dreams; and this is not surprising.' *Verses from a tragedy by Attius Brutus*, quoted by Cicero, *De Div.* I, xiii.

other. I dislike a crowd of dishes and courses as much as I do any other crowd. I am easily satisfied with a few meats, and disagree with Favorinus's* view that, at a banquet, a dish should be snatched away from you as soon as you have taken a liking to it, and a new one be put in its place; and that it is a niggardly supper if the guests have not been stuffed with the rumps of various birds, the beccafico being the only one that deserves to be eaten whole.

I commonly eat salt meats, but I prefer my bread unsalted; and my baker at home, contrary to the local custom, produces no other for my table. In my childhood the chief fault for which I had to be corrected was my refusal of those things that children generally like best – sweets, preserves, and cakes. My tutor fought against this aversion to dainties as if it were a form of daintiness. And indeed it is nothing but a perversity of taste, whatever its object. Even if a child's fondness is for brown bread, bacon, or garlic, when one breaks him of it one is really curing him of greed. There are some who put on an aggrieved and long-suffering air, if deprived of beef and ham when there is plenty of partridge; this is the daintiness of the dainty; it is the taste of one who lives soft and has lost the taste for those common and familiar things 'with which luxury relieves the tedium of wealth'.† Not to find good cheer in what cheers another, to take special care about one's food, that is the essence of this vice:

Si modica coenare times olus omne patella.‡

There is indeed this difference, that it is better to confine one's desires to the things which are easiest to obtain; but it is still a defect to be tied at all. I used to call a relative of mine fastidious because, through service in our galleys, he had learnt to do without a bed, and to sleep without undressing.

If I had male children, I should like them to have the advan-

* See Aulus Gellius, xv, 8, 2. This is not Favorinus's opinion. He argues against it from the same point of view as Montaigne.

† Seneca, *Letters*, xviii.

‡ 'If you are afraid to dine on vegetables in a modest dish.' Horace, *Epistles*, i, v, 2.

tages that I had. The good father whom God gave me and whom I can only repay with gratitude, but certainly with a very hearty gratitude, for his goodness, sent me from the cradle to be brought up in a poor village on his estate, and kept me there so long as I was at the breast and longer, thus training me to the humblest and commonest way of life: 'Liberty consists, in great part, in a well-ordered stomach.'* Never take upon yourselves, and still less entrust to your wives, the care of your children's nurture. Let them be shaped by fortune subject to the laws of nature and the people; let custom train them to be frugal and austere, so that hardship shall be a state they relax from rather than brace themselves for. My father's plan had also another aim: to unite me with the common people, and with that class that needs our aid. He considered it my obligation to consider a man who stretches out his arms to me, rather than one who shows me his back. And this was also the reason why he chose persons of the most lowly fortune to hold me at the font; he wished to bind and attach me to them.

His plan has not succeeded at all badly. I generally feel drawn towards humble men, whether because it is more creditable, or out of natural compassion, which is extremely strong in me. The party that I might condemn in our wars, I should condemn still more bitterly if it were prosperous and flourishing; I should feel somewhat reconciled were I to see it conquered and miserable.

How greatly I admire the noble spirit of Chelonis, daughter and wife of a king of Sparta! So long as her husband Cleombrotus had the advantage over her father Leonidas, during the disturbances in their city, she shared her father's exile and poverty like a good daughter, and opposed the victor. But once the wheel of fortune turned, her will changed with it, and she bravely took her husband's side, accompanying him wherever his disasters carried him. It seems that she had no other choice but to range herself on the side which needed her most, and where she could best show her compassion. I am more naturally inclined to follow the example of Flaminius, who gave himself

* Seneca, *Letters*, CXXIII.

to those who had need of him instead of to those who could benefit him, than that of Pyrrhus, who was prone to humble himself before the great and domineer over the lowly.

Long-drawn-out meals weary and disagree with me. For, perhaps because I formed the habit in childhood, I eat so long as I am at table, for want of anything better to do. Therefore in my own house, though the meals are of the shortest, I generally sit down a little after the rest, after the manner of Augustus. But I do not copy him in leaving the board before the others. On the contrary, I like to sit quietly for a long time afterwards, and listen to the conversation so long as I take no part in it. For it tires me and disagrees with me to talk on a full stomach, although I find loud conversation and argument before meals a very healthy and pleasant exercise. The Greeks and Romans were wiser than we in setting aside for eating, which is an important action in life, several hours and the better part of the night, unless some unusual business kept them from it. They ate and drank less hurriedly than we, who perform all our actions posthaste, and protracted this natural pleasure by the leisurely custom of interspersing their meals with various kinds of useful and agreeable sociability.

Those whose duty it is to look after me could easily deprive me of what they think will do me harm. In these matters, I never desire or miss what I do not see. But if they preach abstinence once a dish is in front of me, they are wasting their time. Should I wish to fast, therefore, I must stay away from supper, and have just so much put before me as is necessary for the diet prescribed. For once I sit down to table, I forget my resolution. When I order that some dish shall be prepared in a different way, my family knows what it means: that my appetite has failed and I shall not even touch it.

I like all meats underdone that can be served so, and many I like very high, even to the point of smelling. It is only toughness that I usually object to. Over other qualities I am as indifferent and as tolerant as any man I have met. So much so that, contrary to common taste, I even find some kinds of fish too fresh and firm. It is not the fault of my teeth, which have always been exceptionally good, and which age is only now beginning to threaten. From childhood I have had the habit of rubbing them with a napkin, both in the morning and before and after meals.

God is kind to those from whom He takes life by degrees; that is the only blessing of old age. The final death will be so much the less complete and painful; it will kill no more than a half or a quarter of a man. One of my teeth has now fallen out painlessly, and without being pulled; it had reached the natural term of its existence. Both this part of my being and several others are dead already, and others are half-dead, though they were some of the most active and important during my years of vigour. Thus I melt and steal away from myself. How foolish I should be to let my mind feel this decline, which is already so advanced, as if it were a fall from the very peak. I hope it will not do so.

In truth, the chief comfort that I find when I think of my death is that it will be proper and natural, and that henceforth any favour I may ask or hope of destiny will be undeserved. Men have persuaded themselves that in former times we were not only taller but had longer lives. But Solon, who lived in those days, fixes life's extreme duration at seventy. Shall I, who have been such a worshipper, in all things, of the *golden mean* of antiquity, and have regarded the average measure as the most perfect, shall I lay claim to a measureless and unnatural old age? Anything that is contrary to the course of nature may be disagreeable, but whatever accords with it should always be pleasing. 'All things that are done according to nature are to be accounted good.'* For this reason, says Plato, let such death as comes by wounds or sickness be considered violent, but such as overtakes us when old age is at our side is the easiest of all, and in some degree pleasant. 'It is violence that takes life from the young; it is maturity that brings it to the old.'†

Death mingles and confuses itself with our life throughout. Decay anticipates its time, and even insinuates itself into the course of our growth. I have portraits of myself at 25 and at 35,

* Cicero, *De Senectute*, XIX.   † ibid.

and I compare them with one of the present time. How very unlike me they are! How much more different my present face is from those than from what it will be at my death! It is too great an abuse of nature to drag her so far that she is compelled to leave us, and abandon the care of us – of our eyes, our teeth, our legs, and the rest – to the mercy of assistance begged from strangers. Weary of accompanying us herself, she will resign us into the hands of art.

I am not excessively fond of salads or of any fruit except melons. My father disliked every kind of sauce; I like them all. Over-eating makes me uncomfortable; but as to quality, I do not yet know for certain that any food disagrees with me. Nor have I observed that I am affected by a full or new moon, by autumn or spring. We are subject to irregular and inexplicable changes. Take radishes, for example; once they agreed with me, then I found them indigestible, and now they agree with me again. Over a number of things I find my digestion and appetite varying in this way. I have more than once changed from white wine to red, and then back from red to white again. I am very fond of fish; for me lean days are fat, and fast days are feasts. Besides I believe that, as some people say, fish is easier to digest than meat. As I make it a point of conscience not to eat meat on a fish day, so my palate has scruples against mixing fish and flesh; the difference seems to me too great.

Ever since my youth, I have occasionally omitted a meal, sometimes to sharpen my appetite for the next day. But whereas Epicurus used to fast and eat poorly in order to accustom his greedy stomach to do without abundance, I do it, on the contrary, in order to prepare mine to take better advantage and make livelier use of it. Sometimes, on the other hand, I have gone short in order to preserve my vigour for the performance of some mental or physical action. For both my body and my mind are cruelly dulled by repletion; and I hate above all things a foolish coupling of the healthy, sporting goddess* with that little indigestible, belching god,† all bloated with the fumes of his liquor. I may fast also in order to cure an upset stomach,

* Venus.　　　　　　　† Bacchus.

or because I have no congenial company. For I say with Epicurus that one should not so much consider what one eats as with whom one eats it. And I admire Chilo, who would not promise to attend Periander's feast before he learned who were to be the other guests. There is no dish so sweet to me, and no sauce so appetizing, as those derived from the company.

I think that it is healthier to eat at greater leisure and less, and to eat oftener. But I would give appetite and hunger their due. I should take no pleasure in dragging through three or four sparse meals a day under the constraint of a medical diet. Who could assure me that I should recover at supper-time the good appetite which I had in the morning? Let us old men, in particular, seize the first opportunity that comes to us. Let us leave the making of dietaries to almanac-makers and physicians. The greatest benefit that I gain from health is physical pleasure; and let us seize the first recognizable pleasure that comes to hand. I refuse to observe these laws of fasting strictly. If a man wishes a habit to be of service to him, he should avoid following it consistently. For then we become hardened to it, and our powers are dulled. Six months later we shall find our stomach so habituated to it that the only advantage we have acquired will be the loss of our freedom to do otherwise, except at our peril.

I do not cover my legs and thighs any more warmly in winter than in summer; I wear silk hose and nothing more. I have gone so far as to keep my head warmer, to guard against colds, and my belly too, because of my colic. But in a few days my maladies became used to this; and scorned my common precautions. From an indoor cap I rose to a head-shawl, and from a bonnet to a lined hat. The padding of my doublet now only serves as a decoration; it is no good, unless I add a hare's skin or a vulture's, and wear a skull-cap under my hat. Follow these gradations, and you will make fine progress. I shall take care not to do so, and I would gladly go back to where I began, if only I dared. Suppose you develop some new trouble, these remedies will be of no avail; you have grown accustomed to them, and must find new ones. Thus it is the ruin of a man to let himself be fettered by these enforced rules, and to cling to them superstitiously. He will need more and more and still more after that; there is no end to it.

For the benefit of our work and for our pleasure, it is much more convenient that we should go without dinner, as the ancients did, and put off our convivial meal till the hour of retirement and repose, rather than cut up the day. This was once my practice. But I have learnt since by experience that, for health's sake, it is better, on the contrary, to dine, and that one digests better while awake.

I am not very subject to thirst, either in health or in sickness. In the latter case, my mouth is very often dry, but I am not thirsty. As a rule I drink only from a desire that comes on me when eating, and fairly late in the meal. I drink pretty freely for a man of the average sort; in summer, and at an appetizing meal, I not only exceed the limits of Augustus, who drank precisely three times; but, not to infringe the rule of Democritus, who forbade men to stop at four since it is an unlucky number, I go on at a pinch to a fifth glass – about a pint and a half. For I favour little glasses, and like to drink them to the bottom; which others consider impolite and refuse to do. I dilute my wine, generally with a half, but sometimes with a third part of water. And when I am at home, following an old habit prescribed by my father's physician, which both he and my father followed, so much as I need is mixed in the buttery some two or three hours before it is served. Cranaus, King of the Athenians, is said to have been the inventor of this practice of diluting wine with water; whether it is a good one or not has been a subject of debate. I think it more proper and wholesome for children not to drink wine before they are sixteen or eighteen. The most usual and common way of life is the best, I think; any singularity ought to be avoided, and I should hate to see a German dilute his wine with water as I should a Frenchman drinking his neat. General usage dictates the laws in such matters.

I dread a stuffy atmosphere, and I mortally detest smoke. The first repairs that I had done in my house were to the chimneys and the privies, which are commonly defective in old buildings, and in such cases intolerable; and among the discomforts of war I count the thick clouds of dust which swathe us for a whole day's march in the heat of summer. My breathing is free and easy, and my colds generally disappear without affecting my lungs or giving me a cough.

Summer's rigours are more harmful to me than winter's. For besides the discomforts of heat, which are less easily remediable than those of cold, and besides the beating of the sun's rays on my head, my eyes are hurt by any brilliant light. I could not now sit at dinner facing a bright, blazing fire. In the time when it was my habit to read more than I do now, I used to place a sheet of glass on my book to deaden the whiteness of the paper, and this gave me great relief. Even to this day I have never had to use spectacles, and can see as far as ever I did, or as any other man. It is true that towards nightfall I begin to feel some dimness and weakness of sight as I read; but reading has always tried my eyes, especially at night. This is a backward step, but hardly perceptible. Soon I shall be taking one more, then after the second a third, after the third a fourth, but all so gently that I shall be stone blind before I notice that my vision is failing and ageing. So do the Fates untwist the skein of our lives! In the same way, I cannot make up my mind that my hearing is beginning to grow dull; and you will see that when I have half lost it, I shall still be blaming the voices of those who speak to me. We must put the soul under great stress if we are to make it feel how it ebbs away.

My step is quick and firm; and I do not know which of the two, my mind or my body, I have found most difficult to bring under control. Any preacher is a good friend to me who can compel my attention through a whole sermon. On ceremonial occasions, when everyone wears the most constrained expression, and when I have seen ladies keep even their eyes quite still, I have never succeeded in preventing some part of me from stirring all the time. Though I may be sitting, I am anything but relaxed. As the philosopher Chrysippus's maid said of her master that he was only drunk in his legs – for he had the habit of shifting them about, whatever position he was in; and she mentioned it at a time when his companions were affected by wine, but he not at all – so it might have been said of me from my childhood that I had either madness or quicksilver in my feet, so active and restless are they, in whatever position I put them.

To eat greedily, as I do, is not only harmful to the health, and even to one's pleasures, but is unmannerly into the bargain. So hurried am I that I often bite my tongue, and sometimes my fingers. When Diogenes noticed a boy eating like this, he gave the tutor a cuff on the ear. There were men at Rome who taught the art of chewing gracefully, as they did deportment. My greed leaves me no time for talk, which gives so pleasant a seasoning to a meal so long as the conversation is suitable, pleasant, and brief.

Our pleasures are jealous and envious of one another; one clashes and conflicts with the next. Alcibiades, a man who understood how to make good cheer, banished even music from his table because it might disturb the pleasantness of the conversation. His reason for doing so, according to Plato, was that it is a practice of vulgar men to bring players of instruments and singers to their feasts for want of such good talk and agreeable entertainment as men of intelligence are able to provide for one another. Varro gives the following prescription for a banquet: a gathering of persons attractive in appearance and pleasing in their conversation, who are neither mute nor loquacious; cleanliness and refinement both in the fare and the room, and fine weather. To give a good dinner requires no slight skill and gives no small pleasure; neither the great commanders nor the great philosophers have disdained to learn and practise the art. My mind has preserved the memory of three such occasions, at different moments in my more flourishing years, which chance made particularly delightful to me. For each guest brings the principal charm with him, which depends on the good state of body and mind in which he is at the time.

I, who am a very earthy person, loathe that inhuman teaching which would make us despise and dislike the care of the body. I consider it just as wrong to reject natural pleasures as to set too much store by them. Xerxes was a fool when, lapped in all human delights, he offered a reward to anyone who would invent others. But hardly less of a fool is the man who curtails those pleasures which nature has found him. They should neither be pursued nor shunned; they should just be accepted. I accept them a little more liberally and kindly, and very readily let myself follow my natural inclination. We have no reason to exaggerate their emptiness; it makes itself sufficiently felt and seen, thanks to our sickly and kill-joy mind, which disgusts us with them and with itself as well. For it treats both itself and all that it receives, now well, now badly, according to its insatiable, unstable, and changeable nature.

*Sincerum est nisi vas, quodcumque infundis, acesit.**

I who boast of embracing the pleasures of life so eagerly and so deliberately, find in them, when I consider them so minutely, little more than wind. But what of that? We are all wind. And the wind itself, wiser than we, takes pleasure in blustering and veering round, and is content with its own functions. It does not desire stability or solidity, qualities that do not belong to it.

Those pleasures that are purely of the imagination as well as its unmixed pains are, according to some, greater than all others, as was suggested by Critolaus and his scales.† This is not to be wondered at; for the imagination composes them to its own liking, and cuts them out of the whole cloth. Every day I see remarkable, and perhaps desirable, examples of this. But I who am made of mixed and coarse stuff, cannot bite only at one simple object presented by the imagination, but must ever be clumsily pursuing those immediate pleasures to which universal laws make us subject: pleasures that are perceived by the mind, and conveyed to it by the senses. The Cyrenaic philosophers hold that bodily delights, like bodily sufferings, are the more rational. There are some who out of savage stupidity, as Aristotle says, depise them; I know some who do so out of

* 'Unless the vessel is clean, all that you pour into it turns sour.' Horace, *Epistles*, 1, ii, 54.

† In which the foods of the soul outweighed all those of the body. See Cicero, *Tusculans*, v, 7.

ambition. Why do they not forswear breathing also? Why do they not live solely on their own resources, and refuse light because it shines for nothing and costs them neither mental nor physical effort? Let them look for sustenance to Mars, or Pallas, or Mercury, instead of to Venus, Ceres, and Bacchus, and see what happens. Are they not the sort who will be trying to square the circle as they lie with their wives! I hate to be told that my spirit should be in the clouds while my body is at table. I would not have the mind pinned or sprawling there, but I would have it attentive; it should sit, not recline. Aristippus spoke for the body only, as if we had no soul; Zeno dealt only with the soul, as if we had no body; and both were mistaken. Pythagoras, they say, followed a philosophy that was all contemplation, while that of Socrates was all deeds and conduct; Plato found a mean between the two. But they say this for the sake of argument, and the true mean is to be found in Socrates. Plato is much more Socratic than Pythagorean, and it is better that he should be.

When I dance, I dance; when I sleep, I sleep: Yes, and when I am walking by myself in a beautiful orchard, even if my thoughts dwell for part of the time on distant events, I bring them back for another part to the walk, the orchard, the charm of this solitude, and to myself. Nature has with maternal care provided that the actions she has enjoined on us for our need shall give us pleasure; and she uses not only reason but appetite to attract us to them. It is wrong to infringe her rules. When I see Caesar and Alexander, in the thick of their greatest labours, so fully enjoying those pleasures which are natural, and therefore right and necessary, I do not say they are relaxing their minds. I say that they are bracing them, subordinating their strenuous activities and burdensome thoughts, by strength of the spirit, to the usages of everyday life. How wise they would have been, if they had believed this to be their ordinary vocation and the other an extraordinary one!

We are great fools. 'He has spent his life in idleness,' we say, and 'I have done nothing today.' What! have you not lived? That is not only the fundamental, but the most noble of your occupations. 'If I had been put in charge of some great affair, I might have shown what I could do.' Have you been able to reflect on your life and control it? Then you have performed the greatest work of all. To reveal herself and do her work, nature has no need of fortune. She manifests herself equally at all levels, and behind curtains as well as in the open. Our duty is to compose our character, not to compose books, to win not battles and provinces, but order and tranquillity in our conduct. Our great and glorious masterpiece is to live properly. All other things – to reign, to lay up treasure, to build – are at the best but little aids and additions.

I delight to see the general of an army at the foot of a breach that he is just about to assault, giving himself up wholly and freely to conversation with his friends; and Brutus, with heaven and earth conspiring against him and the freedom of Rome, stealing an hour from his nightly rounds to read and annotate Polybius, at absolute leisure. It is a small soul, buried beneath the weight of affairs, that does not know how to get clean away from them, that cannot put them aside and pick them up again:

> *O fortes peioraque passi*
> *mecum saepe viri, nunc vino pellite curas;*
> *cras ingens iterabimus aequor.**

Whether it is in jest or in earnest that the *Theologians' wine*† of the Sorbonne has become proverbial, as have their banquets, I think it reasonable that they should dine more comfortably and more pleasantly for having devoted the morning profitably and seriously to the teaching of their classes. The consciousness of having spent the other hours well is a good and appetizing sauce for the table. Thus did the sages live; and that inimitable striving after virtue which excites our admiration in the two Catos, that austere disposition of theirs which they carried to the point of extravagance, was accustomed gently and complacently to submit to the laws of human nature, and of Venus and Bacchus. They followed the precepts of their sect, which

* 'O brave companions, who have often suffered worse things with me, now banish your cares with wine; tomorrow we will set out again over the boundless sea.' Horace, *Odes*, i, vii, 30.

† *Vin théologal*, a good and strong wine.

demand that the perfect sage shall be as skilled and practised in the enjoyment of natural pleasures as in every other duty of life, 'that he who has a sensitive conscience shall also have a sensitive palate'.*

Ease of manner and the ability to unbend are most honourable and fitting qualities in a strong and generous soul. Epaminondas did not think that to join the lads of his city in a dance, to sing, to play an instrument, and to give his whole mind to these amusements, in any way detracted from the honour of his glorious victories, or from the complete reformation of character that he had attained. And amongst all the admirable deeds of Scipio the younger† – all things considered, the first of the Romans – there is nothing that shows him in so charming a light as to see him strolling with Laelius along the seashore, gaily engaged in the childish amusement of picking up and selecting shells, and playing ducks-and-drakes; or, in bad weather, entertaining himself with the ribald writing of comedies, in which he reproduced the most ordinary and vulgar actions of men.‡ With his mind taken up by that marvellous campaign against Hannibal and Africa, he visited the schools in Sicily, and attended lectures on philosophy, so assiduously as to exacerbate the blind envy of his enemies at Rome.§ Nor is there anything more remarkable in Socrates than that he found time, in his old age, to take lessons in dancing and the playing of instruments, and that he thought this time well spent.

This same man was seen to stand rapt for a whole day and night in the presence of the entire Greek army, his mind caught and transported by some profound thought. First among all the valiant men in that army, he was seen to run to the help of Alcibiades, who was being borne down by the enemy. Socrates covered him with his body, and extricated him from the press

* Cicero, *De Finibus*, ii, viii.

† In the edition we are following, Montaigne changed this to 'Scipio the elder, a person who deserved the reputation that he was of heavenly origin'. But the earlier reading, in the edition of 1588, corresponds with the facts, set out in Livy, xxvi, 19.

‡ Rumour had it that he was part-author of Terence's comedies. See Suetonius, *Life of Terence*.

§ Here Montaigne is speaking of Scipio the elder.

by sheer force of arms. And he was the first among all the people of Athens, incensed like him by the shameful spectacle, to spring to the rescue of Theramenes, who was being led to his death by the satellites of the Thirty Tyrants. And, though followed by only two others, he would not desist from his bold attempt until warned to do so by Theramenes himself. Though pursued by a beauty with whom he was in love, he was known at need to exercise a severe abstinence. At the battle of Delium he was seen to pick up and rescue Xenophon, who had been thrown from his horse. He was observed always to march into battle and tread on the ice with bare feet, to wear the same cloak in winter and summer, to outdo all his comrades in the endurance of hardships, and to eat no more at a banquet than at an ordinary meal. He was seen for twenty-seven years to put up with hunger, poverty, the rebelliousness of his children, the clawings of his wife, and finally with calumny, tyranny, imprisonment, fetters, and poison, all without change of demeanour. But if ever this man was challenged to take part in a drinking-bout he would accept as a matter of courtesy and come off best in it out of the whole army. He never refused to play for nuts with the children, or to race with them on a hobby-horse, and he did this nimbly. For all actions, says philosophy, are equally fitting and equally honourable in a wise man. We have material enough, and should never tire of presenting the portrait of this personage as a pattern and ideal of every kind of perfection. There are very few examples of a pure and perfect life, and it is harmful to our education that we should have put before us every day weak and defective models, hardly good in a single feature. These are more likely to pull us backwards, to corrupt us rather than to correct us. The people go astray; it is very much easier to follow the side-path, where the edges serve as a check and a guide, than to keep to the middle of the road, which is broad and open. It is easier to follow art than nature but it is also much less noble and commendable. The soul's greatness consists not so much in climbing high and pressing forward as in knowing how to adapt and limit itself. It takes all that is merely sufficient as great, and shows its distinction by preferring what is moderate to what is outstanding. There is nothing so fine as to play the man well and fittingly, and there is nothing so difficult to learn as how to live this life well and naturally; and the most unnatural of our diseases is to despise our being.

If anyone has a mind to detach his soul, let him do so boldly, if he can, when his body is sick, and thus free it from the contagion. At other times, however, let it help and comfort the body, and not refuse to take part in its natural pleasures, but delight in them like a wife. Let it bring to them, if it be the wiser, some moderation, for fear that, through lack of discretion, they may become mingled with pain. Excess is the bane of pleasure, and temperance is not its scourge but its seasoning. Eudoxus, who considered it the sovereign good, and his fellow-philosophers, who set so high a value on it, relished it in all its charm and sweetness by reason of this temperance, which they practised to a singular and exemplary degree.

I bid my soul look upon pain and pleasure with the same level gaze – 'since it is as wrong for the soul to expand in joy as to contract in sorrow'* – and with the same firmness, but to greet the one cheerfully, the other austerely, and, in so far as it can, to try as hard to cut short the one as to prolong the other. A sane view of good will result in a sane view of evil. And pain has some quality in its gentle beginnings that should not be avoided, as pleasure has something to be shunned in its final excess. Plato couples them together, and maintains that it is a brave man's duty to fight equally against pain and against the immoderate charms and blandishments of pleasure. They are two springs, and whoever draws from them where, when, and as much as is needful – be the drawer a city, a man, or a beast – is very fortunate. The first must be taken medicinally and when needed, but more sparingly; the other for thirst, but not to the point of drunkenness. Pain and pleasure, love and hatred are the first things that a child feels; if when reason comes, these things are governed by it, that is virtue.

I have a special vocabulary of my own. I *pass* the time when

* Cicero, *Tusculans*, IV, xxxi.

it is bad and disagreeable; when it is fine I have no wish to *pass* it, I savour it and keep it back. One must hurry over what is bad, and dwell on what is good. These common phrases, *pastime* and *passing the time*, reflect the usage of those prudent folk who think they can turn their life to no better account than to let it slip by, and to escape from it, to while it away, to deflect it and, in so far as it is in their power, to ignore it and avoid it as if it were something tiresome and contemptible. But I know it to be otherwise, and find it both agreeable and valuable, even in its last decline, in which it is with me. Nature has put it into our hands enhanced with so many favourable circumstances that we have only ourselves to blame if it is a burden to us or escapes from us unprofitably. 'A fool leads a thankless and anxious life, given over wholly to the future.'*

And yet I am resigned to lose it without regret, but as something whose nature it is to be lost, not as a troublesome burden. Moreover, not to dislike the idea of dying is truly possible only in one who enjoys living. It needs good management to enjoy life. I enjoy it twice as much as others, for the measure of enjoyment depends on the greater or less attention that we give to it. Now especially, when I feel mine to be so brief in time, I am anxious to increase it in weight. I wish to check the rapidity of its flight by quickly laying my hands upon it, and by using it vigorously to make up for the speed with which it passes. The shorter my possession of life the deeper and fuller I must make it.

Others feel the charm of contentment and prosperity. I feel it as well as they, but I feel none in letting it pass and slip by. Life must be studied, relished, and meditated upon, so that we may give adequate thanks to Him who grants it to us. They enjoy other pleasures, as they do that of sleep, without being conscious of them. Rather than let sleep insensibly escape me, I used once to have myself woken up, in order that I might catch a glimpse of it.

I dwell upon any pleasure that comes to me. I do not skim over it, but plumb its depths and force my mind, which has

* Seneca, *Letters*, xv.

grown peevish and listless, to take it in. Suppose I am in a calm state, suppose I am tickled by some sensual appetite, I do not allow it to be stolen by the senses; I bring my mind to it, not to be sucked in but to get on terms with it, not to lose itself but to find itself. And I apply it to its own task of viewing itself in this prosperous state, of weighing and valuing its happiness, and of amplifying it. It calculates the extent of its debt to God for being at peace with its conscience and free from other intestine passions, for having the body in a natural state of health, and in orderly and proper enjoyment of those tender and delicious functions with which He is graciously pleased to compensate us for the sufferings which His justice inflicts on us in its turn. The mind considers also its great advantage in being so placed that wherever it casts its eyes the heavens are calm around it, in having no desire, no fear or doubt to disturb the air, and no difficulty, past, present, or future, over which its thoughts may not wander scatheless. This meditation is much enhanced by a comparison with conditions different from my own. Thus I call up a thousand pictures of those who are carried away and storm-tossed by fate or by their own errors, and of those others who, more like me, accept their good fortune so negligently and with such indifference. These are the people who really *pass their time*; they pass beyond the present and what they possess, to make themselves slaves of hope, lured by shadows and vain images that fancy puts before them,

> *Morte obita quales fama est volitare figuras,*
> *aut quae sopitos deludunt somnia sensus,* *

which hasten and prolong their flight, the more they are pursued. The fruit and the object of this pursuit is the pursuit itself, as Alexander said that the end of his labour was to labour,

> *Nil actum credens cum quid superesset agendum.*†

For my part then, I love life and cultivate it in the form in which it has pleased God to bestow it on us. I do not go about

* 'Like the shades that, they say, flit about after death, or the visions that mock our senses in sleep.' Virgil, *Aeneid*, x, 641.

† 'Believing that nothing was done so long as anything remained to do.' Lucan, ii, 657. This refers not to Alexander but to Caesar.

desiring that it should be free of the need for eating and drinking; and it would seem to me just as inexcusable an error to desire that this need should be doubled – 'a wise man is a most earnest seeker for nature's treasures'* – or that we should be nourished simply by putting into our mouths a little of that drug by which Epimenides took away his appetite and kept himself alive; or that we might beget children dully with our fingers or our heels – or beget them, with reverence be it spoken, voluptuously with these same heels and fingers – or that the body should be without desire and titillation. These are thankless and wicked complaints. I heartily and gratefully accept what nature has done for me, and I am pleased and proud of myself that I do. It is a wrong against that great and omnipotent giver to refuse, nullify, or spoil her gift. Being herself all good, she has made all things good. 'All things that are according to nature are worthy of esteem.'†

Of philosophical opinions I embrace for preference those that are most substantial, that is to say most human, and most natural to us. My reflections, in keeping with my actions, are humble and unassuming. Philosophy is, to my mind, quite childish when it preaches to us in hectoring tones that a marriage of the divine and the earthly, the reasonable and the unreasonable, the harsh and the indulgent, the upright and the crooked, is an unnatural alliance; that carnal pleasure is brutish and unworthy to be enjoyed by the wise man – the sole pleasure he may derive from possessing a young wife being the pleasure in his consciousness that he is performing a proper action, like putting on his boots for a necessary ride. What if philosophy's followers had no more right or sap or sinew for the deflowering of their wives than is contained in this lesson!

That is not what our master Socrates says, himself a teacher of philosophy. He values, as he should, the pleasures of the body, but he prefers those of the mind, as having more strength, stability, ease, variety, and dignity. This pleasure, according to him, by no means stands alone – he is not so fantastic – it merely stands first. For him temperance is the

* Seneca, *Letters*, CXIX. † Cicero, *De Finibus*, III, vi.

moderator, not the enemy of pleasures.

Nature is a gentle guide, but no more wise and just than she is gentle. 'We must penetrate the nature of things, and thoroughly discover what she requires.'* I seek her footprints everywhere. We have concealed her tracks by artificial means, and so the sovereign good of the Academics and Peripatetics, which is to *live according to nature*, has become difficult to define and explain, as has the closely allied ideal, of the Stoics also, which is to acquiesce in nature. Is it not a mistake to consider any actions less worthy because they are necessary? Yet no one will ever convince me that the marriage of pleasure with necessity – for which, as one of the ancients remarks, the gods always conspire – is not a very suitable one. What reason can we have to dismember by divorce a fabric woven of so close and brotherly a correspondence? On the contrary, let us strengthen it by mutual service. Let the mind rouse and enliven the heaviness of the body, and the body check and steady the frivolity of the mind. 'He who extols the nature of the soul as the chief good, and condemns the nature of the flesh as evil, is carnal both in his pursuit of the soul and in his shunning of the flesh, since he is prompted by human vanity, not by divine truth.'† In this gift that God has made to us, there is no part that is unworthy of our care; we stand accountable for it even to the last hair. And the charge enjoined upon man to live his life according to his condition is no mere formal one; it is positive, plain, and of the first importance; and the Creator has imposed it upon us strictly and seriously. Authority alone can influence a common understanding; and it carries greater weight in a foreign language. Let us make fresh use of it here: 'Who will deny that it is a sign of folly to do what has to be done in a slothful and rebellious spirit, or to drive the body in one direction, the soul in another, and thus to be torn between the most conflicting impulses?'‡

So then, to make proof of this, ask some ordinary man to tell you one day the ideas and fancies with which he fills his head,

* Cicero, *De Finibus*, v, xvi.
† St Augustine, *The City of God*, xiv, 5.   ‡ Seneca, *Letters*, lxxiv.

and for which he diverts his thoughts from a good meal, even grudging the time he spends in eating it. You will find that not one of all the dishes on your table has so little flavour as the fine things with which he is entertaining his mind – for the most part, we should be better to go fast off to sleep than to stay awake for the thoughts of our waking hours – and you will find that all his talk and aspirations are worth less than your warmed-up stew. Were they the mental raptures of Archimedes himself, what of it? I am not referring here to those venerable souls, exalted by the ardour of devotion and religion to a constant and scrupulous meditation upon divine things. I do not confuse them with the monkey rabble of us common men, occupied with our vain thoughts and desires. Anticipating by the strength of their strong and vigorous hope the enjoyment of eternal nourishment, the final and highest stage of Christian desires, the sole constant and incorruptible pleasure, they scorn to attach themselves to our poor, fleeting, and dubious possessions, and readily leave to the body the provision and enjoyment of sensual and temporal food. Theirs is a study for the privileged. Supercelestial thoughts and subterrestrial conduct are two things, let me tell you, that I have always found to agree very well together.

That great man Aesop saw his master pissing as he walked. 'What!' he exclaimed, 'ought we then to shit as we run?' Let us manage our time as well as we can, there will still remain much that is idle or ill-employed. Our mind has probably not enough hours to spare for the performance of its business, if it does not disassociate itself from the body for that brief space that it requires for its needs. People try to get out of themselves and to escape from the man. This is folly; instead of transforming themselves into angels, they turn themselves into beasts; instead of lifting, they degrade themselves. These transcendental humours frighten me, like lofty and inaccessible heights. There is nothing in the life of Socrates that I find so difficult to swallow as his ecstasies and daemonic states, and nothing so human in Plato as that for which they say he was called divine. And of our sciences, those seem to me the most earthly and low that have made the highest flights. And I find nothing so lowly and mortal in the life of Alexander as his fancies about becoming an immortal. Philotas stung him wittily with his retort, when he wrote congratulating him on the oracle of Jupiter Ammon, which had placed him among the gods: 'For your sake, I am very glad about it, but I am sorry for those men who have to live with and obey one who has exceeded the proportions of a man and is discontented with them.'

*Dis te minorem quod geris, imperas.**

That delightful inscription with which the Athenians commemorated Pompey's visit to their city is in agreement with my view:

*D'autant est tu dieu comme
Tu te recognois homme.†*

The man who knows how to enjoy his existence as he ought has attained to an absolute perfection, like that of the gods. We seek other conditions because we do not understand the proper use of our own, and go out of ourselves because we do not know what is within us So it is no good our mounting on stilts, for even on stilts we have to walk with our own legs; and upon the most exalted throne in the world it is still our own bottom that we sit on.

The finest lives are, in my opinion, those which conform to the common and human model in an orderly way, with no marvels and no extravagances. Now old age stands in need of slightly more tender treatment. Let us commend it to that god who is the protector of health and wisdom – but of a gay and companionable wisdom:

*Frui paratis et valido mihi
Latoe, dones, et, precor, integra
cum mente, nec turpem senectam
degere, nec cithara carentem.‡*

* 'It is because you carry yourself lower than the gods that you reign.' Horace, *Odes*, III, vi, 5.

† 'You are a god only in so far as you recognize yourself to be a man.' Quoted from Plutarch's *Life of Pompey* in Amyot's translation.

‡ 'Grant me, Apollo, that I may enjoy with healthy body and sound mind the goods that have been prepared for me, and that my old age be honourable and no stranger to the lyre.' Horace, *Odes*, I, xxxi, 17.

READ MORE IN PENGUIN

In every corner of the world, on every subject under the sun, Penguin represents quality and variety – the very best in publishing today.

For complete information about books available from Penguin – including Puffins, Penguin Classics and Arkana – and how to order them, write to us at the appropriate address below. Please note that for copyright reasons the selection of books varies from country to country.

In the United Kingdom: Please write to *Dept. JC, Penguin Books Ltd, FREEPOST, West Drayton, Middlesex UB7 0BR*

If you have any difficulty in obtaining a title, please send your order with the correct money, plus ten per cent for postage and packaging, to *PO Box No. 11, West Drayton, Middlesex UB7 0BR*

In the United States: Please write to *Penguin USA Inc., 375 Hudson Street, New York, NY 10014*

In Canada: Please write to *Penguin Books Canada Ltd, 10 Alcorn Avenue, Suite 300, Toronto, Ontario M4V 3B2*

In Australia: Please write to *Penguin Books Australia Ltd, 487 Maroondah Highway, Ringwood, Victoria 3134*

In New Zealand: Please write to *Penguin Books (NZ) Ltd,182–190 Wairau Road, Private Bag, Takapuna, Auckland 9*

In India: Please write to *Penguin Books India Pvt Ltd, 706 Eros Apartments, 56 Nehru Place, New Delhi 110 019*

In the Netherlands: Please write to *Penguin Books Netherlands B.V., Keizersgracht 231 NL–1016 DV Amsterdam*

In Germany: Please write to *Penguin Books Deutschland GmbH, Friedrichstrasse 10–12, W–6000 Frankfurt/Main 1*

In Spain: Please write to *Penguin Books S. A., C. San Bernardo 117–6° E–28015 Madrid*

In Italy: Please write to *Penguin Italia s.r.l., Via Felice Casati 20, I–20124 Milano*

In France: Please write to *Penguin France S. A., 17 rue Lejeune, F–31000 Toulouse*

In Japan: Please write to *Penguin Books Japan, Ishikiribashi Building, 2–5–4, Suido, Tokyo 112*

In Greece: Please write to *Penguin Hellas Ltd, Dimocritou 3, GR–106 71 Athens*

In South Africa: Please write to *Longman Penguin Southern Africa (Pty) Ltd, Private Bag X08, Bertsham 2013*

READ MORE IN PENGUIN

A CHOICE OF NON-FICTION

Bernard Shaw Michael Holroyd
Volume 2 1898–1918 The Pursuit of Power

'A man whose art rested so much upon the exercise of intelligence could not have chosen a more intelligent biographer ... The pursuit of Bernard Shaw has grown, and turned into a pursuit of the whole twentieth century' – Peter Ackroyd in *The Times*

Shots from the Hip Charles Shaar Murray

His classic encapsulation of the moment when rock stars turned junkies as the sixties died; his dissection of rock 'n' roll violence as citizens assaulted the Sex Pistols; superstar encounters from the decline of Paul McCartney to Mick Jagger's request that the author should leave – Charles Shaar Murray's *Shots From the Hip* is also rock history in the making.

Managing on the Edge Richard Pascale

The co-author of the bestselling *The Art of Japanese Management* has once again turned conventional thinking upside down. Conflict and contention in organizations are not just unavoidable – they are positively to be welcomed. The successes and failures of large corporations can help us understand the need to maintain a creative tension between fitting companies together and splitting them apart.

Just Looking John Updike

'Mr Updike can be a very good art critic, and some of these essays are marvellous examples of critical explanation ... a deep understanding of the art emerges ... His reviews of some recent and widely attended shows ... quite surpass the modest disclaimer of the title' – *The New York Times Book Review*

Shelley: The Pursuit Richard Holmes

'Surely the best biography of Shelley ever written ... He makes Shelley's character entirely convincing by showing us the poet at every stage of his development acting upon, and reacting to, people and events' – Stephen Spender

READ MORE IN PENGUIN

A CHOICE OF NON-FICTION

Citizens A Chronicle of the French Revolution Simon Schama

'The most marvellous book I have read about the French Revolution in the last fifty years' – Richard Cobb in *The Times*. 'He has chronicled the vicissitudes of that world with matchless understanding, wisdom, pity and truth, in the pages of this huge and marvellous book' – *Sunday Times*

Out of Africa Karen Blixen (Isak Dinesen)

Karen Blixen went to Kenya in 1914 to run a coffee-farm; its failure in 1931 caused her to return to Denmark where she wrote this classic account of her experiences. 'A work of sincere power ... a fine lyrical study of life in East Africa' – Harold Nicolson in the *Daily Telegraph*

Yours Etc. Graham Greene
Letters to the Press 1945–1989

'An entertaining celebration of Graham Greene's lesser-known career as a prolific author of letters to newspapers; you will find unarguable proof of his total addiction to everything about his time, from the greatest issues of the day to the humblest subjects imaginable' – Salman Rushdie in the *Observer*

The Trial of Lady Chatterley Edited By C. H. Rolph

In October 1960 at the Old Bailey a jury of nine men and three women prepared for the infamous trial of *Lady Chatterley's Lover*. The Obscene Publications Act had been introduced the previous year and D. H. Lawrence's notorious novel was the first to be prosecuted under its provisions. This is the account of the historic trial and acquittal of Penguin Books.

Handbook for the Positive Revolution Edward de Bono

Edward de Bono's challenging new book provides a practical framework for a serious revolution which has no enemies but seeks to make things better. The hand symbolizes the five basic principles of the Positive Revolution, to remind us that even a small contribution is better than endless criticism.

READ MORE IN PENGUIN

A CHOICE OF NON-FICTION

The Time Out Film Guide Edited by Tom Milne

The definitive, up-to-the minute directory of over 9,500 films – world cinema from classics and silent epics to reissues and the latest releases – assessed by two decades of *Time Out* reviewers. 'In my opinion the best and most comprehensive' – Barry Norman

The Remarkable Expedition Olivia Manning

The events of an extraordinary attempt in 1887 to rescue Emin Pasha, Governor of Equatoria, are recounted here by the author of *The Balkan Trilogy* and *The Levant Trilogy* and vividly reveal unprecedented heights of magnificent folly in the perennial human search for glorious conquest.

Berlin: Coming in From the Cold Ken Smith

'He covers everything from the fate of the ferocious-looking dogs that formerly helped to guard East Germany's borders to the vast Orwellian apparatus that maintained security in the now-defunct German Democratic Republic ... a pithy style and an eye for the telling detail' – *Independent*

Cider with Rosie/As I Walked Out one Midsummer Morning
Laurie Lee

Now together in one volume, Laurie Lee's two classic autobiographical works, *Cider with Rosie* and *As I Walked Out One Midsummer Morning*. Together they illustrate Laurie Lee's superb descriptive powers as he conveys the poignancy of a boy's transformation into adulthood.

In the Land of Oz Howard Jacobson

'A wildly funny account of his travels; abounding in sharp characterization, crunching dialogue and self-parody, it actually is a book which makes you laugh out loud on almost every page ... sharp, skilful and brilliantly funny' – *Literary Review*

READ MORE IN PENGUIN

A CHOICE OF NON-FICTION

The Time of My Life Denis Healey

'Denis Healey's memoirs have been rightly hailed for their intelligence, wit and charm ... *The Time of My Life* should be read, certainly for pleasure, but also for profit ... he bestrides the post-war world, a Colossus of a kind' – *Independent*. 'No finer autobiography has been written by a British politician this century' – *Economist*

Chasing the Monsoon Alexander Frater

'Frater's unclouded sight unfurls the magic behind the mystery tour beautifully ... his spirited, eccentric, vastly diverting book will endure the ceaseless patter of travel books on India' – *Daily Mail*. 'This is travel writing at its best. Funny, informed, coherent and deeply sympathetic towards its subject' – *Independent on Sunday*

Isabelle Annette Kobak

'A European turned Arab, a Christian turned Muslim, a woman dressed as a man; a libertine who stilled profound mystical cravings by drink, hashish and innumerable Arab lovers ... All the intricate threads of her rebellious life are to be found in Annette Kobak's scrupulously researched book' – Lesley Blanch in the *Daily Telegraph*

Flying Dinosaurs Michael Johnson

Hundreds of millions of years ago, when dinosaurs walked the earth, we know that there also existed great prehistoric beasts call pterosaurs that could fly or glide. Now you can make these extraordinary creatures fly again. *Flying Dinosaurs* contain almost everything you need to construct eight colourful and thrillingly lifelike flying model pterosaurs – from the pterodactylus to the dimorphodon.

The Italians Luigi Barzini

'Brilliant ... whether he is talking about the family or the Mafia, about success or the significance of gesticulation, Dr Barzini is always illuminating and amusing' – *The Times*. 'He hits his nails on the head with bitter-sweet vitality ... Dr Barzini marshals and orders his facts and personalities with the skill of an historian as well as a journalist' – *Observer*

READ MORE IN PENGUIN

A CHOICE OF NON-FICTION

Riding the Iron Rooster Paul Theroux

Travels in old and new China with the author of *The Great Railway Bazaar*. 'Mr Theroux cannot write badly ... he is endlessly curious about places and people ... and in the course of a year there was almost no train in the whole vast Chinese rail network in which he did not travel' – Ludovic Kennedy

Ninety-two Days Evelyn Waugh

In this fascinating chronicle of a South American journey, Waugh describes the isolated cattle country of Guiana, sparsely populated by an odd collection of visionaries, rogues and ranchers, and records the nightmarish experiences travelling on foot, by horse and by boat through the jungle in Brazil.

The Life of Graham Greene Norman Sherry
Volume One 1904–1939

'Probably the best biography ever of a living author' – Philip French in the *Listener*. Graham Greene has always maintained a discreet distance from his reading public.This volume reconstructs his first thirty-five years to create one of the most revealing literary biographies of the decade.

The Day Gone By Richard Adams

In this enchanting memoir the bestselling author of *Watership Down* tells his life story from his idyllic 1920s childhood spent in Newbury, Berkshire, through public school, Oxford and service in World War Two to his return home and his courtship of the girl he was to marry.

A Turn in the South V. S. Naipaul

'A supremely interesting, even poetic glimpse of a part of America foreigners either neglect or patronize' – *Guardian*. 'An extraordinary panorama' – *Daily Telegraph*. 'A fine book by a fine man, and one to be read with great enjoyment: a book of style, sagacity and wit' – *Sunday Times*